WRITER'S RESOURCES
From Sentence to Paragraph

Annotated Instructor's Edition

Writer's Resources

From Sentence to Paragraph

Julie Robitaille · Robert Connelly

THOMSON

WADSWORTH

Australia · Canada · Mexico · Singapore · Spain · United Kingdom · United States

THOMSON ™
WADSWORTH

Writer's Resources: From Sentence to Paragraph
Julie Robitaille & Robert Connelly

Publisher: *Michael Rosenberg*
Acquisitions Editor: *Stephen Dalphin*
Development Editor: *Christine Caperton*
Editorial Assistant: *Steve Marsi*
Production Manager: *Michael Burggren*
Production Editor: *Samantha Ross*
Director of Marketing: *Lisa Kimball*
Senior Print Buyer: *Mary Beth Hennebury*
Cover Image: © *Diaphor Agency/Index Stock Imagery*

Compositor: *Argosy*
Project Manager: *Edalin Michael*
Photography Manager: *Sheri Blaney*
Cover Designer: *Dick Hannus*
Text Designer: *Jean Hammond*
Printer: *QuebecorWorld Versailles*

For permission to use material from this text or product contact us:
Tel   1-800-730-2214
Fax   1-800-730-2215
Web   www.thomsonrights.com

ISBN: **0-15-505084-2**   **(Student Edition)**
        0-7593-9833-X   **(Annotated Instructor's Edition)**

International Division List

ASIA (excluding India)
Thomson Learning
60 Albert Street #15-01
Albert Complex
Singapore 189969

AUSTRALIA/NEW ZEALAND
Nelson/Thomson Learning
102 Dodds Street
South Melbourne
Victoria 3205 Australia

CANADA
Nelson/Thomson Learning
1120 Birchmount Road
Scarborough, Ontario
Canada M1K 5G4

LATIN AMERICA
Thomson Learning
Seneca, 53
Colonio Polanco
11560 México D.F. México

SPAIN
Thomson Learning
Calle Magallanes, 25
28015-Madrid
España

UK/EUROPE/MIDDLE EAST
Thomson Learning
Berkshire House
168-173 High Holborn
London, WC1V 7AA, United Kingdom

Contents

Preface

Writer's Resources: From Sentence to Paragraph meets the most pressing needs of the developmental writer for motivation, modeling, and practice. The text uses cooperative learning techniques to foster a sense of belonging and increase persistence and retention. Active learning activities such as free writing keep students involved in the writing process. For the concrete learner, accessible student models are presented for writing assignments. Readings from popular periodicals help motivate students by highlighting individuals who have overcome obstacles and accomplished goals.

Along with covering the traditional topics of an entry-level developmental writing course, *Writer's Resources: From Sentence to Paragraph* also addresses first-year-in-college skills such as getting organized, managing time, setting goals, and overcoming obstacles. Additionally, the text incorporates workplace skills such as working in teams and using the computer. Most significantly, the text is reinforced by *Writer's Resources CD-ROM*, which provides a multimedia treatment of most of the text material and offers students animated explanations of concepts, practice using the skills, and testing and recording of skill acquisition.

About the Text

Writer's Resources provides the support that students need to develop into successful writers. The resources to which the title refers include instruction in the writing process for a paragraph, common rhetorical patterns, basic grammar and punctuation skills, and numerous peer and professional models of good writing. We break down rules and concepts into manageable pieces that allow students to focus on one concept at a time and to build understanding and mastery incrementally. Concepts are presented in simple, clear language, supported with numerous examples, and reinforced by frequent practice exercises that allow students to apply what they have learned.

Organization

Part I: Making the Transition to College

The chapters in Part I help students adjust to the demands of college. Chapter 1 introduces students to the textbook, the peer models, and their classmates and provides activities to help them organize their materials and schedule their time. In Chapter 2, students define long- and short-term goals and learn strategies for overcoming the inevitable obstacles they will face as they pursue their goals.

Part II: Beginning College Writing

The chapters in Part II cover the essentials of college writing. In Chapter 3, students learn to use journals to clarify, explore, and develop ideas. In Chapter 4, students use the writing process to brainstorm, plan, draft, revise, and edit paragraphs. Chapter 5 covers the most common rhetorical patterns used in college to develop paragraphs.

Part III: Grammar, Punctuation, and Mechanics Skills

Part III covers the basic skills beginning college writers need to write fluent paragraphs free of distracting errors. Every chapter includes opportunities for cooperative learning, practices after each concept, exercises to integrate the skills in writing, review exercises to test mastery, and editing exercises. In addition, a CD icon throughout the text directs students to more information and practice on *Writer's Resources CD-ROM*.

Part IV: Readings

Part IV begins with a section on successful reading strategies to help students get the most out of their reading. The readings cover a variety of topics of interest, from video games to the job market; moreover, students will read about people like themselves who are succeeding and making a difference in their communities. Marginal glosses of words, names, and events are provided to aid students' understanding of words in context and to improve their understanding of the essay as a whole. The professional essays are followed by comprehension questions, journal topics, discussion questions, and suggestions for writing topics.

Features

- **Critical First-Year-in-College Skills** such as organization, time management, and problem solving help students develop the attitudes and habits that will allow them to succeed in the academic environment.

- **Peer Models** demonstrate the process of writing and the paragraphs that students can produce. These models also help students understand how readers come to know writers through their writing.

- **Group Activities** give students experience working in groups, which is both an effective way to learn and a crucial job skill.
- **The Writing Process** is introduced in Chapter 4 as students learn to write a paragraph by following the steps in the writing process. The writing process is reinforced in Chapter 5, "Patterns of Development," where writing process prompts are tailored to each pattern.
- **Skill Practices** follow every major concept in the grammar and punctuation chapters. Review exercises and editing practices test mastery. Students also generate their own sentences and edit their own writing for target skills.

Supplements

Writer's Resources CD-ROM

The CD-ROM offers the advantage of multimedia technology used to reinforce skill acquisition and provides more than two thousand additional scored practices. The use of color, graphics, animation, and audio in the lessons helps focus student attention and appeals to a variety of learning styles. The audio in animations reinforces but does not repeat the text on screen, and students are free to pause, stop, and replay animations. The CD enables students to review skills and concepts independently.

In the margins of the text you will frequently see CD-ROM icons accompanied by an abbreviation and a number. Each abbreviation refers to one of the four sections found on the Writer's Resources CD-ROM, 2.0, that came with your text: Writing Process (WP); Writing Elements (WE); Rhetorical Patterns (RP); and Grammar, Punctuation, and Mechanics (GPM). The number refers to a specific page (within that section of the CD-ROM) on which you will find additional information relating to the topic being discussed in the text (eg. WE: 1.2). Subsequent pages on the CD-ROM contain additional examples and practice exercises on the topic. Finding the pages on the CD-ROM is easy: first, go to the Main Menu (Contents) on the CD-ROM, click on the section you want, and then click on the appropriate numbered page.

Instructor's Manual

In addition to providing the answers to exercises in the text, the instructor's manual written by Robitaille and Connelly contains chapter-by-chapter suggestions for implementing the material, sample syllabi, and additional tests and proofreading exercises.

Acknowledgments

We wish to thank the instructors who generously provided thoughtful comments about our manuscript during the writing of this book: Jessica I. Carroll, Miami-Dade Community College, Wolfson Campus; Randy D. Freeman,

Colorado Christian University; Timothy J. Jones, University of Oklahoma; Kaye Kolkman, Merced Community College and Modesto Junior College; Dennis Keen, Spokane Community College; Patsy Krech, University of Memphis; and Rebecca S. Mann, Guilford Technical Community College.

And, we wish to thank our editors who have supported this version of *Writer's Resources* text and CD-ROM, especially Steve Dalphin and Christine Caperton. Julie would like to thank her husband, Steve Robitaille, and her two sons, Jean Paul and Jordan, for their support and patience. Bob wishes to thank his significant other, Claudia Munnis, for her continued support.

About the Authors

Julie Robitaille received a B.A. in English from Emory University, an M.A. in English literature from the University of North Carolina at Chapel Hill, and an M.A. in creative writing from the University of Florida. For twenty years, she has directed the Writing Lab at Santa Fe Community College in Gainesville, Florida. In addition to teaching and writing textbooks, she enjoys writing fiction and screenplays.

Bob Connelly received his B.A. from the University of Florida and then attended the University of Chicago, where he received an M.A. in English literature. He has been teaching writing for over twenty years at Santa Fe Community College in Gainesville, Florida. In his spare time, Bob competes in triathlons, practices meditation, and writes.

To the Student

Writing clearly is essential to your success in school and on the job. Rest assured that this textbook and the course you are enrolled in will prepare you for the writing challenges you will face in college. You will learn strategies to become a more organized and active learner and techniques to help you overcome the challenges you will face as you pursue your goals. You will learn to use the writing process to clarify, organize, and develop your ideas, and you will learn the grammar and punctuation rules that will allow you to communicate those ideas clearly. Most importantly, you will learn about yourself, what you think, and how you work, alone and with others. We hope you enjoy this book and the writing you will do this term. We respect the courage and determination to succeed that you are showing by working to improve your writing.

While the materials in this book will help you learn to write well, we believe that the attitude that you bring into the class is the most important ingredient in your success.

Believe in yourself. You have enrolled in college, and you are qualified to do the work, but to succeed, you must be willing to believe in yourself and your ability to achieve your goals and dreams. Think of all the people you know who have not gone to college. Think of the people you know who wish that they had taken this opportunity. You want to succeed, and probably family and friends want you to do well. With hard work, you can get what you want.

Work with yourself. So often we are our own worst enemy. We are critical of everything we do, and we are fearful when presented with new material, especially if we don't think we will do well. Learning to learn is the primary skill in college. Everything else—including writing—is secondary. Think of this course as basic training in learning to work with yourself as you learn.

Rely on your instructor. Your instructor is your guide and wants you to do well. Most students report that their relationship with their instructors is one of the most valuable parts of their education. Work at developing a relationship of trust and respect by attending every class, arriving prepared and on time, and asking questions when you don't understand material. Most importantly, see your instructor if you have any trouble with the class.

Create a community for learning. Your classmates can be valuable allies in your learning. They are going through the same experiences as you. Most students report better attendance and grades when they feel part of the class. Think of the class as a community. You are a member of the community and can help yourself and other members to succeed. Most students get the names and phone numbers of a few classmates in order to get missed assignments or to clarify class work. Consider forming a study group with peers. Most people review material better in a group.

Stay focused. A school term is a long time. To succeed you have to complete the course. Set a pattern of attending every class and doing every assignment. Participation brings achievement. Writing is a skill, and practicing writing and the skills will help you to learn.

Part I

Making the Transition to College

Chapter 1
Getting Started

In this chapter, you will

- Become familiar with the principal parts of your textbook and CD-ROM
- Get to know your classmates and learn their names
- Meet the four student peers who share their writing throughout the book
- Introduce yourself to your classmates and instructor

Write for 10 minutes about how you feel about starting college. How do you think that being in college will change your lifestyle? How will getting a degree improve your life?

Getting to Know Your Materials

Writer's Resources: From Sentence to Paragraph

Each chapter of *Writer's Resources: From Sentence to Paragraph* is a unit of work that will help you learn the skills necessary to be successful in college and in the workplace. In addition to learning how to write clearly and avoid grammatical errors, you will learn a variety of skills that will prepare you to be successful in the classroom and on the job. You will learn how to become a more organized and efficient learner, how to work effectively with groups, how to set goals, and how to become actively involved in your learning.

One of the best ways to learn is to see clear examples of what you are asked to do. Therefore, *Writer's Resources: From Sentence to Paragraph* provides four student peers to share their work throughout the book. Their writing is not as sophisticated as the professional essays generally included in textbooks, but the peers provide examples of writing that communicates their ideas in a clear, well-organized fashion. You can learn to write as clearly and as persuasively as they do, especially when you take ownership of your writing and care about what you say and about how clearly you communicate your ideas.

Another key factor in learning to write well is practice. Like anything else—like learning to play basketball or the piano—the more you practice, the better you get. Developing the skill of writing is like developing any skill. It takes a combination of isolated drills to develop certain muscles and performance practice to sharpen the skill of writing. *Writer's Resources: From Sentence to Paragraph* will introduce you to the basic grammar and punctuation skills needed for success in college and will provide a variety of activities to help you learn the rules. Each skill chapter includes cooperative learning strategies, a variety of practices, and an editing exercise. In addition, you will write your own sentences with the target skill, and you may practice editing your journal writing for the skills you are learning.

Writer's Resources: From Sentence to Paragraph will also give you lots of practice using writing to explore and express ideas. The best way to improve your writing is to write every single day. Journal and Freewriting assignments encourage you to use writing to "prime the pump," come up with ideas, and figure out what you think. They are not graded for grammar or correctness and may take the form of lists or phrases, not necessarily complete sentences. Journal and Freewriting topics give you daily practice thinking on paper. You will also get lots of practice responding to topics and writing paragraphs, all of which will prepare you for the types of writing required in college and on the job.

How to Use Writer's Resources: From Sentence to Paragraph

A textbook's preface, table of contents, appendix, and index are usually not assigned reading at the beginning of a term, but becoming familiar with them can help you get oriented to the book and help you locate material easily.

Preface

In the preface, located at the beginning of your textbook, the authors point out the overall aims and features of the textbook.

Practice **1.1**   **Read the preface and answer the following questions.**

1. What features of the textbook do the authors highlight in the preface?

    First Year in College Skills, Peer Models, Group Activities, The Writing

    Process

2. Of the features mentioned, which do you think will be the most useful to you?

_____

_____

Table of Contents

The table of contents, located after the preface, gives you an outline of the contents and organization of each chapter. By studying the table of contents, you can discover what topics are covered in a textbook and how those topics are organized.

Practice **1.2**   **Examine the table of contents and list the titles of the four parts of the textbook.**

1. Making the Transition to College

2. Beginning College Writing

3. Grammar, Punctuation, and Mechanics Skills

4. Readings

Chapter Organization

Next, it is a good idea to examine a chapter to see how it is structured. Turn to Chapter 11. Leaf through the chapter and take note of the headings and subheadings in the chapter. Notice any graphic elements such as illustrations, boxed elements, and icons. Each time you begin a new chapter, it is a good idea to preview the chapter to get an idea of what you will be learning.

Practice **1.3**   **Look at Chapter 11 to answer the following questions.**

1. What introductory information does the chapter begin with?

    A boxed preview of the chapter

2. How many review exercises end the chapter?

    4

Appendix

The appendix, located at the end of the book, is the section of the book where additional materials such as error lists and English as a Second Language (ESL) materials are located.

Practice **1.4**   **Turn to the appendix (pages 353–393) and list the parts that are included in the appendix.**

ESL Appendix, Spelling, Creating a Portfolio, Checklists

_____

Index

The index, located at the very back of your textbook, allows you to look up specific topics or terms. The index is the fastest way to find information on specific topics because it lists the pages that contain a reference to the topic you are searching for.

Practice **1.5**   **Look at the index and list the page numbers that contain information about topic sentences.**

pages 39–42, 46-47

Play the "Tour"

Writer's Resources CD-ROM

Writer's Resources CD-ROM is meant to accompany your textbook and provide additional resources and practice with the skills your instructor covers in class. The CD provides audio and visual reinforcement for instruction and provides many additional practice exercises with feedback after each item.

How to Use the CD-ROM

1. Store the CD in a hard case to avoid cracking the disc.
2. Play the introductory tour for the Writing Process, Writing Elements, and Grammar sections to learn how the CD works.

Practice **1.6**   **Using the CD-ROM, look at the menu screen and list the main lessons covered by the CD-ROM.**

Writing Process, Writing Elements, Rhetorical Patterns,

Grammar/Punctuation/Mechanics

Getting to Know Your Classmates

Your classmates will be a valuable resource in helping you succeed in this course. Getting to know their names is the first step in forming a strong bond with the class and your peers. Here are some techniques that will help you remember your classmates' names.

1. Take notes. As your classmates introduce themselves or are introduced by others, write down their names and write down anything that will help you remember them (hair color, distinguishing features, etc.).
2. Use mnemonic devices. A mnemonic device is an association that will help you remember a piece of information. Associate a picture or a rhyme with a student's name in order to help you remember the name.

3. Quiz yourself. Before class starts each day, see how many of your class-mates' names you remember. Pay particular attention as those students whose names you couldn't remember introduce themselves or answer the roll.

The Peers Introduce Themselves

I'm **Beth Kamiski**, and I'm a single mom with two kids to raise. I'm back in school because I need a degree to find the kind of job that will allow me to support my kids. Before I had kids, I worked for a couple of years in various retail stores, but I stopped working eight years ago when I had my son, Kyle. I also have a daughter, Kristy, who is five. When my marriage ended, I had to go back to work, but with no degree and not much experience, I was stuck in minimum wage positions going nowhere fast. Even though my ex-husband was helping with child support, I could barely make ends meet. When my parents suggested I try going back to school and offered to help with tuition, I jumped at the chance. Going back to school is scary because I've been out of school for a while, but I'm determined to make it because I need to be able to support my kids. My mom is a nurse, and I think I'd like to become some sort of health professional because I like taking care of people and because salaries in the health professions tend to be above average.

I'm **Tony Anderson** and I'm from Atlanta. Atlanta is a great city and offers lots of opportunities for African Americans, but I didn't take advantage of most of them because in high school, I hung out with a crowd of serious partiers. In a city the size of Atlanta, there is always a party going on somewhere. When I graduated from high school, I knew that if I didn't get out of town, I would end up hanging out with my friends and going nowhere, so I decided to join the Army and see the world. I did two tours of duty, one in Berlin, Germany and one in North Carolina and in Panama. I learned a lot in the Army, and I gained confidence in my abilities and myself. I realized that I had a good head on my shoulders and that I had good "people skills." After spending eight years in the military and being promoted to the rank of Sergeant, I realized that I had developed the discipline and work habits necessary to be successful in school. I'm glad I didn't try to go to college right out of high school because when I was eighteen, I didn't have the motivation and discipline that I do now.

Hi, I'm **Alicia Martinez**. I just graduated from Loma Prieta High School outside of Los Angeles. I grew up speaking Spanish at home and English with my friends. Being bi-lingual is an advantage, especially in southern California. In high school, I worked at Sophisticated You, an upscale clothing store in the mall, and I discovered I was good at retail sales. My goal is to major in business administration and eventually to open a clothing store of my own. After I graduate, I'd like to gain experience by working for a large retail organization such as Sears or Macy's or Bloomingdale's. I know that if I work hard and learn how to run a business, I will eventually be able to open my own business and be successful.

My name is **Dan Tribble**, and I figure I'm probably the oldest student in this class. I'm coming back to school after having worked for quite a few years in retail sales. After being assistant manager of two different stores, I realized that without at least an AA, I wasn't going to get promoted. Going back to school isn't easy, but staying assistant manager and watching younger and less experienced employees get promoted over me is harder. I figure I need to bite the bullet and come back to school to get the training I need to earn the kind of salary it takes to support a family these days. I'd like to major in something to do with computers, maybe Web-page design or programming of some sort. It's hard feeling like I missed the boat by not going to school when I was younger, but I was too busy working and earning money at the time to realize that my potential earnings were limited by not having a degree. "Better late than never," my wife tells me, and I appreciate her support. I have two kids, one a freshman and one a junior in high school, so I figure I had better get started now or they will go to college before me.

Writing Assignment 1.7   Introduce yourself to your instructor and your classmates in one to two pages. You might want to include where you are from, what your interests, goals, and hobbies are, and anything else you think is important or might help your classmates get to know you.

Working with Classmates

In college and in the workplace, you will be working with people from different backgrounds, ages, races, nationalities, and religions. One of the most essential skills for becoming successful in school and at work is to learn to cooperate with people who are different from you. When employers are asked about what they value most in their employees, they consistently list the ability to communicate clearly and the ability to get along with others.

In the work world, employers are increasingly using work groups to accomplish tasks. Teams are often formed to complete projects, and an employee may be a member of a number of teams or task forces. Work in the 21st century is projected to become increasingly group-oriented.

Working in groups in this class will give you practice in making connections with others. The activities in this book are meant to make your leaning become more effective through your participation in groups. You will find that lots of learning can take place in relaxed and fun activities with peers.

Writing Practice   **Describe a work group that you have participated in or a school or community group that you are familiar with.**

_____

_____

_____

_____

_____

Creating Group Rapport

Working together with small groups of classmates will create a valuable resource during the term. Your group partners will support your learning. Group members compare notes, study material, and prepare for tests together. In addition, networking with your classmates can help you stay motivated and connected to the class and the school.

Productive work relationships are built upon good rapport—knowing something about your peers and respecting their point of view. Getting to know your classmates will help you enjoy the group process. The following activity will help you break the ice.

Group Activity **1.9**   **Complete the following roster with your classmates.**

Roster of Classmates

Name/Nickname	Hometown	Major	Favorite music	Study times	Hobbies

Roster of Classmates (continued)

Name/Nickname	Hometown	Major	Favorite music	Study times	Hobbies

Forming a Study Group

As the term progresses, you may wish to form a study group to review material and prepare for tests. An effective study group includes two to five members. You should look for students with whom you can create productive partnerships. Identify students in your class who have similar motivation. They should be available for study at the same time you are. Be sure that you feel comfortable and safe making plans to study with these students. It is wise to schedule study sessions at school. Wait to choose study partners until you have a chance to observe your classmates in class.

Alicia

Our study group formed after about four weeks of the term. The group work in class gave us a chance to get to know one another. Also, we talked before and after class. Then we just decided to try studying for the first test together. Although we are different in just about every way including age, sex, ethnicity, single, married, we are all serious about succeeding. We have found that each of us is good at a different part of the course. When we have to get ready for a punctuation test, Tony leads. When we are writing a paper, Beth gets us to brainstorm, and Dan is good at revising. I have also found that even when one of us doesn't know the material, teaching that person a concept helps me to learn it better.

Getting Organized

The start of a new term is an exciting and busy period. In the first couple of weeks, you will not only start new classes with new instructors and classmates, but you will also establish the routines and habits that will carry you through the term. What follows are steps you can take to get off to a good start.

Schedule Study Time

Most students who start college find that they need to change their lifestyles to accommodate challenging college classes. As a rule, college classes require 1 to 2 hours of out-of-class work for every hour of class. The best way to avoid falling behind in classes is to understand from the beginning how much time will be required to keep up and then to create a schedule that allows you to devote a minimum of 1 hour of out-of-class study time for every hour in class.

Strategies for Finding Study Time and Reducing Distractions

Alicia: Use time between classes to study rather than to socialize, and don't study with the TV on.

Tony: Wake up an hour early (before your family or roommates are up to distract you). If you have loud roommates, you may need to study at the library rather than going home to face their distraction.

Dan: Make it clear to your housemates that you need study time in order to be successful, or stay at school for an extra hour or two and study in the library or a lab.

Beth: If you have children, you may need to arrange play dates or have a family member or babysitter cover your kids several hours during the week while you study.

Use a Notebook

One way to get and stay organized is to use a notebook to keep all the materials for this class. Use a three-ring binder (preferably with pockets) so that you can file papers. Create dividers for each section of the notebook (Handouts, Class Notes, Journal, Skill Notes, and Writing Assignments). By the end of the term, you will have an organized record of the work you have produced.

Take Notes

Taking notes in class and on course materials is an essential skill in college. Learning to take notes and make good use of them will help you learn difficult material, keep up with assignments, and prepare for exams.

The purpose of taking notes in class is to remember important material covered in class and to remember assignments, due dates, and exam dates. Because every instructor and every class is slightly different, there is no one best method of taking notes. Today more than ever before, instructors vary their presentation styles. They break up their lectures with discussion and activities.

Note-Taking Guidelines

1. Date the top of a clean sheet of paper for each day of class.

2. For lecture presentations, write down the key words, definitions, and examples the instructor presents.

3. Write down the information the instructor writes on the board.

4. Write down any information that your instructor repeats or that he or she emphasizes with words, with gestures, or with examples.

5. For activity-centered class periods, write down the activities and any information that you learned from an activity. For example, if the instructor develops a model paragraph on the board, copy the paragraph in your notes so that you can review it later. If a group activity focuses on the acquisition of a certain skill, describe the activity and what you learned. For instance, if you brainstorm ideas as a group activity, write as many of the ideas as possible in your notes because you may well be asked to complete an assignment based on the ideas your group generated.

6. Write down all assignments, all test dates, and all due dates. Before you leave class, make sure you understand what you are supposed to do before the next class period.

Use Your Notes

The best strategy for using your notes is to look them over as soon as possible, preferably at the beginning of the study time you have scheduled for each class period.

1. First, transfer test dates or due dates to your calendar.

2. Next, complete reading and writing assignments you have been given.

3. Last but not least, review your notes to make sure you understand the concepts presented in class. If you are unclear about a point covered in class, try to look up the information in your textbook before the next class period or ask your instructor before class.

Writing Practice 1.10 Write for 10 minutes about your experience so far this term in your writing class. Recall your first class or two. Describe your experience, what you liked and disliked, what was surprising or interesting about the class so far.

Chapter 2
Setting Goals and Overcoming Obstacles

In this chapter, you will learn about

- Examining your attitudes and expectations about college
- Setting long-term goals
- Setting short-term goals
- Setting weekly and daily goals
- Steps to solving problems

Write for 10 minutes in response to the following topic. Have you ever set a goal and worked to achieve it? What obstacles did you face? Were you successful in achieving your goal? Why or why not? How did you feel as a result?

T he beginning of the term is a good time to examine your orientation toward school. Your attitudes and expectations will have a lot to do with your success in college. In addition, the goals that you set, long-term and short-term, and how you solve the inevitable problems of juggling your many responsibilities will play a crucial part in your success.

Examining Attitudes and Expectations

Attitude is an important factor in success in any endeavor. Ask anyone who is successful, and he or she will tell you that the desire to succeed and the willingness to work toward a goal are as important as anything else. You will improve your chances of success by examining your attitudes and making changes in those attitudes and behaviors that affect your success.

Activity 2.1   **Complete the following Self-Assessment Survey to examine your current motivation, attitudes, and skills.**

Self-Assessment Survey

1= Strongly Disagree   2= Disagree   3= Don't Know   4= Agree   5= Strongly Agree

1. I am highly motivated to succeed in school.
      1   2   3   4   5

2. I am able to discipline myself in order to be successful.
      1   2   3   4   5

3. I see a clear relationship between school and achieving my goals.
      1   2   3   4   5

4. Being successful in school is important to me.
      1   2   3   4   5

5. I am confident in my ability to work successfully with people who are different from me.
      1   2   3   4   5

6. I regularly set goals and accomplish them.
      1   2   3   4   5

7. I use my time productively.
      1   2   3   4   5

8. I feel confident in my ability to speak in front of people I do not know.
      1   2   3   4   5

9. I know how to use the computer in school and in the workplace.
      1   2   3   4   5

10. I am confident that I can clearly communicate my ideas in writing.
      1   2   3   4   5

Add up your total points, and refer to the scale below to evaluate your motivation, self-esteem, and assessment of skills.

10–20 = Your motivation, self-esteem, and skill assessment are below average.

21–35 = Your motivation, self-esteem, and skill assessment are average.

36–50 = Your motivation, self-esteem, and skill assessment are above average.

If you are like many beginning college students, you probably did not score as high on the Self-Assessment Survey as you would like. Many students do not start college with clearly defined goals or with the motivation, behaviors, and skills that will help them be successful. If you do have clear goals and good work habits, you are ahead of the crowd. If you don't, the important concept to understand is that you can develop the behaviors and skills that will help you be successful.

Success begins with the willingness to change behaviors that stand in your way and learn behaviors that will help you succeed. The first step is to identify the behaviors that will help you be successful.

Practice 2.2   **List five to ten specific behaviors that make a student successful in college.**
Answers will vary.

In-class behaviors	Out-of-class behaviors
attending class every day on time	scheduling study time
paying attention	completing assignments
taking notes	preparing for tests
asking questions	

Group Activity 2.3   **In a group of three or four students, share your ideas about behaviors that make students successful in college. You should add ideas from other group members to the list that you began generating in Practice 2.2. Groups should share their lists with the class.**

Setting Long-Term Goals

Successful people are not successful by accident. They have specific long-term goals that they steadily work toward. They also develop work habits that make their efforts pay off. They focus on what they want to accomplish by defining long-term goals, and they set short-term goals that move them along the path toward their goals.

Developing concrete long-term goals can help you succeed in college in a number of ways. First, the more concrete and specific your goal, the easier it will be for you to work toward it by selecting the right courses. Also, having a reason to be in college—long-term goals—can help you maintain your motivation to do well in school.

Many students start college with general goals such as being happy or wealthy, but with very little idea of how they will reach their goals or what career they want to pursue. If you do not have a clear idea of what sort of career you want to pursue, you might want to explore your interests and abilities with an academic advisor. Academic advisors can give you a personality inventory that will help you determine what line of work would be most satisfying to you. Advisors can also help you map out the courses that are required to complete a degree in the fields that interest you.

Writing Assignment 2.4 What is your dream? Using your own paper, describe your long-term goals and/or the life you would like to lead.

Peer Examples

Two student peers describe their dreams and long-term goals.

Beth

My dream is to get my RN degree and work with infants. I want to do work that I consider meaningful and that I'm respected for. Because nurses are in demand everywhere, I could move anywhere I wanted and be able to find work. I also like the idea of having a job that is fairly secure so I won't have to worry about being laid off or losing my job. Nursing would allow me to earn a decent salary so that I can support my kids as they get older. I'd like to be able to afford my kids' activities and the things they will want as they get older. One day, I'd like to be able to buy a house. One of the advantages of being a nurse is having a flexible schedule. Ideally, I will be able to arrange a schedule that allows me to be home with my kids in the afternoons and evenings.

Dan

I can recognize a trend when I see one, and computers are the trend of the future. The more I surf the Web, the more I realize the business potential the Internet represents. Every business needs a Web site, and I'm hoping to get a degree that will allow me to create Web sites for businesses. If I play my cards right, I hope I can start my own Web design business. My ideal job is to be able to work from home, but if that doesn't work out, I don't mind working for a big company. I'd like to be able to do work that is interesting and challenging, and I'd like to do work that I am respected and rewarded for. It may sound silly, but I'd also like my wife and kids to be proud of the work I do.

Setting Short-Term Goals

A journey of a thousand miles must begin with a single step. • Lao-tzu
(604 B.C.–531 B.C.)

Making your dreams into reality begins with breaking your goals down into smaller, achievable goals. The only way to accomplish any large task is to break it down into small, manageable steps. Writers write essays one paragraph at a time. Skyscrapers are built one steel girder at a time. Businesses are built one customer at a time. Unless you break your goals down into realistic, manageable steps, it will be easy to get discouraged or distracted and lose your focus.

Setting Weekly and Daily Goals

Most successful people are in the habit of making weekly and/or daily goals, a "to-do" list of things they would like to accomplish. They may not get through everything on the list, but having the list makes it more likely that they will complete some or all of the tasks.

First of all, making a list helps you clarify what you need or would like to accomplish. If you never tell yourself that you need to study for a test, you're not likely to do it. In fact, you may forget the test altogether.

Second, a to-do list helps you prioritize your goals and decide which are the most important. Few people have enough time to accomplish everything they'd like to in a given day or week. You have to decide which of the items on your to-do list are the most important and try to accomplish those.

Steps to Setting Short-Term Goals

➡ Set a realistic short-term goal.

➡ Break the goal down into specific steps.

➡ Set a daily schedule for accomplishing each step.

➡ Assess your progress regularly and modify your plan accordingly.

Problem Solving

Character cannot be developed in ease and quiet. Only through experiences of trial and suffering can the soul be strengthened, vision cleared, ambition inspired and success achieved. • Helen Keller

Learning to overcome the many obstacles that arise in life will help you succeed in your personal life, in school, and at work. No one sails through life without encountering obstacles. In fact, many successful individuals have had to overcome obstacles that others would consider impossible to overcome. Many students think that successful people have succeeded without facing difficulties or disappointments. Nothing could be further from the truth. In "Consider This" (page 288), Jack Canfield provides many examples of famous people who have overcome obstacles in order to become successful.

Steps to Solving Problems

All too often, people give up when they encounter an unexpected obstacle. Giving up when confronted with obstacles can become a habit like so many other habits that keep individuals from realizing their dreams. However, the "I give up" response can be changed through conscious effort.

Overcoming obstacles is a skill that anyone can learn, and the best way to learn the skill is to practice it. The more you practice solving problems, the better at it you will be, and the more confident you will be in your ability to overcome any obstacle, large or small.

A problem well-defined is half solved. • John Dewey

Step 1: Define the problem

Take a few minutes to make sure you understand the problem. Ask yourself the following questions:

> What is the problem?
>
> What caused the problem?
>
> Can the problem be divided into parts that can be solved separately?
>
> Does one part of the problem have to be solved before another?
>
> What have I learned about solving similar problems in the past?
>
> How have similar problems been solved by others in the past?
>
> What is the time frame for solving the problem?
>
> Where should I start in solving the problem?

Now, summarize the problem in a sentence or two.

Step 2: Brainstorm possible solutions

Come up with as many possible solutions to the problem as you can. Don't worry about how silly or unrealistic the solutions you come up with are. Don't judge or criticize any of the ideas you or group members come up with. Ideas help generate other ideas, and you never know what might work in solving a problem.

Step 3: Seek advice

Sometimes the best way to solve a problem is to seek information or advice. For example, if you're trying to decide which of two cars to buy, you may want to have a mechanic evaluate the two cars to give you advice on which is the most reliable. Similarly, if you are trying to figure out how to solve a problem you have no experience with, asking the advice of someone who has had experience with the problem may be your best solution.

Step 4: Evaluate the solutions and choose one

Look over the solutions you generated and/or the advice you received and consider each one. Ask yourself, what are the positive and negative outcomes of each solution? Narrow the choices by selecting what you think are the best solutions. You may want to try ranking the solutions in order from best to worst. After weighing the pros and cons of each solution, select one solution. Several of the solutions may work, but at this stage, you should select the one you think will work the best.

Step 5: Develop a plan to implement the solution

Even a good solution to a problem will not work if it is not carried out. Break the solution down into specific, concrete steps. Develop a schedule or plan of how and when you will accomplish each step.

Step 6: Anticipate possible obstacles

If you fail to anticipate obstacles to your plan, you are more likely to get discouraged and give up on implementing your solution. Use one of the brainstorming techniques described in step 2 to generate a list of things that might interfere with your solution. For example, if the problem you are trying to solve is turning in a paper by the due date, one of the obstacles you might anticipate is that you or your child gets sick. How can you overcome such an obstacle? Anticipating possible obstacles and making a plan to overcome each one is one of the best ways to ensure the success of your plan.

Step 7: Evaluate your progress regularly

One way to ensure the success of your plan is to regularly evaluate your progress toward your goal. If you make a plan but don't check your progress until it is too late to make corrections, you are setting yourself up for failure.

> *The marvelous richness of human experience would lose something of rewarding joy if there were no limitations to overcome. The hilltop hour would not be half so wonderful if there were no dark valleys to traverse.* • Helen Keller

Writing Assignment 2.5 Choose a problem you face in your personal life, in school, or at work and apply problem-solving strategies to help you come up with a solution to your problem.

Step 1: Define the problem.

_____

_____

_____

_____

Step 2: Brainstorm solutions.

_____

_____

_____

_____

Step 3: Get advice.

_____

_____

_____

_____

Step 4: Choose a solution.

_____

_____

_____

_____

Step 5: Implement the solution.

_____

_____

_____

_____

Step 6: Possible obstacles.

_____

_____

_____

_____

Step 7: Evaluate progress.

_____

_____

_____

_____

Results.

_____

_____

_____

_____

Peer Example:

Beth

Step 1: Problem

Getting the kids out of the house on time is a major problem for me in the morning. No matter what I do, something always goes wrong—Kristy can't find her shoes or a toy she just *has* to bring to day care with her, or Kyle can't find his safety patrol belt or his math book. I end up yelling at them, one or both of them end up in tears, and we are still ten to fifteen minutes late leaving the house. It's no way to begin the day because everyone starts out feeling frazzled.

I identified the biggest causes of delay as 1) not being able to find things (clothes, books, lunchboxes, shoes, etc.)

2) everyone moving slower than I anticipate.

Step 2: Solutions

The two solutions I came up with were 1) getting the kids' clothes and backpacks together the night before and 2) setting my alarm 15 minutes earlier and getting the kids started out the door 5–10 minutes earlier than I do now.

Step 3: Advice

I called my mom, explained my problem, and asked for her advice. She suggested getting the kids to help by setting aside 15 minutes before their baths and asking them to get their clothes out for the next day, make sure their backpacks are packed, and organize their lunches. They can put their lunch boxes on the counter and put in non-perishable items like snacks, cookies, and napkins.

Step 4: Choose a solution

I'm going to try both solutions simultaneously because it'll take both to make it work.

Step 5: Implement the solution

I'll start by talking to the kids about the problem. They hate it as much I do that mornings are so stressful. I will need to get them to buy into the solution, which may mean I will have to come up with some sort of a reward. I'll have them come up with suggestions for rewards, but they will only get the reward if we have a week of smooth, on-time exits.

We'll start on Sunday evening, and I'll give them plenty of positive reinforcement for their cooperation. Maybe I can suggest going out to a movie on Friday afternoon as a reward if we are successful the first week.

Step 6: Possible obstacles

The kids may like the idea, but I suspect it won't be easy to get them to organize their things the night before. They will want to keep watching TV, and I will have to pull them away (more stress). That means I will have to get their agreement to stop TV by 7:00 so we can finish dinner, have 15 minutes to get ourselves organized, and forty-five min for baths and reading before bedtime at 8:30.

I will have to remind myself to look at the clock and get them started every night right after dinner so that it becomes a habit. If I get distracted by schoolwork and forget to remind them, I know they won't do it on their own. It will be up to me to stick to a schedule and remind them. Maybe I can make doing the dishes my clue to get them started.

Step 7: Evaluate progress

It will help if we review our success or failure right when we get in the car. I'll ask them to tell me what went right and what went wrong and what we need to do differently the next day.

Results

I admit it took effort to get the kids to pick out their clothes the night before and make sure both of them thought about everything they needed to take to school with them the next day (and I did the same), but it paid off the next morning. I set my imaginary departure time ten minutes earlier than usual. By the time everyone got their teeth brushed and shoes on and was out the door, we were right on time for the first time I can remember. Instead of yelling "hurry up, we're late," I congratulated them on having done a great job getting out on time. What a difference it makes to start the day feeling that you've done something right instead of feeling that you've failed. I can't believe it's taken me this long to figure out how to get control of the situation, but better late than never. Now the challenge will be to consistently follow the plan.

Part II

Beginning College Writing

Chapter 3
Using a Journal

In this chapter, you will

- Learn the benefits of writing in a writer's journal
- Learn what, when, and how to write in your journal
- Read examples of peer journals

Write for 10 minutes in response to the following topic. Have you ever kept a journal or diary? If so, what was the experience like? If not, how might the habit of recording your thoughts and feelings each day improve your attitude and abilities as a writer?

It is wise to write on many subjects, to try many themes, that so you may find the right and inspiring one. Be greedy of occasions to express your thought. . . . You must try a thousand themes before you find the right one, as nature must try a thousand acorns to get one oak. • Henry David Thoreau

What Is a Writer's Journal?

The word *journal* comes from the French word meaning "daily." As the name implies, journal writing is daily writing. For hundreds of years, writers have used journals to record and explore experiences, ideas, and feelings. Daily journal writing is one of the best ways to improve your writing because writing every day helps you practice expressing your ideas on paper. The more you practice expressing your ideas on paper, the easier and more natural it will become, and the more confident you will feel in your ability to express your ideas clearly and effectively.

Beth

I started keeping a journal when my kids were little. I'd write down the funny things they said and did. My journal was a way of recording their growth and a way of hanging on to the memories. Then when I went through my divorce, my journal changed to being focused on feelings, and writing became my way of figuring out how I felt.

Dan

I like writing in the journal because I don't get graded on errors. Journal writing lets me explore and develop my ideas without worrying about how well I'm writing. I'm often surprised at how much I can write and how many ideas I can come up with in ten to fifteen minutes.

Exploring Experiences and Ideas

I write to discover what I think. • Daniel Boorstein, author of *The Ascent of Man*

You can use a journal to record what you see, hear, feel, and experience. You can also use a journal to record your thoughts and ideas. Writing down your thoughts in a journal generates more thoughts and more ideas. As you write, you often begin to understand how your ideas fit together, how you feel, or what the ideas mean to you.

Tony

I've learned that by writing in my journal, I figure out what I think. I start writing about something that happened or something that's been on my mind, and by the time I'm finished with the entry, I have a pretty good idea what I think. Writing in my journal definitely helps me process feelings and ideas.

Alicia

I use my journal to try out ideas. Every time I write a paper, I sit down and write a journal on the topic. Writing in a journal helps me figure out what I think and what I want to say.

Your Journal

Two of the primary purposes of a journal are to help you overcome your fear of writing and to help you see writing as a way to explore ideas. The more you write, the less you will fear it, and the more you will see how useful writing can be in helping you generate ideas and figure out what you think.

How and What to Write

- Use loose-leaf paper.
- Keep your journal entries in a separate section of your class notebook.
- Respond to topics suggested in the textbook or by your instructor.
- Write as much as you can about the topic.
- Don't worry about writing correctly.

When and Where to Write

Some of your journal entries may be completed in class, and some may be completed at home.

Try to write in a comfortable spot, one where you will not be disturbed, and try to write at the same time every day. The habit of writing in a journal is just that, a habit, and you encourage the habit by practicing it regularly in a familiar spot. You may be tempted to skip a day and write several entries in one day, but the entries will sound tired and repetitious, and you won't benefit from the journal in the same way you will if you write daily.

Set aside a half-hour every day for reflection and writing. You will be surprised how such a habit can improve the clarity of your perceptions, feelings, and ideas.

Peer Journals

The four student peers share several of the journal entries they have written in response to journal topics that they were given by their instructor. You may be assigned daily journal topics by your instructor, or you may be allowed to choose some or all of your own topics. As you can see from the peer examples, journal entries come in all shapes and forms. As you read the peer journals, remember that the main purpose of journal writing is to explore and experiment with ideas.

Beth

Topic: *Choose a quote that seems particularly significant to you, copy it into your journal, and explain what the quote means to you or why it is important.*

> Character cannot be developed in ease and quiet. Only through experiences of trial and suffering can the soul be strengthened, vision cleared, ambition inspired and success achieved. • Helen Keller

This quote from Helen Keller sums up something that I'm just beginning to realize. I used to think that happiness meant never having anything go wrong in your life. First of all, I don't think anyone has a perfect life, and if they did, they wouldn't get the chance to grow the way you do through coping with difficulty. I thought my life was over when my husband left me, but now I see that I'm a stronger, more self-confident person because I was able to stand on my own and keep it together for my kids. I could have done without all the pain, but if it hadn't happened, I wouldn't have decided to go back to school and become a nurse. I would be sitting at home watching TV and not feeling like I was worth much. Being on my own helped me figure out who I was and what I wanted for myself. I don't think I could have done that any other way.

Tony

Topic: *How much do you feel that you control your fate?*

I control my fate much more now than I did when I was younger. In high school, I didn't think of the decisions I was making as decisions. I just went along with what everyone else was doing, so I didn't have control. It wasn't until I made the decision to leave Atlanta and join the Army that started to exert some control over my life. Getting away was the best thing I ever did because it gave me the perspective to think about what I did and didn't want in my life. Going back to school is a big step for me, but it's a choice I'm making, so I feel good about it.

Dan

Topic: *What will pose the biggest challenge to your success in this class this semester?*

The biggest problem I'm having so far is feeling like I'm too old to be in college. It's hard to ignore that I'm the oldest person in the class, and I keep feeling like a fish out of water. Going back to school seemed like a good idea, but now I wonder if I haven't made a big mistake. I keep feeling like I shouldn't be here. Do these kids think I'm a loser for being in this class at my age? Or is it me who is starting to feel like a loser?

I've got to get over this feeling or I won't be able to stick it out. But just thinking about quitting school makes me feel like more of a loser than anything else would. How could I face Diane and the kids if I quit? No way. Going to school is a step in the right direction for me—I just know it. I know what I want and why I'm here, which is more than most of the kids in the class can say. In some ways I'm more ready to be here than they are. I just have to get over this hump of feeling out of place.

Alicia

> **Topic:** *Describe a custom or celebration in your culture that others may not understand.*

Everyone thinks Christmas is celebrated on December 25th, but in many Latin countries, gifts are given, not on Dec. 25th but on Jan. 5th, Three Kings' Day, or El Dia de Los Reyes. Three Kings's Day was chosen for the exchange of gifts because it marks the day the three kings brought gifts to the baby Jesus. As a child I remember putting out hay and water for the three kings' camels rather than milk and cookies for Santa. I admit that as a kid it felt strange to be exchanging gifts at a different time than all of my friends, but now I'm glad my parents held on to their traditions. Exchanging gifts on Three Kings' Day was also practical for my family because my parents could avoid the crowds of Christmas shoppers and take advantage of the after Christmas sales. When I have children, I plan to continue the tradition of exchanging gifts on Jan. 5th both to avoid the stress of the Christmas season and to keep my kids in touch with their heritage.

Suggested Journal Topics

1. What will pose the biggest challenge to your success in this class this semester? How can you overcome one or more of those challenges? For example, if you have trouble getting to class on time, what causes you to be late, and what can you do about it? What makes it difficult for you to complete assignments at home? Brainstorm ways of overcoming the difficulty.

2. Do you consider yourself organized? How would improving your organization improve your life? How could you begin to improve your organization in small ways?

3. What are the characteristics of successful people? Which of these characteristics do you share? How could you develop more of their characteristics?

4. Describe a situation in which you felt powerless. How might you avoid being in situations like that again?

5. List five things that improving your writing will help you do better.

6. What are you most proud of in your life thus far? What do you most hope to accomplish in your life?

7. How much do you feel that you control your fate? Does living as though you control your own destiny lead to a more powerful life? How might you begin to take control of your life?

8. How often do you step back and reflect upon the way you are living and where you are headed? How could regular reflection on your life and goals help improve your life?

9. In what way will reaching your goals make your life more satisfying?

10. Write a mission statement for your life.

Chapter 4
Writing a Paragraph

In this chapter, you will learn how

- To understand the assignment
- To narrow the topic
- To determine the writing context
- To formulate a topic sentence
- To develop the topic sentence with supporting details
- To generate ideas for support
- To create a first draft
- To revise the paragraph
- To edit the paragraph

Often in school and the workplace you will be asked to present your ideas in a paragraph. The paragraph is the basic building block of essays and reports. A paragraph presents a main idea and supports the main idea in a number of sentences. While a paragraph is usually only five to ten sentences in length, it demands a coherent organization in which all the sentences are unified in developing the main idea. Writers must use the writing process in order to create a well-structured paragraph.

Because the best way to learn the writing process is to practice it, we suggest that you choose one of the following writing topics and develop it into a paragraph by completing the Writing Practice for each step of the process.

Your Assignment: Choosing a Writing Topic

Choose one of the following topics to write a paragraph about.

1. Choose a place of business that you are familiar with and prove that this business is a good business for students like you to use.

2. Explain why a particular kind of electronic device such as a computer or cell phone is useful to college students.

(continues)

3. Explain why your hometown is a good or bad place to live for a specific group of people (such as young people, families, or retirees).

4. Choose a business that you would like to work for and prove to the employer that you would make a good employee.

5. Assignment from your instructor:

_____

_____

The process for writing a paragraph begins with understanding the writing assignment and then narrowing the topic to an idea that can be developed in just one paragraph.

WP: 1.2

Understanding the Assignment

To make sure that you understand the assignment, you should write down all of the requirements or guidelines that your instructor gives you. Be sure to ask questions if anything is unclear about what you are supposed to do.

Beth

I remembered the date my paragraph was due but not the day or the length until after I asked my instructor for clarification. I've found it helpful to write down this important information.

Assignment: Write a paragraph that proves that a place of business is a good place for students like me to use.
Length: 7–10 sentences
Due date: Friday, October 2

Writing Process Step 1: Understanding assignment

Fill in the information for your assignment.

Assignment: _____

Length (number of sentences in the paragraph): _____

Due date: _____

Narrowing the Topic

While some writing topics do not need to be narrowed, many topics are too general to write about without first narrowing to a subject that can be developed in one paragraph. Often the topic will define a particular subject to write about such as a business, and the writer must narrow to a particular business. Sometimes, choosing a particular audience will narrow the topic.

WP: 1.7

Brainstorming Techniques

One way to narrow a general topic is to work individually or in a group to **brainstorm** a more specific topic. This is a particularly important part of the process. Your task here is to narrow the writing topic to a subject that you can write about effectively. If you find a subject that you have lots of experience with and care about, you are more likely to write a strong paragraph because you will find it easier to think of a good topic sentence and generate support with lots of specific detail.

Most writers have trouble starting a paper. All the brainstorming techniques discussed below are designed to get your thought processes going. You will focus your attention on the topic and write down ideas that come to mind. Many writers combine brainstorming alone and in a group.

WP: 1.5

Narrowing Tree

We can narrow a topic by dividing the topic into its parts or by thinking of specific examples. The parts of the topic and/or specific examples cut the topic down to size and lead us to think of more ideas. A narrowed topic can be covered in just one paragraph.

Follow the activity of your mind, and jot down all the ideas that come to mind. Many writers use a graphic organizer to make a picture of the ideas that come to mind.

Tony

I like using a narrowing tree. You see here that I started very general with kinds of businesses that I use and then narrowed to particular places.

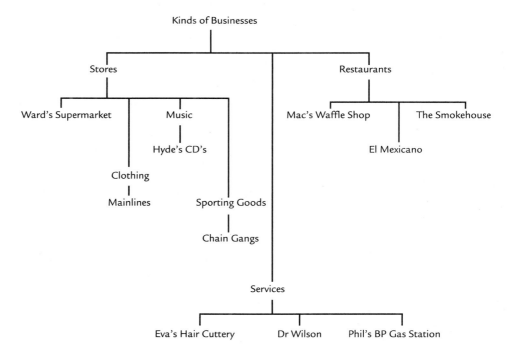

WP: 1.21

Freewriting

Sometimes you may simply want to write for five minutes on the topic to get your ideas flowing. Don't worry about what you write; simply focus on the assignment and write whatever comes to mind. This method can be used in combination with the other methods too.

Beth

If I stick with a topic for ten minutes and write down my ideas, I usually am surprised with what I can come up with.

I'm not sure what I want to write about. I really lucked out with this topic, though, because as a single mom I do an awful lot of shopping. Most of my shopping is for groceries. The store down the street is ok, but it doesn't have everything I want. I could write about the grocery store I used to go to.

The instructions are to write about a business I'd recommend to another student. My instructor says my writing will be more convincing if I pick a place that I really do like. There's that fancy restaurant Bill took me. I can't remember its name, and I've only been there once. I like the people at Child Space. Mrs. Nichols is great, and Colin loves it there.

Last week I had my brakes done, and the mechanic was really nice. What do I know about a garage? There was good service. I don't know if the price was the best or not.

Today I've got to pick up my dress from Nina's. Bill is taking me out to dinner again. Wow! I can't wait, and I'm glad Nina could fix the seam. She was really nice about doing the alteration on short notice. She's a single mom too. What a funky place she has. It's so easy to get to on the way to school. Her work is cheap.

Yes! Nina's Alteration would make a good narrowed topic. I could also write about Child Space. It has a lot to offer parents and kids. Nina's is better because I believe enough in it to recommend it to another student, and I know a lot about the business.

WP: 1.7

Group Brainstorming

Brainstorming ideas with group members is another excellent way to generate suggestions for narrowing a topic. Each individual contributes ideas, which in turn stimulate other ideas. In the work world, groups often brainstorm creative solutions to problems.

Example:

Tony: Let's go through our day and think about the places where we spend money.

Beth: I spend money all the time, mostly on my kids, but today I'm getting a dress altered and going to the grocery store before I pick my kids up at Child Space.

Tony: This morning I grabbed a donut on the way to school. The shop is on my route from the house. Later, I had coffee at the student center near Walker Hall. This afternoon I'm stopping by Chain Gang's to get a new seat for my bike.

Beth: I like that little coffee shop at the student center. The windows look out on the commons area. It's amazing that we came up with the coffee shop because I hadn't even thought of it as a place of business.

Tony: I want to write about a business I really care about.

Beth: A place where I don't mind spending money.

Tony: I want to write about a place I enjoy going and that I do recommend to other students.

Beth: What do you think about the bike shop you mentioned? I've got to get my son's bike overhauled.

Writing Process Step 2: Narrowing the Topic

Use one or more brainstorming methods to narrow your topic.

Writing topic: _____

Narrowed topic: _____

WP: 1.10–1.15

Determining the Writing Context

Determining the writing context means defining your purpose in writing, your audience, and perhaps the tone you wish to use.

Purpose

The purpose of your writing is the reason you are writing. Key words in the writing topic usually define the purpose. **Explain** means to make clear, give the reasons for, or analyze in a step-by-step fashion. **Prove** means to provide evidence to persuade the reader that a statement is true. Most topics ask you to inform the reader about the topic and persuade the audience to accept your main idea. You are trying to convince the audience of your paragraph to accept your ideas.

Audience

Each writing assignment specifies a particular audience. The audience will affect the kinds of information that you provide. For example, if you were trying to prove that a place of business such as a grocery store is a good place to shop for retirees, you would focus on very different products and services than you would if you were proving the same grocery store is good for children.

Group Activity 4.1   **Circle the audience in each writing topic and discuss how the audience will determine what information should be included in the paragraph.**

1. Choose a place of business you are familiar with and prove that this business is a good place for students like you.

2. Explain why a particular kind of electronic device such as a computer or cell phone is useful to college students.

3. Explain why your hometown is a good or bad place to live for young people.

4. Prove to a particular employer that you would make a good employee.

Tone

Most college writing is intended to be serious and formal. No slang or profane language should be used. Depending upon the audience, humor may be appropriate.

Group Activity 4.2   **Discuss the use of tone in the following situations.**

1. Explain how you might use humor to explain the advantages of owning a cell phone for teenagers.

Answers will vary.

2. Discuss why you would use a serious tone to explain why a hospital in your town is a good place of business for someone with a life-threatening illness.

Answers will vary.

_____

_____

_____

Example of Determining the Writing Context:

Tony

I worked through all the steps to determine the writing context.

Purpose: To convince a student to use Chain Gang's for bike needs

Audience: A college student who depends on a bicycle for transportation

Tone: Serious and enthusiastic

Writing Process Step 3: Determining the Writing Context

Decide on the purpose, audience, and tone of your current assignment.

Purpose: _____

Audience: _____

Tone: _____

WE: 5.4–5.8

Formulating a Topic Sentence

The main idea of a paragraph is stated in the topic sentence. The topic sentence is a statement that can be developed with sentences in the body of the paragraph. Often the topic sentence expresses a **feeling**, **attitude**, or **point of view** about the topic. In other words, the topic sentence states an **opinion**.

Examples:

College students who depend on their bikes for transportation should shop at Chain Gang's Bike Stop.

Nina's Alterations meets the sewing needs of students.

A cell phone can be very useful to students.

College students enjoy living in Portland, Oregon.

The topic sentence should focus on a **controlling idea** that can be developed in one paragraph. The controlling idea is the part of the topic sentence that controls what the rest of the paragraph will develop.

Examples:

> College students who depend on their bikes for transportation <u>should shop at Chain Gang's Bike Stop</u>.
>
> Nina's Alterations <u>meets all the sewing needs of students</u>.
>
> Phil's Service Station <u>helps students keep their cars running</u>.
>
> A cell phone <u>can be very useful to students</u>.
>
> College students <u>enjoy living</u> in Portland, Oregon.

Practice 4.3   **Underline the controlling idea in the following topic sentences.**

1. A home computer <u>provides wonderful entertainment</u>.
2. There are <u>many valuable features</u> in a word processing program.
3. A laptop computer is a <u>good option for students</u>.
4. Recording music is <u>easy on the computer</u>.
5. Communication has been <u>revolutionized by the Internet</u>.

The topic sentence is usually **not a cut-and-dried fact**. A fact needs no development because it is either true or false. Normally, a paragraph develops or supports an idea that needs reasons behind it. The paragraph explains or proves the topic sentence, and a fact usually does not need to be proven. The following statements are facts. They do not express an idea that needs to be developed in a paragraph. The ideas might be contained in a paragraph, but these statements could not be used as the main idea of a paragraph.

Examples:

> I shop at Chain Gang's Bike Stop.
>
> Nina's Alterations can alter the hem line of a dress.
>
> Students use cell phones.
>
> Many college students live in Portland, Oregon.

Practice 4.4   **Place an F next to statements that are facts, and place O next to opinions.**

    F 1. Computer Experts sells and services computers.

    O 2. The Computer Experts is very helpful to students.

    F 3. Computer Experts is located on University Avenue.

    O 4. Computer Experts offers a wonderful selection of computers and computer services.

    O 5. Students enjoy the benefits of shopping at Computer Experts.

Most often, the topic sentence will be the **first sentence** of the paragraph. It begins the paragraph by stating the main idea that the paragraph will develop. The first sentence of the paragraph should be indented five spaces in from the margin to show the reader where the paragraph begins.

Example:

> Nina's Alterations meets the sewing needs of students. This fine shop offers service in one hour. Students can drop off pants to be hemmed or a blouse that is missing buttons and pick up the clothing on the way home from school. . . .

Generating a Topic Sentence

Often the topic sentence for a paragraph is suggested by the **writing topic**. The topic is a general subject to write about. Often the writing topic is in the form of a **prompt** or **discussion question** that gives directions to write about a general subject. Most writing prompts can be turned into a topic sentence by using the important words from the prompt to make a statement.

Example:

> Writing topic: Choose a place of business you are familiar with and prove that this business is a good place for students like you.

> Topic sentence: Ward's is a great supermarket for college students.

Practice 4.5   **Use the *important words* in the writing prompt to make a statement.**

1. Explain why a particular kind of electronic device such as a computer or a cell phone *is useful to college students.*

   Topic sentence: A cell phone is useful to college students _____ .

   Topic sentence: A computer is useful to college students _____ .

2. Explain why your hometown is a good or bad place to live for young people.

   Topic sentence: _____ is a good place to live for young people _____ .
                    (your hometown)

3. Prove to an employer that you would make a good employee.

   Topic sentence: I would make a good employee _____ .

Examples of Tentative Topic Sentences

Beth's tentative topic sentence:

I like using Nina's Alterations.

Tony's tentative topic sentence:

College students who depend on their bikes for transportation should shop at Chain Gang's Bike Stop.

Practice 4.6 **Keeping your purpose, audience, and tone in mind, formulate a tentative topic sentence.**

Tentative topic sentence:

_____

_____

WE: 5.19

Developing the Topic Sentence with Supporting Details

The topic sentence of the paragraph is like a promise to the reader. It promises the reader that the paragraph will develop the main or controlling idea with support details. Supporting details **illustrate**, **explain**, or **prove** the topic sentence. Usually, a paragraph will provide three to five supporting details.

The supporting details for the topic sentence have a **unity** of purpose. In other words, every sentence should support the controlling idea.

Practice 4.7 **Cross through sentences that do not support the <u>controlling idea</u>.**

Topic sentence: My computer <u>provides me with valuable resources</u>.

I can play music using the CD drive.

~~The computer only cost six hundred dollars.~~

The word processing program helps me find errors in my papers.

I enjoy communicating with friends through e-mail because I don't have to pay for long distance phone calls.

~~My computer is only six months old.~~

WP: 1.19–1.24

Generating Ideas for Support

Focusing on the controlling idea in the topic sentence is the secret to generating ideas for support. The controlling idea determines what is needed to support the main idea. Experienced writers come up with ideas for support before they begin writing.

In fact, the brainstorming techniques you used to narrow the topic are even more important in generating ideas to support your topic sentence. You will be surprised at how many ideas you can come up with using these techniques. They are like keys that unlock information stored in your brain that you may not be able to access if you rely on writing the paragraph "off the top of your head."

Some writers like to brainstorm by themselves using freewriting, listing, and clustering. Other writers enjoy brainstorming in a group. Many writers use a combination of individual and group work to generate ideas. You should experiment with all the brainstorming techniques presented here. You may find that one of the techniques is more natural to you than others. You may also find that some techniques work with particular topics better than others. By the end of the term, you should be comfortable with a few of these ways of generating ideas.

Focus on the Main Idea to Generate Support

The first step in generating support is determining what the main idea of your paragraph demands as support. Focus on the controlling idea in the topic sentence because it controls or limits what the paragraph will develop.

Tony

Before I began brainstorming supporting details for my paragraph about Chain Gang's, I identified the controlling idea in my topic sentence and underlined it. I focused on what information or support I could use to show why students "should shop at Chain Gang's Bike Stop."

Tentative topic sentence: College students who depend on their bikes for transportation should shop at Chain Gang's Bike Stop.

Beth

I have had plenty of experience with Nina's Alterations because I used to be twenty pounds heavier, and then when I lost weight, I had to take in all my clothes.

Tentative topic sentence: I enjoy using Nina's Alterations.

Practice 4.8   **Underline the key words in your tentative topic sentence that must be developed, explained, or supported in your paragraph.**

Topic sentence:

_____

_____

Freewriting

Sometimes the easiest way to begin gathering ideas for supporting the main idea is to begin writing down all the ideas that come to mind when you try to explain or develop your topic sentence. Write as much and as fast as you can, without worrying about spelling or grammar. Remember that you are just exploring your thoughts on the main idea with this freewriting, not trying to write a polished paragraph.

Tony

Chain Gang's rules! I can give lots of reasons. I really like the people there. They're nice and they are knowledgeable. Kyle has been racing for fifteen years, and the campus road riders meet at the shop on Saturdays before a long ride. It's great getting free air and borrowing a wrench if I need to adjust something before we head out on the road. I also bought my new bike there even though I thought of getting it over the Internet. The free service and discount prices are great.

Dividing

Dividing generates ideas by breaking the topic into its component parts. Use the journalistic questions of **who**, **what**, **where**, **when**, **why**, and **how** in order to divide a topic.

Ask yourself, "How can I divide the topic to prove my idea about the topic?" One technique is to imagine yourself in your topic—at a place of business, for example—and move through the event or the experience chronologically. What happens first, second, third? What issues do you have to face at each moment of the task or situation? Dividing a topic is useful in building support for your main idea.

Once you have divided a topic into its component parts, you will be able to generate specific ideas about each part. Focus on each part and think of specifics that will support your point of view about your topic.

Beth

I imagined myself, or any student for that matter, going to Nina's with clothing that needs alterations. I tried to imagine every step of the process.

1. taking clothes to shop—located behind Hume Hall

2. leaving clothes to fix—can pick up at end of day

3. women working on clothes have lots of experience

4. seamstresses can do any job from buttons and hems to alterations

5. pick up clothes at end of day; pay with cash or credit card—cheap prices

Listing

Another way to generate ideas is listing. Don't worry about trying to write in sentences; just list words or phrases that come to mind when you focus on your main idea. Focus on your topic by visualizing it, and write a list of everything that comes to mind. Try to see the topic in your mind's eye and be aware of all the senses—sight, hearing, taste, smell, and touch.

Tony

Cool inside & cool music too

Kyle's big grin when he shows off latest bikes

Monica's pretty

Tool room is awesome with every wrench and tool hanging on wall

Couch in showroom to relax and read cycling magazines

Clustering

Clustering is a visual representation of ideas. Because you cluster related ideas together, clustering begins the process of grouping or organizing your ideas. Many writers begin by freewriting or listing and then cluster those ideas into related groups that generate further ideas. When you cluster, you write down words or images you associate with your topic. These words may be parts of your topic. Then cluster related ideas together by drawing lines between them.

Beth

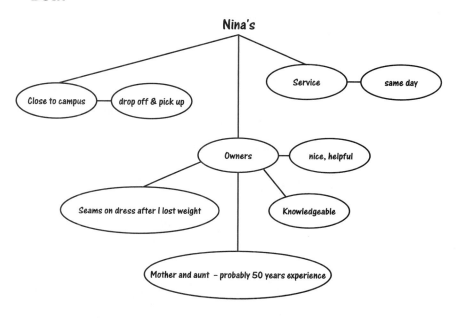

Group Brainstorming

Two or more people can help each other generate ideas by brainstorming together. The group focuses on each individual's narrowed topic and tentative main idea statement, and everyone contributes as many ideas as possible.

Example:

Beth: Tell me about this bike store. My son is getting into bikes and I could use some information.

Tony: It's the shop over on University Avenue, next to Kara's Coffee. I bought my bike there and go there a lot.

Beth: Well, it sure is convenient. I walk by it every day on my way to school. I like the music they play.

Tony: Exactly, and people in there are cool.

Beth: What do you mean by cool?

Tony: Well, they know a lot about bikes, and they are laid back, no sales pitch. I went in a hundred times checking out different bikes before I bought mine.

Beth: Why did you buy your bike there? I thought the best deals are on the Internet.

Tony: The prices I found on the Internet looked good until I factored in shipping and the lack of choices on options. Chain Gang's gives a flat 10–15% off list, and Kyle, the owner, offers free service for the life of the bike.

Beth: I've heard a lot of good reasons to shop at Chain Gang's.

Tony: Don't worry; I've been taking notes. Thanks for the helpful questions. You've made me think about my reasons for liking this place so much.

Writing Process Step 4: Generating Ideas for Support

Use one or more brainstorming techniques to generate ideas for supporting your tentative topic sentence.

Refining the Topic Sentence

Before you began generating supporting ideas, you formulated a topic sentence with a tentative main idea, the point you thought your paragraph would be about. Take a look at the ideas you generated through brainstorming, freewriting, listing, clustering, or dividing. Did you stick with your original main idea, or did you change it as you generated supporting ideas? You may find that you narrowed your focus or changed your focus slightly. Examine your original topic sentence to see if it still fits the ideas you generated or if you need to restate your main idea.

As you formulate and refine your main idea statement, keep your assignment, audience, purpose, and tone in mind. Make sure your main idea statement is appropriate for the length and type of assignment you are completing and for the audience to whom you are directing your writing.

Make sure your topic sentence indicates your purpose, whether it is to inform, persuade, or entertain. Also, make sure your topic sentence matches your desired tone, whether it is serious, sarcastic, or humorous.

Beth

When I looked back at my assignment and audience, I realized that I should write the paragraph to convince other students like me to use Nina's instead of proving that I enjoy Nina's.

Tentative topic sentence:

I enjoy using Nina's Alterations.

Revised topic sentence:

Nina's Alterations meets the sewing needs of students.

Practice **Review your brainstorming of supporting ideas and revise your topic sentence if needed.**

Tentative topic sentence:

_____

_____

Revised topic sentence (if different):

_____

_____

Tailoring Support to the Audience

Once you have decided on a topic sentence and have brainstormed support ideas, you are ready to select the strongest ideas to include in your paragraph. Keep in mind your controlling idea and your audience to determine the most effective supporting ideas. The controlling idea tells you what to focus on in developing the paragraph, and the audience tells you who you are addressing and helps you decide on the most convincing support.

Practice **Suppose that you must prove that a supermarket is a good place to shop. Working alone or in groups, circle the five ideas that would be most convincing to the specified audience.**

Audience 1: retirees

Which five items would be most likely to persuade retirees that a particular supermarket is a good store?

1. fresh vegetables

2. vitamins & minerals

3. candy

4. soda

5. discounts for senior citizens

6. toys

7. health foods

8. prescription medicine

9. comic books

10. cereals

Audience 2: children

Which five items would be most likely to persuade children that the supermarket is a good store?

1. vegetables

2. vitamins

3. candy

4. soda

5. discounts for senior citizens

6. toys

7. health foods

8. prescription medicine

9. comic books

10. cereals

Examples of Tailoring Support

Beth

I have to keep in mind that I am writing for college students, both male and female. I should include information about alterations that men will find convincing like getting pants shortened.

My best supporting ideas:

Location

Service

Owners

Services

Prices

Tony

I'm writing for students who depend on their bikes for transportation. I don't want to present information that is too technical or just aimed at serious riders like myself.

Ideas for support:

Bikes & accessories to buy

Owner & staff

Free stuff

Prices

Location

Practice 4.11 **Keeping in mind your audience, select the four or five strongest supporting ideas that you brainstormed.**

1. _____

2. _____

3. _____

4. _____

5. _____

WE: 5.25

Adding Specific Detail to Supports

Strong support includes lots of specific detail about each supporting idea. Readers want specific or concrete facts to back up supporting ideas. Specific details are usually **facts**, **examples**, **illustrations**, **statistics**, and **descriptions** of the supporting ideas.

Tony

I knew that I needed to give lots of facts about Chain Gang's. I challenged myself to select details that would actually convince students that this bike shop is great. I tried to use facts like the names of the staff and statistics like how many years they've been in business.

Support: Owner & staff

Specifics: Kyle, Toby, and Monica who have been in business for over 10 years

Support: merchandise

Specifics: over 10 name brand bikes for sale and accessories like locks and seats

WE: 5.26

Relating Specific Detail to the Main Idea

Strong support often explains how the specific details support the main or controlling idea. The relation to the topic sentence can be a descriptive word or any information that shows **how and why the specific details support the main idea**.

Tony

I tried to explain how the specific details prove that college students who depend on their bikes should shop at Chain Gang's.

Support: Owner & staff

Specifics: Kyle, Toby, and Monica who have been in business for over 10 years

Relation to main idea: knowledgeable about trends in bikes

Support: merchandise

Specifics: over 10 name brand bikes for sale and accessories like locks and seats

Relation to main idea: meets needs of students

Organizing Supporting Ideas

Organizing your ideas on paper before you start writing is an important step in creating a successful paragraph. Using a **map** or **outline** can help you plan your supports so that you don't leave out important supports or wander away from your main idea. Some writers like to use a map because it shows supporting ideas on one line. Others are familiar with the outline form and prefer it. What matters is that your find a way to plan and organize your ideas before you start writing.

As you work on creating a map or outline for your paragraph, you may find that you haven't generated enough ideas to support your topic sentence adequately. If so, use one of the brainstorming techniques to support your main idea.

Mapping

A paragraph map is like a road map: it shows you how to get from point A to point B without getting lost. A map can take many forms, but in it you plan and order your supporting ideas and details. Such a map takes only a few minutes to complete, and yet it can make the difference between a well-organized paragraph and a disorganized one.

A basic paragraph map consists of a topic sentence, a list of supports in the order they will be presented, and a list of the specific details that will be used to develop each area of support. A more detailed map may contain an indication of the reasoning behind each support or a statement of how or why your supports relate to the topic sentence. Making your reasoning explicit ensures that both you and the reader clearly understand how your supporting ideas relate to your topic sentence.

Beth's map

Keeping in mind that I am convincing college students to go to Nina's Alterations, I came up with the strongest ideas. I had to work at getting lots of specific details and not just relying on general ideas. I added the actual dollar amounts for different alterations and the actual location because my audience would want to know this information. I completed my map by thinking of the reasons that the support should convince students like me. In other words, I related each supporting idea back to the controlling idea in the topic sentence.

Topic sentence: Nina's Alterations meets the sewing needs of students.

Areas of Support	Specific Details	Relation to Topic Sentence
1. location	behind Hume Hall	close to campus
2. service	same day service	convenient
3. owner & family	Nina 20 years/ mom & aunt 30 years	know what they are doing
4. services	buttons, hems, alter seams	all sewing needs
5. prices	Pants hems $5 & buttons $1	reasonable

Outlining

An outline is a formal structure that helps you organize support topics and subtopics. Outline form is broken down into main headings (I, II, III, IV); support headings (A, B, C); and details (1, 2, 3). Use as many main headings, support headings, and details as you need to develop your topic. However, each heading that is broken down should have at least two subheadings. For example, if you have an A, you need a B; if you have a 1, you need a 2. Remember that the number of main topics, supporting ideas, and details is up to you and will vary depending on the ideas you have generated.

Many students find it difficult to outline a paragraph because outline form is somewhat rigid. You should adapt the form presented here to fit the ideas you are presenting. The form will help you incorporate both specific details and a relation to the topic sentence if one is appropriate.

Outline format

Topic sentence:

I. Support 1

    A. Specifics

    B. Relation

II. Support 2

    A. Specifics

    B. Relation

III. Support 3

    A. Specifics

    B. Relation

IV. Support 4

    A. Specifics

    B. Relation

Tony's outline

I like using an outline because I can see the different parts of my supports on different lines.

Topic sentence: College students who depend on their bikes for transportation should shop at Chain Gang's Bike Stop.

I. Owner & staff

    A. Kyle, Toby, and Monica; 10 years

    B. knowledgeable about trends

II. merchandise

    A. bikes & locks

B. meets biking needs

III. Service

A. free air & tune ups

B. keep bikes rolling

IV. Prices

A. 10–15% off other shops

B. save money

V. Location

A. 2 blocks from campus

B. convenient

Writing Process Step 5: Organizing Ideas

1. Examine the ideas you have generated and your revised topic sentence.

2. Select your strongest supporting ideas and place them in the map or outline template in the order you would like to use them. Do more brainstorming if you do not have enough supports to develop your topic sentence.

3. Generate specific details for each of your supports.

4. You may wish to state how each support relates to or proves the topic sentence.

Map Template

Topic sentence:

_____

_____

Area of Support	Specific Details	Relation to Topic Sentence
1.		
2.		
3.		
4.		
5.		

Outline Template

Topic sentence:

_____

_____

I. Support 1 _____

   A. Specifics _____

   B. Relation _____

II. Support 2_____

   A. Specifics _____

   B. Relation _____

III. Support 3 _____

   A. Specifics _____

   B. Relation _____

IV. Support 4 _____

   A. Specifics _____

   B. Relation _____

V. Support 5_____

   A. Specifics _____

   B. Relation _____

WP: 2.10

Drafting

Once you have organized your ideas, you're ready to write a first draft of the paragraph. To write a first draft, you follow your map or outline and put your ideas into sentences. In the first draft, you focus on presenting your ideas as clearly as possible, without worrying about mechanical errors such as spelling or punctuation.

Beth

I wrote a draft of my paragraph by writing a sentence or two for each area of support on my map.

Topic sentence: Nina's Alterations meets the sewing needs of students.

Areas of Support	Specific Details	Relation to Topic Sentence
1. location	behind Hume Hall	close to campus

Draft:

The location of Nina's is behind Hume Hall and close to campus.

Areas of Support	Specific Details	Relation to Topic Sentence
2. service	same day service	convenient

Draft:

There is same day service, which is convenient.

Areas of Support	Specific Details	Relation to Topic Sentence
3. owner/family	20 years/ 30 years	know what they are doing

Draft:

The owner and her family have been in the business for a long time and know what they are doing.

Areas of Support	Specific Details	Relation to Topic Sentence
4. services	buttons, hems, alter seams	all sewing needs

Draft:

The services include all sewing needs such as buttons, hems, and seams.

Areas of Support	Specific Details	Relation to Topic Sentence
5. prices.	Pants hems $5 & buttons $1	reasonable

Draft:

The prices are reasonable.

Tony

Using my outline, I tried to include the concrete facts about my favorite bike shop. I give the names of the staff and the number of years the shop has been in business. I supply the statistic of the ten to fifteen percent discount, and I was sure to include the specifics about the shop's location so my readers could find Chain Gang's after I convince them to shop there.

I made sure that the reader understood why I was including the specific details for each support. I didn't want the reader to ask, "So what?" after reading the supports, so I explained how each support related to my topic sentence.

College students who depend on their bikes for transportation should shop at Chain Gang's Bike Stop. This fine bike shop is owned and run by cyclists who put their experience and knowledge to work serving customers. The owner, Kyle Sommers, has been in the business for over ten years, so he is very knowledgeable about all brands of bikes and the newest trends in cycling. Kyle, Toby, and Monica can suggest the perfect bike for a beginner or the accessories like locks, seats, and lights for college students to get to and from class. Students can get free air for their tires, and the shop offers free adjustments for the life of any bike bought at Chain Gang's. The prices of bikes are usually ten to fifteen percent cheaper than other shops, and the mechanics only charge twenty dollars per hour to work on a bike. Best of all, the Gang is located just two blocks from campus, and the shop is a meeting place for student bike clubs, welcoming experienced and new riders alike.

> ## Writing Process Step 6: Drafting
>
> Write a draft of your paragraph by creating a sentence or sentences for each area of supports on your map or outline. Incorporate your specific details and, where appropriate, the relation to the topic sentence.

WE: 5.36

Writing the Conclusion

When you have completed writing the topic sentence and support, you will need to finish with a concluding sentence. The conclusion isn't usually planned in the map or outline, because it is not until you develop your paragraph that you will know how to conclude.

The conclusion is usually one sentence that restates the main idea in different words than the topic sentence.

Beth

In my conclusion, I wanted to remind the reader that students should go to Nina's for sewing needs. I kept the words sewing needs from the topic sentence but changed the other words.

Nina's Alterations is the place for students with sewing needs.

Tony

I tried to be creative with my conclusion and play on the image of a chain gang, which is the name of the bike shop. Since a chain gang is prison punishment, I included the word punishment in my conclusion, but I remind the reader that shopping at this store is a pleasure.

Going to Chain Gang's is a pleasure, not a punishment.

Practice **Write a concluding sentence for your paragraph. The conclusion should remind the reader of your main idea.**

_____

_____

WE: 5.38

Writing the Title

When a paragraph stands alone as a piece of writing, it is appropriate to give the paragraph a title. You should ask your instructor whether a title is required or not. The title should be written as a sentence fragment centered above the paragraph, and the first word and all important words should be capitalized. Good titles give the reader clues about the topic and controlling idea. Writers try to be creative and create interest with the title.

Beth

I wanted to be creative with my title. Here are some of my alternatives and the one I finally used. I hope you like the one I finally settled on.

Nina's Alterations

Sewing Needs

Sew Fine

Tony

I started with a simple title, but after seeing Beth's title, I tried to be more creative. I focused on the image of a gang to write my title. I didn't capitalize the article *the* or the preposition *at* in the middle of the title, just the important words.

Chain Gang's Bike Stop

Shop at the Stop

Stop at Chain Gang's

Join the Gang

Practice 4.13   **Write a title for your paragraph. Remember that it should be a sentence fragment, and all important words in the title should be capitalized.**

_____

_____

Revising

Revising is the process of examining the content and organization of your writing to see how they could be improved. Whenever possible, it is a good idea to let someone else read your first draft and give you feedback on what works and what doesn't work, what is and is not clear. If you can't get feedback, use the Paragraph Revision Checklist on page 60 to help you revise your own writing. In revising, you focus on developing and clarifying your ideas. You may decide you need more supporting details, or you may decide to delete details that don't relate to your topic sentence.

When you revise, you also work on polishing the presentation of your ideas. You may want to consider using more precise language and appropriate vocabulary. The more specific your writing is, the better.

Polishing your writing may also mean improving your sentence structure. You should try to alternate long and short sentences and use different sentence patterns such as compound sentences and complex sentences.

Peer Feedback

Your peers can give you a good idea of what is and is not working in your draft. If anything in your draft isn't clear to a reader, you will probably want to go back and reexamine or revise it. Listen carefully to the comments of your peer reviewers, but remember that in the end you are the one who decides what to include or not include in your paper.

Note to peer reviewers: When giving feedback on someone else's paragraph, remember that you are trying to help the writer communicate his or her ideas as clearly and effectively as possible. It won't help the writer if you're polite and say only that everything is fine, especially if you have trouble following the meaning or the logic of the paragraph. It is your responsibility to pay careful attention as you read or listen to your classmate's draft, and then to be as helpful as possible. The questionnaire below can help you let the writer know where you have trouble following the ideas or logic in the paragraph.

Beth

I asked Tony to review my paragraph, and I tried to use his comments to improve my paragraph.

First draft:

Sew Fine

Nina's Alterations meets the sewing needs of students. The location of Nina's is behind Hume Hall and close to campus. There is same day service, which is convenient. The owner and her family have been in the business for a long time and know what they are doing. The services include all sewing needs such as buttons, hems, and seams. The prices are reasonable. Nina's Alterations is the place for students with sewing needs.

Tony

I learned a lot by reading Beth's paragraph. She had a better title than I did, and some of the issues that we discussed helped me in my paragraph. I asked to see Beth's map of supports, and we both saw that we should follow our map or outline and include as much information as possible. When I read her paragraph, I tried to put myself in the position of wanting to be convinced of the main idea. I looked at each support and asked myself if there was enough information to convince me. I tried to give constructive feedback and not be critical. I thanked Beth for the opportunity to learn from her writing.

Tony's Peer Review Questionnaire of Beth's Paragraph

1. Is the topic sentence clear? Restate it in your own words.

Nina's is a good place for alterations.

2. Does the paragraph adequately explain or develop the topic sentence? List the areas of support used.

Location, service, owner/mother/aunt, alterations/sewing, prices

3. Does the order of supports seem logical?

Yes, the supports are organized from the first issue of how to get there to the last issue of payment for alteration.

4. Is there enough information or support to develop the topic sentence? What additional information or supporting ideas could the writer have included?

Support #1: Relate location to why good for students

Support #2: What does same day service mean? Give specifics or examples.

Support #3: Give number of years in business and explain "know what they are doing."

Support #4: I don't understand "sewing needs such as buttons." Explain what the need is.

Support #5: Mention specific prices for different jobs.

5. What did you like most about the paragraph?

I thought information about the owner and family was interesting. I want to take some clothes to this business.

6. What seemed most unclear about the paragraph?

The support about prices didn't have any specific detail.

7. Did you notice mechanical errors in the paragraph?

Not many. I wish that I could write this well!

Beth's revision

Mainly, I needed to follow my map of support and include the specific details that I had on my map. I found that I could change the way I express ideas and that I actually enjoyed the chance to improve my paragraph. (I bolded my changes.)

Sew Fine

Nina's Alterations meets the sewing needs of students. The shop is located in the plaza behind Hume Hall, **so students can stop in on their way to or from school.** This fine shop offers same day service. **Students can drop off pants to be hemmed or a blouse that is missing buttons and pick up the clothing on the way home from school.** Nina, the owner, has been sewing clothes for over **twenty years,** and her mother and aunt also work there and have **another thirty years experience.** Whether the job is a **buttonhole or a formal gown that needs to be let out or taken in,** these seamstresses know what to do. What are truly amazing are the inexpensive prices. Pants hems cost **five dollars** and a missing button will be replaced for **just a dollar.** Nina's Alterations is the place for students with sewing needs.

Peer Review Questionnaire: Paragraph

Directions: Read the paragraph carefully and answer the following questions as specifically as possible. Remember, your goal is to help your peer improve his or her paper.

1. Is the topic sentence clear? Restate it in your own words.

2. Does the paragraph adequately explain or develop the topic sentence? List the areas of support used.

3. Does the order of supports seem logical?

4. Is there enough information or support to develop the topic sentence? What additional information or supporting ideas could the writer have included?

5. What did you like most about the paragraph?

6. What seemed most unclear about the paragraph?

7. Did you notice mechanical errors in the paragraph?

Instructor Feedback

Whenever possible, get feedback on the draft of your paragraph from your instructor. You may have an opportunity to submit a draft for review, or you may be able to use your instructor's office hours to get feedback. Instructors generally comment on the strength or weakness of the content and structure of a piece of writing. They may or may not mark errors or list the types of errors they've noticed in your paragraph. Know your instructor's grading symbols (the marks he or she uses to indicate mechanical errors in your writing). If you don't understand your instructor's comments (whether verbal or written), ask him or her to explain. Both seeking feedback on your draft and making sure that you understand it show your instructor that you are serious about improving your writing.

Self-evaluation

If peer or instructor feedback isn't available, or if you prefer self-evaluation, you can use the Paragraph Revision Checklist below to get ideas on how to revise your paragraph. First, it is a good idea to give yourself some distance from what you have written by putting your paragraph aside for as long as you can before coming back to revise it. You may be able to put it aside for an hour or two, or overnight, but if you are writing an in-class paper, you may only have a minute or two before you need to start revising. However much time you have, getting some distance from your ideas will help you spot problems more easily. In revising, you should read your paragraph as critically as possible, looking for areas that could be improved.

Paragraph Revision Checklist

1. **Form**

   Title: Are the major words (including the first and last words) capitalized?

   Does the title reveal the topic and slant of the paragraph?

   Does it catch the reader's attention?

   Is the first sentence indented?

   Does the paragraph have the required number of sentences?

   Does the paragraph have the required organizational pattern?

2. **Topic Sentence**

   Does the topic sentence fit the assignment?

   Is it appropriate for the intended audience and purpose?

   Is the main idea clear?

3. **Support**

   Is there enough support (three to five supports, depending on the assignment) to explain or prove your topic sentence?

   Does each support clearly relate to or develop the topic sentence?

   Are there enough specific details, facts, and examples to convince the reader?

   Are any supports repeated?

   Does anything in the paragraph not relate to the main idea?

   Is the relationship between support sentences clear?

   Are there clear transitions within and between sentences?

   Is the order of supports clear and logical?

   Are the sentences varied in length and structure?

   Is appropriate vocabulary used?

   Is the language clear and precise? (Are there strong verbs, specific nouns, colorful adjectives and adverbs?)

4. **Conclusion**

   Does the conclusion tie together the paragraph?

   Does it introduce any new ideas or arguments that might confuse the reader?

Writing Process Step 7: Revising

Revise your paragraph. If possible, get feedback on your paragraph from peers or your instructor. If your peers or instructor are not available to give feedback, analyze the strengths and weaknesses of your paragraph using the Paragraph Revision Checklist.

Editing

One of the most important skills in writing is editing. All too often, writers receive low grades on their work because they have neglected to edit carefully. No one intends to turn a paragraph in with errors, but finding errors takes time and attention to detail. Using an editing checklist like the one below can help you catch and correct errors in your English. When you edit, you should read your paragraph five or six times, focusing on one type of error each time—fragments, verb errors, comma errors, spelling errors, and so on—paying particular attention to errors you have had trouble with in the past.

One reason it is so hard to spot errors is that we often read what we *intended* to write rather than what is actually on the page. A technique that may help you catch errors is to read your paragraph from the last sentence to the first. Reading backward forces you to focus on the words rather than on the content.

Another technique that may be helpful is tracking, which means using a pencil to point to each word as you read it. Tracking can help slow your reading down so that you can focus on one word at a time.

All of these techniques are intended to help you find and correct errors before you turn in your paragraph.

Editing Checklist

As you learn about the following skills, add them to your checklist.

1. **Check for run-ons and fragments.** Is there one complete sentence—and no more than one complete sentence—between every two periods? (Identify the subject and the verb, and make sure the word group makes sense.)

2. **Check every verb.** Do subjects and verbs agree? Is proper verb tense used? Be sure to check the problem phrases such as *there is/there are* and pay attention to singular subjects such as *everyone*.

3. **Use the dictionary or computer spell check** to catch capitalization errors and misspellings. Remember, however, that the spell check will not catch errors with problem words such as *there/their*.

4. **Remember your personal list of errors.** Check your writing for any of these errors.

5. **Check for apostrophes** in contractions and possessives.

6. **Check commas.**

7. **Check pronouns.** Do they agree with their antecedents? Is the reference clear?

8. **Look for any missing words or letters** by reading the writing slowly from the last sentence to the first.

Writing Process Step 8: Editing the Paragraph

Use the Editing Checklist to proofread your paragraph for errors.

Reviewing the Paragraph Writing Process

Paragraph Writing Process Prompts

The following prompts will guide you in writing paragraphs. You may wish to consult these prompts each time you write a paragraph until the process becomes second nature.

1. **Understanding the assignment**

   Assignment: _____

   Length: _____

   Due date: _____

2. **Narrowing the topic**

   Use one or more brainstorming methods to narrow your topic.

3. **Determining the writing context**

   Decide on your purpose, audience, and tone. Then choose a tentative main idea.

   Purpose: _____

   Audience: _____

   Tone: _____

   Tentative main idea: _____

4. **Generating ideas**

   Generate ideas by brainstorming, free writing, listing, clustering, or dividing. You may find it helpful to use scratch paper. Come up with as many ideas as possible. Keep your purpose and audience in mind as you generate ideas to support your topic sentence.

5. **Organizing ideas**

   a. Examine the ideas you have generated and revise your tentative topic sentence.

   b. Select your strongest support ideas and place them in the map or outline template in the order you would like to use them. Do more brainstorming if you do not have enough supports to develop your topic sentence.

   c. Generate specific details for each of your supports.

   d. You may wish to state how each support relates to or proves the topic sentence.

Map template
Topic Sentence:

_____

_____

<u>Area of Support</u>   <u>Specific Details</u>   <u>Relation to Topic Sentence</u>

1. _____

2. _____

3. _____

4. _____

5. _____

Outline template
Topic sentence: _____

_____

I. Support 1   _____

   A. Specifics _____

   B. Relation _____

II. Support 2   _____

   A. Specifics _____

   B. Relation _____

III. Support 3   _____

   A. Specifics _____

   B. Relation _____

IV. Support 4   _____

   A. Specifics _____

   B. Relation _____

6. **Drafting**

Write a draft of the paragraph by creating a sentence or sentences for each area of support on your map or outline. Incorporate your specific details and, where appropriate, the relation to the topic sentence.

7. **Revising**

If possible, get feedback on your paragraph from peers or your instructor. If feedback is not available, analyze the strengths and weaknesses of your paragraph using the Paragraph Revision Checklist on page 60.

8. **Editing**

Use the Editing Checklist on page 61 and the suggestions of your peer editors to find and correct errors in your paragraph.

9. **Evaluating your paragraph**

Is your paragraph better or worse than you thought it would be?

Could you have done as well by yourself as you did with the group's help? Why or why not?

What was the hardest part of using the writing process for you?

What was the most rewarding part of using the writing process?

How did going through the writing process change what you normally do?

Did using the writing process have a good or bad effect on your writing?

How hard was this paper to write?

How long did you spend on it?

Getting the Paragraph Back

Contrary to popular belief, the process isn't over when you get your graded paper back from your instructor. Part of the process of improving your writing is learning from your mistakes. The last thing most students want to do when they get back a paper is pay attention to the errors that have been marked. However, figuring out what you did wrong is the key to improving your performance, just as it is in sports: you need to listen to your coach if you hope to play your best. Think of your instructor's marks and comments as a way of helping you improve.

First, you need to make sure you understand the errors your instructor has marked. If you do not understand the marks, ask your instructor to explain them. Next, you need to know how to correct the errors. Ask your instructor or classmates when you are unsure of the correction.

You should record the errors your instructor has marked in your paragraph on a **personal error list**. This will help you keep track of the types of errors you have made so that you can avoid repeating them. Although it may take several minutes to record errors on your personal error list, learning to correct past errors is the best way to avoid making those same errors again. A template for your personal error list is available in the appendix at the end of this book. You should review your personal error list before you begin writing another paragraph, so that your past errors are fresh in your mind and you are less likely to repeat them.

Chapter 5

Patterns of Development

In this chapter, you will learn to write

- Narration paragraphs
- Example paragraphs
- Comparison and contrast paragraphs
- Cause and effect paragraphs

In the last chapter, you learned to follow the writing process to develop a paragraph. You learned to narrow your topic, examine the audience, purpose, and context of your writing, formulate a topic sentence, generate and organize supports for your topic sentence, and draft, revise, and edit your paragraph. The model student paragraphs you saw and the paragraph you wrote were arguments. In other words, you were persuading the reader of the main idea you stated in your topic sentence.

There are many ways to develop and structure paragraphs, but all paragraphs share certain characteristics. They develop one main idea (expressed in a topic sentence) with supporting details that explain, prove, or illustrate the main idea. In this chapter, you will learn different ways to develop your ideas using the paragraph form. The four rhetorical patterns you learn here will be useful in all of your classes.

Narration

RP: 2.2–2.3

In narration, the writer tells a story about a series of events. Generally, narratives are told chronologically, in the order the events happened, and they answer the six basic journalistic questions: Who? What? When? Where? Why? How? Narration often uses the first person (I, we) because the writer is recounting personal experience.

Examples of Narration

The Habit of Exercising

The habit of exercising regularly is one that I learned in school and that has stuck with me ever since. I first got interested in exercise in middle school when we did a unit on gymnastics. It was the first year I watched the Olympics, and I couldn't help seeing myself as a Shannon Miller. When different units rolled around, I found I loved soccer, baseball, and track and field as well. I liked the way I felt after exercising, and as I got older, I liked the way exercise helped keep me slim and toned. When I started college, I realized how easy it would be to get caught up in school and work and stop exercising, but I joined a health club and made myself go at least three times a week. The habit of exercising has helped keep me sane over the first few months of college because exercise helps reduce my stress level and helps keep me healthy.

Practice **5.1   Read the example above and answer the questions.**

    1. What general statement does Alicia's story support?

       sentence #1: The habit of exercising regularly is one that I learned. . . .

    2. What major events does she choose to include in her story?

       got interested in middle school watching the Olympics, loved other

       sports, liked the way exercise kept her slim, joined a health club

    3. Underline at least three specific details Alicia includes in her paragraph.

    4. How is Alicia's paragraph organized?

       chronologically—in time order

    5. Circle the words or phrases that help mark the passage of time in Alicia's paragraph.

How I Discovered My Career

Web page design is a field I became interested in gradually. When I worked for an auto parts chain, I realized that computers would be the wave of the future because of how easily they could track inventory and sales. At the time, no one talked about the Web. However, by the time I went to work for an electronics supply store, the Web had blossomed. The company had a Web site to advertise its products, and I was fascinated by the notion of reaching so many people so easily and inexpensively. When business was slow, I would surf the Web looking at competitors' sites. I started noticing that some sites were better designed than others. For example, some sites loaded more quickly, were visually easier to navigate, and had more information whereas other sites took a long time to load, were visually crowded and confusing, and didn't provide useful information. That's when I realized Web page design was something that interested me as a possible career.

Practice **5.2   After reading the narration example above, answer the following questions.**

    1. What general statement does Dan's story support?

       sentence #1: Web page design is a field I became interested in gradually.

    2. What major events does he choose to include in his story?

       auto parts chain—computers tracked inventory & sales electronics supply

       store—Web site for advertising

    3. Underline at least three specific details Dan includes in his paragraph.

4. How is Dan's paragraph organized?

chronologically—in time order

5. Circle the time markers and transitions that Dan uses in his paragraph to help lead the reader through his story.

Professional examples:

Faith Andrews Bedford, "Measles, Mumps, and Chicken Pox," page 281

Leo Buscaglia, "Papa, the Philosopher," page 284

Sandra Cisneros, "The First Job," page 292

Jean Giono, "The Man Who Planted Trees," page 314

Karl Taro Greenfeld, "Blind to Failure," page 322

Mike Rose, From "I Just Wanna Be Average," page 338

Ellen Sherman, "Boys to Men," page 342

RP: 2.5

Organization

Narratives are generally told in chronological order, so the story you are telling will dictate the organization of your paragraph. Try to structure your paragraph around logical divisions in the events you are recounting.

Paragraph Outline

Topic sentence: Subject of story

I. Event or major division 1

    A. Supporting detail

    B. Supporting detail

II. Event or major division 2

    A. Supporting detail

    B. Supporting detail

III. Event or major division 3

    A. Supporting detail

    B. Supporting detail

Topic sentence: The habit of exercising regularly is one that I learned in school and that has stuck with me ever since.

I. Middle school

    A. Gymnastics

        1. Olympics

        2. Shannon Miller

    B. Other sports: soccer, baseball, track and field

II. Older

    A. Liked the way I felt

    B. Liked the way I looked

III. College

    A. Easy to stop exercising

    B. Joined health club

    C. Exercise kept me sane

        1. Reduce stress

        2. Keeps me healthy

Practice **5.3**   **Arrange the following list of events about a car accident in chronological order by numbering them from 1 to 8.**

    __8__ The insurance company raised my rates.

    __2__ A dog ran across the road.

    __1__ My alarm didn't go off and I left the house late.

    __4__ I, in turn, hit the brakes and skidded into the car in front of me.

    __3__ The driver in front of me hit his brakes.

    __7__ The insurance company told me my car was totaled.

    __5__ I got whiplash from the impact.

    __6__ I was wearing my seatbelt or I would have been more seriously injured.

RP: 2.8

Transitions for Narration

Transitions are words or phrases that show the relationship between ideas. Transitions help lead the reader through your paragraph by making the relationship between your sentences clear to the reader. The transitions used in narration are generally time markers, meaning they help relate the events in time.

afterward	eventually	next
at last	finally	soon after
at the same time	first, second, third, etc.	subsequently
at this point	in the end	then
by this time	meanwhile	to begin with

Topics for Writing

1. Tell a story that explains what you were like in high school.

2. Tell the story of one of the most memorable events in your life.

3. Recount the most exciting or scariest moment in your college experience.

4. Recount an experience with friends that helped you learn something about yourself.

5. Have you ever felt powerless? Recount the events that made you feel that way.

6. Describe the experience of applying for a job or your first day on the job.

7. Tell the story of an incident in which you embarrassed your family or your family embarrassed you.

8. Tell the story of a moment in which you realized something important about yourself.

9. Recount an incident in which you helped someone.

10. Describe what it was like to be sick when you were a child.

Writing Process Prompts for Narration

1. Select the subject for your narration.

2. Determine your purpose, audience, and tone.

   Purpose:

   Audience:

   Tone:

3. Write a tentative main idea statement or topic sentence.

4. List what happened in chronological order.

   1.

   2.

   3.

   4.

   5.

   (Add more as needed.)

5. Examine the list to make sure you haven't left out anything the reader needs to know in order to understand or follow your story.

6. Use the following outline to help organize your ideas. Add as many supports and specifics as needed for your topic.

   Topic sentence: Subject of story

   I. Event or major division 1

      A. Supporting detail

      B. Supporting detail

   II. Event or major division 2

      A. Supporting detail

      B. Supporting detail

   III. Event or major division 3

      A. Supporting detail

      B. Supporting detail

7. Working from your outline, write a draft of your narration.

8. Get feedback on your writing to find out if your story is clear and vivid to your reader. Is it entertaining?

9. Revise your writing using the feedback you received or using the Revision Checklist on page 60.

10. Edit your writing using the Editing Checklist on page 61.

RP: 3.2–3.3

Illustration or Example

One of the best ways to help a listener or reader understand a point you are making is to give examples. Examples are concrete, specific cases that explain, clarify, or demonstrate a general idea or concept. We tend to remember examples better than we remember generalizations, because examples are more tangible and therefore easier to understand. Examples keep the reader's attention and make writing vivid and memorable.

Examples of Illustration or Example

Exercise Options

Most clubs offer a variety of aerobic and non-aerobic classes and exercise options. Aerobic classes include <u>step aerobics</u>, <u>dance aerobics</u>, <u>boxing aerobics</u>, and <u>water aerobics</u>. Aerobic workouts are also provided by using equipment such as the <u>treadmill</u>, <u>stationary bike</u>, <u>stair machine</u>, and <u>rowing machine</u>. Large health clubs also offer a variety of non-aerobic exercise classes such as <u>yoga</u> and <u>tai chi</u>. What most clubs call the "line" of exercise machines provides <u>non-aerobic strength training</u> for specific muscle groups. These machines help <u>tone muscles</u> and <u>build strength</u> in the <u>upper body</u> (<u>triceps</u>, <u>biceps</u>, <u>pectorals</u>, <u>back</u>) and the <u>lower body</u> (<u>quadriceps</u>, <u>hamstrings</u>, <u>inner</u> and <u>outer thigh</u>, and <u>calves</u>). The exercises have the added benefit of helping to build <u>and strengthen bones</u> as <u>well as muscles</u>. Both aerobic and non-aerobic exercises work together to provide a balanced exercise regime to <u>firm and tone muscles</u> as well as <u>burn calories</u> and provide a <u>cardiovascular workout</u>.

Practice **5.4**   **Read the example paragraph above and answer the questions that follow.**

1. **What general statement does Alicia support in her paragraph?**

sentence #1: Most clubs offer a variety of aerobic and non-aerobic classes

2. **What examples does she use to support her general statement?**

aerobic classes; step aerobics, dance aerobics, boxing aerobics, water

aerobics

aerobic workouts: treadmill, stationary bike, stair machine, rowing machine

non-aerobic classes: yoga, tai chi

non-aerobic machines build strength in upper body & lower body

3. **Underline at least three specific details Alicia includes in her paragraph.**

4. **How is Alicia's paragraph organized?** A/B aerobic/non-aerobic

5. How does Alicia conclude her paragraph?

Both types of exercise work together

Web Site Functions

A Web site can perform many functions for a company. First, a Web site is an inexpensive way to advertise. For a relatively small initial investment, a company can reach an unlimited number of people worldwide. Unlike expensive print advertising that is limited to the periodicals' subscribers, Web pages are posted indefinitely and can get thousands of hits (visits) a day. Next, because they reach so many people, Web pages are not only the best way to advertise, but also the least expensive way to sell a product. No expensive storefronts or staff is required to make sales 24 hours a day, seven days a week. A Web site can also provide valuable services such as product returns, customer satisfaction surveys, and new product questionnaires. A simple _employment opportunities_ link can also bring in applications from around the world. With so many services, it's a wonder every company, no matter how small, doesn't have a Web site.

Practice 5.5

Read the paragraph above and answer the following questions.

1. **What general statement does Dan support in his paragraph?**

sentence #1: A Web site can perform many functions for a company.

2. **What examples does he use to support his general statement?**

inexpensive ways to advertise: reach an unlimited number of people,

posted indefinitely, thousands of hits a day

inexpensive way to sell: no storefront or staff, 24/7

services: product returns, customer surveys, product questionnaires,

applications

3. **Underline at least three specific details Dan includes in his paragraph.**

4. **How is Dan's paragraph organized?** _order of importance_

5. **Circle the transitions Dan uses to lead the reader through his paragraph.**

Professional Examples:

Jack Canfield, "Consider This," page 288

Daniel Eisenberg, "The Coming Job Boom," paragraph 4, page 305

Leo Buscaglia, "Papa, the Philosopher," paragraph 2, page 284

Practice 5.6

Generate a list of examples that support each of the following general statements.

1. _____(name of your school) offers numerous services to help students succeed in school.

_____

_____

2. There are a variety of eating options available on or near campus.

_____

_____

3. Missing class can hurt a student's chance of passing a class.

_____

_____

4. TV shows/movies present a _____ (negative/positive) view of
_____(women, men, children, minorities, old people, or other group).

_____

_____

5. Honesty is the best policy.

_____

_____

RP: 3.5

Organization

Example paragraphs begin with a general statement, which is then supported by individual examples and details.

Paragraph Outline
Topic sentence: General or abstract idea

I. Example 1

    A. Supporting detail

    B. Supporting detail

II. Example 2

    A. Supporting detail

    B. Supporting detail

III. Example 3

    A. Supporting detail

    B. Supporting detail

Topic sentence: Most clubs offer a variety of aerobic and non-aerobic classes and exercise options.

I.   Aerobic classes: step, dance, boxing, swimming
II.   Aerobic workouts: treadmill, bike, rowing
III. Non-aerobic classes: yoga, tai-chi
IV. Non-aerobic workouts: line machines

    A. Build and tone specific muscles

    B. Build bone

RP: 3.8

Transitions for Illustration or Example

Transitions are words or phrases that show the relationship between ideas. Transitions help lead the reader through your paragraph by making the relationship between your sentences clear to the reader. In example or illustration, many transitions may be appropriate depending on the content. The following are common transitions that relate specifically to example or illustration:

as a matter of fact	indeed	specifically
certainly	in fact	to illustrate
for example	in other words	
for instance	likewise	

Transitions that show order or sequence are often useful, as are transitions that show addition.

Order or Sequence	Addition
first	also
second	as a matter of fact
next	besides
last	for instance
most important	furthermore
	in addition
	in fact
	likewise
	moreover
	similarly

Topics for Writing

1. Write a paragraph for one of the topics you developed examples for in Practice 5.6.

2. Write a paragraph in which you select three to five examples from Jack Canfield's "Consider This" to support his assertion that many successful people have overcome obstacles. Make sure you present Canfield's examples in your own words.

3. _____(name of person or event) helped me succeed in school.

4. First-year college students face many challenges.

5. Wearing the right shoes for the occasion is important.

6. Playing on a team can teach valuable lessons.

7. Rude behavior is common on campus.

8. A bad boss can make life miserable for employees.

9. _____ taught me many valuable lessons.

10. High school sports can be dangerous.

Writing Process Prompts for Illustration or Example

1. Determine the idea you wish to illustrate or explain.

2. Determine your purpose, audience, and tone.

   Purpose:

   Audience:

   Tone:

3. Write a tentative main idea or topic sentence.

4. Keeping the length of your assignment in mind, decide whether exemplification (several short examples) or illustration (one or more long examples) will work best for your topic.

   A. To use examples, generate a list of specific examples that support or prove your thesis.

      1.

      2.

      3.

      4.

      5.

      (Add more as needed.)

   B. To use illustration, generate one or more concrete examples that support or prove your thesis and develop them in as much detail as possible.

      1.

      (Add more as needed.)

5. Use the following outline to help you organize your ideas. Add as many supports and specifics as you need for your topic.

   Topic sentence: General or abstract idea

   I. Example 1

      A. Supporting detail

      B. Supporting detail

   II. Example 2

      A. Supporting detail

      B. Supporting detail

   III. Example 3

      A. Supporting detail

      B. Supporting detail

6. Working from your outline, write a draft of your example paragraph.

7. Get feedback on your paragraph.

8. Revise your paragraph using the feedback you received or using the Revision Checklist on page 60.

9. Edit your paragraph using the Editing Checklist on page 61.

RP: 5.2–5.4

Comparison and Contrast

Comparisons examine the **similarities** between two subjects, and **contrasts** examine the **differences** between two subjects. For a comparison or contrast to be interesting and useful for a reader, the subjects should have something in common. It wouldn't make sense to compare an orange and a car because the two subjects aren't in the same category. Knowing how to examine the similarities and differences between two subjects is useful because instructors frequently ask comparison and contrast questions on essay exams.

Examples of Comparison and Contrast

Aerobic Exercise and Weight Training

Aerobic exercise and weight training are different but complementary exercise regimes. Aerobic exercise, which is defined as exercise that raises the heart rate for at least 15 minutes, strengthens the cardiovascular system while it burns calories and reduces weight. Aerobic exercises include brisk walking, jogging, swimming, dancing, or any sport that involves rapid movement. The benefits of aerobic exercise are wide ranging. Recent studies have shown that women who engage in aerobic exercise at least three times a week live longer and have lower cholesterol levels and lower levels of heart disease. Unlike aerobic exercise, weight training does not increase the heart rate or take off pounds. Weight training is defined as any exercise that involves weight resistance and it includes all the "line" exercise machines at health clubs, each of which strengthens specific muscle groups. It also includes simple exercises that can be done at home with inexpensive free weights. The benefits of weight training are better-defined and stronger muscles, as well as stronger bones. For older women in particular, weight resistance training is important in maintaining bone density and preventing osteoporosis. Because the two types of exercises have different effects, a balance between the two is necessary for optimal health and appearance.

Practice 5.7   **Read the comparison/contrast paragraph above and answer the questions.**

1. What are the subjects of Alicia's comparison/contrast? _____

   Aerobic exercise & weight training

2. Does she primarily compare or contrast her subjects? _contrast_____

3. Examine the structure of Alicia's paragraph. Does she discuss one subject first and then the other subject, or does she compare/contrast her subjects in alternating sentences (A/B, A/B, A/B)? _Aerobic exercise first and then weight training_

4. Underline at least three specific details Alicia includes in her paragraph.

5. Circle the transitions Alicia uses to lead the reader through her paragraph.

Good and Bad Web Sites

Although it may not be obvious to a novice, the difference between a well-designed and poorly designed Web site is like the difference between night and day. The most obvious difference is how long it takes a Web page to load. Pictures may be pretty, but if they cause a Web site to take to take more than thirty seconds to load, many potential clients won't bother to wait. A well-designed Web page can be graphically interesting without memory intensive pictures and will load in under thirty seconds. The next most important difference is how easy the site is to navigate. A graphically complicated site may leave clients wondering what to click on to get the information they need. A clear structure and links are essential to a successful site. The final difference between a poor site and a good site is maintenance. Everyone has had the unfortunate experience of clicking on dead links. That experience certainly does not inspire confidence in the sponsoring company. A good site must be regularly maintained to ensure that the information is up-to-date and the links are functioning. A well-designed Web page can boost a company's profits, but a poorly designed one can lose business.

Practice 5.8   **Read the comparison/contrast paragraph above and answer the questions.**

1. What are the subjects of Dan's paragraph? Good and bad Web sites

2. Does he primarily compare or contrast his subjects? contrast

3. How does Dan structure his paragraph? Does he discuss one subject first and then the other subject, or does he compare/contrast his subjects in alternating sentences (A/B, A/B, A/B)? alternating sentences (point-by-point)

4. Underline at least three specific details that Dan includes in his paragraph.

5. Circle the transitions Dan uses to lead the reader through his paragraph.

Professional Examples:
Faith Andrews Bedford, "Measles, Mumps, and Chicken Pox," page 281

RP: 5.6

Organization

Comparison/contrast paragraphs are organized around either a subject-by-subject or a point-by-point structure. In a **subject-by-subject** structure, you would cover one subject first and then move on to the second subject. In a subject-by-subject paragraph, the writer would discuss everything about subject A before moving on to discuss subject B. This structure results in larger blocks devoted to each subject.

In a **point-by-point** structure, the writer organizes his or her writing around points of similarity or difference between the two subjects, so each subject is discussed in relation to a point of similarity or difference. This structure results in both subjects A and B being discussed within a paragraph.

Subject-by-Subject Pattern: Outline Form
Topic sentence: Similarities and/or differences in Subject A and Subject B.

I. Subject A

    A. Point 1

    B. Point 2

C. Point 3

D. Point 4

E. Point 5

II. Subject B

A. Point 1

B. Point 2

C. Point 3

D. Point 4

E. Point 5

Alicia's paragraph

Topic sentence: Aerobic exercise and weight training are different but complementary exercise regimes.

I. Aerobic exercise

A. Definition

B. Effects

C. Types of exercise

D. Benefits

E. Example

II. Weight training

A. Definition

B. Effects

C. Types of exercise

D. Benefits

E. Example

Point-by-Point Pattern

Topic sentence: Similarities and/or differences in Subject A and Subject B.

I. Main point 1

A. Subject A

B. Subject B

II. Main point 2

A. Subject A

B. Subject B

III. Main point 3

A. Subject A

B. Subject B

Dan's paragraph

Topic sentence: The difference between a well-designed and poorly designed Web site is like the difference between night and day.

I. Load time

    A. Poor

        1. Too many pictures

        2. More than 30 sec to load

    B. Good

        1. Graphically interesting

        2. Load in under 30 sec

II. Ease of navigation

    A. Poor

        1. Complicated

        2. Users get lost

    B. Good

        1. Clear

        2. Users find information

III. Maintenance

    A. Poor

        1. Dead links

        2. Bad impression

    B. Good

        1. Current information

        2. Live links

Practice **Arrange the following facts about gray whales and humpback whales into a subject-by-subject and a point-by-point outline.**

Feeding habits: Gray whales are bottom feeders. They suck up mud from the sea floor, filter the organisms out of it, and spit the mud out of the other side of their mouths.
Humpback whales gulp sea water, filter out the organisms and small fish, and spit out the water.

Hunting: Gray whales do not hunt cooperatively.
Humpback whales cooperate to round up schools of small fish.

Birth: Gray whales are born tail first and are weaned at eleven months.
Humpback whales are born head first and are weaned at seven to eight months.

Population: There are 15,000–22,000 gray whales in the world. There are 10,000–15,000 humpback whales in the world.

Subject-by-Subject Pattern

Topic sentence: There are many differences between gray whales and humpback whales.

I. Subject A Gray whales

  A. Point 1 Feeding habits

  B. Point 2 Hunting

  C. Point 3 Birth

  D. Point 4 Population

II. Subject B Humpback whales

  A. Point 1 Feeding habits

  B. Point 2 Hunting

  C. Point 3 Birth

  D. Point 4 Population

Point-by-Point Pattern

Topic sentence: There are many differences between gray whales and humpback whales.

I. Main point 1 Feeding habits

  A. Subject A Gray whales

  B. Subject B Humpback whales

II. Main point 2 Hunting

  A. Subject A Gray whales

  B. Subject B Humpback whales

III. Main point 3 Birth

  A. Subject A Gray whales

  B. Subject B Humpback whales

IV. Main point 4 Population

  A. Subject A Gray whales

  B. Subject B Humpback whales

RP: 5.9

Transitions for Comparison/Contrast

Transitions are words or phrases that show the relationship between ideas. Transitions help lead the reader through your paragraph by making the relationship between your sentences clear to the reader. Transitions used in **comparison** generally show similarity or addition. For a list of common transitional devices used to show addition, see page 73.

Transitions used in **contrast** generally show difference or dissimilarity, but many transitions can be appropriate in comparison or contrast depending on the content. The following are common transitional devices used for contrast:

conversely	nonetheless
however	otherwise
instead	on the contrary
nevertheless	on the other hand

Topics for Writing

1. Compare or contrast your classes in high school and college.
2. Compare or contrast two clubs or movie theaters.
3. Compare or contrast two brands of ice-cream, pizza, or other food.
4. Compare or contrast two teachers.
5. Compare or contrast two styles of playing or coaching a sport such as basketball, baseball, or tennis.
6. Compare or contrast you and a brother or sister.
7. Compare or contrast two friends or relatives.
8. Compare or contrast two styles of playing an instrument, dancing, or dressing.
9. Compare or contrast two styles of driving.
10. Compare or contrast two cable, cell phone, or pager services.

Writing Process Prompts for Comparison/Contrast

1. Select the subject for your comparison/contrast. Keep in mind that there should be a reason to bring the two subjects together.
2. Determine the purpose, audience, and tone of your comparison/contrast.

    Purpose:

    Audience:

    Tone:

3. Use a technique such as brainstorming, freewriting, listing, clustering, or dividing to generate a list of similarities and differences for A and B. If you discuss a topic for A, make sure you discuss the same topic for B. Use whichever method is most comfortable or best fits your topic.

Similarities	Differences
1.	1.
2.	2.
3.	3.
4.	4.

Similarities	Differences
Subject A	Subject A
1.	1.
2.	2.
3.	3.
Subject B	Subject B
1.	1.
2.	2.
3.	3.

4. Do A and B share more similarities or differences? Will you discuss only similarities, only differences, or both similarities and differences?

5. Formulate a tentative topic sentence or main idea. Remember to name both A and B and state the focus on either similarities or differences.

6. Choose the outline structure that best suits your topic.

7. What main points do you wish to compare/contrast about A and B?

    1.

    2.

    3.

    4.

8. Focus on each main point and use a technique such as brainstorming, freewriting, listing, clustering, or dividing to generate specific details for what you want to include about A and B.

    A.

    B.

    Repeat for each main point.

9. Use one of the outline templates in prompt 6 to outline your paragraph based on the ideas you have generated.

10. Working from your outline, write a draft of your paragraph.

11. When the draft is completed, request feedback from your instructor or peers.

12. Revise your paragraph using the feedback you received or using the Revision Checklist on page 60.

13. Edit your paragraph or essay using the Editing Checklist on page 61.

RP: 6.2–6.4

Cause and Effect

Causes focus on why things happen, and effects focus on what the results or consequences of actions or events are. **Causes** are the **reasons why** something happened; they answer the question "Why did the event happen?" For example, the causes of a failing grade on a test might be failure to study, lack of understanding of the material, lack of sleep, test anxiety, or illness. Causes occur before the event and make the event happen.

Effects are the direct **results** or **consequences** of an event; they respond to the question "What happened because of the event?" The effects of a failing grade on a test might be depression, a discouraged attitude, or a failing grade in the class; or the effects might be improved study habits and greater effort and attention. Effects come after the event and are the direct results of the event.

Causes and effects are important in many classes and careers. For example, mechanics try to figure out why a car isn't running properly, foresters try to figure out why a bird population is decreasing or what effects fire has on a forest, and physicians try to diagnose the cause of an illness and study the effects of treatments and medications. Historians, scientists, and economists all focus on causes and effects as well.

Tip

Don't confuse **affect** and **effect**.

Affect is a verb meaning "to influence."

The movie seriously affected my mood.

The prescription drug did not affect his driving.

Effect is usually used as a noun meaning "result."

The effects of the flood devastated the community.

The drug seemed to have no effect.

When used as a verb, **effect** means "to make or to cause to happen."

He effected changes in his routine.

I will effect the changes as soon as possible.

Examples of Cause and Effect

The Advantages of Regular Exercise

Regular exercise has a number of beneficial effects. First, aerobic exercise strengthens the cardiovascular system, primarily the lungs and heart, thereby reducing the chance of heart disease and stroke. Regular exercise also reduces cholesterol levels and improves brain functions. Not only can exercise improve one's health, but it can also improve one's appearance. Exercise reduces body fat and strengthens muscle, leading to a thinner, sleeker appearance. Looking good can make a person feel good. In addition to benefiting the body, exercise benefits the spirit as well by relieving stress and boosting energy levels. Vigorous exercise releases serotonin, a powerful brain chemical that produces a sensation of happiness and contentment. Regular exercise can lead to a healthier and happier life.

Practice **Read the cause and effect example on the previous page and answer the questions.**

1. What cause or effect does Alicia examine in her paragraph?

The effects of regular exercise

2. What causes or effects does she give to support her topic sentence?

strengthens cardiovascular system

reduces cholesterol and improves brain function

improves appearance, improves emotional state

3. Underline at least three specific details Alicia includes in her paragraph.

4. How is Alicia's paragraph organized? order of importance of effects

5. How does Alicia conclude her paragraph?

summary statement: Regular exercise leads to health & happiness.

Effects of a Good Web Site

A well-designed Web site can benefit a business in many ways. First, a Web site provides inexpensive advertising that can reach people around the <u>globe twenty-four hours a day, seven days a week</u>. A Web site can provide much more detailed information about a company and its products than can any other form of <u>print media</u>. In addition to advertising a product, a Web site can also <u>field questions about products</u>, <u>gauge customer satisfaction</u>, and <u>recruit potential employees</u>. Most importantly, a Web site is the least expensive way to sell a product. Successful Web sites have <u>boosted sales</u> for some companies as <u>much as 75%</u>. Because there are none of the expensive overhead costs associated with retail storefronts, namely <u>buildings and personnel costs</u>, the company makes a larger profit.

Practice 5.11 **Read the cause and effect paragraph above and answer the following questions.**

1. What cause or effect does Dan examine in his paragraph?

the effects of a good Web site

2. What causes or effects does he give to support his topic sentence?

inexpensive advertising

other services: questions, customer satisfaction, recruit employees

inexpensive way to sell product

3. Underline at least three specific details Dan includes in his paragraph.

4. How is Dan's paragraph organized? order of importance of effects

5. How does Dan conclude his paragraph?

final strong support—larger profit

Professional Examples:

Cathy Dyson, "The Girl Who Helped the Samburu," page 302

John Garrity, "Too Good to Be True," page 311

Daniel Eisenberg, "The Coming Job Boom," page 305

Jean Giono, "The Man Who Planted Trees," page 314

Cynthia Jabs, "Saying Good-Bye," page 332

Mike Rose, From "I Just Wanna Be Average," page 338

Practice **Distinguish between the causes and effects of a car accident by labeling the causes of the accident (why the accident happened) with a C and the effects of the accident (what happened as a result of the accident) with an E.**

___E___ The insurance company raised my rates.

___C___ A dog ran across the road.

___C___ My alarm didn't go off and I left the house late and in a rush.

___E___ The police officer gave me a ticket that cost me over $300.

___C___ I, in turn, hit the brakes and skidded into the car in front of me.

___C___ The driver in front of me suddenly hit his brakes.

___E___ The front of my car was crumpled.

___E___ I got whiplash from the impact.

___C___ The road was slick because it was raining.

___E___ I had to ride the bus to school until my car was repaired.

RP: 6.5

Organization

Cause/effect paragraphs generally focus on the causes or the effects of an event, problem, or phenomenon.

Paragraph Outline

Topic sentence: Causes or effects of an event or phenomenon

I. Cause or effect 1

    A. Supporting detail

    B. Supporting detail

II. Cause or effect 2

    A. Supporting detail

    B. Supporting detail

III. Cause or effect 3

    A. Supporting detail

    B. Supporting detail

Topic sentence: Regular exercise has a number of beneficial effects.

I. Cardiovascular system

    A. Strengthen heart and lungs

B. Reduce heart disease and stroke

C. Reduce cholesterol levels

II. Appearance

A. Reduce fat

B. Strengthen muscles

C. Thinner, sleeker appearance

III. Attitude

A. Reduce stress

B. Boost energy

C. Release serotonin

Transitions

RP: 6.8

Transitions are words or phrases that show the relationship between ideas. Transitions help lead the reader through your paragraph by making the relationship between your sentences clear to the reader. There are no transitions specific to cause. Use those transitions that show you are adding causes to the ones already discussed or those that show sequence.

For a list of common transitional devices used to show **addition**, see page 73.

For a list of common transitional devices used to show **sequence**, see page 73.

There are three transitions especially useful in effect:

> as a result
> consequently
> therefore

Topics for Writing

1. How can friends influence your success or failure in school?

2. Examine the causes or the effects of a problem you are having in school.

3. Discuss the causes or effects of your decision to attend college.

4. Discuss the effects of excessive partying in college.

5. Discuss the causes or effects of working and going to school at the same time.

6. Discuss the effect a good or bad boss can have on a workplace.

7. Discuss the causes or effects of a good or bad decision you made recently.

8. _____(name of person) had a positive or negative influence on my life.

9. Discuss the reasons you eat the way you do or effects your diet has on your health.

10. Discuss the causes or effects of a behavior you consider annoying or harmful.

Writing Process Prompts for Cause and Effect

1. Select the subject for your cause or effect paragraph.

2. Will you examine causes or effects?

3. Determine the purpose, audience, and tone of your paragraph.

   Purpose:

   Audience:

   Tone:

4. Write a tentative topic sentence or main idea statement.

5. List all the causes/effects of your event, problem, or phenomenon.

   1.

   2.

   3.

   4.

   5.

   (Add more as needed.)

   Examine each item on your list to determine that it is an independent cause/effect.

6. Generate support for each of your causes/effects. How can you show your audience how each item you listed in prompt 5 is a cause/effect of your event, problem, or phenomenon?

7. Outline your paragraph using the following outline, changing it to fit your topic.

   Topic sentence:

   I. Cause or effect 1

      A. Support topic

         1. Specific support

         2. Specific support

      A. Support topic

      B. Support topic

   II. Cause or effect 2

      A. Support topic

         1. Specific support

         2. Specific support

      B. Support topic

   III. Cause or effect 3

    A. Support topic

    B. Support topic

     1. Specific support

     2. Specific support

8. Working from your outline, write a draft of your cause or effect paragraph.

9. Get feedback on your writing.

10. Revise your paragraph using the feedback you received or using the Revision Checklist on page 60.

11. Edit your paragraph using the Editing Checklist on page 61.

Part III

Grammar, Punctuation, and Mechanics

Chapter 6

Learning to Write Correctly

In this chapter, you will explore strategies for learning writing skills.

Part III of *Writer's Resources: From Sentence to Paragraph* presents the grammar, punctuation, and mechanics skills you need to write correctly. In this chapter, we present strategies that will make learning this material easier.

Be Curious

Learning is fun if you come to it with an open mind. Curiosity is the most powerful ally you have as a learner. You will end up enjoying what you learn, and you will become a more skillful learner for later when you take courses in your major.

Rely on Your Resources

Your instructor wants to help you learn the skills. Bring questions to class, go to your instructor's office during office hours, or stay after class for clarification of concepts. In other words, show your teacher that you want to learn.

Dan: I try to see my teacher every week. I write down questions in my book as I complete assignments. If I have no questions, I still stop by to tell my instructor how I am doing.

Writing Practice 6.1 | Instructor's office hours: _____

Day and time I will go to the office: _____

Your school may have a **writing lab** or learning resource center where you can get individual help on skills. The tutors in the lab are trained to help students. Set a regular time to go to the lab. If you have no questions or need no help, use the time there to do homework or study.

Alicia: The people in the writing lab are very nice. They've told me more than once that helping students is what they like about their jobs. I've found that a tutor can sometimes make a rule clear for me in just a couple of minutes.

Writing Practice 6.2

Writing lab's hours: _____

Day and time I will go to lab: _____

Consider forming a **study group**. Your classmates are going through the same learning process as you. Perhaps you can learn the material together. Even if you are not having trouble learning the concepts, you will learn more thoroughly if you help others learn.

> **How to study in a group:**
>
> ➡ Check each other's homework.
>
> ➡ Complete exercises together and discuss the answers.
>
> ➡ Teach each other skills. One member explains the skill. Another member asks questions for clarification. One member observes and adds or corrects information.

Beth: Our study group has made the difference in my grade. First, I am more certain to do my work because I don't want to let my friends down. I've found that tutoring group members has helped me solidify my understanding, too.

Writing Practice 6.3

Three students I can study with: _____, _____, _____

Phone numbers: _____, _____, _____

The **Writer's Resources CD-ROM** can provide valuable support for your learning. Complete each lesson on the CD that you cover in class, including all practices and exercises.

Writing Practice 6.4   **What resources will you most likely use to learn the skills and why? Write for five minutes in your journal.**

Become a Skillful Learner

Divide and Conquer

When you are assigned a skill to learn, break down the skill into its parts and concentrate on one part at a time. For example, Chapter 17 includes five different comma rules. You shouldn't try to learn all the rules at once. Tackle one rule at a time. Focus on that one rule during one study session. If you can learn one concept each time you study, you will find the material much easier to process.

> How to learn skills by setting short-term goals:
>
> ➥ Divide each skill into small packages that can be accomplished daily.
>
> ➥ Make a plan for accomplishing each task.
>
> ➥ Evaluate your progress daily.
>
> ➥ At the end of the week, evaluate your success in reaching your goal.

Tony: I was assigned Chapter 17 on commas last week. I divided my time so that I would put in an hour a day for each rule and two hours on the weekend to complete the review exercises. Day 1 I got behind, so I tried to catch up day 2. By day 3 I was worried that I was falling behind. I put in an extra hour on day 4 and did catch up because the last rules were not as hard as the first ones. By the weekend, I was ahead of schedule and only needed one hour to complete the review exercises.

Stay Active

Complete all the practices and exercises in the chapter. Think of the practices and exercises as a way for you to check on your learning.

Take notes and highlight the textbook when you study. You can underline important points, ask questions about material you don't understand, and write down important concepts in your notes. These activities help you become familiar with the material.

Tony: I try to ask questions as I read the textbook. Usually the book answers my questions, but I like being in the questioning mode because it keeps me sharp.

Apostrophes are used to indicate possession. The apostrophe indicates that the second word group belongs to the first word group.   *What is a word group?*

Examples:

The teacher's pet

Many teams' coaches   *Why is there an apostrophe after the s in this example?*

Learn from Your Experience

Review all exercises, tests, and exams. Keep a record of all your errors. When your instructor returns a paper, make sure you understand all the comments. Use the error list provided in the appendix.

Dan: I always write down the errors I have made on *any* work I do. I look over the list before I write or take any sort of test. My goal is not to make the same error twice.

<u>Error list</u>

Error	**Correction**	**Explanation**
Its been raining.	It's (it has) been raining.	Contraction
Peoples' opinion	People's opinion	irregular plural owner

Work with Your Frustration

We all want to do well and learn what we don't know, and we aren't happy until we learn the material, preferably perfectly. We may be nervous about whether we are learning, and then we get impatient that we are not learning quickly enough or that we don't already know what we are learning. There are number of steps you can take to help minimize your frustrations:

➥ Keep tabs on your frustration level.

➥ Take a break if you find yourself getting annoyed or frustrated with a skill.

➥ Let your instructor know when you do feel frustrated. Your teacher has experience with learning the material and may be able to offer valuable insight into your situation.

Writing Practice **6.5** **Write for five minutes about one frustrating experience you have had learning some skill. Explain what you were frustrated about and how you overcame the frustration.**

Know Yourself

Skillful learners monitor their learning. They notice when they really don't understand a concept. They make a point to attack their weak areas themselves rather than wait for the weaknesses to be exposed on an exam. When you identify areas that you are uncertain about after studying, return to your teacher, the lab, or classmates for clarification.

Review Exercise 6.6 **Writing practice**

Write a one-page journal entry about one successful learning experience you have had.

Chapter 7
Capitalization

> **In this chapter, you will learn the rules for capitalizing the**
>
> - First word of sentences and quoted sentences
> - Proper names of people
> - Proper names of places
> - Proper names of things

Capital letters announce to the reader that a word has special importance. The first word of sentences and proper names are always capitalized. You probably know many of the rules for capitalization, but this lesson will acquaint you with all the rules and give you practice testing your knowledge.

Sentence Beginnings

1. Capitalize the **first word of sentences**.

    Example: My car is in the garage.

1.1 The first word of a **quoted sentence** should be capitalized.

    Example: He replied, "Nothing is wrong."

Practice **Add capital letters where needed.**

1. my homework is due tomorrow.

2. justin asked, "may I have this dance?"

3. my mother wanted to know when I would finish my homework.

4. my mother asked, "when are you going to finish your homework?"

5. according to Felix, the exam will be easy.

Proper Nouns

Names of specific people, places, and things are considered proper nouns, and all proper nouns should be capitalized.

> *Example*: **Dana** is going to **New York City** to attend **Columbia University**.

2.   People

2.1   Proper names of people should be capitalized.

> *Examples*: Don Jordan, Lin Ying, LaToya Jones

2.2   Proper titles are capitalized if they are used to replace someone's name.

> *Example*: Are we going shopping on Friday, **Mother**?

2.3   Capitalize titles only if they are used to replace someone's name or if they are used with a proper name.

> *Example*: I told **my uncle** that I would come. *But* I told **Aunt Julia** that I would come. (If a word such as *my* or *the* comes before the title, the title is not replacing a proper name.)

2.4   The pronoun *I* is considered a proper name and should be capitalized.

> *Example*: Juan and **I** will return soon.

Practice **7.2**   **Capitalize the words that should be capitalized.**

king	my mother
aunt julie	delores ramirez
queen elizabeth	doctor punjab
uncle richard	mother teresa
tony paris	professor

GPM: 3.8

There is more practice on this rule on the CD.

3.   Places

3.1   Proper names of specific geographic features and proper place names should be capitalized.

> *Examples*: Mount Everest, Arctic Ocean, Lake Superior, Banff National Park, Tiananmen Square, Namib Desert

3.2   Do not capitalize places that are not proper names.

> *Examples*: the lake, the desert, an ocean, a mountain

3.3   Names of cities, counties, states, regions, countries, continents, and planets should be capitalized.

> *Examples*: Budapest, Dekalb County, Illinois, the South, Romania, North America, Venus

(Prepositions are not capitalized in proper names unless they are the first or last word of the name.)

Example: United States of America

3.4   Directional words ending in *-ern* are not capitalized.

Examples: western, northern, southern

The words north, south, east, west are **not** capitalized if they refer to a direction, but are capitalized if they name a geographical region.

Examples: I'll be heading **south** this winter.

The **West** is known for its abundant wildlife.

Practice   **Capitalize the words that should be capitalized.**

mountain	the rockies
mississippi river	the alps
eastern united states	several mountains
canyon	alaska
times square	new york city

   There is more practice on this rule on the CD.

GPM: 3.12   **4.   Things**

4.1   Proper names of institutions, businesses, and federal agencies should be capitalized.

Examples: Central High School, First National Bank, University of Tennessee, Holiday Inn, Environmental Protection Agency, Chicago Bulls

4.2   Proper names of buildings and historical monuments should be capitalized.

Examples: Statue of Liberty, Parthenon, Kennedy Center, Sistine Chapel

Practice   **Capitalize the words that should be capitalized.**

centerville high school	internal revenue service
miami dolphins	community college
high school band	eiffel tower
high school prom	empire state building
yale university	the white house

4.3   Names of holidays should be capitalized.

Examples: Fourth of July, Thanksgiving, Flag Day, Black History Month

4.4   Days and months are capitalized.

Examples: Monday, Tuesday, Saturday, January, March, December

4.5   Names of seasons are not capitalized.

Examples: spring, summer, fall, winter

Practice 7.5   **Capitalize the words that should be capitalized.**

easter	friday
sunday	halloween
christmas	thanksgiving
summer	father's day
memorial day	autumn

4.6   Names of specific school courses should be capitalized.

Examples: Fundamentals of Algebra, College Composition

4.7   Subject names that are not part of a course title are *not* capitalized.

Examples: math, writing, history

4.8   The first word, last word, and all important words in the titles of books, poems, articles, chapters, academic papers, songs, journals, and magazines should be capitalized.

Examples: *Journal of Education, Paradise Lost, The Grapes of Wrath, Working Woman*

(Prepositions are not capitalized unless they are the first or last word of the title.)

Practice 7.6   **Capitalize the words that should be capitalized.**

english	grammar
the wizard of oz	*hamlet*
history 101	history
the goblet of fire	comedy
the new york times	*alice in wonderland*

4.9   Specific historical events and any eras or periods in history should be capitalized; however, the word "century" should not be capitalized.

Examples: the Civil War, the French Revolution, the Renaissance, the seventeenth century

4.10   Nationalities and languages should always be capitalized.

Examples: Swedish, English, French pastry, Swiss cheese

4.11   Abbreviations for agencies, organizations, trade names, and radio and television stations should be capitalized.

Examples: KCAZ, WFHB, TVA, NASA, NFL

Practice **7.7**   **Capitalize the words that should be capitalized.**

the twentieth century	nba
italian chocolate	the french cinema
abc	rn
the middle ages	german measles
english tea	the paleolithic era

4.12   Capitalize only the words of animal and plant names that refer to a specific place or person.

> *Examples*: German shepherd, Bermuda grass, cardinals, blue whales, roses, oak trees

Practice **7.8**   **Capitalize the words that should be capitalized.**

cantaloupe	fleas
french poodle	scorpions
fruit salad	shetland pony
watermelon	stallion
ticks	horse

GPM: 3.24

There is more practice on this rule on the CD.

Review Exercise **7.9**   **Capitalize the words that should be capitalized.**

1. snapdragon
   daffodil
   bluebell
   banana spider
2. jackson senior high
   high school newspaper
   princeton university
   my college instructor
3. nearby hospital
   santa fe river
   community college
   mercedes elementary school
4. aspirin
   pain reliever
   advil
   excedrin

11. lab assistant
    lawyer
    judge judy
    high school teacher
12. spring
    memorial day
    easter
    summer vacation
13. english terrier
    big horn sheep
    grizzly bear
    alligator
14. rock and roll
    america online
    abc news
    publix

5. jaguar

poodle

blue jay

nile crocodile

6. french

math

biology 101

history

7. denny's

cafeteria

bennigan's

hilton hotel

8. president

madonna

president kennedy

doctor johnson

9. aunt martha

my uncle

my mother

uncle vanya

10. mustang convertible

pick-up truck

mercedes

my uncle's cadillac

15. spanish moss

oak tree

coral reef

condor

16. quarter horse

golden retriever

rattlesnake

bald eagle

17. western ontario

the south

east of the campus

southern louisiana

18. german chocolate cake

green beans

pecan flavored ice cream

shrimp cocktail

19. community college

university

foothills community college

ibm

20. the twentieth century

the middle ages

the french revolution

the paleolithic era

Group Activity **7.10** Divide the twenty items in Review Exercise 7.9 equally among group members. Each group member explains his or her answers to the group. If there is disagreement about an answer, group members should consult the skill rules, the instructor, or a dictionary for answers.

Review Exercise **7.11** Correct any errors in capitalization.

1. My friend went to Manatee High School, but I went to a different High School.

2. You can stay at your College, and I will transfer to Foothills Community College.

3. I like to visit the german area at the Alachua County Fair.

4. She said that German Shepherds should not be bred with Poodles.

5. The Bank gives out calendars every Fall and umbrellas every Spring.

6. I received my fall calendar in October; the Teller gave it to me.

7. Your sister has invited us to tea.

8. I asked Mother to bring raspberry scones and apple pie.

9. *Sense and sensibility* offers a fascinating glimpse into human relationships.

10. *Emily Reads The Book* was written for beginning readers.

Review Exercise 7.12   **Correct any capitalization errors in the following sentences.**

1. I am currently enrolled in a Biology class at Santa Fe community college.

2. Did you take Humanities 101?

3. My favorite class this semester was english.

4. The roots of an Oak tree can descend as far as three miles.

5. She just purchased a new house on oak street.

6. I have heard that Bank presidents always win at Monopoly.

7. Is the Doctor teaching History this year?

8. Should I wear white shoes after Labor Day?

9. Do Britons celebrate the fourth of July?

10. Let's go sailing during the Summer this year.

Review Exercise 7.13   **Identify the capitalization in the following sentences as correct (C) or incorrect (I).**

____I____ 1. Call the Doctor if you think you have the Chicken Pox.

____C____ 2. Ford and Chevrolet are both American made cars.

____C____ 3. I like to visit the zoo at the community college.

____I____ 4. You can get discount tickets for Disney world and Universal studios.

____I____ 5. I bought a pair of jeans, two turtlenecks, and a leather jacket at sears.

____C____ 6. Lydia planted big sunflowers and roses in her garden.

____I____ 7. Her new truck, a little nissan, has bucket seats.

____I____ 8. Her chickens got loose on paynes prairie last summer.

____C____ 9. A book from the public library had information about building a chicken coop.

____C____ 10. At the Fall River Mall, children can participate in activities.

Group Activity 7.14   **Review of exercise**

Each group member answers and explains two items. If there is a disagreement about the correct answer, review the definitions and decide on the correct answer. Each group member records the items he/she missed on the Capitalization Items Missed page in his or her notebook.

Review Exercise 7.15   **Editing for capitalization errors**

Correct all capitalization errors in the passage below.

Fun for the Weekend

What do you like to do for fun on the weekend? There are probably a thousand things to do in Centerville ranging from a quiet stroll through the trails along lake alice to a fun-filled day at an amusement park such as wild waters or silver springs. If it's movies you are in to, you can pick from many movie choices at any one of the seven theaters in town. The state theater offers many plays and movies for just about everyone, including foreign movies and art films. Also, it might be nice to try a restaurant that serves foreign food. If you have never eaten sushi, there are four sushi restaurants in centerville. Sometimes a newcomer may be too timid for this experience, but there are sushi choices that do not include raw fish such as the california roll, which features rice, seaweed, cooked crab, and avocado. The centerville area also has several nature reserves and state parks. Just off of milhopper road are the twin oaks state park and lake placid state reserve. Also, seminole prairie is home to unusual animals such as buffalo, alligators, ibis, roseate spoonbills, and sandhill cranes.

Review Exercise 7.16   Editing your writing

Choose two journal entries and edit them for capitalization errors. Use a different colored pen to make your corrections. Write *capitalization* in the upper right-hand corner of the page to let your instructor know you have edited the entry for capitalization errors.

Review Exercise 7.17   Editing your writing

Write a one-page journal entry in which you pay particular attention to capitalization. When you finish writing, go back and compare your use of capitals to the rules you have learned to see if you have used capitals correctly.

Review Exercise 7.18   Writing practice

Write a one-page journal entry in which you respond to the following writing prompt. When you finish writing, go back and proofread for capital letters.

Explain why you enjoy or don't enjoy family gatherings. Or, tell about a memorable time you spent with your family.

Chapter 8
Problem Words

In this chapter, you will learn about the most commonly confused words through definitions, memory hooks, and examples.

Words that **sound alike but have different spellings and different meanings** can cause spelling errors for writers. Spell-check programs won't catch errors with these commonly confused words because each word exists in the spell-checker's dictionary, and spell-check programs can only identify misspelled, not misused, words. The only way to catch errors with these problem words is to learn the meaning of each word and to proofread your writing carefully for misuses of these words.

List I	List II
Accept/Except	Advice/Advise
An/And	Affect/Effect
Its/It's	All ready/Already
Know/No	All together/Altogether
Passed/Past	Bare/Bear
Peace/Piece	Blew/Blue
Principal/Principle	Brake/Break
Right/Write	By/Buy
Steal/Steel	Capital/Capitol
Suppose/Supposed to	Choose/Chose
Than/Then	Complement/Compliment
Their/There/They're	Fair/Fare
Thorough/Through	Hear/Here
Throw/Threw	Hole/Whole
Through/Threw	Lay/Lie
Though/Thought	Loose/Lose

To/Too/Two	Your/You're
Use to/Used to	Stationary/Stationery
Weather/Whether	Weak/Week
Woman/Women	
Would, could, should, must Have/Of	

There are two easy ways to remember the differences between the words in these groups.

1. Use a memory hook: Associate an image or sound with each word as a way to hook your memory into remembering the word's meaning.

2. Remember an example for each word that illustrates the difference between the words.

Activity 8.1   **Set a goal of learning five words each night. For each problem word, write the definition, the memory hook (if there is one), and an example sentence.**

List 1

GPM: 4.3–4.44

Accept means to take or receive what is offered.

✔ With <u>accept</u> think of <u>accept</u>ance.

I accept your invitation.

Except means what is left out or excluded.

✔ Remember that the **x** in e**x**cept means *not*.

Everyone is here except Joaquin.

An is an article meaning *one* or *any* and is used before words that begin with a vowel or silent *h* sound.

✔ Remember *An apple*

An airline pilot must fly for *an* hour before taking a break.

And means *plus*.

✔ And = +

Jean and Takela went to the store.

Its is the singular possessive pronoun meaning belonging to it.

✔ Its = his, her, their (no apostrophe)

The car lost its antenna.

It's is the contraction of *it is* or *it has*.

✔ It's = it'(i)s.

It's a beautiful day.

Know means to have knowledge of.

✔ <u>Know</u> = <u>know</u>ledge

I know how to sew very well.

No means zero.

✔ No = 0

There is no water in the dry well.

Passed means the past tense of the verb *pass*.

✔ Passed ends in -ed because it's a verb.

I have passed the test.

Past means time that has already gone by or is the adverb meaning *by* or *beyond*.

The bus went past the bus stop every day this past week.

Peace means tranquility.

✔ Remember "**Pea**ce on **Ea**rth!"

There was peace after the war.

Piece means a part of something.

✔ Remember "**pie**ce of **pie**."

A piece of thread is hanging from your sleeve.

Principal means main or most important.

The principal road into town is Main Street.

Principle means a rule or law.

One principle of math is addition.

Right can mean something that is due to a person by law.

✔ Remember that "m**ight** does not make r**ight**."

My neighbor has a right to park in the driveway to his house.

Write means to put words on paper.

✔ Remember "**w**rite looks like scribble."

Please write your name clearly.

Steal means to rob.

✔ Remember that to ste**al** is illeg**al**.

A robber could steal the bicycle.

Steel means a hard metal.

✔ Remember that the **ee** in steel is doubled to make it strong like the metal.

The part for the machine was made of steel.

Suppose means assume. No **d** means suppose is a verb in present tense.

I suppose I will go to the dance unless I am sick.

Supposed to means ought to or should.

✔ *Supposed to* is always preceded by a form of *to be* and followed by *to* plus a verb: is supposed to go.

Children are supposed to respect their parents.

Than is used to make comparisons.

✔ Remember th**an** = comp**a**rison.

Jackie is taller than Raphael.

Then means for a moment in time.

✔ Remember th**e**n = tim**e**.

First, we will go to the movie; then we will go to eat.

Their is a possessive pronoun meaning belonging to them.

✔ Remember their = heir.

The neighbors should cut their lawn.

There can mean a place.

✔ Remember there = not here.

There is a car over there in the parking lot that looks brand new.

They're is the contraction of "they are."

✔ Remember they're = they are.

The children are quiet because they're watching a movie.

Thorough means complete or entire.

✔ Remember that *thorough* has an **o** for c**o**mplete.

The house needs a thorough cleaning.

Through can mean in one side and out the other. Through can also mean finished.

The last person went through the door.

Throw means to launch an object.

The mayor will throw out the first ball at the baseball game.

Threw is the past tense of the verb *throw*.

The pitcher threw the last pitch.

Through means finished or in one side and out the other or in the midst of.

The mechanic is through checking the engine.

Threw is the past tense of *throw*.

The pitcher threw the last pitch.

Though is the short form of *although*.

> Though it's almost winter, the days are still warm.

Thought means the past tense of the verb *think*.

> I thought you had left already.

To is a preposition that indicates direction or a part of the infinitive verb form (to be, to go, to do).

> I am going to the store.

Too means excessively, extremely, or also.

✔ Remember too = too many o's or also.

> It's too hot to play outside.

Two is the number.

> Two boys are fishing on the bridge.

Use to means utilize and is present tense.

> That wood I will use to make a fire.

Used to means having the habit and is past tense.

✔ It always includes to + verb (used to eat).

> The mailman used to arrive before lunch.

Weather means outdoor air conditions.

> The rainy weather is almost over.

Whether indicates alternatives.

> I don't know whether I can come or not.

Woman is the opposite of *man* in the singular form.

> One woman left already.

Women is the plural form of *woman*.

✔ Remember women and men.

> Two women are staying to hear the last speaker.

Would have, could have, should have, and must have are verb phrases.

> The garbage should have been taken out last night.

Would of, could of, should of, and must of: The *of* that follows the verbs begins a prepositional clause.

✔ *Of* is almost never used after these verbs. (*Have* is almost always used after these verbs.)

> You would, of all people, be the first to know my secret.

Your is the possessive pronoun meaning belonging to you.

> Your uncle just called.

You're is the contraction of *you are.*

You're (you are) the most interesting person that I know.

Group Activity **8.2**   **In a group, divide the word pairs equally among group members. Each member should review his or her assigned word pairs and provide a way to remember the difference between words and an example of each for the other group members.**

Review Exercise **8.3**   **Identify the sentences as correct (C) or incorrect (I), and then correct all problem word errors.**

GPM: 4.46

 _I_ 1. The first semester is usually harder <u>than</u> then any other time for college students.

 _C_ 2. Many college students have difficulty accepting responsibility.

 _I_ 3. Some students are not use^d to living on their own.

 _I_ 4. Living away from home allows students to^o meet new friends their own age.

 _C_ 5. Some students find that it's hard to find peace and quiet in their dorm.

 _I_ 6. Often, students find that it[']s better to go to the library to study.

 _I_ 7. Getting a good education is the <u>pal</u> principle reason to attend college.

 _I_ 8. During finals, many students wish that they could <u>have</u> of studied more.

 _I_ 9. Students want to know <u>whether</u> weather they passed their courses or not.

 _I_ 10. After finals, most students look forward to a rest and some recreation <u>too</u> to.

Review Exercise **8.4**   **Identify the sentences as correct (C) or incorrect (I), and then correct all problem word errors.**

 _I_ 1. <u>There</u> Their are not enough books for everyone.

 _I_ 2. It[']s important to wear nice clothes at the office.

 _C_ 3. The cafeteria gets too hot in the summer.

 _C_ 4. Arriving late to work is against the company's principles.

 _I_ 5. The plane should <u>have</u> of avoided the bad weather.

 _I_ 6. The store use^d to be open every day except Sunday.

 _I_ 7. The two women thought that the soup was <u>too</u> to hot to eat.

 _C_ 8. My neighbors don't know when they're returning from their trip.

 _C_ 9. The club lost its principal supporter.

 _C_ 10. Our instructor says that it's not acceptable to write in pencil.

Review Exercise **8.5**   **Identify the sentences as correct (C) or incorrect (I), and then correct all problem word errors.**

 _C_ 1. Two friends from high school lived in an apartment downtown their sophomore year.

 _I_ 2. All of my friends <u>except</u> accept Juan live in apartments with steel bars on their doors.

 _C_ 3. Determine whether you're able to afford to live in an apartment before moving away from home.

 _I_ 4. A woman in my dorm is suppose^d to help me find a new roommate.

    C   5. West End Apartments has a nice pool, but its rooms are too small.

    _{passed}

    I   6. The other day, I past by Crestview Manor, and it looked very peaceful.

    _{than}

    I   7. I will be through this school sooner then I thought.

    C   8. I am not sure whether I will be living in a dorm or in an apartment complex next semester.

    I   9. Some of my friends are attending summer school, and they're working part time to.

    _{too}

    C 10. Change is a principle of life that I have trouble accepting sometimes.

Review Exercise **8.6**   **Editing for problem words, List 1**

Correct all problem word errors.

A Popular Destination

England use to be considered to dull for a vacation, but now it has become a

popular destination for many travelers. Even thought the whether is suppose to be to

rainy for sightseeing, summers often bring cool, misty mornings an sunny

afternoons. For visitors interested in cultural history, London is the link to the

country's passed. Buckingham Palace an The Tower of London introduce tourists to

English royalty threw the ages. Their must of been more then twenty kings an

queens who lived in Buckingham Palace. Most of the royalty lived long lives accept

for some men and woman who died in the Tower of London. Travelers who want to

experience the beauty of England's natural landscapes are suppose to hike thorough

the English countryside. The Yorkshire Moors are a principle attraction in northern

England. They provide tourists with an opportunity to enjoy the piece and quiet of

England's majestic Lake District. Weather travelers seek city life or rural solitude,

England is certain too become there favorite destination.

 List II

GPM: 4.48–4.83

Advice is a noun that means a recommendation.

    My father has given me good advice about my finances.

Advise is a verb that means to counsel.

    The doctor will advise you to stop smoking.

Affect is a verb that means to influence or bring about a change.

✔   Remember *a*ffect is an **a**ction.

    The temperature can affect plants.

Effect is a noun that means a result.

✔   Remember *e*ffect is a r**e**sult.

One effect of exercising is weight loss.

All ready means everyone or everything is prepared.

✔   Remember that if the sentence makes sense without *all*, write "all ready."

My children are all ready for school.

Already means before or previously or by this time.

✔   Remember that if the sentence does not make sense without *all*, write "already."

Dinner has been served already.

All together means everything or everyone together.

✔   Remember that if the sentence makes sense without *all*, write "all together."

The camping gear is all together in the closet.

Altogether means completely or entirely.

✔   Remember that if the sentence does not make sense without *all*, write "altogether."

I have altogether too much work to do tonight.

Bare means uncovered or just enough.

There is barely time to reach the airport before our plane leaves.

Bear means the wild animal OR to carry, to hold up, or to endure.

I can't bear the thought of school starting again after our vacation.

Blew is the past tense of *blow*.

The wind blew all night long.

Blue is the color.

✔   Remember that b**lue** = color or **hue**.

Her eyes are blue.

Brake means a device to stop movement.

The car's brakes needed to be replaced.

Break means an interruption.

I must take a break before I continue working.

By is a preposition.

My sister will stop by our apartment with cookies.

Buy means to purchase.

You need to buy milk.

Capital means the main or most important.

  The capital city of New York is Albany.

Capitol means the government building.

✔   Remember that capit**ol** = d**o**me.

  Congress meets in the Capitol in Washington.

Choose means to pick out.

✔   Remember *choose* has two o's to choose from.

  I will choose a new car.

Chose is the past tense of *choose* and is pronounced with a long *o*.

  The dinner I chose last night gave me food poisoning.

Complement means to make complete or something that completes or makes perfect.

  The blue shirt complements your tan slacks.

Compliment means praise.

  My teacher gave me a compliment about my paper.

Fair means just, good, blond, pale, or carnival. *Fair* is used for all meanings except money.

  It's not fair when someone takes advantage of an elderly person.

Fare means the ticket price.

  The bus fare was only five dollars.

Hear means to perceive by ear.

✔   Remember h**ear** = **ear.**
  I can't hear you when you are in the next room.

Here means location.

✔   Remember **here** = not t**here.**
  Please come here right now.

Hole means an opening.

  The workman used a shovel to dig the hole.

Whole means entire or complete.

  I can't believe that you ate the whole pie.

Lay means to place or put. In present tense, if you can substitute *place* or *put* for *lay*, then *lay* is correct.

✔   Lay = Place

  Please lay the book on the table.

Lie means to recline.

  My grandfather always lies down before dinner.

Loose can mean free.

The doorknob is loose and wobbles when I turn it.

Lose can mean unable to keep.

✔ Remember lose = lost.

People can lose a lot of money gambling.

Stationary means not movable.

The car was stationary when it was hit by the bus.

Stationery means writing paper.

✔ Remember station**ery** = pap**er**.

The letter came on blue stationery.

Weak means the opposite of strong.

A muscle can be weak after an injury.

Week means seven days.

The meeting is next week.

Group Activity 8.7   **Paired note taking**

Student A reads the definition and example of a word while Student B records it. Both students agree on a new example sentence, which Student B records. Repeat the same procedure for the second word. For the next word pair, exchange roles and Student B reads definitions and example sentences aloud while Student A records. Continue through the list, exchanging roles on each word pair. Copy each other's work so that each student has a complete set of notes.

Review Exercise 8.8

GPM: 4.85

Identify the problem words in the following sentences as correct (C) or incorrect (I) and then correct the errors.

   _I_   1. I use the Internet to find the cheapest plane fairs. ^(fares)

   _C_   2. Choosing a topic to write about is not an easy task.

   _I_   3. I all ready have plans for Saturday night. ^(already)

   _I_   4. Rosalie only took the bear necessities on the camping trip. ^(bare)

   _C_   5. My whole family gathers at Thanksgiving.

   _I_   6. I was afraid I was going to loose the game.

   _C_   7. My mother wanted to buy me an extra pair of shoes.

   _C_   8. My instructor advised me to take a foreign language class.

   _I_   9. Many people feel blew over the holidays. ^(blue)

   _I_ 10. Murder is a capitol offense. ^(a)

Review Exercise **8.9**   **Identify the problem words in the following sentences as correct (C) or incorrect (I)
and then correct the errors.**

                                  all ready

   I   1. The Boy Scouts are already to leave for camp.

               o

   I   2. The capital dome was damaged in the ice storm.

   C   3. The teacher did not lose her cool when the incident occurred.

                   break

   I   4. The officer had to brake the bad news to the family.

   C   5. A whole week has gone by and my friend hasn't called.

               fares

   I   6. Bus fairs went up again last week.

   C   7. The stationery on the secretary's desk was neatly arranged.

                               i

   I   8. My boyfriend complemented me on my new dress.

                          altogether

   I   9. The lawyer asked whether I was all together sure of my answer.

               break

   I 10. If you brake my watch, you will have to buy me a new one.

Review Exercise **8.10**   **Identify the problem words in the following sentences as correct (C) or incorrect (I)
and then correct the errors.**

   C   1. Julio has already seen the movie.

   C   2. I can't bear to hurt my friend's feelings.

                                e

   I   3. I need to buy some new stationary.

   C   4. My brother chose to go to work rather than go to college.

              altogether

   I   5. I am all together certain I am right.

              hole

   I   6. There is a whole in my new blue folder.

             fare

   I   7. The train fair to New York is sixty-four dollars.

                    loose

   I   8. Her ring fell off because it was lose.

   C   9. Will you drive me through the capital?

   C 10. I brake for animals.

Group Activity **8.11**   **Review of Review Exercise**

Each group member answers and explains two items. If there is a disagreement
about the correct answer, review the definitions and decide on the correct answer.
Each group member records the items he/she missed on the Problem Words Items
Missed page in his or her notebook.

Review Exercise **8.12**   **Editing for problem word errors, Lists I and II**

GPM: 4.87

Read the following paragraph and correct all problem word errors.

The Sinkhole

                 week

Last weak, my geology class took an educational field trip to a sinkhole. Our

                                            already

instructor wanted to supplement what we had all ready learned in class by showing

                                   there

us some of the changes that have taken place their over the years. From our

                   know

classroom studies, we no that limestone was eroded by minerals in the water table, and underground caves were created. Than, when the weight of the surface rock

Then

became to great, a massive sinkhole opened. Descending to a depth of 120 feet, this

too

whole allows visitors to chose to enter another dimension. As you descend the

hole   *choose*

wooden stairway that winds over the lose soil, the sounds of birds fill the air. Your

loose   *You're*

immediately enveloped by the quiet, dense atmosphere and fragrant, woody

aromas, as thought you had left behind the modern world of pollution, noise, and

smog. The field trip to the sinkhole was an enjoyable experience, and I look forward

too exploring it's amazing scenery again soon.

to   *its*

Review Exercise 8.13   **Editing your writing**

Choose two journal entries and edit them for problem word errors. Use a different colored pen to make your corrections. Write *problem words* in the upper right-hand corner of
the page to let your instructor know you have edited the entry for problem words.

Review Exercise 8.14   **Writing practice**

Write a one-page journal entry in which you respond to the following writing prompt.
When you finish writing, go back and compare your use of problem words to the definitions you have learned to see if you have used the problem words correctly.

Describe the role a special pet plays or has played in your life.

Chapter 9
Parts of Speech

To learn about any subject, you must understand the vocabulary that is used to describe information about the subject. Specialized words have been developed to help explain basic concepts. For example, if your car breaks down, it helps to know the names of the car's mechanical parts when talking to the mechanic. Similarly, you may need to know what terms such as sautéing, blanching, and braising mean if you want to follow a recipe in a cookbook.

The parts of speech are the basic terms used by writers to discuss the words in a sentence. All the rules about writing correct sentences rely on an understanding of the parts of speech. Fortunately, there is nothing mysterious or difficult about understanding the concepts.

The parts of speech define the eight general ways in which words function in sentences. In other words, every word in a sentence can be classified as one of the parts of speech. This chapter will define the parts of speech and discuss the ways the parts are used and misused. Much of the information is background that you will build on in later chapters.

The Eight Parts of Speech

1. Nouns	5. Adverbs
2. Pronouns	6. Prepositions
3. Adjectives	7. Conjunctions
4. Verbs	8. Interjections

GPM: 1.3

1. Nouns

1.1   Nouns name persons, places, things, and ideas.

teacher, church, lamp, energy

1.2   Nouns can be singular (one person, place, thing, or idea) or plural (more than one). To make a noun plural, add -s (or -es, for most nouns ending in *o, x, z, sh, ch, ss, y*).

teacher/teachers	lamp/lamp
church/churches	energy/energies

1.3   Some nouns have irregular plurals (don't end in -s or -es). The most common **irregular plurals** are *men, women, children,* and *people*.

a man/two men	a child/two children
a woman/two women	a person/two people

1.4   Determiners before the noun can help you use the correct ending.

One speaker/**many** speakers

A player/**some** players

The backpack/**many** backpacks

An agent/**several** agents

1.5   The objects in prepositional phrases such as *one of the* _____ and *a couple of the*_____, *a lot of the* _____ are plural.

One of the waiter**s**

A couple of the tree**s**

A few of the cat**s**

Practice   **Circle the correct noun.**

1. Some child/(children) arrive early to school every day.

2. Five churchs/(churches) will have a joint service on Sunday.

3. A few of the student/(students) will be late today.

4. There are a lot of car/(cars) in the parking lot.

5. Some peachs/(peaches) in a few of the barrel/(barrels) are rotten.

6. One of the computer/(computers) is broken.

7. Sunday, a couple of the game/(games) will played in front of thousands of fan/(fans).

8. Some politician/(politicians) make many speechs/(speeches) every day.

9. Only one large (book)/books will fit in a small (book bag)/book bags.

10. A lot of woman/(women) want to have a (career)/careers and raise a (family)/families.

What to Remember about Nouns

Nouns are people and things. If you are unsure whether a word is a noun, ask yourself whether the word names something that can be singular or plural. Nouns are the subjects and objects of sentences. Nouns can be concrete or abstract. Proper nouns (the names of specific people, places, and things) are capitalized.

Connections

Nouns work with verbs and prepositions. Adjectives describe or modify nouns. Pronouns take the place of nouns. Nouns are important in Chapter 11, "Subject–Verb Identification."

GPM: 1.16

2. Pronouns

2.1 Pronouns take the place of nouns (called antecedents) in sentences. Like nouns, pronouns are singular or plural.

> **Antecedent**   **Pronoun**   **Pronoun**
> The **meter reader** parked **her** scooter at the curb so that **she** could write tickets.

> **Antecedent   Pronoun**   **Pronoun**
> Some **actors** ask **their** agent to make dates for **them**.

Pronoun Case

2.2 Different pronoun forms are used in different parts of the sentence.

	Subjective Case	Objective Case	Possessive Case
Singular	I	me	my/mine
	you	you	your/yours
	he/she/it	him/her/it	his/her/its
Plural	we	us	our/ours
	you	you	your/yours
	they	them	their/theirs

Subjective case (pronoun used as subject of sentence)

> S   V
> **She** left the book on the table.

Objective case (pronoun comes after the verb)

> S   V   Obj
> The bus took **us** to the mall.

Possessive case (pronoun used to show possession)

My father enjoyed **our** vacation.

Kinds of Pronouns

2.3   **Personal pronouns** refer to people or things.

I, me, you, it, she, her, they, them

I dropped her off at the bus stop.

2.4   **Possessive pronouns** indicate ownership.

my, mine, your, yours, his, hers, its, theirs, ours

The cat licked its paws.

2.5   **Reflexive pronouns** indicate that the doer and receiver of action are the same.

myself, yourself, himself, themselves

The sick man checked himself into the hospital.

2.5a   Do not use nonstandard forms such as *hisself, theirself, theirselves,* and *themself.*

Practice 9.2   **Correct the nonstandard pronouns.**

1. The boy cooked the meal hisself. *himself*
2. The family rented a house for themself and their friends. *themselves*
3. The children tired theirselves out playing all morning. *themselves*
4. Juan hit hisself on the leg with the bat. *himself*
5. The fans forced theirself to leave the game early. *themselves*

2.6   **Relative pronouns** introduce dependent clauses and refer to a noun or pronoun that comes before them.

who, whom, which, that, whoever, whomever, whatever

The computer **that** is on the table belongs to the man **who** just left the room.

Use *that* and *which* with things and *who* with people.

2.7   **Interrogative pronouns** are used in questions.

who, whom, what

What are the dates of the exams?

2.8   **Demonstrative pronouns** identify or point to nouns.

this, that, these, those

This class meets at nine every morning.

2.9 **Indefinite pronouns** do not refer to any particular person or thing.

any	everyone	nothing
anybody	everything	one
anyone	few	several
anything	many	some
both	neither	somebody
each	nobody	someone
either	none	something
everybody	no one	

2.9a Most indefinite pronouns are singular and take a singular verb and a singular pronoun.

Everyone here **brings his or her** own calculator to class.

2.9b Some indefinite pronouns are plural and take plural verbs and pronouns.

Several of my friends **drive their** cars to school.

2.9c A few indefinite pronouns can be either singular or plural depending on the noun or pronoun to which they refer.

Some of the water **has leaked** out of **its** tank.

Some of the tickets **have been sold** already.

What to Remember about Pronouns

Pronouns always refer to particular nouns (antecedents). The correct form (case) of the pronoun depends on its place in the sentence. Most indefinite pronouns (such as words ending with -*one*, -*body*, -*thing*) are singular.

Connections

Pronouns take the place of nouns and are connected to verbs and sometimes prepositions. Pronouns are important in the following chapters: Chapter 11, "Subject–Verb Identification," and Chapter 18, "Pronoun Agreement."

GPM: 1.43

3. Adjectives

3.1 Adjectives describe or modify nouns and pronouns.

```
Adj   Adj    N         Adj Adj Adj  N       Adj Adj     N
```
The small child rested his little red hand on the glass tabletop.

3.2   Adjectives answer the question "what?" or "which?" about nouns and pronouns.

       N

Computers are inexpensive.

        Adj   **N**

What computers? Personal computers are inexpensive.

         Adj   **Adj**

Which personal computers? New personal computers are inexpensive.

3.3   The **articles** *a, an,* and *the* are adjectives that modify nouns.

A is used before words that begin with a consonant (such as b, c, d, f) or a consonant sound.

    a book, a camera, a zebra, a university

An is used before words that begin with a vowel (*a, e, i, o, u, y*) or silent *h.*

    an astronomer, an expedition, an interest, an honorary degree, an A

Practice **9.3**   **Underline the adjectives in each sentence.**

1. The small child next door has an adorable smile.

2. Her mother walks the little girl in a new blue stroller.

3. Friendly neighbors wave at the pair as they walk on the shady street.

4. Sometimes the young girl cries for her cuddly teddy bear or a warm bottle.

5. On a sunny day, the mother will carry a colorful umbrella to protect the baby from the hot sun.

Group Activity **9.4**   **Each group member should write two sentences using adjectives. Trade papers and underline the adjectives in your partner's sentences.**

Answers will vary.

_____

_____

_____

Practice **9.5**   **Circle the correct article.**

1. Having (a)/ an regular exercise program is important to (a)/ an person's health.

2. A /(An) overweight person needs to be careful, though, not to overdo a /(an) exercise program.

3. Jogging is a /(an) excellent form of exercise, or for (a)/ an low-impact form, swimming is a /(an) outstanding choice.

4. (A)/ An game of basketball offers a /(an) eager sports enthusiast (a)/ an competitive exercise.

5. (A)/ An university or college provides (a)/ an union or center for students who want to play a /(an) engaging game of ping pong or billiards.

3.4   Adjectives can compare nouns **(comparative)** or show that a noun is the best **(superlative)**. For most adjectives of one syllable, add *-er* to form the comparative and *-est* to form the superlative.

> Comparative: Nina is **taller** than Sophie.

> Superlative: Rhea is the **tallest** girl in the class.

3.4a   For most adjectives of more than one syllable, add *more* to form the comparative and *most* to form the superlative. Adjectives that end in *-y* usually form the comparative and superlative by dropping the *-y* and adding *-ier* or *-iest*.

> Comparative: Wali was **more** considerate than Ahmad.

> Superlative: Ben was the **most** considerate.

3.4b   Some adjectives are irregular.

Adjective	Comparative	Superlative
good	better	best
bad	worse	worst

Practice **9.6**   **Circle the correct form of the adjective.**

1. One instructor's explanation was clearer / more clear than another instructor's explanation.

2. My teacher's tests are the hardest / most hard in the department.

3. In fact, my teacher was voted the most outstanding / oustandingest instructor in the department.

4. Nine o'clock is the earliest / most early appointment I could make.

5. My golden retriever is fatter / more fat than my German shepherd.

6. The movie that I saw last night was the worst / baddest film of the year.

7. Miguel's car is one of the fastest / most fast cars I've ever driven.

8. I am happier / more happy than I was last year.

9. This restaurant is expensiver / more expensive than I expected.

10. The scientist is the brilliantest / most brilliant researcher in the field of medicine.

What to Remember about Adjectives

Adjectives are like spice; they add color and flavor to sentences because they are descriptive words. They have different forms when they are used to compare nouns.

Connections

Adjectives describe nouns and can be confused with adverbs.

GPM: 1.29

4. Verbs

4.1   Verbs are words that express action or state of being.

Action verb: Many birds **fly** south in the winter.

State of being verb: The weather **is** hot today.

Kinds of Verbs

4.2   **Action verbs** express an action.

> play, drive, hit, ask, decide, write

The woman **drives** her kids to school.

4.3   **Linking verbs** link the subject to a noun, pronoun, or adjective.

> is, are, was, were, be, been, feel, look, seem, become, smell, sound, taste

The food **smells** good.

4.4   **Helping or auxiliary verbs** link the subject to a verb.

> is, are, was, were, am, be, been, being, was, could, might, will, would,
> shall, should, must, can, may, have, has, had, do, did

The construction **should have been** completed by August.

Group Activity **9.7**   **Write three sentences using active verbs, linking verbs, and helping verbs. Then share sentences with the group.**

Sentences using active verbs:

Answers will vary.

_____

_____

Sentences using linking verbs:

Answers will vary.

_____

_____

Sentences using helping verbs:

Answers will vary.

_____

_____

Verb Forms

4.5   There are three main forms of the verb: the **present**, **past**, and **past participle**. The form of the verb changes according to its **tense** (present, past, future, present perfect, past perfect, future perfect); **number** (singular or plural); **voice** (active, passive); and **mood** (indicative, imperative, subjunctive). The chapters on subject–verb agreement and verb tenses will explain the rules for verb endings in the present and past tenses.

> Present: The dog always **goes** with its owner on a walk.

> Past: Yesterday, the dog and its owner **went** for a long walk.

> Past participle: The dog has **gone** for many walks this week.

4.6   **Verbals** are verb forms that act as another part of speech.

4.6a   **Infinitives** are verb forms introduced by *to*.

> Cassandra wants **to buy** a new car.

4.6b   **Gerunds** are verb forms ending in *-ing* that act as nouns.

> **Running** is good exercise.

4.6c   **Participles** are verb forms usually ending in *-ing* or *-ed* that act as verbs or adjectives.

> The **closed** shop was dark inside.

What to Remember about Verbs

Verbs are action words or being words (is/are, seem). They are always present in a sentence. Verb endings can be tricky and cause major writing errors.

Connections

Verbs join subjects (nouns) to make sentences. Verbs are modified by adverbs. Verbs are covered in the following chapters: Chapter 11, "Subject–Verb Identification;" Chapter 12, "Subject–Verb Agreement;" and Chapter 13, "Verb Tenses."

GPM: 1.50

5. Adverbs

5.1   **Adverbs** describe or modify *verbs*, *adjectives*, and other *adverbs*. Many adverbs end in *-ly*.

>   **V**   **Adv**   **Adv**   **Adv**   **Adj**
> The postman walked **very quickly** because the air was **really** cold.

5.2   Adverbs answer the question "how?" about a verb, an adjective, or another adverb.

>   **Adj**
> I am tired.

                                         Adv   Adj
                    How tired? I am **really** tired.

                                          V
                    The elderly woman walked across the street.

                                                   V   Adv   Adv
                    How did she walk? The elderly woman walked **very slowly** across the
                    street.

Practice 9.8   **Circle the adverbs in each sentence.**

1. The customer asked (firmly) for her money to be refunded.

2. He touched her arm (lightly).

3. The (heavily) seasoned meal gave my father heartburn.

4. The drunken man walked (unsteadily) out the door.

5. (Terribly) tired, the hikers fell (soundly) to sleep.

Practice 9.9   **Write a sentence using the adverb in parentheses.**

(loudly) _Answers will vary._____

(smoothly) _____

(clearly) _____

Adverb/Adjective Confusion

5.3   Do not confuse adjectives and adverbs. Since many descriptive words can be used both as adjectives and adverbs, using the adjective for the adverb is a common error. Only adverbs can modify adjectives.

                            Adj   Adj
            Incorrect: I was **awful** hot.

                            Adv   Adj
            Correct: I was **awfully** hot.

5.3a   *Real* is an adjective and can only modify a noun. *Really* is an adverb and must be used to modify verbs, adjectives, and adverbs.

                    Adj   N   Adj Adj   Adj   N
     Incorrect: The real cowboy had a **real** easy time riding the real horse.

                    Adj   N   Adv Adj   Adj   N
     Correct: The real cowboy had a **really** easy time riding the real horse.

5.3b   *Good* is an adjective and can only modify a noun. *Well* is an adverb and must be used to modify verbs, adjectives, and adverbs.

                            Adj   V   Adj
     Incorrect: The teacher's good class did **good** on the test.

                            Adj   V   Adj
     Correct: The teacher's good class did **well** on the test.

Practice 9.10 **Circle the correct form of the adverb.**

1. Our dog whines steady /(steadily) because she wants a biscuit bad /(badly.)

2. Class begins regular /(regularly) at ten, and the teacher gets real /(really) angry if anyone is late.

3. The cat pounced fierce /(fiercely) on the toy that the child dragged slow /(slowly) across the floor.

4. The team performed good /(well) during practice but played poor /(poorly) during the game.

5. The professional driver operated her car fearless /(fearlessly) in the race.

6. Twins are usually real /(really) close and understand each other very good /(well.)

7. Our car runs terrible /(terribly) in real /(really) cold weather.

8. The computer worked beautiful /(beautifully) after it was skillful /(skillfully) repaired at the shop.

9. The crowd waited noisy /(noisily) for the speaker to begin.

10. My mother speaks French good /(well) and Spanish perfect /(perfectly.)

What to Remember about Adverbs

Adverbs often end in -*ly*. If you are describing the "how" of something, then the adverb is the descriptive form to use. Remember the most common mistakes with *good* and *real*.

Connections

Adverbs describe verbs, adjectives, and adverbs.

Review Exercise 9.11 **Correct all errors with adjectives and adverbs.**

Tattoo Removal

most popular   really

Tattoos are one of the populorest fads today, and getting a tattoo is real easy.

harder

However, removing a tattoo can prove to be much more hard than getting one. Tattoo

parlors proudly claim that tattoos are permanent, but sometimes people want to

cheapest

remove a tattoo. Lasers have become the most cheap way to remove tattoos. Lasers

easily   really   quickly

vaporize the pigment colors easy into real tiny fragments that get absorbed quick

easiest

into the skin. Black tattoos are the most easy to remove because black pigment is

more difficult

absorbed totally into the skin. Other colors are difficulter to remove because they

selectively

only absorb selective into the skin.

more common   really

Dermabrasion and chemical skin peels are becoming commoner now. A real

small portion of skin is sprayed thoroughly with a solution that freezes the area. The tattoo is then sanded lightly with a rotary abrasive instrument. Unfortunately,

                                 unexpectedly   more painful

bleeding and scarring sometimes occur unexpected. Chemical peels are painfuler.

Surgery is also an option to remove a tattoo. The tattoo is cut off, and the wound is

               cleanly   more fearful

sewn up clean. Many people are fearfuller of this method of removal than the others

because scarring occurs the most often of any of the procedures.

GPM: 1.38

6. Prepositions

6.1   A **preposition** explains the relationship between its **object** (the noun or pronoun that follows it) and another word in the sentence. Many prepositions explain time or space relationships.

             Prep   **Prep**

My coat **in** the closet has a stain **on** the arm.

In explains the relationship between *coat* and *closet*. *On* explains the relationship between *stain* and *arm*.

Common Prepositions

about	between	on
above	beyond	on account of
according to	by	on top of
across	despite	out
after	down	outside of
against	during	over
along	except	since
along with	for	through
among	from	throughout
around	in	to
as	in addition to	toward
as far as	inside	under
at	in spite of	until
before	instead of	up
behind	into	upon
below	like	with
beneath	near	within
beside	of	without
besides	off	

Group Activity 9.12   Each member of the group should brainstorm a prepositional phrase for ten prepositions in the list above. Then members share their prepositional phrases.

Practice 9.13   Underline each prepositional phrase in each sentence.

1. On the Fourth of July of last year, the members of our family held a picnic at the
   beach.

2. By the end of the day, I must finish all of my work.

3. During the fall, the school is full of new students.

4. After lunch, the group from the other organization made its presentation to the
   committee.

5. Sometime in April baseball fans around the country get excited about their
   teams.

What to Remember about Prepositions

Prepositions are short words that show relationships between nouns.
(Think of a cloud and a plane. Prepositions describe the relationship of the
plane to the cloud: under, over, in, to, from, within.) Prepositions and their
objects together form **prepositional phrases**. A prepositional phrase can
appear anywhere in a sentence.

Connections

Prepositions will appear in the following chapters: Chapter 11, "Subject–
Verb Identification," and Chapter 17, "Commas."

GPM 1.57–1.60

7. Conjunctions

7.1   Conjunctions join words or groups of words.

7.2   **Coordinating conjunctions** join a word to a word, a phrase to a
phrase, or a clause to a clause.

Coordinating Conjunctions
for, and, nor, but, or, yet, so

Remember *fanboys*: *for, and, nor, but, or, yet, so*

We will take the bus **or** the train to visit Baltimore. (joins two words)

Doing the dishes **and** mowing the lawn are my least favorite chores.
    (joins two phrases)

The room is small, but it has a large window. (joins two independent
    clauses)

Practice 9.14   **Write a sentence using each of the coordinating conjunctions. Check your sentences with a classmate to be sure the coordinating conjunction is used correctly.**

(for)__ Answers will vary. _____

(and)_____

(nor) _____

(but) _____

(yet) _____

(so) _____

7.3   **Subordinating conjunctions** show the relationship between clauses. They connect a dependent clause to an independent clause.

Subordinating Conjunctions

after	that
although	though
as	unless
because	until
before	when
if	where
in order that	whereas
since	while
so that	

Independent Clause   **Dependent Clause**
The audience cheered **because** the band agreed to play another song.

Dependent Clause   **Independent Clause**
When the music stopped, the audience gave the musicians a standing ovation.

Practice 9.15   **Write a sentence using five of the subordinating conjunctions. Share your sentence with another classmate to be sure the subordinating conjunction is used correctly.**

Answers will vary.

_____

_____

_____

_____

7.4 **Conjunctive adverbs** also join clauses.

> ### Common Conjunctive Adverbs
> therefore, consequently, however, moreover, also, furthermore, then, later

For a complete list of conjunctive adverbs, see Chapter 17, page 222.

Conj Adv
The conference met until noon; **however**, we left early.

What to Remember about Conjunctions

Conjunctions, like junctions, join word groups together. The meaning of each conjunction explains the relationship between the word groups.

Connections

Conjunctions are important in the following chapters: Chapter 14, "Sentence Parts and Types," Chapter 17, "Commas," and Chapter 20, "Sentence Combining."

8. Interjections

8.1 An interjection communicates a strong emotion and is separated from the rest of the sentence by a punctuation mark such as a comma or an exclamation point.

> ### Common Interjections
> wow, yikes, watch out, hey, ouch, OK

Ouch! That hurts.

Connections

Interjections are not used in academic writing.

Review Exercise 9.16   **Fill in the blanks.**

1. Nouns are the part of speech that name a <u>person</u>, <u>place</u>, <u>thing</u>, and <u>idea</u>.

2. Which part of speech is an action word? <u>verb</u>

3. What part of speech takes the place of nouns? <u>pronoun</u>

4. *On the floor* is an example of a <u>prepositional</u> phrase.

5. *Good* is an <u>adjective</u>, and *well* is an <u>adverb</u>.

6. Name two kinds of conjunctions: <u>coordinating</u> and <u>subordinating</u>.

7. Adverbs describe or modify what parts of speech? <u>verbs</u>, <u>adjectives</u>, and <u>adverbs</u>

8. Adjectives describe or modify what parts of speech? <u>nouns</u> and
<u>pronouns</u>

9. Name three kinds of verbs: <u>action</u> , <u>linking</u> , <u>helping or auxiliaries</u> .

10. Name three articles: <u>the</u> , <u>a</u> , <u>an</u> .

Group Activity 9.17   **Review of exercise**

Each group member answers and explains two items. If there is a disagreement about the correct answer, review the chapter and decide on the correct answer.

Review Exercise 9.18   **Writing practice**

Write a one-page journal entry in which you respond to the following writing prompt.

Why do you feel love is possible or not possible in the modern world?

Chapter 10
Word Choice

In this chapter, you will

- Learn the difference between abstract and concrete words and between general and specific words
- Learn to use vivid adjectives, specific verbs, and colorful adverbs
- Learn to avoid the pitfalls of
    nonstandard language
    double negatives
    slang
    clichés
    wordiness

To be successful in college and in the work world, you have to be aware of your language. You have to choose words that have the right meaning if you wish to communicate your ideas clearly.

Words are the most basic element our communication, yet most of us don't spend much time thinking about the words we choose. We often use the first word that comes to mind. Sometimes our choice effectively expresses our ideas, and sometimes it doesn't. In writing, perhaps even more so than in speaking, it is important to choose the best words.

Deciding which words to choose is important in two stages of the writing process—drafting and revising. In your first draft, you want to choose concrete, specific language that you are familiar with—nothing fancy, just clear language that communicates your meaning. When you are revising, you can go back and focus on language again. Take a look at your nouns and verbs: are they concrete and specific enough? Take a look at your vocabulary: is it appropriate for the topic? Get rid of slang, clichés, and unnecessary words and expressions. Start thinking about the language you use, and be aware of the language used in the essays you read. Nine times out of ten, what makes writing work, what makes it effective, is the language the author chooses to use.

WE: 1.2

Effective Word Choice

Abstract and Concrete Words

1. Words can be divided into **abstract** or **concrete**. We know concrete words through our senses. You can see, touch, taste, hear, and smell a flower or a car. Abstract words, in contrast, we know through our minds. You can't touch or see abstractions such as *love* and *loyalty*. We have to use abstract words to convey concepts like beauty and truth, but when we want to create a picture in the reader's mind, we should choose specific, concrete words.

> Abstract: The old homestead represents the struggle and endurance of generations of our family.

> Concrete: The backyard tire swing hangs from the spreading branches of a one-hundred-year-old live oak.

Practice 10.1 **Identify the following words as abstract (A) or concrete (C).**

1. __C__ dog
2. __A__ beauty
3. __C__ television
4. __A__ friendship
5. __A__ fear

6. __C__ chair
7. __C__ ambulance
8. __A__ heroism
9. __A__ injustice
10. __C__ window

General and Specific Words

2. Concrete words vary from **general** to **specific**. General nouns, even if they are concrete, won't help the reader see a picture of what you have in mind. After all, there are all kinds of cars, flowers, and bridges. Use specific nouns to create images for the reader.

General	Specific
dog	Irish setter
tree	magnolia tree
pen	felt-tipped pen
mountain	Mount Washington
chair	Windsor chair

General	More Specific
She has a dog.	She has a German shepherd.
We drove our truck.	We drove our Ford pickup truck.
The farm animals made noise.	The horses, cows, and sheep bellowed and bleated.

Practice 10.2   **Identify the following words as general (G) or specific (S).**

1. _G_ book   6. _S_ hamburger
2. _S_ eagle   7. _S_ tuna
3. _G_ car   8. _S_ goldfish
4. _S_ Lake Ontario   9. _G_ tree
5. _S_ potato chips   10. _G_ insect

Vivid Adjectives

3.1   Even when we use specific nouns, we sometimes need adjectives to create a more specific picture of what we have in mind. When appropriate, use **vivid adjectives** to describe nouns, other adjectives, and adverbs.

General			Specific
car	sports car	convertible sports car	white convertible sports car
chair	folding chair	folding beach chair	folding aluminum beach chair
book	antique book	antique leather book	crumbling antique leather book

Example: To generate a clear picture of the cat in the following sentences, we have added increasingly specific words.

> She has a cat.
> She has a **Persian** cat.
> She has a **white Persian** cat.
> She has a **longhaired white Persian** cat.

Adjective Word Order

3.2   Adjectives generally appear in front of the noun they modify, and when there are several adjectives in a row, they appear in the order listed below.

1. Determiners (a, an, the, that, those, some, his, her, our, etc.)
2. Evaluation (subjective) adjectives (perfect, beautiful, ugly, interesting, etc.)
3. Size and shape adjectives (tiny, enormous, square, triangular, etc.)
4. Age (antique, old, young, etc.)
5. Color (blue, rosy, dark, light, etc.)
6. Nationality (American, English, Spanish, etc.)

7. Religion (Baptist, Buddhist, Jewish, Islamic)

8. Material (glass, stone, plastic, wooden, etc.)

9. Qualifying adjectives that are often seen as part of the noun (beach chair, sports car, baby carriage, love letter, etc.)

Examples:

Last summer we rented a large, drafty, old beach house.

We walked for miles on the beautiful white sand beaches, and I collected hundreds of tiny delicately colored seashells.

I drove my brother's brand new red convertible sports car.

Practice **10.3**   **Arrange the adjectives in the correct order.**

1. My brother has the autographs of several American basketball professional players.

several professional American basketball players

2. I wore an evening long black strapless gown to the prom.

a long black strapless evening gown

3. My mother loves Belgian antique lace.

antique Belgian lace

4. I saw a litter of Labrador yellow adorable puppies.

adorable yellow Labrador puppies

5. My friend drives a yellow dirty ten-speed bike.

dirty yellow ten-speed bike

Specific Verbs

4.1   Like nouns, verbs vary from **general** to **specific**. Specific verbs help create an image of an action, just as specific nouns help create an image of people, places, and things.

General Verbs	Specific Verbs
move	gallop, amble, glide, slink, creep
say	yell, scream, whisper, growl, snarl, chatter
drink	gulp, savor, sip, taste, lap

To Be and *To Have*

4.2   The verbs *to be* and *to have* are general verbs. Often, more specific verbs can be used in their place. When you can replace *to be* or *to have* with another verb, your sentence will be stronger and more effective.

Weak: My brother *has* a ten-speed bike.

Strong: My brother *owns* a ten-speed bike.

Weak: The instructor *is* on time for class.

Strong: The instructor *arrives* on time for class.

Practice 10.4 **Identify the following verbs as general (G) or specific (S):**

1. __S__ squirm

2. __G__ is

3. __S__ hiss

4. __G__ has

5. __G__ walk

6. __S__ slither

7. __S__ manipulate

8. __S__ caress

9. __G__ does

10. __G__ was

Practice 10.5 **Replace the general verb with a more specific verb.** Answers will vary.

bark
1. The dogs next door <u>make noise</u> at night.

offers
2. Our school cafeteria <u>has</u> a salad bar at lunch.

lives/vacations
3. My best friend's family <u>is</u> in Jamaica.

borrow
4. Students <u>get</u> books from the library.

caught
5. The child <u>got</u> a cold at school.

deposited
6. I <u>put</u> my money in the bank.

bought
7. The parents <u>got</u> their child a new bike.

sleeps
8. The cat <u>is</u> on my bed.

pick up
9. Some parents <u>get</u> their children at the bus stop.

arrives/delivers mail
10. The postman <u>is</u> here every day before noon.

Colorful Adverbs

5. When appropriate, use **colorful adverbs** to describe verbs, adjectives, and other adverbs.

Examples:

She spoke to the crowd of reporters.

She spoke **tearfully** to the crowd of reporters.

She spoke **angrily** to the crowd of reporters.

She spoke **cautiously** to the crowd of reporters.

Notice how each adverb creates a completely different image.

Simon skied in front of the others.

He skied **confidently** in front of the others.

He skied **awkwardly** in front of the others.

He skied **expertly** in front of the others.

The modifying adverb gives more information about the action.

Practice 10.6   **Write two new sentences by selecting words from the list of descriptive words for each symbol and bold word or phrase.**

1. The ◆ **boy walked** down the ◆ **street**.

Adjective	Noun	Verb	Adjective	Noun
rain-soaked	teenager	stumbled	congested	freeway
runaway	child	sprinted	dark	alley
bearded	youth	pushed	crowded	intersection
crippled	soldier	hobbled	dirty	track
handsome	Boy Scout	strolled	leafy	lane

Answers will vary.

2. The ◆ **vehicle came** to a ◆ stop.

Adjective	Noun	Verb	Adverb
muddy	pickup	slid	screeching
elegant	sailboat	glided	noiseless
chrome	motorcycle	roared	death-defying
souped-up	jalopy	screeched	sudden
red	tricycle	careened	dangerous

Practice 10.7   **Create your own sentences by substituting specific nouns, vivid adjectives, strong verbs, and colorful adverbs.** Answers will vary.

1. The woman walked into the building.

2. The bird flew in the sky.

3. The animal crossed the road.

_____

4. The truck moved down the road.

_____

5. The man spoke to an associate.

_____

Denotation

6.   Choose words that have the right **denotation**, or literal meaning. If you're not absolutely sure the word you have in mind is the right one, look it up in the dictionary. You are better off choosing a word you are familiar with rather than one that you think sounds sophisticated.

Practice 10.8   **Circle the correct word in each sentence. Use a dictionary if you need to.**

1. We like are/(our) new house.

2. We finally reached our (destination)/destiny.

3. The trainer messaged/(massaged) the dancer's foot.

4. My daughter always (feels)/fells better after her nap.

5. The students (were)/where taking an exam.

Practice 10.9   **Within each set of parentheses, circle the most appropriate word or phrase.**

   Welcome back from Christmas break, everyone. I'm sure you are aware of the (currency/(current)) policy which does not (sanction/(allow)) flowers, decorations, or pictures to be (positioned/(placed)) in your (personnel/(personal)) workspace. Because of ((complaints)/complements) from a ((significant)/signifier) number of workers, this policy has been (received/(reversed)) and will ((no)/know) longer be (infringed/(enforced)). It is now (exceptable/(acceptable)) for all managers to personalize ((their)/there) work-space. All employees may feel free to hang plants, pictures, or anything they would like as long as the objects will not offend ((their)/there) co-workers.

WE: 1.26

Ineffective Word Choice

Take care to avoid pitfalls such as using slang, clichés, and wordiness in your writing.

Nonstandard Usage

7.   Avoid **nonstandard usage** (incorrect words and phrases that may be commonly used). Some words are used incorrectly by lots of people, but the words are still incorrect. The dictionary will have these words labeled as nonstandard or incorrect.

Nonstandard	Standard
ain't	am not
gonna	going to
wanna	want to
would of/could of/should of	would have/could have/should have
drive thru	drive through
alright	all right
being that	because
on account of	because
so ____(tired, full, etc.) until	so ____ that

8.   Certain commonly used phrases are also considered nonstandard and imprecise and should be avoided.

> Nonstandard: Being that she was only fifteen, she couldn't go to an R-rated movie without her parents.

> Standard: Because she was only fifteen, she couldn't go to an R-rated movie without her parents.

> Nonstandard: Bill laughed so hard until he cried.

> Standard: Bill laughed so hard that he cried.

> Nonstandard: On account of his height, he couldn't join the Army.

> Standard: Because of his height, he couldn't join the Army.

Practice **10.10**   **Rewrite the following sentences by eliminating nonstandard usage.**

1. It's alright with me if we get hamburgers for dinner at the drive thru.

   It's all right with me if we get hamburgers for dinner at the drive through.

2. I ain't gonna go to the movies.

   I am not going to go the movies.

3. Susana laughed so hard until she cried.

   Susana laughed so hard that she cried.

4. Being that my sister was tuckered out, she went home.

   Because my sister was tired, she went home.

5. I passed the test on account of I studied hard.

   I passed the test because I studied hard.

Double Negatives

9.   Avoid the use of two negatives in a sentence.

Nonstandard	Standard
I'm not going nowhere.	I'm not going anywhere.
I don't want no broccoli.	I don't want any broccoli.
I'm not doing no yard work.	I'm not doing any yard work.

Practice 10.11   **Rewrite the following sentences by eliminating double negatives.**

1. I ain't got no money to spend.

I don't have any money to spend.

2. My cousin swore he wasn't doing no more overtime.

My cousin swore he wasn't doing any more overtime.

3. Larissa is not going nowhere today.

Larissa is not going anywhere today.

4. I don't understand nothing the teacher says.

I don't understand anything the teacher says.

5. Don't tell me no more of your problems.

Don't tell me any more of your problems.

Slang

10.   Avoid **slang** (informal words that have a specific meaning to a group of people) and **profanity** (language that is disrespectful or vulgar). Slang may be colorful, but it is generally considered inappropriate for most writing. One of the problems with slang is that the writer runs the risk of the audience not understanding the intended meaning.

anyways	dis (disrespect)
awesome	far out
bad dude	gross
bro (brother)	gnarly
bummed	hood (neighborhood)
cool	

Practice 10.12   **Rewrite the following sentences to eliminate slang.** Answers will vary.

1. Santos met a totally awesome dude in the hood.

Santos met a fascinating man in the neighborhood.

2. I was bummed out when I got my grade.

I was depressed when I got my grade.

3. Sally dissed her boss and got fired.

Sally talked back to her boss and got fired.

4. On Saturday, I surfed some gnarly waves.

On Saturday, I surfed some exciting waves.

5. It's far out that you won the lottery.

It's fantastic that you won the lottery.

Clichés

11.   Avoid **clichés**, expressions that have been used so much they have lost their freshness. Many clichés are similes, figures of speech that use *like* or *as* to compare two things. Others are simply phrases that we've become so familiar with that they no longer help us see an image.

cold as ice	poor as a church mouse
dumb as an ox	pretty as a picture
go out on a limb	read him like a book
happy as a clam	red as a rose
hot as hell	sink your teeth into
mad as a hornet	strong as a bear
open-and-shut case	

Practice 10.13   **Rewrite the following sentences to eliminate clichés.** Answers will vary.

1. My room is as neat as a pin.

My room is well organized.

2. My sister looked as pretty as a picture in her prom dress.

My sister looked radiant in her prom dress.

3. I'll be as happy as a clam if I can go to the movies.

I'll be happy if I can go to the movies.

4. The horse shot out of the gate like a rocket.

The horse shot out of the gate.

5. He added insult to injury when he scored a goal after tripping the goalie.

He infuriated everyone when he scored a goal after tripping the goalie.

Wordiness

12. Avoid **wordiness**, the use of words that do not contribute to meaning. Often writers end up using more words than they need. In writing, it's best to be concise.

Unnecessary phrases	Intensifiers
In my opinion	So (as in so nice)
I think	Extremely
As far as I'm concerned	Very
Obviously	Really
It goes without saying	Quite
At this point in time	
Due to the fact	
Because of the fact that	

Wordy:

I think that in our American society today, we have **gone too far and** made a **big** mistake in allowing violence **of every sort** to become a part of our **everyday** lives.

Concise:

In America, we have made the mistake of allowing violence to become a part of our lives.

Practice  **Rewrite the following sentences to eliminate wordiness.** Answers will vary.

1. It goes without saying that the party was so very exciting that all of us, my friends and I, had the time of our lives.

   The party was exciting, and my friends and I enjoyed ourselves.

2. I think attendance should not be required in college because in my opinion students should take responsibility for their attendance themselves.

   Attendance should be not required in college.

3. Because of the fact that I have a date Friday night, I can not possibly consider accepting a date from you on the same night that I am already committed to another date.

   I cannot accept a date from you because I already have one.

4. As a matter of fact, the party on Saturday was well attended by many students who appeared to be enjoying themselves while having a good time.

   The party on Saturday was well attended, and students enjoyed themselves.

5. In American society today, parents need to take responsibility for their children's behavior as far as their children's treatment of others is concerned.

   Parents need to take responsibility for their children's treatment of others.

Review Exercise 10.15   **Eliminate slang, clichés, and wordiness from the following sentences.** Answers will vary.

1. In my opinion professional sports has gotten so commercialized that it's not as much fun anymore and people don't enjoy watching it because they feel it's too commercialized.

Because professional sports has become commercialized, fans no longer

enjoy watching it.

2. Why on earth would perfectly ordinary average Americans want to support a policy that so clearly goes against their own best interests and isn't good for them?

Why would Americans support a policy that isn't good for them?

3. By all means, I completely agree that we should leave no stone unturned in trying to get to the bottom of the problem.

We should try to solve the problem.

4. Some people who play golf feel that their leisure time away from work should not be interrupted by distractions such as cell phone calls.

Some golfers feel that their leisure time should not be interrupted by dis-

tractions such as cell phone calls.

5. Being that I like dancing, I like to go out to really cool dance clubs and boogie the night away with totally cool dudes.

Because I like dancing, I like to go to fashionable clubs and dance with

stylish partners.

Review Exercise 10.16   **For each italicized word or phrase, circle the most appropriate choice within the parentheses ([delete] means that the best choice is simply to cut the italicized word or phrase).**

Northern California

In my opinion (([delete])/I think), Northern California ((offers)/offering) tourists *on vacation* (([delete])/on holiday) a variety of *extremely* (([delete])/really) ((interesting)/interested) activities because it is rich in art, history, and culture. In Sacramento, a visitor can tour the capitol building and its (surroundings/(surrounding)) rose gardens, and then he may choose to take in some entertainment at the Memorial Theatre or (sanction/(sample)) the local cuisine at one of the many outdoor cafes. *In actual fact* (([delete])/in reality), a 40-minute drive from the blue skies of

Sacramento will transport the tourist to San Francisco, the foggy city by the bay. West of Sacramento, a tourist may take a (brake/break) and lose himself in the rolling valleys of the Napa and Sonoma wine countries. A drive down to the seaside village of Carmel offers an (universal/unrivaled) view of the scenic coastline's rocky, jagged cliffs and (exotic/extraterrestrial) marine life. *In my opinion* ([delete]/really), with its entertainment, scenery, and variety, Northern California is an (extreme/excellent) vacation spot.

Review Exercise 10.17 **For each italicized word or phrase, circle the most appropriate vocabulary from each set of parentheses.**

I'd like to (impress/inform) all the housekeeping staff of a few (charges/changes) in our security (productions/procedures). First, we now have (a/and) security guard at (nite/night). No employees should be going out to the parking lot after dark without an (escort/escape). Please call the security guard at the end of your shift, and he will walk you out to your car. Also, sometimes staff members come back to (retrieve/rescind) items from (they/their/there) desks but forget their keys. You cannot let employees (in too/in two/into) offices without seeing their hospital picture identification. If employees don't (got/have) their picture identification, tell them to check in with the security guard, but do not let them into (any/no) office. Thank you for your willingness to follow the new rules.

Review Exercise **Writing practice**

Write a one-page journal entry in which you respond to the following writing prompt. Pay particular attention to word choice.

Describe the scene below using concrete words, specific verbs, vivid adjectives, and colorful adverbs.

Chapter 11

Subject–Verb Identification

In this chapter you will learn to identify the subjects and verbs of sentences.

Subjects and verbs are the basic ingredients of the sentence. Learning to identify subjects and verbs will help you to recognize sentences and to avoid sentence fragments and run-on sentences. Also, you will use this skill to understand subject–verb agreement, which is probably the second most important skill after writing complete sentences. The first step is to become familiar with the basic ingredients of the sentence: the subject and the verb.

A sentence is a group of words that contains a **subject** and a **verb** and makes complete sense.

          S   V

The **lifeguard watches** the pool for swimmers in trouble

                             S   V

Every night this week, the **screech** of an owl **has startled** me.

    S   V

Freedom is a citizen's most valuable possession.

Group Activity **11.1**   Examine the list of subjects and verbs below. Add the following words to the list of subjects or verbs: elephant, tries, was taken, Tabitha, attendance, appears.

Subjects	Verbs
mailman	walks
dream	was
weather	has been
Tony and Marco	sell
race	fished
	started
elephant	tries
Tabitha	was taken
attendance	appears

In your group, discuss the reasons why you made the choices you did. What observations can you make about the words in the list of subjects? What do the words in the list of verbs have in common?

GPM: 5.3

1. Subjects

1.1   The subject of a sentence is the word or words that express **who or what the sentence is about**.

My **dream** last night was very scary.

The sentence is about my *dream*.

Every Saturday, **Tony** and **Marco** fish on Tony's boat.

The sentence is about *Tony* and *Marco*.

The **race** started at noon.

The sentence is about the *race*.

What Does "Who or What the Sentence Is About" Mean?

The subject is the foundation of the sentence. In other words, the subject is the word or words that all the other words relate to. In the first example, there are a number of ideas in the sentence (my dream, last night, and very scary), and all these ideas relate to *my dream*. Notice how all the words in the last two examples relate to the subject of the sentence.

Practice **11.2**   **Fill in the blank with a subject.** Answers will vary.

1. _____ meets on Sunday. (Who or what meets on Sunday?)

2. _____ sometimes cooks turkey. (Who cooks turkey?)

3. _____ is my favorite hobby. (What is my favorite hobby?)

1.2   The **simple subject** is the one word or words that name the subject. Words such as *the*, *a*, *an*, and *my* are not part of the simple subject. The **complete subject** includes the simple subject and any words that modify or describe the subject.

Examples:

My oldest niece is going to college.

Simple subject: niece

Complete subject: my oldest niece

Practice **11.3**   **Identify the simple subject and the complete subject.**

1. **The mystery story** had a surprising ending.

   Simple subject: story

   Complete subject: The mystery story

2. **A very old man** has used a rake to clear the garden.

   Simple subject: man

   Complete subject: A very old man

3. Sometimes late at night, **strange green lights** appear on the horizon.

   Simple subject: lights

   Complete subject: strange green lights

GPM: 5.6–5.8

What Kinds of Words Are Subjects?

1.3   Subjects can be **nouns**, **pronouns**, or **gerunds**.

Noun subjects are persons, places, things, or ideas.

My **friends** went on a trip.

The **courthouse** was built by Jonathan Marks.

Attendance is important in this class.

Pronoun subjects take the place of nouns and are words such as he, she, it, they, everyone, something.

I don't like spinach.

Everything in life is not easy.

Gerund subjects are verbs ending in -ing that act as nouns.

Swimming is great exercise.

Doing homework correctly takes time every day.

1.4   A **compound subject** is two or more subjects joined by *and*.

The **cat** and the **dog** are both asleep.

GPM: 5.4

How to Find the Subject

➥ To find the subject, ask yourself, "Who or what is the sentence about?"

➥ The subject usually comes near the beginning of the sentence and before the verb.

➥ The subject is a word or words that name an object (person or thing) or an idea (an object that cannot be touched).

Practice **Circle the subject of each sentence.**

1. The (lawnmower) was very loud.

   (Who or what is the sentence about?)

2. (I) ate an apple this morning.

   (Who or what is the sentence about?)

3. The (rain) will stop soon.

   (Who or what is the sentence about?)

4. Usually (music) makes people happy.

   (Who or what is the sentence about?)

5. (Headaches and backaches) are the most common problems.

   (Who or what is the sentence about?)

Problems with Identifying the Subject

GPM: 5.12

1.5   In command sentences, the subject *you* is **implied**. A command sentence tells you to do something. The word *you* is not stated.

> (**You**) Close the window.

> (**You**) Stop annoying me.

Practice Write a command sentence telling a friend to call you after school.

Answers will vary.

Write a command sentence telling a bus driver to stop the bus.

Write a command sentence telling someone to leave you alone.

Notice that in each sentence, you began with a verb because the sentence is directly addressing a particular person.

1.6   The subject *follows* the verb in sentences that begin with **there** or **here**.

V   S

Here comes my **sister**.

               V   S

There are some funny **scenes** in the movie.

Notice that *here* and *there* are not the words that tell who or what the sentences are about. *Here* and *there* are not nouns or pronouns. They are never the subject of the sentence.

Practice 11.6   **Circle the subject of each sentence by asking who or what the sentence is about. If the sentence is a command sentence, write (You) before the first word of the sentence.**

1. (You) Go home now!

   (Who or what is the sentence about?)

2.   There are many (books) on the shelf.

   (Who or what is the sentence about?)

3.   Here is my (money).

   (Who or what is the sentence about?)

4. (You) Try to figure out the problem.

   (Who or what is the sentence about?)

5.   There was a (light) on.

   (Who or what is the sentence about?)

GPM: 5.16

1.7   The subject is **not found in a prepositional phrase** (a preposition followed by its object).

   Prep Phrase   **S**   **Prep Phrase**

Across the street, a **child** *in the yard* is crying.

> For a list of common prepositions, see Chapter 9, page 128.

Practice 11.7   **Write prepositional phrases in the following sentences.** Answers will vary.

A bird is <u>on</u> _____.

She looked <u>for</u> _____ <u>under the</u> _____.

<u>Near</u> _____, there is a large tree.

Notice that the subject of the sentences is not in the underlined prepositional phrases.

1.8   To find the subject of the sentence, cross out the prepositional phrases and ask who or what the sentence is about.

   ~~On Friday~~, the **teacher** is giving a test ~~in my math class~~.

Practice 11.8   **Cross out each prepositional phrase and circle the subject.**

1. ~~Without a doubt~~, the best (time) ~~of the year~~ is springtime.

2. ~~After class~~, the (teacher) spoke ~~with the student~~.

3. ~~In the room, the~~ (lamp) ~~on the table~~ went out.

4. ~~During the night, a~~ (storm) ~~from the north~~ brought cold weather ~~to the region.~~

5. The (dog) ~~behind the fence~~ barked ~~throughout the day.~~

GPM: 5.22

2. Verbs

2.1   The verb tells the **action** of the subject or the **state of being** of the subject.

> **Action verbs** and their many forms:
> walk, walks, walked, has walked, are walking, have been walking
> try, tries, tried, have tried, is trying
> eat, eats, ate, have eaten
> **State of being verbs** and their many forms:
> is, are, was, were, has been, is being
> seem, seems, has seemed
> feel, felt, has been felt

What Does "Action or State of Being of the Subject" Mean?

A sentence expresses a complete idea about the subject (person or object). The most important part of the idea is the word or words that tell the action or the state of being of the subject. Verbs are often action words (writes, ran, bowls). They tell the action of the subject. Verbs can also state something about the existence of the subject (is, are, were, have, appears, sounds). Verbs that express a state of being don't express an action.

> The **policemen** in our town **bowl** on Wednesdays.

> The idea about the policemen is that they *bowl*.

> The **policemen** in our town **are** courteous to motorists.

> The idea about the policemen is that they *are* courteous. *Are* is the state of being verb.

How to Find the Verb

To find the verb, determine which word expresses the **action** of the subject or which word expresses the **state of being of the subject**. The verb usually comes ***after*** *the subject*, but the verb is not necessarily the next word.

> My best **friend** from high school **goes** to school in Vermont.

> What word expresses the action of *friend*?

> Our **dog** almost always **is** gentle with children.

> What word tells the state of being of our *dog*?

2.2   There are **three classes of verbs**: action verbs, linking verbs, and helping verbs.

> **Action verbs** tell what the subject is doing.
>
> The **mail arrives** in the morning.
>
> The verb *arrives* expresses the action of the subject *mail*.
>
> **Linking verbs** link the subject to words that describe or identify the subject.
>
> The **child** in the back row **looks** happy.
>
> The verb *looks* links the subject *child* to the descriptive word *happy*.

> Common linking verbs: is, feel, look, seem, become, smell, sound, taste, appear

Helping verbs, called **auxiliaries**, help the main verb. The helping verb plus the main verb make a **verb phrase**, which expresses the complete action or state of being of the subject.

> The **salesperson** behind the counter **has checked** our identification.
>
> The verb phrase *has checked* describes the action of the *salesperson*.

> Common helping verbs: is, are, was, were, am, be, been, being, was, could, might, will, would, shall, should, must, can, may, have, has, had, do, did

Practice   **Underline the verb of each sentence.**

1. The teacher <u>asked</u> the class to open their books.

   What word or words expresses the action of the subject *teacher*?

2. I <u>feel</u> sick today.

   What word or words expresses the state of being of the subject *I*?

3. In the living room, the child <u>is watching</u> television.

   What is the subject *child* doing?

4. The computer <u>won't shut off</u>.

   What word or words expresses the action of the subject *computer*?

5. Your voice <u>sounds</u> tired.

   What word or words expresses the state of being of the subject *voice*?

Problems with Identifying the Verb

GPM: 5.28

2.3   The **complete verb** includes a helping verb with present participles (verbs ending in -ing) and past participles (verbs that often end in -ed).

A **song** from my favorite group **was playing** on the radio.

Sometimes the **car** next door **is parked** in our driveway.

Practice   **Circle the subject and underline the complete verb.**

1. Someone has taken my seat in the movie!
2. Our car must be taken to the shop.
3. That motorist should move her vehicle.
4. The bedspread has been washed many times.
5. My parents may arrive today.

2.4   An **infinitive** (to + verb) is *not* part of the complete verb.

My **son wants** *to watch* television tonight.

Practice   **Circle the subject and underline the complete verb.**

1. I want to eat early tonight.
2. Before school today, my child is supposed to finish her homework.
3. On Friday, Maria asked to meet with me.
4. Sometimes before class, the teacher of my class tries to have conferences with students.
5. The man at the table seems to be angry.

2.5   A subject can have a **compound verb** (more than one verb).

Serious **athletes** on our team **train** everyday and **watch** their diets.

Practice   **Circle the subject and underline the complete verb.**

1. A few of the kids eat lunch and watch television in homeroom.
2. The visiting team plays the game at seven and then travels by bus back home.
3. The speaker put on her glasses and began to read her speech.
4. After the performance, the actors took bows and exited the stage.
5. After a long wait, the baseball batter picked up his bat and stepped up to the plate.

2.6   The main verb of the sentence is not found in a **dependent clause** (a group of words beginning with a subordinating conjunction or a relative pronoun).

~~When the rain stopped~~, the **children went** out to play.

The **man** ~~who was mowing his lawn~~ **was injured**.

Dependent clauses begin with words like **because**, **while**, **if**, **although**. Relative clauses begin with **who**, **which**, or **that**. For a complete list of relative pronouns and subordinating conjunctions, see Chapter 9, page 120 and page 130.

Dependent clauses don't include the subject or the verb of the sentence even though they include subjects and verbs. Remember that the subject and verb of the sentence are the foundation of the sentence. Often, you can reduce the sentence to just the subject and the verb and get the main idea of the sentence.

Practice **Circle the subject and underline the complete verb.**

1. The comedians who I enjoy tell funny jokes.

2. The computer that I used in the lab makes a funny noise.

3. When I bought my car, the dealership gave me a free cell phone.

4. My sister doesn't want to help me because she is annoyed with me.

5. If you want to do well in life, you should work hard to make friends who will help you.

Review Exercise **11.14** **Circle the subject and underline the complete verb. (It will be helpful to cross out prepositional phrases and dependent clauses.)**

1. In the lobby of the hotel, the doorman greets guests and helps guests who are carrying suitcases.

2. With a wave of his hand, the policeman was motioning for one lane of traffic to continue.

3. By the time class begins, my classmates and I must have completed the entire assignment.

4. The large bird in the tree was singing a familiar song.

5. My computer that I just bought was made in Japan and shipped to me yesterday.

6. The tree in the front yard has dropped most of its leaves and has begun to sprout new ones.

7. People who enter our house may take off their coats and leave them in the front hall.

8. When the road crews arrived, workers and their foremen jumped out of their trucks and looked at the job to be done.

9. The work on that job was difficult and needed to be completed quickly.

10. Before the workers have lunch, everyone working on the project must meet in the conference room.

Review Exercise **Circle the subject and underline the complete verb. (It will be helpful to cross out prepositional phrases and dependent clauses.)**

1. Playing board games has been popular in America for more than a century.

2. The first popular game was invented by Milton Bradley.

3. The name of the first game was *The Checkered Game of Life*.

4. There were many game inventors who became famous.

5. Along with Milton Bradley, the Parker brothers got rich when they invented Monopoly.

6. With its hotels and railroads, Monopoly is the most popular and well-known game of all time.

7. Because they took people's minds off their troubles, Monopoly and Life were extremely popular during the Depression and were played every night by millions of Americans.

8. Even with all of the computer games today, many children and adults from all over the world still enjoy checkers, Scrabble, and Clue.

9. Some families make up their own games and create the board and the rules.

10. There are even books that explain how to create board games.

Group Activity **11.16**   **Review of exercise**

Each group member answers and explains two items. If there is a disagreement about the correct answer, review the chapter and decide on the correct answer. Each group member records the items he/she missed on the Subject–Verb Identification Items Missed page in his or her notebook.

Review Exercise **11.17**   **Circle the subject and underline the verb in each sentence in the following passage.**

Car Troubles

I am looking forward to taking my car to the shop. While my mechanic gives the car a tune up, I will use the city bus. Surprisingly, traveling by bus can be fun. There is always someone interesting on the bus. Last week, a woman from Japan sat next to me. She and I talked about her homeland. Later that day, some kids and their mother boarded the bus. One of the boys told me about the video game that he liked playing. My best experience of talking to someone on the bus happened just last week. A snowstorm had just begun. I was looking out the window and thinking about how long the ride would take when a beautiful girl got on. Lucky for me, there was only one seat available. She came and sat next to me! Her name was Marissa. We talked for over an hour before I had to get off. However, I did get her phone number.

Review Exercise 11.18   **Writing practice**

Write a one-page journal entry in which you respond to one of the following writing prompts.

Discuss the joys or frustrations of raising a child.

Discuss the advantages of children learning about other cultures.

Chapter 12

Subject–Verb Agreement

In this chapter, you will

- Learn the rules of subject–verb agreement
- Learn to avoid errors with problem subjects and problem verbs

The subject–verb agreement rules describe the way the ending on the verb in standard written English is determined by its subject. Although these rules are not always followed in spoken English, they must be followed in writing, and verb errors are major English errors. What makes these rules difficult to follow and verb errors such a problem in writing is that we learn patterns for subjects and verbs by listening to the adults around us as we grow up. If we grew up around adults who did not use standard verbs, then we probably don't use standard verbs in our speech, and we will have to learn new patterns to write correctly. Fortunately, the rules for making subjects and verbs agree are easy to learn, and through practice, we can learn to use standard verbs in our writing.

Singular and Plural Subjects

A **singular** subject refers to **one** person or thing.

My best friend	he
an exam	the boy
a teacher	a car

Notice that the articles *a* and *an* are used with singular subjects.

A **plural** subject refers to **more than one** person or thing. Most plural subjects end in an **-s**.

my best friends	they
exams	the boys
teachers	cars

Some plural subjects do not end in an **s**. They are **irregular plurals** because they do not follow the rule that plural subjects end in an **s**.

men

women

children

people

Practice 12.1 Identify the following as singular (S) or plural (P).

1. _P_ boys   6. _P_ firemen

2. _P_ rakes   7. _P_ three fans

3. _S_ notebook   8. _P_ the police

4. _P_ cowboys   9. _S_ a woman

5. _P_ children   10. _S_ a mistake

Practice 12.2 Write three singular nouns, three plural nouns, and three irregular plural nouns.

Singular nouns:_____

Plural nouns: _____

Irregular plural nouns: _____

GPM: 8.2

Subject–Verb Agreement Rules

Subjects and **verbs** must **agree** in number. A singular subject takes a singular verb, and a plural subject takes a plural verb.

    S   V

Joe takes his lunch to work every day.

       S   V

The **girls** in the scout troop **take** binoculars to view the wildlife.

In the present tense, the verb has no ending unless the subject is third person singular. If the subject is third person singular, the verb takes an -s or -es ending.

	Singular	**Plural**
1st person	I work	We work
2nd person	You work	You work
3rd person	**He** works	They work
	She works	Students work
	It works	
	A student works	

This formula may help you remember the correct endings for verbs.

    Singular subject begins with **s**, and the verb needs an **-s ending**.

Singular subject	-s on verb
He	walk**s**.

    A **plural subject** doesn't begin with **s**, so the verb needs **no -s**.

Plural subject	no -s on verb
They	walk.

    I and **you** take a verb with no ending.

I/you	no -s on verb
I	walk
You	walk

Subject–Verb Agreement Process

1. Identify the subject and the verb.

2. Determine if the subject is singular (one person or thing) or plural (more than one).

3. Apply present tense subject-verb agreement formula for third person.

   Singular subject → **-s on verb.**
   Plural subject → **no** -s on verb.

Practice 12.3   **In the following passage, circle the subjects and identify whether they are singular or plural by writing an S or a P over them. Next, underline the verbs.**

Grandma Anderson

    My grandmother is a special lady. She stands barely five feet tall and weighs under a hundred pounds, but her will is as strong and fierce as a lion's. Her gray hair is pulled into a tight braid at the back of her head, and she wears a simple cotton housedress. On Sunday, when she goes to church, she puts on the lace trimmed black dress that is shiny with starch and ironing. Her face is small and lined with her years, but her eyes are as bright and attentive as a hawk's. She misses nothing in the world or in you. I still sometimes believe she can read my mind today. Although her frame is bent slightly with her more than eighty years, her smile is as warm and free as a teenager's. Because I love and respect my grandmother, nothing gives me greater pleasure than to sit down at her dinner table and see her face light up when I ask for a second helping of her famous peach cobbler.

GPM: 8.11

Problem Subjects

1. Prepositional Phrases

The subject is never found in a **prepositional phrase**. Because prepositional phrases may come between the subject and the verb, they may distract students from the subject and cause problems with subject–verb agreement.

> For a list of common prepositions and a definition and examples of prepositional phrases, see Chapter 9, page 128.

           S   **V**

The **trees** ~~behind the fence~~ **are covered** with apples.

Even though *fence* appears immediately before the verb *are covered*, what are covered with apples are the trees.

           S   **V**

The **men** ~~in my office~~ **work** late.

Because *office* appears in front of the verb, writers may mistake it for the subject. Mistaking *office* (which is singular) for the subject would cause a verb error.

Practice 12.4   **Cross out the prepositional phrases in the following sentences. Circle the subject, label it as singular (S) or plural (P), and select the correct verb.**

1. The students ~~in the back row~~ (is/**are**) talking.

2. Bicyclists ~~in the city~~ (rides/**ride**) ~~on bike paths~~.

3. One ~~of my friends~~ (**is**/are) coming over this afternoon.

4. The plants ~~above the waterline~~ (is/**are**) dying.

5. The bikes ~~against the wall~~ (belongs/**belong**) ~~to students~~.

Practice 12.5   **Cross out the prepositional phrases in the passage below. Circle the subject, label it as singular (S) or plural (P), and underline the verb.**

Kinds of Meditation

    The three basic (kinds) ~~of meditation~~ are passive meditation, openness meditation, and creative meditation. Passive (meditation) happens when (we) just sit and observe the movement ~~of our breath~~. This (type) ~~of meditation~~ develops our concentration. The (focus) ~~of a second type of meditation~~, openness meditation, is being open ~~to the sensations~~ (we) experience in our bodies. (Sights, sounds, and feelings) ~~in our body~~ become the object ~~of our attention~~. The last (type) ~~of meditation~~, creative meditation, involves using our imagination ~~to unlock creative energy~~. ~~In this type of meditation~~, (we) imagine experiences such as unlocking doors or taking a sauna that will relax us and allow us to realize our potential. Each (kind) ~~of meditation~~ is useful ~~for different purposes~~.

Practice **12.6**   **Write two sentences that include prepositional phrases. Cross out the prepositional phrases. Then circle the subjects and underline the verbs.**

1. _____

2. _____

2. Indefinite Pronouns

Some indefinite pronouns are singular, some are plural, and some can be either singular or plural depending on the meaning of the sentence.

2.1   Most **indefinite pronouns** are singular and take a verb with an *-s* ending.

Singular Indefinite Pronouns	
Pronouns ending in "**-one**" any**one** everyone no one one someone	Pronouns ending in "**-thing**" any**thing** everything nothing something
Pronouns ending in "**-body**" any**body** everybody nobody somebody	Other singular indefinite pronouns each either neither

      S   **V**
Everything seem**s** fine.

      S   **V**
Everybody love**s** a parade.

Practice **12.7**   **Underline the correct verb in the following sentences.**

1. Everyone (loves/love) a parade.

2. Something (is/are) wrong with Eric.

3. Nothing ever (happens/happen) quickly.

4. No one (remembers/remember) the teacher's name.

5. Each of the Girl Scouts (bakes/bake) a dozen cookies.

Practice **12.8**   **Write two sentences in which you use singular indefinite pronouns as subjects. Then circle the subjects and underline the verbs.**

1. _____

2. _____

2.2   Some indefinite pronouns are **always plural**.

> ### Plural Indefinite Pronouns
> both, few, many, several

      S   V

Few of us **want** dessert.

      S   V

Many of my friends **have** jobs.

Practice 12.9 **Underline the correct verb in the following sentences.**

1. Both of my brothers (knows/<u>know</u>) how to swim.

2. Many geese (<u>fly</u>/flies) south in the winter.

3. Several of your answers (is/<u>are</u>) right.

4. Few of us (has/<u>have</u>) a job.

5. Many students (<u>want</u>/wants) to succeed in school.

Practice 12.10 **Write two sentences in which you use plural indefinite pronouns as subjects. Cross out any prepositional phrases. Then circle the subjects and underline the verbs.**

1. _____

2. _____

2.3   Some subjects can be **either singular or plural** depending on the meaning of the sentence. Sometimes the meaning comes in the prepositional phrase that follows these subjects.

> ### Subjects That Can Be Singular or Plural
> a lot, all, any, lots, more, most, none, some

      S   V

A lot of energy **goes** into studying. (Singular)

Energy determines that *a lot* is singular.

      S   V

A lot of students **enjoy** college. (Plural)

Students determines that *a lot* is plural.

      S   V

None of the money **is** missing. (Singular)

Money determines that *none* is singular.

S   V

None of Jason's answers **are** correct. (Plural)

Answers determines that *none* is plural.

Practice 12.11   **Underline the correct verb in the following sentences.**

1. None of the bills (has/<u>have</u>) been paid.

2. All of the sugar (<u>is</u>/are) dry.

3. None of your information (<u>is</u>/are) correct.

4. Most of your advice (<u>has</u>/have) fallen on deaf ears.

5. A lot of what you say (<u>is</u>/are) true.

Practice 12.12   **Write two sentences using the same subject (such as a lot, most, or none). Make one subject singular by adding a prepositional phrase that contains a singular word. Make one subject plural by adding a prepositional phrase that contains a plural word. Then circle the subjects and underline the verbs.**

1. _____

2. _____

3. Collective Nouns

Collective nouns refer to a group of people or things. Collective nouns are usually singular and take a verb with an **-s** ending.

Common Collective Nouns		
a band	a family	an audience
a faculty	a team	a crowd
a number	a committee	a jury
a class	a group	

S   V

The **class** on Monday **meets** in the library.

S   V

My soccer **team practices** twice a week.

Practice 12.13   **Underline the correct verb in parentheses.**

1. The jury (<u>walks</u>/walk) into the courtroom.

2. My family (<u>goes</u>/go) to the beach in the summer.

3. The band (<u>marches</u>/march) at four o'clock.

4. The audience (applaud/<u>applauds</u>) politely after the performance.

5. A team that (work/<u>works</u>) together will succeed.

Practice **12.14**   Write two sentences in which you use collective nouns as subjects. Then circle the subjects and underline the verbs.

1. _____

2. _____

4. Fields of Study

Fields of study are singular subjects and take a verb with an *-s* ending.

> ### Fields of Study
>
> | | |
> |---|---|
> | home economics | news |
> | mathematics | statistics |
> | politics | music |
> | physics | history |

$$\overset{\text{S}}{} \qquad \overset{\text{V}}{}$$

Mathematics require**s** logic to understand.

$$\overset{\text{S}}{} \qquad \overset{\text{V}}{}$$

The **news** always **depresses** me.

Practice **12.15**   Underline the correct verb in parentheses.

1. Biology (is/are) my hardest subject this term.

2. Mathematics (take/takes) attention to detail.

3. Music (is/are) relaxing.

4. Home economics (is/are) no longer taught in many high schools.

5. The news (is/are) on at six o'clock.

Practice **12.16**   Write two sentences in which you use fields of study as subjects. Then circle the subjects and underline the verbs.

1. _____

2. _____

5. Compound Subjects

Compound subjects are two subjects joined by *and*. Compound subjects are plural and take a verb with no ending.

$$\overset{\text{S}}{} \qquad \overset{\text{S}}{} \quad \overset{\text{V}}{}$$

Mary and **Jason walk** home together every day.

$$\overset{\text{S}}{} \qquad \qquad \overset{\text{S}}{} \quad \overset{\text{V}}{}$$

My **brother** and **sister study** for several hours each night.

Practice 12.17 **Circle the subject, and label it as singular (S) or plural (P). Then underline the correct verb.**

    P
1. Math and science (is/<u>are</u>) required for graduation.

    P
2. My cat and dog (plays/<u>play</u>) well together.

    P
3. Trees and bushes (<u>lose</u>/loses) their leaves in the winter.

    P
4. Ants and spiders (has/<u>have</u>) a thorax.

    P
5. My books and papers (<u>fit</u>/fits) in my backpack.

Practice 12.18 **Write two sentences in which you use compound subjects. Then circle the subjects and underline the verbs.**

1. _____

2. _____

6. Gerunds

A **gerund** (an *-ing* word used as a subject) is singular and takes a verb with an *-s* ending.

    S   V
Running take**s** energy.

    S   V
Reading mystery novels **is** a great way to relax.

Practice 12.19 **Circle the subject, and label it as singular (S) or plural (P). Then underline the correct verb.**

    S
1. Writing term papers (<u>is</u>/are) my most difficult task.

    S
2. Exercising with friends (<u>relieves</u>/relieve) stress.

    S
3. As I get older, staying up late to read assignments (<u>is</u>/are) difficult for me.

    S
4. Planting flowers (<u>puts</u>/put) me in touch with nature.

    P
5. Running and swimming (is/<u>are</u>) my favorite sports.

Practice 12.20 **Write two sentences in which you use gerunds (-ing words) as subjects. Then circle the subjects and underline the verbs.**

1. _____

2. _____

7. Subjects That Are Joined by *Or* or *Nor*

When subjects are joined by *or* or *nor*, only one of the subjects performs the action, so the verb agrees with the closest subject.

            S   P ——▸ V
The woman **or** her children answer the phone.

            P   S ——▸ V
Neither the children **nor** their mother answer**s** the phone.

Practice 12.21   **Circle the subject, and label it as singular (S) or plural (P). Then underline the correct verb.**

1. Politics and money (seems/<u>seem</u>) to go hand in hand. [P]

2. Either our entire team or our two best players (is/<u>are</u>) going to the state meet. [P]

3. Taking notes and reviewing them regularly (is/<u>are</u>) the best ways to succeed. [P]

4. Neither my wife nor my brothers (is/<u>are</u>) interested in going to the game. [P]

5. Tom and Lisa (is/<u>are</u>) best friends.

Practice 12.22   **Write two sentences in which you use subjects joined by *or* or *nor*. Then circle the subjects and underline the verbs.**

1. _____

2. _____

Problem Verbs

GPM: 8.30

8. Compound Verbs

When a subject has more than one verb, it is called a **compound verb**. Make sure that that both verbs agree with the subject.

    S   V   V

The letter **carriers stop** at mailboxes and **deliver** mail.

    S   V   V

My history **instructor writes** on the board and **paces** in front of the class.

Practice 12.23   **Underline the verbs in the following sentences.**

1. The students in the back row <u>read</u> and <u>write</u> quietly.

2. My brother <u>plays</u> football after school and <u>studies</u> at night.

3. My best friend <u>types</u> and <u>takes</u> shorthand.

4. The farmer <u>plants</u> corn and <u>weeds</u> between the rows.

5. Jose <u>runs</u> downstairs, <u>grabs</u> his backpack, and <u>races</u> for the bus.

Practice 12.24   **Write two sentences in which you use compound verbs. Then circle the subjects and underline the verbs.**

1. _____

2. _____

9. To Be

The verb **to be** is irregular and should be conjugated correctly. Sometimes, "I be," "he be," "they be" are used in speaking; however, these forms are not Standard English and should be avoided in writing.

	Singular	**Plural**
1st person	I am	We are
2nd person	You are	You are
3rd person	**He** is	They are
	She is	Students are
	It is	
	A student is	

10. Verbs Following *Here* or *There*

When a sentence begins with *there* or *here*, the subject comes **after** the verb. Remember that *Here* and *There* are never the subject of a sentence. The subject will come after the verb in these kinds of sentences. Many people make mistakes with verb agreement in these situations because they say the verb before the subject. In order to avoid a verb error, you must identify the subject (found after the verb) and then choose the correct verb.

        V   S

There **is** a **cat** on the car.

        V   S

Here **come** the **runners**.

Practice 12.25 In the following sentences, circle the subject and write in *is* for singular subjects or *are* for plural subjects.

1. There __are__ a lot of problems with my report.
2. Here __are__ my answers.
3. There __are__ over 40,000 books in the library.
4. Here __is__ the money you requested.
5. Here __are__ everyone's papers.

Practice 12.26 In the following sentences, circle the subject and underline the correct verb in parentheses.

1. There (have/has) been reports of severe thunderstorms in the area.
2. Here (come/comes) the bride.
3. There (go/goes) my best friend.
4. Here (are/is) the information you requested.
5. There (are/is) a favor I need to ask of you.

Practice 12.27 Write two sentences that begin with *There* or *Here*. Then circle the subjects and underline the verbs.

1. _____

2. _____

11. Verbs in Questions

The subject usually comes **after** the verb in **questions**.

V   S

What **are** your **feelings**?

V   S

Where **is** my **pen**?

Practice 12.28   Circle the subject and underline the correct verb.

1. What (am/is) I expected to do with these papers?
2. Where (have/has) your brother gone?
3. When (do/does) the movie start?
4. Why (have/has) the teacher called?
5. How far (is/are) the beach?

Practice 12.29   Write two questions. Then circle the subjects and underline the verbs.

1. _____

2. _____

12. More Than One Subject and Verb

Remember that a sentence can have **more than one subject and verb**. Make sure that each verb agrees with its subject.

S   V   S   V

Kin plays the piano while **his sisters play** the violin.

Practice 12.30   Circle the subject and underline the correct verb.

1. Where (is/are) my new shoes, and where (has/have) you put my hat?
2. After the party (starts/start), I (wants/want) to dance.
3. My brother (loves/love) root beer floats, but his friends (thinks/think) he is crazy.
4. I (wants/want) to go, but my friends (is/are) too tired to come with me.
5. How (do/does) you (expects/expect) me to follow these directions?

Practice 12.31   Write two sentences that have more than one subject and verb. Then circle the subjects and underline the verbs.

1. _____

2. _____

13. Relative Clauses

Relative clauses are groups of words that begin with a **relative pronoun** such as *who, that,* or *which.* Inside a relative clause, the verb that follows a relative pronoun must agree with the **antecedent**, the word *who, that,* or *which* refers to in the sentence.

S   relative clause   V

The **club** in New Orleans *that has the best music* **is** on Main Street.

S   relative clause   V
The **women** *who make the alterations* **are** out sick today.

Practice 12.32   **In the following sentences, circle the subject, and identify it as singular (S) or plural (P). Then underline the appropriate verbs.**

1. The students who (turns/turn) their papers in on time (receives/receive) full credit.

2. Many birds that (flies/fly) south for the winter (stops/stop) in Virginia.

3. All of the merchandise that (is/are) on sale (is/are) marked down 40%.

4. The classes that (is/are) easiest to pass (is/are) not always the most valuable.

5. Everyone who (passes/pass) the final (passes/pass) the class.

Practice 12.33   **Write two sentences that contain relative pronouns. Circle the subjects and underline the verbs.**

1. _____

2. _____

Review Exercise 12.34   **Circle the subject, and label it as singular (S) or plural (P). Then underline the correct verb.**

1. A lot of my problems in school (has/have) to do with procrastination.

2. Walking two miles every morning (is/are) a great way to stay in shape.

3. Neither my friends nor my family (wants/want) to help me raise money.

4. Most of the money (was/were) stolen.

5. Paying attention and taking notes (is/are) the keys to success in class.

6. How many brothers (does/do) she have?

7. There (is/are) some issues we need to discuss.

8. My sisters (plays/play) tennis, but my brother (is/are) interested in golf.

9. The woman who (comes/come) in first in the fifty yard dash (wins/win) the gold medal.

10. The material that my study group (reviews/review) is easy to remember.

Review Exercise 12.35   **Circle the subject, and label it as singular (S) or plural (P). Then underline the correct verb.**

1. None of my friends (is/are) coming to the club.

2. The puppies in the window (barks/bark) playfully.

3. Butterflies in the forest (lives/live) in the treetops.

4. Anybody who (answers/answer) correctly will win a prize.

5. Everything you have heard about me (is/are) true.

6. Politics (is/are) a dirty business.

7. Our team (is/are) winning the game.

8. As I watch, the crowd (pushes/push) forward.

9. The jury (votes/vote) today.

10. Studying for exams (takes/take) discipline.

Review Exercise **Underline the correct verb in the following sentences.**

1. Joe always (play/<u>plays</u>) his music very loudly.

2. Skiing on ocean waters (<u>is</u>/are) my favorite pastime.

3. Everyone says that it (taste/<u>tastes</u>) like chicken.

4. Vegetarians (<u>don't</u>/doesn't) eat chicken.

5. There (is/<u>are</u>) several explanations for the sudden changes in the weather.

6. Either the girls or Andrew (have/<u>has</u>) to wash the car.

7. I wish you would (<u>take</u>/takes) out the trash today.

8. The plan and purpose (<u>are</u>/is) explained clearly in this book.

9. Nobody in my classes ever (bring/<u>brings</u>) an extra pen.

10. Neither the dog nor the twins (has/<u>have</u>) been to the lake before.

Review Exercise **Identify the subject–verb agreement in the following sentences as correct (C) or incorrect (I). Correct the verb errors in the incorrect items.**

__C__ 1. The two dancers gracefully walk onto the dance floor.

__I__ 2. Crying seldom solve^s problems.

__C__ 3. If everyone passes the test, we can have a party.

__I__ 4. Math tests gives̸ me anxiety.

__C__ 5. Doctors frequently recommend a low fat diet.

__C__ 6. There is a championship game this weekend.

__C__ 7. My best friends always walk to school.

__I__ 8. Children doesn't usually do what they are told. *don't*

__I__ 9. Choosing the right answers on a multiple-choice test are hard. *is*

__C__ 10. Each citizen is entitled to vote.

Group Activity **Review of exercise**

After completing a review exercise, divide into groups of five. Each group member explains his or her answers to two items of the review exercise. Explain which subject–verb agreement rule is being tested and summarize the rule. If there is a disagreement about the correct answer, review the rules and decide on the correct answer.

Review Exercise 12.39 **Editing for S-V Agreement**

Correct the subject–verb agreement errors in the following paragraph.

The Sound of Music

Although the music listeners hears̸ on the radio may sound simple, it is often

made up of many different types of instruments working together to create sound.

Woodwind instruments includes̸ saxophones, oboes, and clarinets. Strings are made

up of violins, guitars, and cellos. The brass section include^s trumpets, trombones, and tubas. Most people thinks of drums or congas as the only percussion instrument, but

the piano is actually percussive as well. A piano's sound is produced when a small

                                                        s
hammer hits a string and play a note. The most portable and remarkable instrument,

            is
however, are the human voice. It is capable of producing an amazing array of sounds.

              s
The voice work much like a stringed instrument because air passes over the vocal

                                                                    s
cords, causing them to vibrates and create sound. The singer's brain tell the vocal

cords to relax or tighten, and the proper pitch is produced. From percussion to brass

and strings to woodwinds, it takes many different types of instruments to make music.

Review Exercise **Editing your writing**

Choose two journal entries and edit them for subject–verb agreement errors. Circle
the subject and underline the verb. Use a different colored pen to make your corrections. Write "subject–verb agreement" in the upper right-hand corner of the page to
let your instructor know you have edited the entry for subject–verb agreement.

Review Exercise **12.41** **Writing practice**

Write a one-page journal entry in which you respond to the following writing
prompt. When you finish writing, go back and circle the subjects, underline the
verbs, and check subject–verb agreement.

Explain why extreme sports are attractive or unattractive to you. OR explain why
skateboarding should or should not be outlawed on city streets.

Chapter 13
Verb Tenses

In this chapter you will

- Learn to form the past tense and past participle of regular and irregular verbs
- Review the uses of the present and past perfect tenses
- Learn to recognize passive constructions and learn how to avoid unnecessary passives
- Learn to use the past participle as an adjective
- Learn to use tenses in the correct sequence

Verb tense in a sentence indicates when something takes place. The present tense shows that an action or state of being of the subject takes place in the present. The past tense indicates that the action or state of being took place before the present moment. As you learned in the last chapter, adding an -s or -es ending to third person singular verbs signals present tense, and no ending is added to verbs other than for third person singular.

Past tense is signaled in several ways. Regular past tense verbs are formed by adding -ed. Irregular verbs, however, are much more complicated because their forms change. The past participle verb form uses a helping verb, usually *has/have/had* or *was/were*. Because many people don't use the past tense and past participle of verbs correctly in their speech, you should review the correct forms and practice using them.

In addition, the past participle can be used in a number of ways—in passive constructions and as adjectives, for example—and it is important to know how and when to use it. Once you have learned about verbs in the present and past tenses, you will be ready to edit your writing for verb shifts.

Forming the Past Tense and Past Participle

GPM: 9.2

1. Regular Verbs

1.1   To form the past tense or past participle of **regular verbs**, add -ed to the verb.

Examples:

He walk**ed** to school yesterday. (Past)

He has walk**ed** to school every day this week. (Past Participle)

They talk**ed** to their coach about the problem. (Past)

They have already talk**ed** to their coach. (Past Participle)

Notice that the past tense and past participle of regular verbs have the same form.

Spelling of Regular Past and Past Participles

1.2   When adding the *-ed* ending to verbs, pay attention to the spelling rules.

If the verb ends in *e,* drop the extra *e.*

Examples:

imagined, filed, stored, hired

If the word is one syllable and a vowel comes before the final consonant, double that consonant.

Examples:

stopped, dripped, fitted, slipped

Practice **13.1**   **Fill in the past and past participle of the verb in parentheses.**

1. Jose _____returned_____ (to return) the coat yesterday.

   Jose had _____returned_____ (to return) the coat by the time I got home.

2. The villain of the movie _____robbed_____ (to rob) a bank when he needed money.

   The criminal has _____robbed_____ (to rob) twenty banks.

3. As a child, I _____learned_____ (to learn) my multiplication tables quickly.

   Rosario has _____learned_____ (to learn) to dance.

4. My sister _____talked_____ (to talk) on the phone for two hours last night.

   I have never _____talked_____ (to talk) on the phone for more than thirty minutes.

5. Michael Jordan _____played_____ (to play) for the Chicago Bulls in 1995.

   The team has _____played_____ (to play) three games this week.

6. Tillie _____danced_____ (to dance) until midnight.

   I could have _____danced_____ (to dance) all night.

7. I _____raked_____ (to rake) the yard and _____earned_____ (to earn) five dollars.

   If I had _____raked_____ (to rake) the yard, I could have _____earned_____ (to earn) ten dollars.

8. Last night, I _____wished_____ (to wish) upon a star.

   I have always _____wished_____ (to wish) for a best friend.

9. My father _____dropped_____ (to drop) out of school before graduating.

   Now he wishes he had never _____dropped_____ (to drop) out of school.

10. Stewart _____worked_____ (to work) late last night.

    I have never _____worked_____ (to work) so hard in my life.

GPM: 9.4

2. Irregular Verbs

Unlike the past and past participle of regular verbs, the past and past participle of irregular verbs are not formed by adding -*ed*.

Example:

Michael **drives** a sports car. (Present)

Yesterday, Michael **drove** his father's sports car to school. (Past tense)

Michael's father **has driven** sports cars since he was a young man. (Past participle)

Note: Good dictionaries list the past tense forms of irregular verbs. A typical dictionary entry on an irregular verb looks like this:

go (go) v. went, gone, going

The first word listed after the v. (which indicates that the word is a verb) is the past tense—*went*. The second word listed is the past participle—*gone*. The third word listed is the present participle—*going*. If only two forms are listed, then the past and past participles are the same.

Practice 13.2   **Use a standard college dictionary to look up the following verbs. Write the three verb forms listed after the base form of the verb and label each as the past, past participle, and present participle.**

past past part. pres. part
take: took, taken,   taking

past   past part. pres. part
write: wrote, written,   writing

past past part. pres. part
sing: sang, sung,   singing

Are these verbs regular or irregular? irregular

2.1 Irregular Verbs That Do Not Change Forms

Some irregular verbs keep the **same form** in the present tense, past tense, and past participle.

Irregular Verbs That Do Not Change Forms:		
bet	hurt	shut
burst	let	slit
cast	put	split
cost	quit	spread
cut	read	wet
hit	set	

Examples:

The canoes **cost** only ten dollars each per day. (Present)

Yesterday, the two canoes **cost** twenty dollars. (Past)

The canoes have **cost** only forty dollars for the two days. (Past participle)

Practice 13.3 **Fill in the correct form of the verb.**

1. Last week, I _____ read _____ (to read) three chapters of English.

   I have _____ read _____ (to read) two chapters so far this week.

2. My mother _____ shut _____ (to shut) the windows when she saw the storm coming.

   I have always _____ shut _____ (to shut) my windows at night.

3. My brother _____ set _____ (to set) the table last night.

   I had _____ set _____ (to set) the table by the time my mother got home from work.

4. Hank Aaron _____ hit _____ (to hit) home runs in one season.

   I have _____ hit _____ (to hit) two pop flies so far this season.

5. My brother _____ quit _____ (to quit) his job last night.

   My little sister had _____ quit _____ (to quit) bothering me by the time I was in high school.

6. Last month, my friend _____ let _____ (to let) me borrow his bike.

   He has not _____ let _____ (to let) me borrow it since.

7. The fisherman _____ cast _____ (to cast) his lure far out into the stream.

   The fisherman had _____ cast _____ (to cast) his lure hundreds of times before he caught a trout.

8. This morning before school, I _____ spread _____ (to spread) the word about the party.

   I have _____ spread _____ (to spread) the mulch around the oak trees.

9. Last night, the pipes _____ burst _____ (to burst) when they froze.

   By the time I woke up, the pipes had _____ burst _____ (to burst).

10. My father _____ split _____ (to split) wood all day Saturday.

    My father has _____ split _____ (to split) wood for four hours.

2.2 Irregular Verbs That Do Change Forms

Most irregular verbs, however, take **different forms** in the present tense, past tense, and past participles. There is no set pattern to form the past or past participle of **irregular verbs**. You must memorize the forms.

Example:

I often **go** on a trip. (Present)

Last week, I **went** on a trip. (Past)

I **have gone** on a trip every summer. (Past participle)

PRESENT	PAST	PAST PARTICIPLE	PRESENT	PAST	PAST PARTICIPLE
arise	arose	arisen	lose	lost	lost
awake	awoke	awakened	make	made	made
bear	bore	born	mean	meant	meant
beat	beat	beaten	meet	met	met
become	became	become	pay	paid	paid
begin	began	begun	quit	quit	quit
bend	bent	bent	read	read	read
bet	bet	bet	ride	rode	ridden
bind	bound	bound	ring	rang	rung
bite	bit	bitten	rise	rose	risen
bleed	bled	bled	run	ran	run
blow	blew	blown	see	saw	seen
break	broke	broken	seek	sought	sought
bring	brought	brought	sell	sold	sold
build	built	built	send	sent	sent
burn	burned	burned/burnt	set	set	set
burst	burst	burst	shake	shook	shaken
buy	bought	bought	shave	shaved	shaved
cast	cast	cast	shine	shone	shone
catch	caught	caught	shoot	shot	shot
choose	chose	chosen	show	showed	shown/showed
cling	clung	clung	shrink	shrank	shrunk
come	came	come	shut	shut	shut
cost	cost	cost	sing	sang	sung
creep	crept	crept	sink	sank	sunk
cut	cut	cut	sit	sat	sat
dare	dared	dared	sleep	slept	slept
deal	dealt	dealt	slide	slid	slid
dig	dug	dug	slit	slit	slit
do	did	done	speak	spoke	spoken
draw	drew	drawn	speed	sped	sped
dream	dreamed	dreamed/dreamt	spend	spent	spent
drink	drank	drunk	spin	spun	spun
drive	drove	driven	split	split	split
eat	ate	eaten	spread	spread	spread
fall	fell	fallen	spring	sprang	sprung
feed	fed	fed	stand	stood	stood
feel	felt	felt	steal	stole	stolen
fight	fought	fought	stick	stuck	stuck
find	found	found	sting	stung	stung
fling	flung	flung	strike	struck	struck
fly	flew	flown	string	strung	strung
forget	forgot	forgotten	swear	swore	sworn
forgive	forgave	forgiven	sweep	swept	swept
freeze	froze	frozen	swim	swam	swum
get	got	gotten/got	swing	swung	swung
give	gave	given	take	took	taken
go	went	gone	teach	taught	taught
grind	ground	ground	tear	tore	torn
grow	grew	grown	tell	told	told
hang	hung/hanged	hung/hanged	think	thought	thought
have	had	had	throw	threw	thrown
hear	heard	heard	understand	understood	understood
hide	hid	hidden	wake	woke	woke
hit	hit	hit	wear	wore	worn
hold	held	held	weave	wove	woven
hurt	hurt	hurt	wed	wed	wed
keep	kept	kept	weep	wept	wept
know	knew	known	wet	wet	wet
lay	laid	laid	win	won	won
lead	led	led	wind	wound	wound
leave	left	left	wring	wrung	wrung
lend	lent	lent	write	wrote	written
let	let	let			
lie (to relax)	lay	lain			
light	lit/lighted	lit/lighted			

Practice **13.4**   **Write the correct form of the irregular verb in the space.**

1. The boy _____ did _____ (to do) what he was asked to do.

   I have _____ done _____ (to do) my homework every day this week.

2. The baby _____ drank _____ (to drink) his bottle too quickly.

   The boy has already _____ drunk _____ (to drink) too many sodas.

3. I _____ hid _____ (to hide) my sister's doll yesterday.

   They have _____ hidden _____ (to hide) the clues all over town.

4. Joe _____ stole _____ (to steal) two chocolates from the box last night.

   I have never _____ stolen _____ (to steal) anything.

5. Alyssa _____ was _____ (to be) here yesterday.

   My two best friends have _____ been _____ (to be) fighting for over a week.

6. Yesterday I _____ went _____ (to go) to a movie.

   My friend has already _____ gone _____ (to go) downtown.

7. Someone _____ saw _____ (to see) the accident happen.

   We have _____ seen _____ (to see) that movie three times.

8. Last year, my mother _____ bought _____ (to buy) me a new suit.

   My best friend has _____ bought _____ (to buy) three new pairs of shoes this week.

9. Yesterday I _____ wore _____ (to wear) my new dress to church.

   I have never _____ worn _____ (to wear) my hair long.

10. Last week, I _____ taught _____ (to teach) my dog to sit.

    Life has _____ taught _____ (to teach) me many lessons.

2.3 The Verb *To Be*

One of the most irregular verbs is *to be*. It has different forms for different persons in the past tense.

Present	**Past**	**Past Participle**
Singular	*Singular*	*Singular*
I am	I was	I have been
You are	You were	You have been
He is	He was	He has been
She is	She was	She has been
It is	It was	It has been
Plural	*Plural*	*Plural*
We are	You were	You have been
You are	We were	We have been
They are	They were	They have been

Practice 13.5   **Write the correct form of the verb *to be* in the space.**

1. Larry and I _____were_____ friends in first grade.

2. Susana _____is_____ my best friend now.

3. My brothers _____were_____ outstanding athletes in high school.

4. I _____am_____ proud of my family.

5. I have never _____been_____ here before.

6. They _____are_____ not afraid of the dark.

7. The twins have always _____been_____ inseparable.

8. Jules and Jim _____were_____ here a moment ago.

9. My brother _____is_____ also my best friend.

10. Those bushes _____were_____ planted yesterday.

Using the Past Participle

GPM: 9.22

3. The Present Perfect Tense

3.1   The **present perfect tense** expresses an action that began in the past and is continuing in the present. The present perfect tense is made with the present tense of *to have* and the past participle.

Examples:

I **have gone** to the same school for two years.

Marta **has lived** in San Antonio since she was a child.

3.2   The present perfect tense can also describe an action that has just been completed or an action that was completed at an undetermined time in the past.

Examples:

We **have just finished** washing the dishes.

My instructor **has posted** our grades on-line.

Practice 13.6   **Underline the correct verb in present perfect tense.**

1. Kim (drives/has driven) her car to school every day this week.

2. Ashley and Tina (are/have been) friends for years.

3. LaTosha (wears/has worn) a different hairstyle every day she comes to class.

4. The kittens (grow/have grown) quickly.

5. My speedometer (is/has been broken) for over a month.

6. I (spend/have spent) most of my allowance this week.

7. Preparing for the marathon (takes/has taken) me four months.

8. I (study/have studied) Spanish for four years.

9. Ever since I was a child, I (want/<u>have wanted</u>) to learn to dance.

10. Norman (is/<u>has been</u>) popular for years.

GPM: 9.24

4. The Past Perfect Tense

The **past perfect tense** is used to emphasize that an action occurred in the past before another past action or point in time. It is always used when *already* or *just* is in a sentence in which one action occurred in the past before another past action. The past perfect tense is made with the past tense of *to have* and the past participle.

Examples:

I **had** already **been** in college for two years before I decided on my major.

I **had** just **become** a recreation major when I met my future husband.

Practice **13.7   Underline the correct verb in the past perfect tense.**

1. I (turned/<u>had just turned</u>) the corner when I saw the downed tree.

2. Marcus (finished/<u>had finished</u>) school by the time he received his first job offer.

3. Justin (read/<u>had already read</u>) the book when the teacher assigned it.

4. Naomi and her friends (succeeded/<u>had succeeded</u>) in achieving their goals by the time they were fifteen.

5. By the time I arrived, Karla (left/<u>had left</u>) for the movie.

6. I (have finished/<u>had finished</u>) the exam by the time the fire alarm went off.

7. Eduardo (has taken/<u>had taken</u>) soccer lessons for five years when he won the trophy.

8. Clarissa's poodle (has been accepted/<u>had been accepted</u>) to compete in the dog show before she left.

9. By the time I finished cooking, the guests(have been seated/<u>had been seated</u>.)

10. My friends (have been/<u>had been</u>) on restriction the week before the prom.

GPM: 9.26

5. Passive Voice

In the **passive voice**, the subject of the sentence receives the action of the verb. The passive voice is made with a form of the verb *to be* and the past participle.

Examples:

This seat **is taken** by my husband.

The dinner **was paid** for by Bill.

The explanation **will be given** by the president's spokesman.

(Notice that the passive voice takes the emphasis away from who or what is doing the action and puts the emphasis on who or what is receiving the action.)

In most writing, the **active voice** is preferable to the passive voice because active voice communicates clearly and directly the subject completing the action. However, the passive voice is acceptable when the doer of the action is unknown or unimportant.

Examples:

The crime **was committed** at 11:31 P.M. (No one knows who committed the crime.)

The explosion **was recorded** on videotape. (Who recorded the videotape is unknown or unimportant.)

When you use a word processing program, your program will underline passive constructions and recommend using active construction.

Practice 13.8

Underline the passive verb forms in the following sentences. Next, rewrite the sentences in active voice if the passive is not appropriate.

1. The assignment <u>was completed</u> after midnight by the student.

   The student completed the assignment after midnight.

2. The dog food <u>was gobbled</u> up by the hungry puppy.

   The hungry puppy gobbled up the dog food.

3. The house <u>was robbed</u> sometime after midnight.

   passive acceptable because doer of action is unknown

4. The town <u>was devastated</u> by a tornado last year.

   A tornado devastated the town last year.

5. The steak <u>was undercooked</u>.

   passive acceptable

6. The letter <u>was received</u> by my mother.

   My mother received the letter.

7. The exam <u>was taken</u> by the students last week

   The students took the exam last week.

8. A new college president <u>has been hired</u> by the Board of Trustees.

   The Board of Trustees hired a new college president.

9. The speech <u>was broadcast</u> live.

   passive acceptable

10. Our soccer team <u>was awarded</u> a gold cup.

    passive acceptable

GPM: 9.28

6. Using the Past Participle as an Adjective

The past participle form of the verb may be used as an adjective (a modifier).

Examples:

a piece of **broken** glass

some **fried** chicken

a **closed** book

Practice   **Correct all errors with past participles used as adjectives.**

1. The broke ⁿ window cost fifty dollars to repair.
2. It is against the law to leave a load ᵉᵈ gun in the reach of children.
3. The exhausted runner crossed the finish line.
4. The program was close ᵈ captioned for the hearing impaired.
5. The wreck ᵉᵈ car was towed away.
6. The accuse ᵈ man asked to speak to a lawyer.
7. A retire ᵈ police officer saved the young boy.
8. A well bake ᵈ cake is a thing of beauty.
9. This restaurant's specialty is blacken ᵉᵈ tuna.
10. I don't want a dog that isn't house broke ⁿ.

GPM: 9.30

Avoiding Shifts in Tense

7.   Avoid shifting tenses within a piece of writing unless the time of the action changes. For example, if the actions took place in the past, remain consistent in using past tenses for verbs; if the actions are taking place in the present, remain in the present throughout the writing.

Tense shift (from past to present to past):

When I <u>asked</u> the grocer about the vegetables, he <u>says</u> to me that they <u>came</u> in fresh that morning.

Consistent tense (all in past):

When I <u>asked</u> the grocer about the vegetables, he <u>said</u> to me that they <u>came</u> in fresh that morning.

Practice 13.10   **Correct the verbs in the following sentences to avoid shifts in tense by putting all the verbs in the same tense, present or past.**

1. When I drove into the yard, I see ˢᵃʷ my door standing open, and I know ᵏⁿᵉʷ something is ʷᵃˢ wrong.
2. By the time I got to the game, the first inning is ʷᵃˢ over.
3. I like ice cream, so I ate ᵉᵃᵗ it every night for dessert.
4. Juliana is my best friend, and she turned ˢ sixteen next month.

ed
5. The mayor visited a rest home and plays cards with the residents.

6. I like to listen to music when I weeded the yard.

s
7. My teacher always writes dates on the board when she announced a test.

was
8. My father joined the service when he is eighteen.

s
9. After a mechanic removes a flat tire, he checked the tire alignment.

gives
10. Shoppers should always check their change when the cashier gave it to them.

Review Exercise 13.11   **Correct all verb errors in the following sentences. Rewrite sentences in the passive voice to put them in the active voice. (*Note:* Some verbs are correct and should not be changed.)**

ed
1. My neighbors' grass is green because they have water their lawn every day this week.

en
2. The sunk boat was raised by the recovery crew. The recovery crew raised the sunken boat.

3. The fifty-yard dash was won by my brother. My brother won the fifty-yard dash.

laid
4. Five hundred workers were lay off yesterday.

5. The boat was damaged in the storm.

ed
6. I was treated by a well-train doctor. A well-trained doctor treated me.

ed
7. The party was cater by my aunt. My aunt catered the party.

d
8. My favorite Italian meal is bake lasagna.

9. I am tired of listening to complaints.

10. The woman was disgusted by what she saw.

Review Exercise 13.12   **Identify the verbs in the following sentences as correct (C) or incorrect (I) and correct the verb errors.**

___C___ 1. The man was arrested outside our house.

overcome
___I___ 2. The child was overcame with grief.

ed
___I___ 3. The car was being tow by a truck when the accident occurred.

n
___I___ 4. My son had two broke bones after his fall.

hidden
___I___ 5. The candy has been hid in the closet since Halloween.

n
___I___ 6. The stole bike was recovered by the police.

___C___ 7. My son has watched TV for two hours.

ridden
___I___ 8. My best friend has rode his bike to school for years.

___C___ 9. The teacher extended the deadline because many students were sick.

d
___I___ 10. When I was five, my family move to New York City.

Review Exercise 13.13   Correct all errors with verb tenses, unnecessary passives, and past participle forms used as adjectives.

Moving to the United States

When I was ten years old, I ~~have~~ moved to the United States from Puerto Rico. It

was ~~is~~ hard at first because I don't know *didn't* how to speak English very well. However, I learn*ed*

to speak English in six months, and as a result, I *met* meet a lot of new friends. I was able

to ~~learned~~ English much faster than my parents or my older brothers and sisters.

have been   *feel*   *have*
Now that I ~~am~~ in the United States for twelve years, I felt like I had a pretty good

visit me
grasp of the English language. Today when ~~I am visited by~~ my parents, I still

don't   *d*
sometimes have to act like a translator, but I didn't mind. I am very glad that I move

was
to the United States when I ~~am~~ a young girl because knowing how to speak two

she can learn
languages can be an advantage. When I have a child, I hope two languages ~~can be~~

~~learned by her~~ also.

Review Exercise 13.14   Correct all verb errors (subject–verb agreement, verb tenses, unnecessary passives, and past participle forms used as adjectives).

Moving to a New Town

is   *don't*
Moving ~~are~~ a real hassle. Because I don't have a lot of furniture, I didn't usually

d
hire a moving company when I move. Since moving to Indiana, I have relocate

become
twelve times in four years. My friend, Teresa, says that moving has became a

I rearrange
pastime for me. Unfortunately, the furniture ~~is rearranged by me~~ several times

ied   *d*
before I am satisfy. My clothes are always wrinkle, and if I don't have time to iron, I

d
have to wear wrinkle shirts to work. This past moving experience was probably the

d
worst for me, but it got better when I receive help from my friends.

Review Exercise   **Correct all errors with subject–verb agreement, verb tenses, unnecessary passives, and past participle forms used as adjectives.**

Queen Bess, Daredevil Aviatrix

was
Bessie Coleman, the first African-American female flier, is born in Texas in 1892.

d
Bessie worked hard to get an education, and at the age of 23, she move to Chicago.

had
For years, Bessie have wanted to be someone special, and on a dare from her

d
brother, who had serve in France during World War I, she decided to learn to fly.

Because it was impossible for an African-American woman to take flying lessons in

d
the United States, she had to go to France to attend flight school. In 1921, she receive

have
her international pilot's license, the first black woman ever to done so. When she

was
returned to New York, she is greeted by hundreds of reporters. She performed in air

a
shows across the country and become known as "Queen Bess, Daredevil Aviatrix." In

1926, Bessie Coleman died in an accident while she was scouting a parachute jump

d
she was schedule to perform.

Review Exercise 13.16   **Editing your writing**

Choose two journal entries and edit them for verb tense errors. Use a different colored pen to make your corrections. Write "verb tense" in the upper right-hand corner of the page to let your instructor know you have edited the entry for tenses.

Review Exercise 13.17   **Writing practice**

Write a one-page journal entry in which you respond to the following writing prompt. When you finish writing, go back and circle the subjects, underline the verbs, and check your tenses to make sure all are correct.

How does contact with the natural world of plants, animals, and nature make you feel?

Chapter 14

Sentence Parts and Types

In this chapter you will

- Become familiar with the parts of a sentence: phrases and clauses
- Learn about the four sentence types: simple, compound, complex, and compound-complex
- Understand the different sentence purposes: declarative, interrogative, imperative, and exclamatory

The sentence is the basic building block of all writing because it communicates a complete thought. This chapter will define the structure of the sentence: the parts, the types, and the different purposes of the sentence. The concepts and vocabulary you will learn will prepare you to use the different sentence types and avoid the major sentence structure errors of run-on sentences and sentence fragments.

WE: 2.2

Definition of a Sentence

A group of words needs three ingredients to be a complete sentence: a subject, a verb, and a complete thought.

The **subject** is who or what the sentence is about (a noun—person, place, thing, or idea).

The **verb** is what the subject does (action) or is (state of being).

A **complete thought** means that the subject and verb together convey an idea that makes sense by itself.

S   V

The **raccoon scurried** across the road.

WE: 2.4–2.5

Definition of a Clause

The subjects and verbs in a sentence are contained in word groups called clauses. Clauses are the most important ingredients of a sentence; putting clauses together in different ways creates the different sentence structures.

An **independent clause** is a group of words that contains a subject and a verb and expresses a complete thought.

        S   **V**

My cell **phone rang**.

An independent clause can stand alone as a *sentence*, and every type of sentence will include at least one independent clause.

A **dependent clause** is a group of words that contains a subject and a verb but *does not* express a complete thought.

        S   **V**

Because **I forgot** to turn off the ringer.

A dependent clause is a *fragment* and cannot stand alone; it is dependent upon an independent clause to complete its meaning. Dependent clauses start with subordinating conjunctions or relative pronouns.

Subordinating Conjunctions

after	even though	until
although	if	when
as	since	whereas
because	though	whether
before	unless	while

Relative Pronouns

that	whoever
which	whom
whichever	whomever
who	whose

WE: 2.6

Definition of a Phrase

A **phrase** is a group of words that doesn't include a subject and a verb. Phrases add information to sentences, and most sentences include at least one phrase. The most common phrases are

➥ **Noun phrases** (a noun and its modifiers):

    The old gray station wagon turned the corner.

➥ **Verb phrases** (a verb and its modifiers):

    The computer **has been broken** for two weeks.

➡ **Prepositional phrases** (a preposition and its object):

There are two oak trees **in my yard**.

➡ **Verbal phrases** (a phrase beginning with a gerund, an infinitive, or a participle):

Taking a walk is fun. (gerund phrase)

My dog loves **to take walks**. (infinitive phrase)

Founded in the 1820s, the college is one of the best in the country. (past participial phrase)

Group Activity **Group members should write two examples of independent clauses, dependent clauses, and phrases.** Answers will vary.

Practice 14.2 **Identify each word group as an independent clause (IC), a dependent clause (DC), or a phrase (PH).**

_PH_ 1. On the table in the kitchen next to the telephone.

_DC_ 2. After I left the party at Don's house.

_IC_ 3. The tree fell in the road during the storm.

_DC_ 4. Although the floor is clean.

_PH_ 5. During the play at the theatre downtown.

There are grammatical rules for putting clauses and phrases together into sentences. We learn most of the rules when we learn to speak the language. In writing, we revisit the rules to learn how to combine ideas clearly and effectively and how to punctuate them correctly.

Sentence Types

Clauses can be combined into four different sentence types. These sentence types may include phrases.

A **simple** sentence contains one independent clause.

       S   V

One **neighbor watched** our house for a week.

A **compound** sentence contains two independent clauses.

   Independent Clause   **Independent Clause**

One neighbor watched our house for a week, and another neighbor picked up our newspaper.

   Independent Clause   **Independent Clause**

One neighbor watched our house for a week; another neighbor picked up our newspaper.

   Independent Clause   **Independent Clause**

One neighbor watched our house for a week; furthermore, another neighbor picked up our newspaper.

Notice that the two independent clauses can be joined into a compound sentence using a number of different punctuation marks. You will learn the punctuation rules in the chapter on commas.

A **complex** sentence contains one independent clause and one or more dependent clauses.

    Dependent Clause   **Independent Clause**

While we were on vacation, one neighbor watched our house for a week.

A **compound-complex** sentence contains two independent clauses and one or more dependent clauses.

    Dependent Clause   **Independent Clause**

While we were on vacation, one neighbor watched our house for a week, and another neighbor picked up our newspaper.

        Independent Clause

Because the compound-complex sentence type is a combination of the compound and complex types, there are many ways to combine dependent and independent clauses.

Group Activity **Group members should work together to write two examples of each type of sentence. Use the examples above as models.** Answers will vary.

Practice **14.4** **Identify the following sentences by their type: S (simple), CD (compound), CX (complex), or compound-complex (CDCX).**

  CX 1. Computers have come a long way since they were first introduced.

  CDCX 2. The first computers filled a room, but now because of advances in the technology, they can be as small as a pad of paper.

  CD 3. The prices have improved; for example, a new personal computer has dropped in price over the past five years.

  CX 4. Also, the computer now has more uses that help us in our everyday lives.

  S 5. Computers will probably continue to improve for years to come.

Sentence Purposes

WE: 2.14–2.18

Every sentence can be classified by its purpose of communication.

A **declarative** sentence makes a statement and ends with a period.

Maria does her homework every night.

An **interrogative** sentence asks a direct question and ends with a question mark.

Does Maria do her homework every night?

An **imperative** sentence makes a command and ends with a period.

Do your homework, Maria.

An **exclamatory** sentence expresses strong emotion and ends with an exclamation point.

Maria does her homework every night!

Group Activity **14.5**   **Group members should write a sentence for each sentence purpose. Then members should exchange papers and label the sentence purposes of a partner.**

(declarative) _Answers will vary._

(interrogative) _____

(imperative) _____

(exclamatory)_____

Practice **14.6**   **Identify the purpose of each sentence: D (declarative), IN (interrogative), IM (imperative), or EX (exclamatory).**

_IM_ 1. Stop playing with the dog.

_EX_ 2. This room looks like a tornado hit it!

_IN_ 3. What time will you get home?

_IM_ 4. Take out the garbage before you leave.

_D_   5. Parents seem to complain a lot.

Review exercise **14.7**

1. What are the three necessary ingredients of a sentence?

Subject, verb, a complete thought

2. What are the two ingredients of a clause?

Subject and verb

3. Which kind of clause can stand alone as a sentence?

Independent clause

4. Give three words that begin dependent clauses.

Answers will vary.

5. Name two kinds of phrases.

Answers will vary.

6. Which kind of clause is in a simple sentence?

Independent clause

7. How many independent clauses are in a compound sentence?

two

8. What two types of sentences contain a dependent clause?

Complex, compound-complex

9. Which kind of sentence asks a question?

Interrogative

10. Which kind of sentence makes a statement?

Declarative

Group Activity 14.8   **Review of exercise**

Each group member explains two items. If there is a disagreement about the correct answer, review the definitions and decide on the correct answer.

Review Exercise 14.9   **Choose two paragraphs of a journal entry and identify the type of each sentence and purpose of each sentence. Use a different colored pen. Write "sentence types and purposes" in the upper right-hand corner of the page.**

Review Exercise 14.10   **Writing practice**

Write a one-page journal entry in which you respond to the following writing prompt. Try to use at least three types of sentences and three sentence purposes at least once. When you finish writing, go back and label the sentence type and purpose of each sentence.

Discuss the advantages and/or disadvantages of cell phones.

Chapter 15
Sentence Fragments

In this chapter you will

- Be introduced to the four kinds of sentence fragments
- Learn to recognize and correct fragments

A sentence fragment is a part (or fragment) of a sentence. We often speak in fragments. However, in writing, fragments create a break-down in communication between writer and reader because the reader is left asking questions. Readers are confused when they see the signs of a sentence (a capital letter at the beginning and a period at the end) but read an incomplete thought. Sentence fragments are major writing errors.

Read the newspaper while eating dinner.

(Who read the newspaper?)

Mary read the newspaper while eating dinner. (subject added)

My sister who lives in Los Angeles.

(What about my sister who lives in Los Angeles?)

My **sister** who lives in Los Angeles **works** for the government. (verb added)

Because many players get knee injuries.

(What happens because many players get knee injuries?)

Because many players get knee injuries, new **rules** about tackling **have been added** this year. (subject and verb added)

Group Activity 15.1 When you check in with your group, try to identify the sentence fragments that group members use in conversation. Listen for short word groups of one to four words. The answers to questions are often fragments.

Types of Fragments

Fragments do not express a complete thought. They are missing one or more of the three ingredients that make a complete sentence: a subject, a verb, or a complete thought.

GPM: 6.4

1. Missing-Subject Fragments

When sentence fragments are missing the subject, the reader is left wondering who or what is doing the action of the verb. To correct these fragments, add a subject (a noun: a person, place, thing, or idea).

Works for the sheriff's department in Collier County.

(Who works for the sheriff's department?)

My **aunt works** for the sheriff's department in Collier County.

Broke down at the end of last week.

(What broke down?)

The washing **machine broke** down at the end of last week.

Practice 15.2   **Correct the fragment by adding a subject.** Answers will vary.

1. Walks on the beach every day.

Joann walks on the beach every day.

2. Received permission from the doctor to begin exercising.

I received permission from the doctor to begin exercising.

3. Was crying during the night.

The baby was crying during the night.

4. Is on television every night at six o'clock.

The news is on television every night at six o'clock.

5. Tried to call last night from the airport.

My husband tried to call last night from the airport.

GPM: 6.6

2. Missing-Verb Fragments

Some fragments have a subject but are missing the verb. To correct these fragments, add a complete verb (an action word or a state of being word). The verb and the words that complement the verb complete the meaning of the sentence.

The elderly **woman** with the large shopping bag.

(What about the woman?)

The elderly **woman** with the large shopping bag **sits** at the bus stop.

The long **limb** of the oak tree in the back yard.

(What is the action or state of being of the limb?)

The long **limb** of the oak tree in the back yard **is** ready to fall.

2a.   Fragments also occur when the verb of the sentence is not complete. For example, present participles and past participles are not complete verbs. To correct this kind of fragment, add a helping verb or a complete verb.

> The elderly **woman** sitting next to me on the bus.
>
> (What is the action or state of being of the woman sitting next to me?)
>
> The elderly **woman** sitting next to me on the bus **offered** me an apple. (a complete verb added)
>
> The tree **knocked** over during the storm.
>
> (What is the action or state of being of the tree?)
>
> The tree **was knocked** over during the storm. (a helping verb added)

Practice 15.3   **Correct the fragment by adding a verb.** Answers will vary.

1. The television broken by the kids.

The television was broken by the kids.

2. The old dog under the tree.

The old dog under the tree wants water.

3. Some days this week.

Some days this week will be hectic.

4. The glasses in the cupboard.

The glasses in the cupboard are clean.

5. The air conditioner sitting behind the house.

The air conditioner sitting behind the house does not work.

GPM: 6.16–6.19

3. Missing-Subject-and-Verb Fragments

Phrases have no subject or verb. Phrases may communicate an idea, but there is no complete thought. To correct these fragments, add a subject and a verb.

> To buy a house with plenty of room. (infinitive phrase)
>
> Most young **families try** to buy a house with plenty of room.

3.1   Phrase fragments can often be corrected by connecting the phrase to a sentence before or after the fragment.

> (Sentence) The refugees were in danger of contracting disease. (fragment) From the unsanitary living conditions.
>
> (Sentence) The refugees were in danger of contracting disease from the unsanitary living conditions.

Practice **15.4**   **Correct the fragment by adding a subject and a verb.** Answers will vary.

1. With high winds and lots of rain.

The cold front arrived with high winds and lots of rain.

2. Sleeping soundly on the couch in the living room.

The cat is sleeping soundly on the couch in the living room.

3. Built by the best construction company in the state.

The stadium was built by the best construction company in the state.

4. On the table since yesterday morning.

The newspaper has been on the table since yesterday morning.

5. In order for the children to arrive at school on time.

Our family gets up at six in order for the children to arrive at school on time.

Group Activity **15.5**   **Bring a magazine or advertising flyer to class and choose two full-page advertisements. Identify and correct all of the fragments. Compare the number of fragments each group has found and how the fragments are corrected. Why do you suppose that advertisers use fragments?**

GPM: 6.9–6.10

4. Dependent Clause Fragments

Dependent clauses are fragments that start with a **subordinating conjunction** or **relative pronoun** and contain a subject and a verb. Dependent clauses should be added to an independent clause (sentence). Removing or adding words can also make dependent clauses into sentences.

For a list of subordinating conjunctions and relative pronouns, see Chapter 14, page 190.

Although the weather has turned freezing.

(Add the dependent clause to an independent clause to make a complete sentence.)

Although the weather has turned freezing, we will still take a hike in the woods.

OR

The weather has turned freezing. (The subordinating conjunction is removed to make the dependent clause into sentence.)

Which allow writers to revise and spell-check their work easily.

(A dependent clause starting with *who*, *which*, and *that* is always a fragment that needs to be added to a sentence.)

Personal computers have wonderful word processing capabilities, which allow writers to revise and spell-check their writing easily.

Practice   **Correct the fragment by adding or removing words.** Answers will vary.

1. When I want to go out at night for entertainment.

I want to go out at night for entertainment.

2. Which is my favorite place to eat.

We ate at The Rotunda, which is my favorite place to eat.

3. If everyone wants to go bowling.

If everyone wants to go bowling, we should leave now.

4. Who was my last English teacher.

I liked Mrs. Jackson, who was my last English teacher.

5. After class is over today.

After class is over today, I must go to work.

Group Activity 15.7   **Write two examples of each kind of fragment and exchange them with members of your group. Correct the fragments from another group member, and then share your work.**

Identifying and Correcting Fragments

To recognize sentence fragments in your own writing, you should identify the subject and verb of the sentence and make sure that the group of words or the sentence expresses a complete thought. When you identify a fragment, add the missing part to complete the thought.

Subject = who or what the sentence is about (a noun—person, place, thing, or idea)

Verb = what the subject does (action) or is (state of being)

Complete thought = an idea that the subject and verb together convey that makes sense by itself. (In other words, if someone said the words of the sentence to you, would you have enough information to understand the point of the sentence?)

Academic dishonesty on final exams.

(The subject is *dishonesty*. There is no action word or being word that completes the thought about dishonesty, so add the missing verb to complete the thought.)

Academic **dishonesty** on final exams **can cause** serious problems for students.

5. Problems Identifying Fragments

5.1   Command sentences are sometimes mistaken for fragments because the subject (you) is understood but not stated.

Stop watching television.

(The subject *you* is understood but not stated.)

Take out the garbage.

(This command is being addressed to *you*.)

5.2 Dependent clauses have a subject and a verb, but they don't make complete sense by themselves. You can recognize dependent clauses by the subordinating conjunctions or relative pronouns that begin them.

While the last **game** of the year **was being played**.

(This dependent clause fragment contains a subject and a verb but doesn't make complete sense. To correct this fragment, add an independent clause with a subject and a verb or delete the subordinating conjunction *while*.)

While the last game of the year was being played, the **band prepared** to march.

(Notice that the subject and verb of the complete sentence are different from the subject and verb of the dependent clause.)

The **plumber** who fixed the leak in our bathroom.

(This fragment has a subject but no complete verb. The dependent clause includes a verb, but the complete verb of the sentence is never in the dependent clause. To correct this fragment, add a complete verb.)

The **plumber** who fixed the leak in our bathroom **must return** to our house.

Practice 15.8   Circle the subject and underline the complete verb in each item. If the word group is missing a subject or complete verb or doesn't make a complete thought, label it (F). Label sentences (S).

F   1. The (cars) that are parked in front of our house.

S   2. Our (neighbors) have a lot of guests visiting them.

F   3. From California and Texas.

F   4. To celebrate Wanda's birthday on Saturday.

S   5. (you) Invite your friends to the party.

Review Exercise 15.9   Label each item as Fragment (F) or Sentence (S) and correct the sentence fragments. Corrections will vary.

S   1. Many homeowners don't look forward to having to call a plumber.

_____

F   2. Dread the cost of repairing a leaking pipe.

_____

F   3. Fifty dollars per hour or more for some plumbers.

_____

S   4. Some plumbers will come at any hour of the day or night.

_____

_F_   5. Can cost more if at night or on the weekends.

_S_   6. Call a plumber during the day to save money.

_F_   7. Our plumber who has thirty-five years in the plumbing business.

_F_   8. Very knowledgeable.

_F_   9. When the plumber arrives at the house.

_F_ 10. Which can be very costly for homeowners.

Review Exercise **15.10** Label each item as Fragment (F) or Sentence (S) and correct the sentence fragments. Corrections will vary.

_F_   1. Making a meal for a family.

_F_   2. A real challenge to satisfy everyone's tastes.

_S_   3. Some cooks take a vote to decide what to cook.

_F_   4. Kids who like only a few foods like peanut butter and jelly.

_S_   5. Teenagers usually love pizza and hamburgers.

_F_   6. Which can be fattening for adults.

_S_   7. Don't try to please everyone.

_F_   8. Because most cooks don't have a lot of time to make a meal.

_F_   9. Cooked in the oven for half an hour.

_F_ 10. A favorite recipe that my mother gave me.

Group Activity 15.11   Review of exercise

Each group member answers and explains two items. If there is a disagreement about the correct answer, review the chapter and decide on the correct answer. Each group member records the items he/she missed on the Fragment Items Missed page in his or her notebook.

Review Exercise 15.12   Editing for fragments Corrections will vary.

Edit the following passage by correcting all the sentence fragments. (Some word groups are sentences.)

Bing Crosby

Bing Crosby was a popular singer of our grandparents' generation. Also, *he was* popular with musicians like Elvis Presley and the Beatles. Now remembered for his *he is* contribution to American music. Ideal figure to track popular culture in the twentieth *Bing Crosby is an* century. Played an important role in the development of the recording, radio, and *He* film industries. Over 400 hit singles. More hits than any other musician. Crosby got *Crosby had   He had* his start in radio. Had a hit radio show, Which was listened to by half of America in *He   ,* the 1930s. In the '40s, tops at the box office with three of the most popular movies. *he was*

Nicknamed Der Bingle by the press, Crosby got the name of Bing at the age of 7, *He* Because he sang a short song called "The Bingville Bugle." Helped make jazz *Crosby   ,* popular. Learned to sing jazz from Louis Armstrong, Who was "the beginning and *He* the end of American music," in Bing Crosby's opinion. Bing Crosby was really a *he was* swing singer, Who had a perfect sense of the music's beat. Also, the first to *He* understand how to use the microphone as an instrument that made his voice more personal and expressive. Took silly songs and transformed them with his voice. *learned from him.*

Frank Sinatra learned from Bing Crosby. Also, later singers like John Lennon,

Review Exercise 15.13   Editing your own writing

Choose two journal entries and edit them for fragment errors. Circle the subject and underline the complete verb in each sentence, and make sure that the word group expresses a complete thought. Use a different colored pen to make your corrections of any fragments. Write "fragments" in the upper right-hand corner of the page to let your instructor know you have edited the entry for fragments.

Review Exercise 15.14 **Writing practice**

Write a one-page journal entry in which you respond to the following writing prompt. When you finish writing, go back and check each word group to make sure you have a subject and a complete verb that make a complete thought.

What are your dreams for the future?

Chapter 16

Run-ons

In this chapter you will learn how to recognize and correct

- fused sentences
- comma sentences

Run-ons are two or more sentences that have been run together without the proper punctuation. They are major English errors. Run-ons are incorrectly joined sentences, not merely sentences that are too long and run on and on.

The two word groups below are run-ons. Two complete sentences (subject + verb) have been joined incorrectly.

Fused Sentence

        S   **V**   **S**   **V**

The math **test took** two hours **it was** hard.

      Sentence   Sentence

Comma Splice

S   **V**   **S**   **V**

I answered all the easy questions, then **I completed** the hard ones.

     Sentence   Sentence

Group Activity 16.1   **Working with another student, draw a line between the two complete sentences. Then check your answers with others.**

Example: The dog barked, someone was knocking on the door.

1. Losing weight can be difficult/it takes motivation and knowledge.

2. You may need to change your diet,/also you should exercise regularly.

3. Experts believe changing lifestyle is the key to weight control/people must make changes in the way they live.

4. Two out of three successful dieters change some habits,/for example, they may stop eating late at night.

5. Change takes awareness of the problem,/it helps to identify habits that may be adding pounds.

6. Establishing a goal for weight loss helps people get motivated/they can then visualize what they need to accomplish.

7. Concrete goals are better than vague ones,/set small goals that are realistic like only eating ice cream twice a week.

8. Dieters must keep track of their activities/they should write down how much they are exercising each week.

9. With a clear picture of their behavior, dieters can see when they are not sticking to their diet and exercise,/modifying activity is easier when we know what we need to change.

10. Consulting a fitness counselor may help/a nutritionist can also help with diet.

GPM: 7.2–7.4

Types of Run-ons

Run-ons occur when two sentences are fused together without punctuation or when a comma is used incorrectly to splice together two sentences.

Fused Sentence Run-ons

1.   A fused sentence incorrectly joins or fuses two sentences (independent clauses) without any punctuation.

        S   V   S   V

Joaquin is giving the party **it will be held** at his house.

Fused Sentence Run-on = Sentence + sentence.

Comma Splices

2.   A comma splice incorrectly joins or splices together two sentences with only a comma.

        S   V   S   V

Joaquin is giving the party, **it will be held** at his house.

Comma Splice Run-on = Sentence, sentence.

The comma splice is a particularly common error. Remember that **a comma by itself cannot join two sentences**.

Group Activity 16.2   **Label the run-ons in Activity 16.1 as either FS (fused sentence) or CS (comma splice).**

Practice 16.3   **Write two fused sentences and two comma splices.** Answers will vary.

Use the following subjects for your run-ons: sports, school, jobs, and music.

FS _____

FS _____

CS _____

CS _____

Identifying and Correcting Run-ons

GPM: 7.5

A sentence contains a subject and a verb and expresses a complete thought. Identifying subjects and verbs that make a complete thought can help you determine whether there is more than one sentence in a word group.

1. Identify the subjects and the verbs in a word group that ends with a period.

2. If the subjects and verbs can be divided into two complete thoughts that are not joined with the proper punctuation, then the word group is a run-on.

3. If the word group cannot be divided into two complete thoughts (with two subjects and verbs), it is not a run-on.

Group Activity 16.4 Break into pairs and use the fused sentence and comma splice run-ons your partner wrote in 16.3 to practice identifying subjects and verbs and complete thoughts. Each member should circle the subjects and underline the complete verbs in the partner's run-ons.

Practice 16.5 Circle the subjects and underline the verbs in the following word groups to determine how many complete thoughts are in each word group. If there are two complete thoughts fused without punctuation or spliced together with a comma, indicate the run-on with RO. Identify the sentences with S.

RO　1. Sheboygan, Wisconsin, is located on Lake Michigan the town is known for its bratwurst.

S　2. A bratwurst is a sausage and is known as a brat, which rhymes with pot.

RO　3. A brat is spicier than a hot dog, bratwurst is thicker than a hot dog too.

RO　4. In Sheboygan, cooks grill their sausages no one boils or fries them.

RO　5. Every civic, charitable, and sporting event features bratwurst for sale everyone loves the stout little sausage.

S　6. A few butchers in Sheboygan make their own bratwurst by stuffing pork and beef in casing and spicing the sausage with salt, pepper, and nutmeg.

S　7. Tradition dictates that the brat must be served on a hard roll, which is called a semmel.

S　8. Since Wisconsin is the dairy state, a brat bun should have butter spread on it.

RO　9. Most brat lovers prefer brown mustard on their sandwich, some people add ketchup.

RO　10. Bratwurst originated in Germany the most famous German brats come from a town called Nuremberg.

Ways to Correct Run-ons

GPM: 7.8

To correct run-ons, you must use a correct form of punctuation and sometimes a connecting word (conjunction) between the two sentences. The easiest way to correct run-ons is to separate the two sentences with a period.

However, there are other methods that involve using commas, conjunctions, and semicolons.

$$\overset{\text{S} \quad \text{V}}{} \qquad \overset{\text{S} \quad \text{V}}{}$$

Run-on: **Joaquin is** giving the party **it will be held** at his house.

3. Separate the two sentences with a **period**, and start the second sentence with a **capital letter.**

Joaquin is giving the party. It will be held at his house.

Practice 16.6 **Correct each run-on by separating the sentences with a period.**

1. The economy is good right now/ ¡there are lots of job openings. .T
2. Interest rates are low ¡people can afford to buy a new house. .P
3. Banks are making loans ¡almost everyone can qualify. .A
4. Consumers are buying new cars in record numbers. Last month over ten thousand new cars were bought in this state.
5. Sometimes saving money is the wise course of action/ ¡ater you can use the money for a down payment on a house or car. .L

4. Join the two sentences with a **comma** and a **coordinating conjunction.**

Coordinating conjunctions: for, and, nor, but, or, yet, so

Joaquin is giving the party**, and** it will be held at his house.

Practice 16.7 **Correct each run-on by joining the two sentences with a comma and a coordinating conjunction.** Answers may vary in choice of coordinating conjunction.

1. I love walking on the beach, I like to look for shells. and
2. Mornings are the loveliest time evenings are pretty too. , but
3. People walk alone to think, friends spend quality time talking as they walk. yet
4. At midday, sunburn is a real danger, it is important to wear a cap and keep sunscreen on all exposed parts of the body. so
5. Also, the weather can play a part in any beach walk walkers should keep an eye on the clouds for any approaching storm. , so

5. Join the two sentences with a **semicolon,** a **transition word,** and a **comma.**

Common conjunctive adverbs and transitional expressions: moreover, however, therefore, for example

For a complete list of conjunctive adverbs and transitional expressions, see Chapter 17, page 222.

Joaquin is giving the party**; therefore,** it will be held at his house.

5.1 If you use a conjunctive adverb or transitional expression to join two sentences, you must use a semicolon before the connecting word or words and not a comma. Joining two sentences with a comma and a conjunctive adverb or transitional expression creates a run-on.

Run-on: History is a fascinating subject**,** however, there are lots of dates and facts to remember.

Sentence: History is a fascinating subject; however, there are lots of dates and facts to remember.

Practice 16.8   Correct each run-on by joining the two sentences with a semicolon, a conjunctive adverb or transitional expression, and a comma. Choice of conjunctive adverb or transitional expression may vary.

1. Neighbors can be a source of support; however, the people in the neighborhood can also be a source of annoyance or danger.

2. Neighbors can help one another in times of need; for example, they might give their next door neighbor a ride when her car breaks down.

3. Neighbors watch out for the houses around them; therefore, they will investigate or call the police if they see something suspicious.

4. Getting a smile and a wave on the way home feels good; moreover, someone putting the paper on the doorstep or delivering a package creates a sense of support.

5. Neighbors contribute to our quality of life; indeed, most people appreciate their neighbors.

6. Join the two sentences with a **semicolon.** A semicolon can join two closely related sentences.

Joaquin is giving the party; it will be held at his house.

6.1 Because a semicolon is appropriate only when two sentences are closely related and their relationship clear to the reader, it is often better to use a period between two sentences.

Incorrect: Our meeting is at nine; after I drop off my kids, I'll drive over from their school.

Correct: Our meeting is at nine. After I drop off my kids, I'll drive over from their school.

Practice 16.9   Correct the run-ons by joining the two sentences with a semicolon.

1. Good neighbors are a blessing; not everyone has good neighbors.

2. Noise from neighbors can be a real hassle; no one likes to be awakened at two in the morning by someone's idea of good music.

3. A neighbor's dogs can be a problem; they bark all the time.

4. Trash in the yard is another problem; no one likes to look at a mess.

5. Bad neighbors can make life miserable; everyone wants to move away.

7. Join the two clauses with a **subordinating conjunction.**

Subordinating Conjunctions

after	even though	until
although	if	when
as	since	whereas
because	though	whether
before	unless	while

Joaquin is giving the party **since** it will be held at his house.

Practice 16.10   **Correct the following run-ons by joining the two clauses with a subordinating conjunction.** Answers will vary.

1. Neighborhood organizations can help a neighborhood come together [because] they provide a way for neighbors to meet and discuss common concerns.
2. These organizations also tackle problems/ [when] neighbors may have specific complaints.
3. [If] There are services that the neighborhood wants the city may work well with the organization.
4. Some neighborhoods have organized themselves/ [although] many neighborhoods do not have any organization to represent the residents.
5. [While] Many organizations were formed in the 1970s, now such organizations are quite common.

Practice 16.11   **Use one of the methods you have learned to correct the run-ons in 16.1.** Answers will vary.

Practice 16.12   **Use one of the methods you have learned to correct the run-ons in 16.5.** Answers will vary.

Group Activity 16.13   **Using the run-ons you created in Practice 16.3, group members should correct the run-ons from another member in your group using the different methods.**

Review Exercise 16.14   **Label each word group as Run-on (RO) or Sentence (S), and correct the run-ons using one of the methods you have learned.** Corrections will vary.

____RO____ 1. Living a fulfilling life isn't hard/ it just takes being conscious of choices.

____S____ 2. Relying on family members for love and encouragement is important, and friends are important too.

____S____ 3. Wise ones suggest that we sing every day if we want to cultivate joy in our lives.

____RO____ 4. Colorful surroundings will lift our spirits/ [; therefore,] paint a room in bold colors.

____RO____ 5. Successful people don't play it safe/ [.T] they take risks and try new things all the time.

____S____ 6. Although it sounds corny, singing every day brings passion to our lives, so go ahead and sing along with the radio when the urge grabs you.

____RO____ 7. Being fulfilled in life isn't about money/ it's about joy.

____RO____ 8. Too much work and no play make us dull [, so] we should have fun and even be silly sometimes.

____S____ 9. Quiet moments without the television or radio can restore our inner peace, which is important for our sense of self.

____RO____ 10. A life filled with everyday joy is our birthright/ [.W] we just need to develop the habits keep us in touch with our best selves.

Review Exercise 16.15   **Label each word group as Run-on (RO) or Sentence (S), and correct the run-ons using one of the methods you have learned.**

____RO____ 1. Many people don't get enough sleep, [and] one in three adults suffers from sleeplessness.

_RO_ 2. Experts advise people who have trouble sleeping well to go to bed only when they feel drowsy/ otherwise, they will get frustrated trying to fall asleep.

_S_ 3. If you can't fall asleep in twenty minutes, you should get up and leave your bedroom for some quiet time elsewhere.

_RO_ 4. Exercising regularly helps .T the exercise should be done early in the day.

_RO_ 5. Coffee doesn't help us sleep .I it keeps us awake, so coffee lovers shouldn't drink coffee in the evening.

_S_ 6. Some people drink alcohol to sleep better, but it doesn't help problem sleepers and should be avoided.

_RO_ 7. We all love naps , but they should be kept under one hour in the mid-afternoon.

_RO_ 8. Large meals seem to make us sleeping, and indigestion keeps us awake.

_S_ 9. Smokers have a particularly hard time sleeping because nicotine is a stimulant.

_RO_ 10. Sleeping pills should be used conservatively because they can lead to addiction.

Group Activity **16.16**   **Review of exercise**

Each group member answers and explains two items. If there is a disagreement about the correct answer, review the chapter and decide on the correct answer.

Review Exercise **16.17**   **Editing for run-ons and fragments**

Correct the run-ons and fragments in the passage. Corrections will vary.

Golf Balls

Golf balls are a profitable industry in the United States and around the world. Consumers buy hundreds of millions of balls each year, and the manufacturers make over one billion dollars each year. For such a profitable product, it is strange that all balls are very similar. Balls must be certified by the United States Golf Association (U.S.G.A.)/ .T they must meet strict performance tests. The maximum weight is 1.62 ounces , and the minimum diameter is 1.68 inches. Balls must be round, and their velocity or speed in the air and overall distance when hit by a machine must meet the standards set by the U.S.G.A.

There are fewer than a dozen companies that compete for golfers' dollars, and the most popular balls are made by Titleist, Callaway, and Nike. A dozen balls cost anywhere from thirty to fifty dollars , and golfers use a lot of balls. They may use Anywhere from one to three balls each time they golf. Many golfers use the brand that their favorite golfer uses. Tiger Woods, who is the most popular golfer in the world, recently changed brands, and many gofers switched to his new brand.

The ball, an important component of a golfer's game, ~~The ball~~ can affect
because
performance, some balls seem to travel farther than others. Golfers like the feel of
e
their particular brand, Even though the materials are the same for most brands. The
like
most popular ball has a solid core. Many professional golfers who use the brand,
it very much.   because
Companies continue to develop new balls, amateur golfers are always looking for an

advantage to improve their game.

Review Exercise 16.18   Editing your own writing

Choose two journal entries and edit them for run-ons. Circle the subject and underline the complete verb in each sentence. When a word group expresses two complete thoughts, make sure that they are joined correctly. Use a different colored pen
to make your corrections of any run-ons. Write "run-ons" in the upper right-hand
corner of the page to let your instructor know you have edited the entry for run-ons.

Review Exercise 16.19   Writing practice

Write a one-page journal entry in which you respond to the following writing
prompt. When you finish writing, go back and check each word group to make sure
you have written no run-ons.

Where in the world would you like to visit? What attracts you to this place?

Chapter 17

Commas

In this chapter you will learn about the most important rules for using commas in:

- Compound sentences
- Introductory elements
- Transitions
- Series
- Dates and addresses

This chapter will cover the most important rules. These rules cover 80 to 90 percent of the times you will need to use commas. To help you learn the rules, we have broken down the rules into formulas and key words. You will see the formulas and key words used in sentences, and you will get practice using commas and writing sentences that use the comma rules.

The Purpose of Using Commas

Commas help writers organize information in sentences. Commas set off certain word groups, often with the help of connecting words, called conjunctions. Writers also use the comma rules to add variety to the types of sentences they write.

The Two Most Important Comma Rules: Compound Sentences and Introductory Elements

1. Compound Sentences

GPM: 10.11

1.1   Use a comma between **two independent clauses** joined by **a coordinating conjunction**.

| | Coordinating | |
| Independent clause | conjunction | Independent clause |

One car skidded to a stop, but the other car had to pull off the road.

Remember that an independent clause contains a subject and a verb and expresses a complete thought. An independent clause can stand alone as a complete sentence.

Punctuating Compound Sentences

There are three steps to placing commas in compound sentences:

1. Locate the coordinating conjunction in the sentence.
2. Confirm that there are independent clauses on both sides of the coordinating conjunction by identifying the subject and verb in each independent clause.
3. Place a comma before the coordinating conjunction.

$$\text{S} \qquad \text{V} \qquad\qquad\qquad \text{S} \qquad \text{V}$$

The **music stopped** playing, **and** the **dancers returned** to their seats.

Independent clause   Coordinating   Independent clause
conjunction

Formula

Independent clause (sentence), coordinating conjunction independent clause (sentence.)

Key Words

Coordinating conjunctions: **for, and, nor, but, or, yet, so**
(Remember *fanboys* for the first letter of these key words.)

$$\text{S} \quad \text{V} \qquad\qquad \text{S} \qquad \text{V}$$

We raked the leaves, **and** **we mowed** the lawn on Saturday.

Independent clause Coordinating Independent clause
conjunction

$$\text{S} \quad \text{V} \qquad\qquad \text{S} \qquad \text{V}$$

The **test is** on Monday, **but** **it will not take** the entire hour of class.

Independent clause Coordinating   Independent clause
conjunction

Practice 17.1 **Add a comma before the coordinating conjunction in each compound sentence.**

1. The dance will be held on Saturday, and a live band will provide the music.
2. I want to ask Takesha to go to the dance with me, or I might ask Juanita.
3. My friends want to go to the dance too, but they don't have dates.
4. Tickets to the dance are inexpensive, for they only cost five dollars.
5. I may not get a date for the dance, so I will go with my friends.

Misuses

1.2 Do not use a comma before a coordinating conjunction that does not join two independent clauses (sentences).

Independent clause (sentence), coordinating conjunction fragment.

$$\text{S} \quad \text{V} \qquad\qquad\qquad \text{V}$$

Incorrect: My cell **phone is broken,** and **won't receive** calls.
(The word group following the conjunction is not an independent clause because it does not have a subject.)

Correct: My cell phone is broken and won't receive calls.

Correct: My cell phone is broken, and it won't receive calls.

Practice 17.2   **Use the formula for compound sentences to add commas where needed. Check your answers by circling the subject and underlining the verb in each independent clause and placing a double underline under the coordinating conjunction. (Some sentences may not need a comma.)**

Example: Televisions are on sale downtown, so I am going to buy one.

1. My neighbors are gone a lot during the day, and their dogs get bored.

2. The dogs run along the fence and bark at people walking on the street.

3. One dog has a loud bark, and the other dog likes to whine.

4. People are afraid of the dogs and cross the street to avoid the dogs.

5. I have made friends with the dogs by giving them bones, so the dogs don't bark at me.

1.3   Do not use a comma between word groups that are not joined by one of the seven coordinating conjunctions. (Remember the seven coordinating conjunctions.)

Incorrect: Working while going to school is a challenge, because there is not enough time for everything.

Correct: Working while going to school is a challenge because there is not enough time for everything.

Practice 17.3   **Use the formula for compound sentences to add commas where needed. Check your answers by circling the subject and underlining the verb in each independent clause and by placing a double underline under the coordinating conjunction. (Some sentences may not need a comma.)**

1. Andy must write a paper, and he is supposed to work until eleven.

2. He plans to leave work early in order to get his paper written.

3. The assignment is due by noon if Andy doesn't want to be penalized for being late.

4. The essay must be three pages long, but it shouldn't be longer than five pages.

5. Andy is confident he can write the paper in two hours because he has already written a first draft.

1.4   Do not use a comma before *so* when *so* means *so that* because the word group after the *so* is not an independent clause.

Incorrect: I am on a diet, so (that) I can lose weight.

Correct: I am on a diet so (that) I can lose weight.

Practice 17.4   **Make sure each sentence fits the compound sentence comma rule before placing a comma before the coordinating conjunction *so*. (If you can substitute *so that* for *so*, no comma is needed.)**

1. There has been no rain in two weeks, so the plants need to be watered.

no comma   2. Many gardeners use soaker hoses so they don't waste water.
(that)

no comma   3. Watering is important when there is no rain so plants don't become weak and
(that)
die.

4. Water is precious, so a gardener should only water when necessary.

5. Last winter was very dry, so now plants are in need of extra water.

Group Activity 17.5   **Review the compound comma rule with a partner.**

1. Make flash cards with the formula and key words (coordinating conjunctions.)

2. Practice applying the rule by creating a compound sentence using each of the coordinating conjunctions.

3. Proofread your sentences by circling the subject and underlining the verb in each independent clause to make sure your sentences fit the formula.

Practice 17.6   **Use the formula for compound sentences to add commas where needed. Check your answers by circling the subject and underlining the verb in each independent clause and by placing a double underline under the coordinating conjunction. (Some sentences may not need a comma.)**

1. We chose to drive on the turnpike, for we needed to get home quickly.

2. Joe and Ted play football together and help each other with their homework each night.

3. Our dog can run hard to catch a cat yet will only walk slowly when he is called back home.

4. My car broke down, so I had to take it to a mechanic.
(that)
5. I exercise regularly so I can stay in good condition.

When to Use Compound Sentences in Your Writing

The compound sentence pattern is one of the most common and powerful sentence types. Writers use compound sentences when they want to express two related ideas in one sentence.

Group Activity 17.7   **In a group of two or three students, write a compound sentence using each of the coordinating conjunctions. Choose one of the following topics as the subject of your group's sentences.** Answers will vary.

1. Attending college

2. A sport or sporting event

3. A store

4. Studying for tests

5. Applying for a job

Practice   **Add commas where needed. (Some sentences may not need a comma.)**

1. Some plants need a lot of watering, but many plants only need to be watered once a week.

2. The hat that I bought at the stadium is too small for me, so I gave it to my brother.

3. The photographer took pictures of my family for my sister's wedding.

4. The street was deserted, yet it was only 9 P.M.

5. The patrol car was hidden so ⁽ᵗʰᵃᵗ⁾ the police could catch speeders coming around the corner.

GPM: 10.21

2. Introductory Elements

2.1 Use a comma after an **introductory element**. An introductory element is a sentence fragment, either a dependent clause or a phrase, that introduces an independent clause.

Formula
Dependent clause or phrase, independent clause.

Examples:

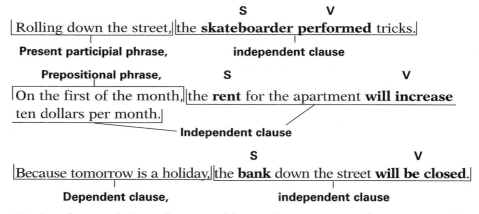

Notice that each introductory element is a sentence fragment, and a comma separates the fragment from the independent clause that follows the comma. The subject and verb of the independent clause usually follow after the comma.

Punctuating Introductory Element Sentences
There are three steps to placing commas in introductory element sentences:

1. Locate the independent clause of the sentence by identifying the subject and verb of the sentence.

2. Identify the introductory element of the sentence. It should be a sentence fragment (a dependent clause or a word phrase) that comes before the independent clause.

3. Separate the introductory element from the independent clause with a comma. Usually the comma comes immediately before the subject and verb of the independent clause.

Example:

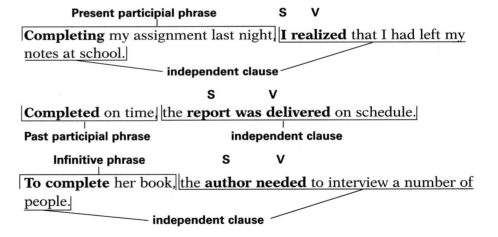

Sentence fragment (phrase)   S   V

On the first Saturday of each month, the **club cleans** up trash on the roadside.

                        ── Independent clause

Key Words

Most introductory elements begin with particular types of words. Becoming familiar with these words will help you recognize when you are using introductory elements in your writing. The three kinds of words that create introductory elements are **verbals, prepositions**, and **subordinating conjunctions**.

2.1   Verbal phrases begin with present participles, past participles, or infinitives. Verbals are verb forms, but they are not used as verbs. Present participles are the verb form ending in -ing. Past participles often end in -ed. Infinitives are *to* plus the base form of the verb.

Present participles	Past participles	Infinitives
Completing	Completed	To complete
Passing	Passed	To pass
Trying	Tried	To try
Finding	Found	To find

Examples:

Present participial phrase   S   V

Completing my assignment last night, **I realized** that I had left my notes at school.

                    ── independent clause

                          S   V

Completed on time, the **report was delivered** on schedule.

Past participial phrase   independent clause

Infinitive phrase   S   V

To complete her book, the **author needed** to interview a number of people.

                ── independent clause

Practice 17.9   **Underline the verbal that begins the verbal phrase introductory element and place a comma after the introductory element and before the independent clause in each sentence. Remember that the subject and the verb of the independent clause usually follow the comma.**

1. Working on her homework assignment, Tameka discovered that she had left her notes at school.

2. Sunk in the Indian Ocean in 1956, the ship was thought to be carrying a million dollars.

3. To meet his future wife's parents, the young man was forced to travel across the country in an old pickup truck.

2.3 **Prepositional phrases** begin with a preposition.

Common prepositions: in, on, from, by, at, as, during, under
 For a complete list of prepositions, see Chapter 9, page 128.

$$$$
                                                            S   V

During the last game of the season, the team's star **player was injured.**

          Prepositional phrase,   **independent clause**

          Prepositional phrase   **S**   **V**

Under cross-examination by the prosecutor, the **defendant admitted** to lying.

                              Independent clause

Practice **17.10**   Circle the preposition that begins the prepositional phrase introductory element and place a comma after the introductory element and before the independent clause in each sentence. Remember that the subject and the verb of the independent clause usually follow the comma.

1. (In) Chapter 3 of the textbook, there is an explanation of global warming.

2. (At) the end of this month, our store will have a close-out sale.

3. (Behind) the back room of the office, someone has pinned up last year's calendar.

2.4 **Dependent clauses** begin with a subordinating conjunction and include a subject and a verb.

Subordinating conjunctions: after, although, because, since, if, while, when
 For a complete list of subordinating conjunctions, see Chapter 14, page 190.

                                           S   **V**

Although it rained all night, the **morning was** clear and cold.

          Dependent clause,   **independent clause**

                                          S   **V**

Because snow was expected soon, the **hikers wore** their heavy coats.

          Dependent clause,   **independent clause**

Notice that there are a subject and a verb in the dependent clause, but they are not the subject and verb of the sentence.

Practice **17.11**   Circle the subordinating conjunction that begins the dependent clause introductory element and place a comma after the introductory element and before the independent clause in each sentence. Remember that the subject and the verb of the independent clause usually follow the comma.

1. (While) many birds migrate in the winter, some common birds remain in one place all year.

2. (Since) our dog is so healthy, we are planning to take it with us hiking this summer.

3. When the bank manager gets to work each morning, she turns off the alarm in the safe.

4. Because there has been no rain in more than a month, brush fires are a hazard now.

5. If there is no rain in the next week, the county will start mandatory water rationing.

Misuses

2.5   A comma is usually **not** needed if the dependent clause or phrase **follows** the independent clause.

Incorrect: You'll have to pay for gas, if you drive my car.

Correct: You'll have to pay for gas if you drive my car.

Practice 17.12   **Circle the key word (verbal, preposition, or subordinating conjunction) that begins the introductory element and place a comma after the introductory element and before the independent clause in each sentence. Remember that the subject and the verb of the independent clause usually follow the comma. (Some sentences may not need a comma.)**

1. After the storm swept through the area, many residents went outside to clean up the debris.

2. One homeowner found a tree limb on top of the roof of his car.

3. Raking the yard was a common activity for many people in the neighborhood.

4. To restore electricity after the storm, the power company sent three service trucks to repair downed power lines.

5. Since the roads were flooded, many motorists had to leave their cars and walk.

When to Use Introductory Element Sentences in Your Writing

The introductory element sentence pattern allows writers to introduce information before writing the independent clause. Writers use introductory elements when they want to introduce the independent clause with a secondary idea.

Group Activity 17.13   **In a group of two or three students, write introductory element sentences using five of the key words. Choose one of the following topics as the subject of your group's sentences.**

1. Attending college
2. A sport or sporting event
3. A store
4. Studying for tests
5. Applying for a job

Practice 17.14   **Circle the key word (verbal, preposition, or subordinating conjunction) that begins the introductory element and place a comma after the introductory element and before the independent clause in each sentence. Remember that the subject and the verb of the independent clause usually follow the comma. (Some sentences may not need any commas.)**

1. (Although) spring just arrived, the temperatures will not reach above freezing tonight.

2. (Through) the window in the kitchen, I can watch my children playing in the back-yard.

3. (Carved by) hand five hundred years ago, the violin has a beautiful sound when played by a master musician.

4. (To receive) a full refund, you must bring the broken appliance back to the store where you bought it.

5. The budget was passed in March by the legislature.

Group Activity **17.15**   **Review the introductory element comma rule with a partner.**

1. Make flash cards with the formula and key words (include at least fifteen key words.)

2. Practice applying the rule by creating sentences using eight different key words to begin an introductory element.

3. Proofread your sentences by circling the key word that begins the introductory element and underlining the independent clause that follows the introductory element.

Other Useful Comma Rules: Transitions, Series, Dates

GPM: 10.44–10.45

3. Transitions

3.1   Use commas to set off **transitions** that interrupt the flow of the sentence. In other words, if the transition can be removed from the sentence without changing the meaning of the sentence, it is an interrupter. These interrupters can be **conjunctive adverbs or transitional expressions**. Transitions and transitional phrases can be placed anywhere in the sentence and should be separated from the rest of the sentence by commas when they interrupt the flow of the sentence.

> **Most importantly**, the weather conditions are dangerous for small boaters today.

> Winds are gusting up to fifty miles per hour, **for example**.

> The sailing club has, **therefore,** canceled its race today.

Formula

Transition, sentence.

Sentence, transition.

Sentence beginning, transition, sentence ending.

Key Words

Conjunctive Adverbs

accordingly	also	anyway	besides
certainly	consequently	conversely	finally
furthermore	hence	however	indeed
instead	likewise	meanwhile	moreover
nevertheless	next	nonetheless	otherwise
similarly	specifically	still	subsequently
then	therefore	thus	

Transitional Expressions

after all	all in all	as a result	as a matter of fact
at the same time	by the same token	first	for example
for instance	in addition	in brief	in comparison
in conclusion	in any event	in fact	in other words
in spite of	in sum	in this instance	last
lately	most importantly	of course	on the contrary
on the other hand	on the whole	previously	second
surely	third	to conclude	suddenly
to summarize	to sum up	to illustrate	

Punctuating Transitions in Sentences

There are three steps to placing commas in sentences that use transitions:

1. Locate the transition or transitional expression.

2. Make sure the transition or transitional expression is interrupting the flow of the sentence. In other words, you should be able to remove the transition or transitional expression without changing the meaning of the sentence.

3. Separate the transition or expression from the sentence. Place a comma after a transition or transitional expression at the beginning of the sentence, place a comma before a transition at the end of the sentence, and place commas before and after a transition or transitional expression in the middle of the sentence.

> **Moreover**, he had trouble reading the test because he didn't have his eyeglasses.

> One of the problems in the design it that there is no space for wheel-chair access, **for instance**.

> The reason, **however**, for the delay was the severe thunderstorm.

Practice 17.16   **Use commas to separate the transition or transitional expression from the sentence.**

1. First, the train was late arriving at the station.

2. Also, there were no seats on the train.

3. The air was hot and stuffy, furthermore.

4. The passengers were, in fact, very uncomfortable.

5. Consequently, many riders were complaining loudly.

Misuses

3.2 A transition or transitional expression that is a **necessary** word in the sentence should not be separated by commas. If the transition cannot be removed from the sentence without changing the meaning of the sentence, it is a necessary part of the sentence and not an interrupter.

> Incorrect: My best friend is, also, my neighbor.
>
> (*Also* is a necessary word and not an interrupter in this sentence.)
>
> Correct: My best friend is also my neighbor.

Practice 17.17 **Add commas where needed. (Some sentences may not need any commas.)**

1. As a matter of fact, my trip to Los Angeles was not very expensive.

2. Luckily, I found a discount airfare for under three hundred dollars.

3. My hotel room was, in addition, very reasonably priced.

4. Thus, I did not spend more than six hundred dollars for my room and meals.

5. Consequently, I also had money for seeing the sights around LA.

Group Activity 17.18 **Review the transition comma rule with a partner.**

1. Make flash cards with the formula and key words (include at least eight transitions or transitional expressions).

2. Practice applying the rule by creating a sentence using eight different transitions or transitional expressions. Make sure to use at least one transition at the end or in the middle of the sentence.

3. Proofread your sentences by circling the transition or transitional expression and making sure that you can remove the word or phrase without changing the meaning of the sentence.

GPM: 10.7–10.8

4. Series

4.1 Use commas to set off items in a **series**. A series is a list of at least three items. The items may be single words, phrases, or clauses.

> *Examples:*
>
> The fruit for sale includes apples, oranges, and bananas.
>
> Going to the movies, playing music, and jogging are all excellent ways to relax.

Although the comma before the final *and* is optional, using the last comma makes the series clear to the reader.

Misuses

4.2 Don't use commas when there are only two items.

> Incorrect: A neighborhood needs good schools, and parks for children.

Correct: A neighborhood needs good schools and parks for children.

4.3   Don't use commas when *and* or *or* joins each item.

Incorrect: A neighborhood needs good schools, and parks, and recreation centers for children.

Correct: A neighborhood needs good schools and parks and recreation centers for children.

4.4   Don't use a comma after the last item in the series.

Example:

Incorrect: Red, white, and blue, are my favorite colors.

Correct: Red, white, and blue are my favorite colors.

Practice **17.19**   **Place commas where needed. (Some sentences may not need commas.)**

1. Accounting, business, and psychology are popular majors for college freshmen.

2. Elderly people should take vitamins, exercise regularly, and get plenty of rest in order to stay healthy.

3. My favorite meal would be a hamburger with French fries and a chocolate shake.

4. An economical car should cost under fifteen thousand dollars, come with a five year warranty, and get over thirty miles to the gallon.

5. Most people like to read the newspaper at breakfast, during lunch, or before dinner.

GPM: 10.3–10.4

5. Dates and Addresses

5.1   Use commas between items in **dates** and **addresses.**

The oldest resident of the town was born on Friday, July 7, 1906, in Springfield, Illinois, of German immigrants.

Misuses

5.2   Don't separate the month from the year if the date is not given.

Incorrect: The first class of the school graduated in May, 2000.

Correct: The first class of the school graduated in May 2000.

Review Exercise **17.20**   **Place commas where needed. (Some sentences may not need any commas.)**

1. A conference was held in Seattle, Washington, on May 25, 2000, and scientists presented research on the subject of caffeine.

2. Coffee is one of the most popular beverages in the world, and caffeine is the active ingredient that gives coffee its jolt.

3. Because so many people drink coffee every day, caffeine is probably the most widely used drug in the world.

4. In fact, more than 85 percent of Americans consume significant amounts of caffeine daily.

5. Coffee is full of caffeine, for one cup holds around 100 milligrams of caffeine.

6. The most sensitive coffee drinkers can feel a lift from as little as 20 milligrams of caffeine, but many people don't notice any effects until they have taken in more than 350 milligrams.

7. Along with coffee, caffeine is present in teas, colas, and chocolate.

8. Since caffeine is a stimulant, many people think they are sharper after drinking coffee or tea or soda.

9. Also, some people report getting headaches when they don't have their usual dose of caffeine.

10. Caffeine speeds up brain activity and increases concentration for most people.

Review Exercise **Place commas where needed. (Some sentences may not need any commas.)**

1. Lately, scientists have been studying the effects of caffeine on the body.

2. By stimulating the brain, caffeine in coffee, tea, or soda helps fight fatigue.

3. Because caffeine increases the production of stomach acid, a moderate amount of coffee or tea can help digestion.

4. Too much caffeine, however, can cause stomach pains and nausea.

5. Also, a little caffeine helps the pumping action of the heart.

6. On the other hand, too much caffeine can overstimulate the heart and cause palpitations.

7. With a mild dose of caffeine, athletes may improve their performance, moreover.

8. A little caffeine can give us energy, yet too much caffeine can cause muscles to twitch.

9. In June 2000, a conference was held to discuss the scientific findings.

10. Scientists agree that caffeine is a powerful drug, so research will continue to be done.

Group Activity **Review of exercise**

Each group member should answer and explain two items. If there is a disagreement about the correct answer, review the chapter and decide on the correct answer.

Review Exercise **Editing for commas**

Place commas where needed.

Coffee Time

I live for my cup of coffee every morning. Before I go to bed, I grind fresh coffee.

Then, I put it into my automatic coffee maker and set the timer for the next morning.

When I awake, I smell the aroma of fresh brewed coffee that fills the apartment. I

usually drink two cups with my toast, eggs, and bacon.

On the weekends, I make special coffees such as espresso or latte. For my weekend breakfasts, I like to make pancakes, bake fresh cinnamon rolls, or cook an omelet to have with my coffee. On Saturdays, I will only drink a cup or two before hitting the road on my bike. However, on Sundays, I enjoy brewing a whole pot of coffee and eating a big breakfast of home fries and eggs. I spread out the newspaper, and I read all the articles and go through the classified ads.

My love affair with coffee drinking extends to the weekdays. Frequently, I sit in a local coffee shop between classes so that I can study. After my morning classes, I go to the Local Grounds Coffee Shop, for it is located close to my afternoon classes. The owner lets me study for a couple of hours before my biology class. Once in a while, the shop gets noisy, yet I find that I can concentrate well as long as I am drinking my java. I study quietly, or I watch the people going by on the street. Coffee is, indeed, an important part of my life.

Review Exercise 17.24   **Editing your writing**

Choose two pages of your journal and edit them for commas. Use a different colored pen to add commas or cross out commas that are not needed. Write "commas" at the top of the pages to let your teacher know that you edited for commas.

Review Exercise 17.25   **Writing practice**

Write a one-page journal entry in which you respond to the following writing prompt. Use at least two compound sentences, two introductory element sentences, and one series.

What sport do you enjoy playing? Explain why you enjoy this sport or describe one memorable game or activity.

Chapter 18
Pronoun Agreement

In this chapter you will learn about

- Antecedents
- Pronoun agreement
- Avoiding shifts in number and person
- Limiting the use of the second person

Pronouns are words that take the place of nouns. Pronouns cause confusion if the incorrect pronoun is used or if the pronoun does not refer clearly to the correct noun. Many people misuse pronouns in their speech. Therefore, writers sometimes have difficulty identifying pronoun errors because the errors do not sound wrong. In order to use pronouns correctly, you should pay attention to the rules and not rely on your ear to guide you.

Below are the personal pronouns. Other types of pronouns include relative pronouns, reflexive pronouns, and interrogative pronouns.

	Subjective case	**Objective case**	**Possessive case**
Singular	I	me	my/mine
	you	you	your/yours
	he/she/it	him/her/it	his/her/its
Plural	we	us	our/ours
	you	you	your/yours
	they	them	their/theirs

GPM: 12.3

Antecedents

Pronouns take the place of nouns (see Chapter 16). The noun to which the pronoun refers is called the **antecedent.**

    antecedent   **pronoun**
The **employee** filled out **her** time card incorrectly.

    antecedent   **pronoun**
Our **neighbors** lost **their** dog.

    antecedent   **pronoun**
The **college** registers **its** students by phone.

GPM: 12.6–12.8

Pronoun Agreement

1. A pronoun must **agree in number** with its antecedent. If the antecedent is **singular**, any pronouns referring to the antecedent must also be singular.

Examples:

My favorite **restaurant** raised **its** prices last week.

The **girl** took **her** mother's hand.

The **boy** grabbed **his** coat.

Practice 18.1   **Write two sentences in which you use singular subjects and singular pronouns to refer to them. Now circle the antecedents and underline the pronouns.**

1. _____

2. _____

1.1 If the antecedent is **plural**, any pronouns referring to the antecedent must also be plural.

Examples:

The **dogs** wagged **their** tails.

The **trees** lost **their** leaves.

The **women** passed **their** exams.

Practice 18.2   **Write two sentences in which you use plural subjects and plural pronouns.**

1. _____

2. _____

Avoiding Sexist Language

2. Pronoun use is changing to **avoid sexist language.** Always using *he* to refer to an unspecified individual is considered sexist and should be avoided. There are many options for avoiding sexist language when referring to an unknown singular antecedent.

2.1 Use *his or her.*

A **student** left **his or her** umbrella in the auditorium.

2.2 Use *his/her.*

A **student** left **his/her** umbrella in the auditorium.

2.3 Alternate *he* and *she.*

A **student** left **his** umbrella in the auditorium.

Another **student** left **her** book in the auditorium.

2.4   Use an article instead of a pronoun.

A **student** left **an** umbrella in the auditorium.

2.5   Change the antecedent to a plural.

Some **students** left **their** umbrellas in the auditorium.

Each of these alternatives requires careful practice to avoid sounding awkward. Because there is no single accepted solution to the problem of how to refer to an antecedent that may be male or female, it is best to consult with your instructors for their preferences.

Agreement Errors

3.   Pronoun **agreement errors** occur when the pronoun does not agree in number with its antecedent (the noun it refers to). The most common error is the use of a plural pronoun with a singular antecedent.

Incorrect: A **student** forgot **their** book bag.

The word student is a singular noun, and their is a plural pronoun. The pronoun must agree with the noun.

Correct: A **student** forgot **his or her** book bag.

Correct: **Students** forgot **their** book bags.

Practice   **Cross out any incorrect pronouns and write a correct pronoun above.**

1. A football player left their gym bag in the locker room. *his or her*

2. The bird escaped from its cage.

3. The student who passed their test received an award. *his or her*

4. The Police Academy requires their recruits to attend six weeks of basic training. *its*

5. The flower dropped its petals on the table.

Problem Antecedents

4.   **Compound antecedents** joined by *and* are plural and require plural pronouns.

Sarah and Julie decided to try **their** luck at the game.

Students and teachers enjoy **their** spring break.

Practice   **Cross out any incorrect pronouns and write a correct pronoun above.**

1. Boys and girls rarely share their toys.

2. Bob and Ray bring his lunch to school. *their*

3. The cats and dogs played with its toys. *their*

4. My sister and her best friend like to braid their hair.

5. Claudia and Deb paint her fingernails on Saturday. *their*

5. With compound **antecedents joined by** *either . . . or* or *neither . . . nor*, the pronoun should agree with the nearest antecedent.

Neither my sister nor her **friends** can find **their** tickets to the play.

Neither my friends nor my **sister** can find **her** ticket to the play.

Practice 18.5   **Cross out any incorrect pronouns and write a correct pronoun above.**

1. The bike and skateboard were moved from their original location.

   her
2. Either my brothers or my sister left their keys on the table.

3. The players and coaches celebrated their victory.

   their
4. Neither my brother nor my friends brought his car.

5. Either the painting or the sketch has doubled its value overnight.

Practice 18.6   **Write two sentences in which you use compound subjects and plural pronouns to refer to them. Then circle the antecedents and underline the pronouns.**

1. _____

2. _____

Indefinite Pronouns

6. **Indefinite pronouns** refer to nonspecific nouns. Indefinite pronouns can themselves serve as antecedents to personal pronouns. Most indefinite pronouns are singular, but some are plural. Writers must pay careful attention to agreement between indefinite pronoun antecedents and the pronouns that refer to them. For a complete list of indefinite pronouns, see Chapter 9, page 121.

Common singular indefinite pronouns: everything, everyone, someone, somebody, each, anybody, anyone

Everybody should know **his/her** license number.

Someone forgot **his or her** book.

No one is bringing **his or her** family to the party.

Practice 18.7   **Cross out any incorrect pronouns and write a correct pronoun above.**

   his or her
1. Everyone chose their favorite dessert to bring to the picnic.

2. Each of the boys remembered his homework.

   his or her
3. Someone left their headlights on.

   her
4. Each of the Girl Scouts brought their badges to the meeting.

   his or her
5. Any driver caught without their license will be ticketed.

Practice 18.8   **Write two sentences in which you use singular indefinite pronouns as subjects and singular pronouns to refer to them. Then circle the antecedents and underline the pronouns.**

1. _____

2. _____

6.1   Some indefinite pronouns are always plural.

Plural indefinite pronouns: both, few, many, several

Few are chosen to lead **their** country.

Many of my friends have lost **their** jobs.

Practice 18.9   **Cross out any incorrect pronouns and write a correct pronoun above.**

1. Both of my brothers love ~~his~~ *their* bikes.

2. Many students enjoy their spring break.

3. Several papers have holes in them.

4. Few athletes understand the importance of academics in ~~his~~ *their* future.

5. Many trees have lost their leaves.

Practice 18.10   **Write two sentences in which you use plural indefinite pronouns as subjects and plural pronouns to refer to them. Then circle the antecedents and underline the pronouns.**

1. _____

2. _____

6.2   A few indefinite pronouns may be **either singular or plural** depending on the noun or pronoun to which they refer.

Indefinite pronouns that can be singular or plural: a lot, all, any, lots, more, most, none, some

None of the money has lost **its** markings. (Singular)

None of the books are missing **their** pages. (Plural)

A lot of the candy had lost **its** flavor. (Singular)

A lot of students spend **their** Saturdays studying. (Plural)

Practice 18.11   **Cross out any incorrect pronouns and write a correct pronoun above.**

1. None of the teachers had met ~~his~~ *their* new students.

2. Most of the campers forgot their insect repellent.

3. I must do a lot of homework because it is due tomorrow.

4. All of the glasses have chips in them.

5. Some of the chairs have stains on ~~its~~ *their* seats.

Practice 18.12   **Write two sentences using the same indefinite pronoun as a subject. In one example, the pronoun should be singular and include a singular pronoun to refer to it, and the other example should use a plural antecedent and include a plural pronoun to refer to it. Then circle the antecedents and underline the pronouns.**

1. _____

2. _____

Collective Nouns

7.   **Collective nouns** are words that refer to one whole made up of parts. Most collective noun antecedents are singular and take a singular pronoun.

> **Common Collective Nouns**
>
> | | |
> |---|---|
> | a band | a committee |
> | a faculty | a group |
> | a number | an audience |
> | a class | a crowd |
> | a family | a jury |
> | a team | |

A **business** just moved **its** operations into the building next door.

The **team** elected **its** best player as captain.

The **school** and **its** principal were featured in the newspaper.

Practice **Cross out any incorrect pronouns and write a correct pronoun above.**

1. The college expects their students to pay for classes on the day of registration.
   its
2. The class meets their teacher on Monday.
   its
3. My favorite restaurant flame-broils its hamburgers.
4. The soccer team won their second game of the season.
   its
5. A team should consider their options before deciding on a strategy.
   its

Practice 18.14 **Write two sentences in which you use collective nouns as subjects and singular pronouns to refer to them. Then circle the antecedents and underline the pronouns.**

1. _____

2. _____

GPM: 12.21–12.22

Avoiding Shifts in Number and Person

8.   While it's important to check for pronoun agreement within a sentence, it is also important to be consistent from sentence to sentence. Do not shift from singular subjects to plural subjects or vice versa within a paragraph.

Incorrect:

A **dentist** can be scary. **They** almost always have needles next to **their** examination chairs.

Do not shift from singular *dentist* to plural *they*. Remain consistent in using plural subjects or singular subjects.

Correct:

Dentists can be scary. **They** almost always have needles next to **their** examination chairs.

OR

A **dentist** can be scary. **She** almost always has needles next to **her** examination chair.

Practice 18.15   **Correct any pronoun errors.**

1. If students want to register easily, he should register online. *[they]*

2. Diners can enjoy a wide selection of menu items, and he can also choose from a wide variety of specialty drinks. *[they]*

3. The girl claimed she left her backpack on the bus.

4. The school will not allow students to register if they have not paid their fees.

5. Athletes should keep up with school work so that he doesn't lose his scholar- ships. *[they don't] [their]*

9.   Pronouns are classified according to **person:** first person (I, me, we); second person (you); and third person (he, she, it, they). Do not shift from one person to another within a sentence or paragraph.

Incorrect:

I like golf because **you** can enjoy nature while **you** exercise.

Do not shift from *I* to *you* when the same person is clearly meant. Remain consistent in using the same person.

Correct:

I like golf because **I** can enjoy nature while **I** exercise.

Practice 18.16   **Cross out any pronouns that shift in number or person and write a correct pronoun above.**

1. When a person opens a bank account, you can sign up for a variety of member services. *[he or she]*

2. Players should attend all practices. If a player does not participate regularly, they may not be allowed to play. *[he or she]*

3. If a driver hears or sees a siren, you must pull to the side of the road. *[he or she]*

4. Golfers must reserve playing times, and he or she must pay higher fees for weekend time slots. *[they]*

5. Students who are concerned about doing well in their classes will do everything they can to stay healthy. If students visit the infirmary on campus, they can get a free flu shot.

Limiting Use of the Second Person

10.   Although the second-person pronoun, *you*, is frequently used in speech, its use is discouraged in most academic writing because it is considered vague and sometimes illogical because the use of *you* implies that the reader is being addressed personally.

> Incorrect: **You** should pay **your** fees before **your** classes are canceled.

> It is not clear who the *you* in this sentence is. Be specific in naming the subject.

> Correct: A **student** should pay **his** or **her** fees before **his** or **her** classes are canceled.

> OR

> **Students** should pay **their** fees before **their** classes are canceled.

Correcting Related Agreement Errors

11.   When correcting pronoun errors, correct any related errors (such as verb errors).

> Incorrect: **Every** student should pay **their** fees before **they** lose **their** classes.

> If an incorrect pronoun is used with a verb, sometimes the verb ending must be changed if the pronoun is corrected. Be sure to make pronoun subjects agree with their verbs.

> Correct: **Every** student should pay **her** fees before **she loses her** classes.

Practice 18.17   **Rewrite the following sentences to eliminate the use of *you*. Think of a specific noun or pronoun to replace *you*. Be sure to correct related errors such as verbs.**

1. When you drink and drive, you endanger your life and the lives of others.
   drivers   they   their lives

2. If you break the law, you will have to pay the consequences.
   a criminal s   he or she

3. Unless you study regularly, you will find it difficult to keep up with your classes.
   students   they   their

4. You should always water your lawn in the mornings or evenings.
   Homeowners   their   s

5. If you are looking for low prices, go to discount department stores.
   shoppers   they should

Review Exercise 18.18   **Correct any pronoun errors.**

1. The jury has reached its verdict.

2. The puppies and the kitten played in their cages.

3. Either my brother or my parents will contribute their time to the food drive.

4. Anybody who answers their door without looking through the peep-hole first is foolish.
   his or her

5. None of the computers have been taken out of its boxes.
   their

6. If a ~~student~~ want value for their money, they should go to the campus bookstore.
   (above: s · students)

7. When you register for classes, they make you pay your fees immediately.
   (above: the school s them   their)

8. Everyone who finished their dinner may have dessert.
   (above: his or her)

9. The dentist will close their office on Saturday.
   (above: her)

10. The store gives their regular customers a discount.
    (above: its)

Review Exercise 18.19   **Correct any pronoun or verb errors. Make sure that both verbs and pronouns agree with their subjects.**

1. Someone have left their calculator on the table.
   (above: has   his or her)

2. The awards committee have made their decision.
   (above: has   its)

3. None of the students have taken their final exams.

4. Every athlete who wants to excel in sports knows they have to practice regularly.
   (above: he or she has)

5. All of my friends have promised that they will attend my party.

6. Each movie has their own story line.
   (above: its)

7. Neither my mother nor my aunts has lived in her house for long.
   (above: have   their)

8. A teacher who doesn't treat their students fairly loses their respect.
   (above: his or her)

9. Elena and Tasha are meeting at their favorite restaurant for dinner.

10. My brother and his friend has given me his word to return my car by eleven.
    (above: have   their)

Review Exercise 18.20   **Identify the pronouns in the following sentences as correct (C) or incorrect (I) and correct pronoun and verb errors.**

___I___ 1. A child who doesn't do what they are told can get into trouble.
   (above: he or she is)

___C___ 2. Policemen are paid well because of the risks they take.

___C___ 3. Bob and Mariko have been friends all their lives.

___I___ 4. Each of the teachers has their own opinion.
   (above: his or her)

___I___ 5. The committee gave their decision to the president.
   (above: its)

___I___ 6. Everyone enjoys themselves on their day off.
   (above: him or herself his or her)

___I___ 7. Either my best friend or my sister always brings their lunch to school.
   (above: her)

___I___ 8. If you study, you will succeed in school.
   (above: students   they)

___C___ 9. Children fear going to the doctor because they are afraid of painful shots.

___C___ 10. My best friend won her second math award this week.

Group Activity 18.21   **Review of exercise**

Each group member should answer and explain two items from the selected Review Exercise. If there is a disagreement about the correct answer, review the rules and decide on the correct answer.

Review Exercise **18.22**   **Editing for pronoun errors**

Correct all pronoun errors and related verb errors. Substitute specific nouns for the second person pronoun *you*.

Valley View Mall

It has

The new Valley View Mall is fantastic. ~~They have~~ terrific stores, restaurants, and

shoppers   they   Shoppers

theaters, and ~~you~~ can find almost anything ~~you~~ want. ~~You~~ are certain to find the

it   has

latest in back to school fashions and accessories because ~~they have~~ over thirty

department stores and specialty stores. The mall also offers a food court with twelve

Shoppers

restaurants and dining emporiums. ~~You~~ can choose between fine Italian dining and

Tired   s

snack shops that specialize in ice cream, hot pretzels, or smoothies. A shopper can

rest their feet and relax on one of the many benches in the garden courtyard, or

they

~~he~~ can take a break and go to one of the sixteen movies showing in the movie

Shoppers

theater. ~~Everybody~~ like the new mall because it is such a clean and friendly place,

they   they

and ~~you~~ can find just what ~~you~~ are looking for.

Review Exercise **18.23**   **Editing your writing**

Choose two journal entries and edit them for pronoun agreement errors. Circle the antecedent and underline the pronoun. Use a different colored pen to make your corrections. Write "pronoun agreement" in the upper right-hand corner.

Review Exercise 　　**Writing practice**

Write a one-page journal entry in which you respond to the following writing prompt. When you finish writing, go back and circle the antecedents, underline the pronouns, and check pronoun agreement.

Explain what kind of music you listen to and why you like it, including your favorite artists and why you like them.

Chapter 19

Apostrophes

In this chapter you will learn to use apostrophes in

- Contractions
- Possessive phrases
- Letters and numerals

Apostrophes are usually signals to the reader of the relationship between words. They show that words have been put together into contractions or that words are in a possessive relationship. Apostrophes can also be used to make letters and numerals plural. This chapter will teach you when and where to use apostrophes.

Group Activity 19.1 **Each member should find at least two apostrophes used in other chapters of this textbook or another book. Discuss the reasons that you think the apostrophes are being used.** Answers will vary.

Contractions

GPM: 11.3

1.1   Apostrophes are used in contractions to indicate missing letters. Contractions are words that combine two words into one by replacing the missing letters with an apostrophe.

> he'll = he will
>
> there's = there is
>
> you're = you are
>
> shouldn't = should not
>
> won't = will not
>
> it's = it is

1.2   Be sure to place the apostrophe correctly. The apostrophe takes the place of the missing letter(s).

> Incorrect: is'nt
>
> Correct: isn't (The apostrophe takes the place of the missing *o* in *is not*.)

Group Activity 19.2 **The group should brainstorm twenty contractions. Compare the list with other groups.** Answers will vary.

Practice 19.3 **Add an apostrophe in the contractions in the following sentences.**

1. There's a major brand of car that won't be on the streets anymore.
2. ~~The~~ Oldsmobile aren't manufactured now because people weren't buying enough of the cars.
3. Some people haven't stopped loving these cars, though.
4. They're going to be valuable for collectors before long.
5. It's a shame when beloved symbols like Oldsmobile cars are discontinued, but they'll never die for some people.

GPM: 11.6–11.8

Possession

2.1   Apostrophes are used to indicate possession. The apostrophe indicates that the second word group belongs to the first word group.

The teacher's pet = the pet of the teacher

Someone's new book = new book of someone

Many teams' coaches = coaches of many teams

A few people's brilliant ideas = brilliant ideas of a few people

Determining Possession

2.2   The most important step in using possessive apostrophes correctly is recognizing possessive phrases. A possessive phrase is a word group in which the first word or words *owns* or *possesses* the second word or word group.

Wanda's sisters (the sisters belong to Wanda)

The hikers' map (the map belongs to the hikers)

Children's parents (the parents belong to the children)

In reality, possession means that an **object** (a noun: a singular or plural person, place, thing, or idea) belongs to an **owner** (a noun). A possessive phrase looks like this:

owner's object or several **owners' object.**

Practice 19.4 **Fill in the blank with a noun (person, place, thing, or idea) to make a possessive phrase.** Answers will vary.

1. Bill's _car_
2. the car's _muffler_
3. a few men's _jobs_
4. two girls' _mothers_
5. my mother's _ring_

Group Activity 19.5   The group should make a list of twenty-five possessive phrases. (Don't worry about where the apostrophes go yet.) Use the following topics to help generate possessive phrases: family, pets, sports, friends. Later you will use this list to practice testing for apostrophes.

Tests for Ownership

Remember that not every word that ends in *s* needs an apostrophe. You must check carefully for a possessive relationship. To make sure that a word group is a possessive phrase that needs an apostrophe to show possession, convert the form of the phrase from **owner's object** to **the object of the owner or object that belongs to the owner.** The restated phrase should clearly show the relation of ownership.

> **owner's or owners' object = <u>object</u> of the <u>owner</u>**
>
> the car's parking place = parking place of the car (apostrophe needed)
>
> the cars parked = parked of the cars (no apostrophe needed)
>
> my parents' house = house of my parents (apostrophe needed)
>
> my dog's collar = (object) _____collar_____ of (owner) _____my dog_____

Another way to test for ownership is to ask whether the second word or word group **belongs** to the word before it.

> the car's parking place: *parking place* belongs to *car,* so there is a possessive relationship.
>
> the cars parked: *parked (verb)* doesn't belong to *cars,* so no apostrophe is needed to show possession.
>
> the house's roof: Does *roof* belong to *house*? (Yes, so the apostrophe is correct.)

Word Order in a Possessive Phrase

2.3   The object owned must immediately follow the owner. The only words that might come between the owner and the object owned are words that describe the object. If the words are in any other arrangement, no apostrophe is needed.

> Maria's long black hair = long black hair of Maria
>
> Maria has long black hair = has of Maria (no apostrophe needed because a noun can't own a verb)

Practice 19.6   Fill in the blanks to determine whether the apostrophe is needed in each sentence. Remember that if phrase makes no sense when you rearrange the words then no apostrophe is needed. Cross out the apostrophe if it is not needed.

Example:

the book's last page = <u>last page</u> of <u>the book</u>

1. Mr. Major's job = _____job_____ of _____Mr. Major_____

2. the yard's need water = _____needs water_____ of _____the yard_____

3. a pool's diving board = ___diving board___ of ___a pool___

4. my friend's father = ___father___ of ___my friend___

5. the key/s to the car = ___to___ of ___the key___

6. Sheila's ninety year old grandmother = ninety year old grandmother of ___Sheila___

7. an essay's concluding paragraph = concluding paragraph of ___an essay___

8. a store's return policy = ___return policy___ of ___a store___

9. some people's most important dream = most important dream of ___some people___

10. the room/s contain furniture = ___contain___ of ___the room___

Group Activity 19.7   **Group members should compare answers for the above practice and come to an agreement. Then check to make sure all of the phrases in the list your group brainstormed in 19.5 are possessive phrases.**

Placement of Apostrophes in Possessive Phrases

Once you are aware of possessive phrases, the rules for where to place the apostrophe are relatively easy to use.

Singular Owners

3.1   To make a **singular** noun possessive, add **'s**.

the girl's feelings	Chris's teacher
Jorge's lunchbox	my neighbor's house
the woman's husband	the singer's voice

Remember that a singular noun is one person, place, thing, or idea. Usually when writers use possessive phrases, they write the -s and may need to go back when editing to **add the apostrophe before the -s.**

3.2   When a singular word ends in -s, add **'s.**

the class's teacher

Ms. Hess's purse

the dress's buttons

Practice 19.8   **Add apostrophes where needed.**

1. One man's love for music has benefited the world of music and many jazz musicians.

2. Milton Gabler's store, the Commodore Music Shop, was New York City's most comprehensive and knowledgeable record shop.

3. This jazz lover's other claim to fame was his record label's support of jazz musicians like Billy Holiday.

4. This record label's recording of Billy Holiday's music helped keep her music alive.

5. Music lovers give Milton Gabler credit for contributing to jazz's history.

Plural Owners

4.1 To make a **regular plural** noun possessive, add an apostrophe after the final **s**.

> three girls' sweaters   many workers' jobs
>
> some students' test   the wives' invitations

4.2 Remember that the number of owners determines the placement of the apostrophe before or after the final -s, not the number of objects owned. One owner can own more than one object, just as two or more owners can own one object.

> one musician's musical instruments
>
> two sisters' mother

Practice 19.9   **Add apostrophes where needed.**

1. Two twins' experiences with school can be very different as they grow up.

2. The twins may find that many teachers' opinions of them are not identical.

3. Their parents' attention may also not be consistent, and one or both of the parents may favor one of the twins over the other.

4. Many kids say that they wish they had a twin, but twins don't always enjoy the attention they receive.

5. Friends' opinions about each of the twins can cause hard feelings when one twin is more popular than the other.

Determiners

5. To avoid mistakes with possessive apostrophes, pay attention to words around the possessive phrase that determine whether the owner is singular or plural.

> **Determiners that signify singular owners:** a, an, one, each, every
>
> **Determiners that signify plural owners:** all, many, most, some, few
>
> one friend's work   some friends' work
>
> an apple's color   all apples' color
>
> a company's employees   many companies' employees

Practice 19.10   **Add apostrophes where needed.**

1. Many new cooks use a cookbook's recipes, but some recipes' instructions are difficult to follow.

2. Also, a few dishes' ingredients may be hard to find in the grocery store.

3. There are hundreds of ways to make stew, and most chefs' favorite recipe will include variations on the standard ingredients.

4. A new cook's best bet is to ask for a couple of experienced cooks' favorite recipes.

5. My mother's meat loaf is a recipe everyone in my family loves, but my two sisters' variations on the recipe are very tasty too.

Irregular Plural Owners

6. Some nouns are plural without an **-s** ending. To make irregular plurals possessive, add **'s**. The most common irregular plurals are *women, men, children,* and *people.*

the women's coats	the people's preference
the men's volleyball team	the children's room

Practice 19.11 **Add apostrophes where needed.**

1. Most people's home is their castle because it's the place where they relax.

2. The children's room often contains a television set and a computer.

3. A home's backyard is many men's favorite place to relieve stress.

4. When living an apartment, some people's choice for a place to relax is the patio or porch.

5. Some women's hobbies include sewing, so a sewing room is great addition to the house and a place for a woman's sewing machine and materials.

Group Activity 19.12 **Each group member should make up five sentences that use apostrophes. Include contractions and singular, plural, and irregular plural possessive phrases. In each sentence, leave the apostrophes out or put them in the wrong place. Then switch papers with another group member and edit each other's sentences. Check your answers with the group.** Answers will vary.

Possessive Pronouns

7. Possessive pronouns have the normal function of showing possession, so they don't need apostrophes.

Possessive pronouns: his, hers, ours, theirs, its, yours

His book has lost its cover.

You don't need to bring your car because you can ride in ours.

Practice 19.13 **Add apostrophes where needed.**

1. The teacher accepted Kayla's answer but not yours.

2. The dog buried its bone behind Brianna's house.

3. My father left his car in his oldest brother's carport.

4. Takela's allowance is bigger than ours.

5. I went to my class, and Jose and Kia went to theirs.

Letters and Numerals

8. Use an apostrophe to make a letter or numeral plural.

There were many A's on the last test.

Some R.N.'s at the hospital have been nurses for over twenty years.

Some writers make their 1's and 7's alike.

The 1940's were an interesting time in American history.

Practice **Add apostrophes where needed.**

1. Clothing styles from the 1960's are popular again with today's teenagers.

2. Handheld computers are called PDA's.

3. The temperatures will be in the 90's today.

4. Many companies' health plans are run by HMO's (health management organizations).

5. The top golfers in the tournament shot in the 60's yesterday.

Review Exercise **Add apostrophes where needed.**

1. One family's dog tore up a neighbor's yard.

2. During the night, some people's sleep was interrupted by the loud noise coming from the factory's warehouse.

3. The class's tests are always given on Mondays.

4. Some classes' exam periods will be at night this term.

5. One boy's mother told the other children's mothers about some of the kids' misbehavior.

6. A song's lyrics can stay in people's minds for a long time.

7. A letter's weight determines how much the stamps will cost.

8. The student's teacher asked her to give a presentation to the class.

9. Last week, the teachers' union told them that they would be getting a raise in the next year's budget.

10. Many families' health insurance protects them in times of crisis.

Review Exercise **Add apostrophes where needed.**

1. Sometimes people's beliefs are tested during times of crisis.

2. The players had a gentlemen's agreement that the losers would buy the winners sodas after the match.

3. In the game's final minutes, a player's lucky shot put her team ahead.

4. There's too much research to do for the few Ph.D.'s on the staff.

5. I can't figure out what is wrong with Maria's cat.

6. The students are using the school's computers because they left theirs at home.

7. The secretary's duties include keeping track of her boss's schedule.

8. The hospital's nurses rotate shifts, and most nurses' schedules include three days off each week.

9. Every morning, it's my dog's job to fetch the newspaper.

10. One plant's pot is cracked, but the other plant's pot is in perfect condition.

Group Activity   **Review of exercise**

Each group member should answer and explain two items. If there is a disagreement about the correct answer, review the definitions and decide on the correct answer.

Review Exercise 19.18   **Editing for Apostrophes**

Add apostrophes where needed, and circle unnecessary apostrophes.

One of This Country's Most Important Holidays

Thanksgiving is one of America's most celebrated holidays. It's held on the fourth or last Thursday of November of each year. Thanksgiving was first celebrated by the Pilgrims' in 1621. It's purpose was to give thanks for the Pilgrim's' harvest and other blessings during the year. Today, those traditions are still strong with children and their parents' who gather from near and far for the annual festivitie's. As with all holidays, Americans' devote a great amount of time and effort toward making everyone's holiday memorable. While the cooks' frantically stuff turkeys' and prepare the feast, it is the children's job to steer clear of the kitchen and harm's way. Many men's favorite Thanksgiving pastime is watching football's collegiate playoffs on television. The beauty of Thanksgiving is the way in which people and families' gather and give thanks for their good fortune. Some are so touched with the spirit of giving that they will spend their holiday's' time in a soup kitchen or a homeless shelter in order to give back to the community and share with those less fortunate.

Review Exercise   **Editing your own writing**

Choose two journal entries and edit them for apostrophe errors. Add apostrophes where needed and circle unnecessary apostrophes. Use a different colored pen to make your corrections. Write "apostrophes" in the upper right-hand corner of the page to let your instructor know you have edited the entry for apostrophes.

Review Exercise **Writing practice**

Write a one-page journal entry in which you respond to the following writing prompt. When you finish writing, go back and circle the apostrophes, and check to make sure they are placed correctly.

Do you enjoy or not enjoy living in your neighborhood?

Chapter 20
Sentence Combining

In this chapter you will learn

• To use coordination and subordination strategies to combine sentences.

Often in a first draft, we write the way we speak. We use the same sentence patterns over and over, and we don't worry about how we present the information. When we are speaking, we can use as many sentences as we want to express ourselves and answer questions about what we mean. However, in writing, our relationship with our audience is different. Readers want each sentence to hold significant information. They get impatient when the sentences are all simple sentences with only one piece of information.

Sentence combining is a set of strategies that writers use in the revision process to build a variety of sentence structures from simple sentences. Writers combine the information in two sentences into one stronger sentence. When ideas are combined, writers have to explain the relationship of the ideas. Readers will understand the writing better when the relationship between ideas is clear and extra words are cut out.

There are two steps to sentence combining:

1. Begin with two simple sentences (or ideas) that are related.

   Eating a hearty breakfast is important.
   Breakfast gives us the fuel we need to start the day.

2. Combine the sentences into one sentence that expresses the relationship between the ideas.

   Eating a hearty breakfast is important because breakfast gives us the fuel we need to start the day.

By combining the two simple sentences, the writer helps the reader understand the relationship between the ideas. Sometimes, the writer also cuts down on unnecessary words.

Junk foods like chips and ice cream taste good.

Chips and ice cream are full of sugar and fat.

> **Combined:** Junk foods like chips and ice cream taste good but are full of sugar and fat.

There are two main strategies for combining sentences: **coordination** and **subordination**. You will use both when you combine sentences. In fact, you will usually see a possibility for combining sentences without thinking about which strategy you are using.

WE: 4.3

Coordination

Coordination means to make equal parts work together.

Compound Sentences

One coordination strategy is to combine two simple sentences (independent clauses) into a compound sentence. For more information about compound sentences, see Chapter 17, pages 213-217.

> Compound sentence = independent clause, coordinating conjunction independent clause.

A healthy breakfast provides the necessary nutrition to start the day.

A solid meal gives us energy.

> **Combined:** A healthy breakfast provides the necessary nutrition to start the day, and a solid meal gives us energy.

Building a compound sentence from simple sentences is an easy method of combining. You simply join two sentences with a comma and a coordinating conjunction (*for, and, nor, but, or, yet, so*).

Practice 20.1   **Combine each pair of sentences into a compound sentence by joining the first sentence to the second with a comma and a coordinating conjunction. Then compare answers with a classmate.** Answers may vary.

> *Example:*   Water skiing is fun.
>
> It can be dangerous.

Water skiing is fun, but it can be dangerous.

1. Skiers need to be in good shape.

   They should warm up before skiing.

   Skiers need to be in good shape, and they should warm up before skiing.

2. Skiers can hurt their back or arms.

   Skiing is very hard on the upper body.

   Skiers can hurt their backs or arms, for skiing is very hard on the upper body.

3. Boats don't have brakes.

   Skiers are in danger of being run over in the water.

   Boats don't have brakes, so skiers are in danger of being run over in the water.

4. Skiers should remain aware of boats and obstacles in the water. They should have someone in the boat looking out for them.

   Skiers should remain aware of boats and obstacles in the water, and they should have someone in the boat looking out for them.

5. Tired skiers have the most accidents. They should signal to stop before becoming exhausted.

   Tired skiers have the most accidents, so they should signal to stop before becoming exhausted.

Choosing the right coordinating conjunction is the most difficult step in making strong compound sentences out of simple sentences. The coordinating conjunction in a compound sentence tells how the two independent clauses relate to each other. Knowing the meaning of each coordinating conjunction can help you pick the appropriate conjunction to join two sentences.

For suggests "because."
I can't type my paper, for my computer is broken.

And adds two ideas that are similar.
The sun is shining, and the temperature is hot.

Nor negates both ideas.
I didn't do well on the assignment, nor did I do well on the test.
(Notice that the verb comes before the subject in the second independent clause in compound sentences using *nor*.)

But contrasts two ideas.
The temperature outside is freezing, but the air is hot inside the house.

Or offers the ideas as equal choices.
I will do homework before dinner, or I will mow the lawn.

Yet limits or contrasts two ideas.
The team lost the game, yet it is still in first place.

So suggests results.
The weather is supposed to be rainy, so I will take my umbrella to class.

Group Activity **20.2** **Working in pairs, add the coordinating conjunction that best expresses the relationship between the two independent clauses. Sometimes more than one conjunction can be used.**

1. The new car was expensive, (contrast) but or yet I got a good price on the car I traded in.

2. The new car cost a lot of money, (results) ____so____ I had to get a car loan for six years.

3. The new car can be ordered with many luxury options, (equal choices)　or　the car can be ordered without options.

4. The car will take six weeks to be delivered, (because)　for　it comes with special options that must be added at the factory.

5. I don't like the silver exterior color, (negation)　nor　do I like the gold color.

6. Burgundy is the color I ordered, (addition)　and　I asked for the cream interior.

7. The engine of my new car is very powerful, (limits or contrast) yet or but it has good fuel efficiency.

Compound Predicates

Another coordination strategy is to combine the predicates (the verb and all the words that modify the verb) of two sentences.

> A black eye is known medically as "periorbital hematoma."

> It can last a few days to a month.

> **Combined:** A black eye is known medically as "periorbital hematoma" and can last a few days to a month.

The complete predicate of the sentence begins with the verb and includes all the words after the verb. If the subject of two sentences is the same or a pronoun of the same subject, then the predicates can often be joined with a coordinating conjunction. No comma is used when joining two predicates.

Group Activity **20.3** **With a partner, combine the pairs of sentences. First, underline the predicate of each sentence. Then combine the predicates with a coordinating conjunction.**

> *Example:*
>
> Alzheimer's disease affects the brain.
>
> It causes memory loss.
>
> Alzheimer's disease affects the brain and causes memory loss.

1. Alzheimer's disease robs millions of older people of their memory.

   It causes devastating heartbreak for their families.
   Alzheimer's disease robs millions of older people of their memory and causes devastating heartbreak for their families.

2. About four million Americans are afflicted with Alzheimer's.

   They have little hope of being cured.
   About four million Americans are afflicted with Alzheimer's and have little hope of being cured.

3. Doctors don't know what causes Alzheimer's.

   They don't have a cure for the disease.
   Doctors don't know what causes Alzheimer's and don't have a cure for the disease.

4. Some drugs slow progress of the disease.

   The drugs don't stop the disease.

Some drugs slow progress of the disease but don't stop the disease.

5. Researchers <u>are trying to find a vaccine to prevent the disease</u>.

They <u>have not been successful so far</u>.

Researchers are trying to find a vaccine to prevent the disease but have not been successful so far.

Practice 20.4 **Combine the two sentences using a compound sentence or a compound predicate.** Answers will vary.

1. Children love to stay up late at night.

Getting a good night's sleep is important.

Children love to stay up late at night, yet getting a good night's sleep is important.

2. Parents must put their kids to bed on time.

The kids will not get enough sleep.

Parents must put their kids to bed on time, or the kids will not get enough sleep.

3. Staying up too late can hurt children the next morning.

They will wake up tired and cranky.

Staying up too late can hurt children the next morning, for they will wake up tired and cranky.

4. Some parents make deals with their children.

The parents offer a bribe like ice cream before bed.

Some parents make deals with their children and offer a bribe like ice cream before bed.

5. Young children like to be told stories.

Parents read to their children at bedtime.

Young children like to be told stories, so parents read to their children at bedtime.

6. Parents should establish a set time for bed.

They should stick to that set time every night.

Parents should establish a set time for bed and stick to that set time every night.

7. Children may try to bend the rules.

Parents should be consistent.

Children may try to bend the rules, but parents should be consistent.

8. Parents must be firm with their kids.

They must stick to the bedtime they set.

Parents must be firm with their kids and stick to the bedtime they set.

9. Most youngsters enjoy watching television or movies late at night.

They like to play video games too.

Most youngsters enjoy watching television or movies late at night, and they like to play video games too.

10. Going to bed on time is no fun at all.

Children look forward to growing up.

Going to bed on time is no fun at all, so children look forward to growing up.

WE: 4.14

Subordination

Subordination means to relate the parts so that one part is less important.

Complex Sentences

The most important subordination strategy is to combine two sentences into a complex sentence. One sentence is subordinated by adding a subordinating conjunction to make it a dependent clause, and it is added to the other sentence (independent clause). For more information about complex sentences, see Chapter 14, page 192.

Complex sentence = independent clause + dependent clause.
OR
Complex sentence = Dependent clause, independent clause.

Getting the mail has always meant going to the mailbox.

Many people now receive most of their mail electronically on their computers.

Combined: While getting the mail has always meant going to the mailbox, many people now receive most of their mail electronically on their computers.

OR

Getting the mail has always meant going to the mailbox although many people now receive most of their mail electronically on their computers.

When you make a complex sentence from two simple sentences, you use a subordinating conjunction to make one sentence (independent clause) into a dependent clause. Note that a comma follows an introductory dependent clause at the beginning of a sentence. If the dependent clause comes at the end of the sentence, no comma is needed. (Review Introductory Elements on page 217 in Chapter 17.)

Choosing an appropriate subordinating conjunction is the most important step in making strong complex sentences out of simple sentences. The subordinating conjunction in a complex sentence tells how the two clauses relate to each other. Knowing the meaning of each subordinating conjunction can help you pick the right conjunction.

One idea is a **contrast** of the other
> although
> even though
> though
> whereas
> while

It is raining outside **although** the sun is shining.

One idea is a **consequence** of the other
> as
> because
> since

Because it is raining outside, I will take my umbrella.

One idea is a **condition** of the other
> if
> unless

I will wait to go to my car **if** it is raining outside.

One idea is **related in time** to the other
> after
> as
> before
> until
> when
> while

Before I leave for work, I will check the weather outside.

Group Activity **20.5** **Working in pairs, add the subordinating conjunction that best expresses the relationship between the two clauses. Some sentences can use more than one conjunction.** Answers will vary.

1. Our math teacher is very popular (contrast) <u>although</u> she gives homework every night.

2. Some teachers give very little homework (consequence) <u>because</u> they have their students do their assignments in class.

3. (condition) <u>If</u> teachers give a lot of homework, they should warn their classes.

4. (time relation) <u>When</u> our teacher is going to give us a big assignment, she tells us a few days in advance so that we can plan for it.

5. I have trouble studying outside of class (condition) <u>unless</u> I get together with a study group.

6. (consequence) <u>Since</u> I learn best by interacting with people, I learn from my study partners.

7. (contrast) <u>Even though</u> my study partners and I spend time socializing, our study time is valuable.

8. My study group usually gets together for coffee and a short review (time relation) _before_ we take a big test.

Practice **20.6** **Use a subordinating conjunction to combine the two sentences into a complex sentence.**

1. Some people will only go fishing during the day.

   Other people love fishing at night.

   While some people will only go fishing during the day, other people love fishing at night.

2. Fishing at night can be enjoyable.

   The air is cool without the sun beating down.

   Fishing at night can be enjoyable because the air is cool without the sun beating down.

3. Fishermen need to see what they are doing in the dark.

   They use a flashlight or lantern for light.

   When fishermen need to see what they are doing in the dark, they use a flashlight or lantern for light.

4. Fishing in the dark water is fun.

   It can be hazardous too.

   Although fishing in the dark water is fun, it can be hazardous too.

5. Night time fishing from bridges is dangerous.

   It's a good idea to wear bright clothing that motorists can see.

   Because night time fishing from bridges is dangerous, it's a good idea to wear bright clothing that motorists can see.

6. It's also a good idea to keep valuables in something waterproof that floats.

   The fisherman doesn't want to lose keys and wallet in the water.

   It's also a good idea to keep valuables in something waterproof that floats if the fisherman doesn't want to lose keys and wallet in the water.

7. Serious fishermen want to catch fish at night.

   Most people just want to enjoy the outdoors.

   Serious fishermen want to catch fish at night though most people just want to enjoy the outdoors.

8. Taking a boat out on the water at night presents challenges.

   Only experienced boaters should venture out into the dark waters.

   Because taking a boat out on the water at night presents challenges, only experienced boaters should venture out into the dark waters.

9. Boaters should wear preservers at all times.

   They want to remain safe should the boat capsize or sink.

   Boaters should wear preservers at all times since they want to remain safe should the board capsize or sink.

10. Being out on the water at night can present challenges.

    The best fishing is out in the middle of the water.

    While being out on the water at night can present challenges, the best fishing is out in the middle of the water.

WE: 4.29–4.30

Using Coordination or Subordination

Understanding the relationship between sentences is the most important ingredient in sentence combining. Once you know what the relationship is, you can often choose coordination or subordination to combine the ideas into a strong sentence. The three most common relationships between sentences are **addition of similar ideas, contrast of opposing ideas,** and **consequence of resulting ideas.** Below are the conjunctions used to show these relationships.

	Addition	**Contrast**	**Consequence**
Coordinating conjunctions	and	but yet	so for
Subordinating conjunctions	along with in addition to	even though although	because since while though

Addition

The Volkswagen Beetle has had an interesting history.

The Beetle has enjoyed enormous popularity.

Compound sentence: The Volkswagen Beetle has had an interesting history, **and** the Beetle has enjoyed enormous popularity.

Complex sentence: **Along with** having an interesting history, the Beetle has enjoyed enormous popularity.

Contrast

The Beetle is a German car.

It gained the most popularity in America.

Compound: The Beetle is a German car, **yet** it gained the most popularity in America.

Complex: **Even though** the Beetle is a German car, it gained the most popularity in America.

Consequence

The Beetle has a round shape.

It was nicknamed the "Bug."

Compound: The Beetle has a round shape, **so** it was nicknamed the "Bug."

Complex: **Since** the Beetle has a round shape, it was nicknamed the "Bug."

Review Exercise **20.7**   **Combine the following pairs of sentences according to the directions following each pair. Refer to the chart of connectors to choose an appropriate conjunction and sentence pattern. Check your answers with the other members of your group.** Answers will vary.

1. The Volkswagen Beetle has become popular again.

   It can be seen on freeways and in parking lots everywhere.

   Use a coordinating conjunction in a compound sentence.
   The Volkswagen Beetle has become popular again, and it can be seen on freeways and in parking lots everywhere.

   Use a coordinating conjunction in a compound predicate.
   The Volkswagen Beetle has become popular again and can be seen on freeways and in parking lots everywhere.

   Use a subordinating conjunction in a complex sentence.
   Because the Volkswagen Beetle has become popular again, it can be seen on freeways and in parking lots everywhere.

2. The new Beetle has the same shape as the old one.

   It even comes with a flower vase on the dashboard like the original Beetle.

   Use a coordinating conjunction in a compound sentence.
   The new Beetle has the same shape as the old one, and it even comes with a flower vase on the dashboard like the original Beetle.

   Use a coordinating conjunction in a compound predicate.
   The new Beetle has the same shape as the old one and comes with a flower vase on the dashboard like the original Beetle.

   Use a subordinating conjunction in a complex sentence.
   The new Beetle has the same shape as the old one in addition to coming with a flower vase on the dashboard like the original Beetle.

3. The old Beetle had its engine in the rear.

   The new Beetle has its engine in the front.

   Use a coordinating conjunction in a compound sentence.
   The old Beetle had its engine in the rear, but the new Beetle has its engine in the front.

   Use a subordinating conjunction in a complex sentence.
   While the old Beetle had its engine in the rear, the new Beetle has its engine in the front.

4. The "Bug" is a small car.

   It is fun to drive.

   Use a coordinating conjunction in a compound sentence.
   The "Bug" is a small car, but it is fun to drive.

   Use a coordinating conjunction in a compound predicate.
   The "Bug" is small and fun to drive.

   Use a subordinating conjunction in a complex sentence.
   Although the "Bug" is a small car, it is fun to drive.

5. The original Bug had an air-cooled engine.

   The new Beetle has a water-cooled engine.

   Use a coordinating conjunction in a compound sentence.
   The original Bug had an air-cooled engine, yet the new Beetle has a water-cooled engine.

   Use a subordinating conjunction in a complex sentence.
   While the original Bug had an air-cooled engine, the new Beetle has a water-cooled engine.

6. The new Beetle has a small engine.

   It is economical to drive.

   Use a coordinating conjunction in a compound sentence.
   The new Beetle has a small engine, so it is economical to drive.

   Use a coordinating conjunction in a compound predicate.
   The new Beetle has a small engine and is economical to drive.

   Use a subordinating conjunction in a complex sentence.
   Since the new Beetle has a small engine, it is economical to drive.

7. The earlier Beetle came in a large number of colors over the years.

   The new Beetle is offered in far fewer colors.

   Use a coordinating conjunction in a compound sentence.
   The earlier Beetle came in a large number of colors over the years, but the new Beetle is offered in far fewer colors.

   Use a subordinating conjunction in a complex sentence.
   The earlier Beetle came in a large number of colors over the years, while the new Beetle is offered in far fewer colors.

8. Earlier models of the Beetle cost about three thousand dollars.

   The new Beetle costs more than seventeen thousand dollars.

   Use a coordinating conjunction in a compound sentence.
   Earlier models of the Beetle cost about three thousand dollars, yet the new Beetle costs more than seventeen thousand dollars.

   Use a subordinating conjunction in a complex sentence.
   Even though earlier models of the Beetle cost about three thousand dollars, the new Beetle costs more than seventeen thousand dollars.

9. The sport model even boasts a turbo engine.

   It costs close to twenty-five thousand dollars.

   Use a coordinating conjunction in a compound sentence.
   The sport model even boasts a turbo engine, and it costs close to twenty-five thousand dollars.

   Use a coordinating conjunction in a compound predicate.
   The sport model even boasts a turbo engine and costs close to twenty-five thousand dollars.

   Use a subordinating conjunction in a complex sentence.
   Because the sport model even boasts a turbo engine, it costs close to twenty-five thousand dollars.

10. The old Beetle was most popular with young people.

The new Beetle is most popular with young people and those who grew up with the Beetle in the 1960's.

Use a coordinating conjunction in a compound sentence.

The old Beetle was most popular with young people, and the new Beetle is most popular with young people and those who grew up with the Beetle in the 1960s.

Use a subordinating conjunction in a complex sentence.

While the old Beetle was most popular with young people, the new Beetle is most popular with young people and those who grew up with the Beetle in the 1960s.

Review Exercise **20.8**   **Editing to combine sentences**

There are eighteen sentences in this passage. Rewrite the passage by combining sentences so that there are twelve sentences or fewer. Answers will vary.

A Good Night's Sleep

Sleeping well is difficult for many people. Over thirty percent of the population *, and*

is believed to have trouble sleeping at night. Sleep problems can be related to *While*

age. Problems can also be caused by medications, alcohol, or caffeine. Lifestyle *, P*

plays a part in how we get to sleep. Some people don't get much exercise. They may *, so*

have too much energy left at the end of the day to fall asleep.

Experts offer some guidelines on how to get a good night's sleep. People should

maintain a regular time to go to bed. They should also get up at the same time *and*

every day. A regular exercise schedule can help. Drinking alcohol or smoking *While* *,*

cigarettes can hurt. It's important to establish relaxing rituals before bed. Some *, and*

people take a bath or have a cup of non-caffeine tea. People should get up after

twenty minutes of not falling asleep. ~~They should~~ do something quiet like read. They *and*

will feel drowsy soon. Sleep is too important to miss.

Review Exercise **20.9**   **Editing your own writing**

Revise a journal entry by using sentence combining to reduce its length. Use a different colored pen to cross out words and add conjunctions and commas. Write "sentence combining" in the upper right-hand corner of the page to let your instructor know that you have edited the entry by combining sentences.

Review Exercise **Writing practice**

Write a one-page journal entry in which you respond to the following writing prompt.

Tell about one good or bad experience you have had with a doctor or medical facility.

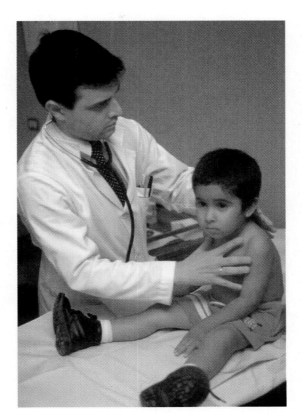

Chapter 21

Sentence Variety

In this chapter you will learn to vary sentences by

- Varying the beginnings of sentences
- Varying the lengths of sentences
- Varying the placement of important information

Communicating effectively in writing requires getting and holding the reader's attention. In written communication, unlike spoken communication, the writer is not present with the reader. Since writers cannot use physical actions like hand gestures and voice volume, they must use other means to keep the reader focused on the writing.

Good writers continually change sentence patterns and wording to keep their writing fresh and interesting for the reader. The sentence variety techniques you learn here are used during the writing and revision process. You will become sensitive to the patterns in your writing and practice varying the patterns in order to keep your writing engaging.

Read the paragraph below that Tony wrote and his revision after using the sentence variety techniques.

Tony: I wrote this paragraph for a cooking class that I am taking. When I read the paragraph out loud, it sounded choppy and simple. I knew that I had included the information I wanted, but something wasn't right about the way the way it sounded.

Good Cooks

Home cooks have the same goals as professional chefs. Home cooks demand top-quality ingredients. Home cooks are concerned with how a meal looks when it is served. They want it to taste delicious too. They carefully prepare the meal by following the recipe. They also may modify it some for their families. Home cooks and professional chefs are similar.

Group Activity 21.1 **Two members should read Tony's paragraph out loud to the group. (Often you can actually hear the poor sentence variety.) Discuss Tony's comment that the paragraph sounds choppy and simple. Do you agree? What would you do to fix the paragraph?**

There are three basic sentence variety strategies that writers use to make their ideas flow for the reader:

1. Vary sentence beginnings

2. Vary the length of sentences

3. Vary the placement of important information in sentences

You will practice each strategy, but study Tony's revision using the sentence variety techniques.

Tony: My instructor found the content of my paragraph interesting, and she liked the details I included. She pointed out, however, that I started most of the sentences with the same words. I also used sentences of about the same length. The important information was at the end of every sentence, and each of my sentences was a simple sentence. I used the sentence variety techniques to improve my paragraph without changing any of the ideas.

Good Cooks

Good home cooks have the same goals as professional chefs. They demand top-quality ingredients. The home chefs are concerned with how a meal looks when it is served, and they want it to taste delicious too. Although home cooks carefully prepare the meal by following the recipe, they also may modify it some for their families. The amateur and the professional are similar.

Group Activity **21.2**   **One member should read the revised paragraph out loud to the group. Does the paragraph flow better and sound less choppy than the first draft? Is there more rhythm to the sentences? Try reading the first draft again and then the revision. Which would receive a better grade?**

Sentence Variety Techniques

WE: 3.3

Vary the Beginnings of Sentences

One of the easiest ways to give your sentences variety is to use different words to begin each sentence. When sentences begin with the same words, the writing can seem boring. In general, do not start any two consecutive sentences with the same words.

Alicia: This is the first draft of a report that I wrote for my merchandising class. I know that I repeated the name Barbie at the beginning of each sentence.

The Barbie Doll

Barbie is the most popular doll in the world. Barbie made her debut in 1959. Barbie was the brainchild of the wife of a toy company executive. Barbie was named for their daughter. Barbie's boyfriend was named for their son Ken. Barbie has changed a lot over the years. Barbie has had over 80 careers. Barbie has been a fashion model, a soccer player, and even a presidential candidate.

The following methods can be used to vary sentence beginnings.

Use a Synonym (a Word with the Same Meaning)
Use different words with the same meaning for repeated words at the beginning of sentences.

> Barbie is the most popular doll in the world. **The toy** made her debut in 1959. **The plastic doll** was the brainchild of the wife of a toy company executive.

Practice **Cross out the words in italics and replace them with synonyms. No two consecutive sentences should start with the same words.** Answers will vary.

Motorists
Drivers must not drink and drive. *Drivers* who drink are endangering their lives and
Vehicle operators   Motorists
others. *Drivers* who drink have slower reflexes. *Drivers* may not be able to stop in

time when the car in front of them stops.

Use a Pronoun
Use a pronoun (*he, she, it, they,* etc.) that takes the place of the subject of the previous sentence.

> *Example:*

> Barbie was named for their daughter. **Her** boyfriend was named for their son Ken. **She** has changed a lot over the years.

Practice 21.4 **Cross out the words in italics and replace them with pronouns. No two consecutive sentences should start with the same words.**

It
Swimming is great exercise. *Swimming* uses all the major muscles. Swimmers exer-
They
cise arms, legs, and back. *Swimmers* also condition their hearts and lungs.

Use a Transition
Transitions or transitional expressions make the relationship between sentences clear and help the writing flow smoothly.
Common transitions and transitional expressions: first, finally, also, moreover, however, therefore, in fact, for example

For a complete list of conjunctive adverbs and transitional expressions, see Chapter 17, page 222. Note that a comma follows a transition or transitional expression when it introduces a sentence.

> Barbie has changed a lot over the years. **In fact**, Barbie has had over 80 careers. **For example**, Barbie has been a fashion model, a soccer player, and even a presidential candidate.

Practice **Fill in the blanks with transitions or transitional expressions. No two consecutive sentences should start with the same words.**

Registering on line for classes is easier than doing it in person. __For example__, registering on line can be done any time of the day or night. __Also__, on line registering can be accomplished anywhere there is a computer with Internet access.

Students only need their student identification number to register by computer. <u>Otherwise</u>, students will have to visit an advisor on campus before school begins.

Group Activity **Read aloud Alicia's revision and compare it to her first version. Why does it sound more like college writing?**

The Barbie Doll

Barbie is the most popular doll in the world. **The toy** made her debut in 1959. **The plastic doll** was the brainchild of the wife of a toy company executive. Barbie was named for their daughter. **Her** boyfriend was named for their son Ken. **She** has changed a lot over the years. **In fact,** Barbie has had over 80 careers. **For example,** Barbie has been a fashion model, a soccer player, and even a presidential candidate.

Practice 21.7 **Rewrite Tony's paragraph using the techniques for varying sentence beginnings. No two consecutive sentences should start with the same words.** Answers will vary.

Tony: Here are some ways I figured out to replace *flag* as the first word of every sentence:

1. Use synonyms for *flag*: Old Glory, the stars and stripes, our flag.

2. Use the pronoun it for flag.

3. Use transitions like *also*, *moreover*, and *in addition* at the beginning of sentences.

Proper Respect

The American flag should be respected. ~~The flag~~ ^{Our} should only be flown from sunrise to sunset. ~~The flag~~ ^{It} can only be flown at night if properly lit. ~~The flag~~ ^{Old Glory} should always be displayed with the blue field in the upper left corner. ^{In addition,} The flag should not be allowed to touch anything beneath it. ~~The flag~~ ^{Moreover, it} should be kept clean and repaired. ~~The flag~~ ^{Stars and Stripes} can be donated to a veterans' group when it frays for proper disposal.

 WE: 3.18

Vary Sentence Length

Another easy way to improve sentence variety is to vary the lengths of sentences. In general, you should alternate long sentences with short ones. When most of the sentences are short, the writing will sound simple and choppy. You can use the sentence combining techniques you learned about in Chapter 20 to make some of the sentences longer. When all the sentences are long, break some of them into smaller sentences. Alternating long and short sentences will give your writing a rhythm that is pleasing to read.

Dan: This paragraph sounds choppy, and I know that I need to get better sentence variety when I revise it.

The Spy Museum

The International Spy Museum celebrates spying. It is located in Washington, D.C., on the Mall. The museum is near the FBI headquarters. It contains a fascinating collection. There are poison pens and two-way mirrors. The telephone bugs were used in the Soviet Union. It also includes surveillance cameras and a spy satellite. The most interesting exhibit is an interactive display of disguises. Visitors can try on fake mustaches and hairpieces. The museum proves that espionage is an art full of gadgets of deception.

Group Activity 21.8 **Each member of the group should read the paragraph aloud. Do you agree with Dan that it sounds choppy? Discuss ways to make the sentences flow more smoothly.**

The surest way to vary sentence length is to use a variety of sentence types in your writing.

Simple sentence = one independent clause
Compound sentence = two independent clauses
Complex sentence = one independent clause + one (or more) dependent clauses
Compound-complex sentence = two independent clauses + one (or more) dependent clauses

Complex sentence: Since it is located on the Mall in Washington, D.C., the museum is near the FBI headquarters.

Compound sentence: There are poison pens and two-way mirrors, and the telephone bugs were used in the Soviet Union.

Compound-complex sentence: Although it also includes surveillance cameras and a spy satellite, the most interesting exhibit is an interactive display of disguises, and visitors can try on fake mustaches and hairpieces.

Group Activity 21.9 **Read aloud Dan's revision and compare it to his first version. Why does it sound less choppy and flow better?**

The Spy Museum

The International Spy Museum celebrates spying. Since it is located in Washington, D.C., the museum is near the FBI headquarters. There are poison pens and two-way mirrors, and the telephone bugs were used in the Soviet Union. Although it also includes surveillance cameras and a spy satellite, the most interesting exhibit is an interactive display of disguises, and visitors can try on fake mustaches and hairpieces. The museum proves that espionage is an art full of gadgets of deception.

Practice 21.10 **Rewrite Beth's paragraph using the techniques for varying sentence lengths. No two consecutive sentences should be the same sentence type.** Answers will vary.

Beth: Here are the ways I thought about combining sentences in my paragraph to vary the sentence lengths:

1. Combine sentences 2 and 3 into a complex sentence starting with *Because*.

2. Combine sentences 4 and 5 into a compound sentence.

3. Combine sentences 6 and 7 and 8 into a compound-complex sentence.

Honeybees

Honeybees may be the most important insects in the world. (2) ~~They~~ ^{Because} pollinate almost every food crop, (3) Most of our food would not grow without the help of bees. (4) Farmers have used honeybees for millions of years, ^{, and} (5) Bees were brought to this continent by the earliest settlers. (6) ^{Because} Bees also give us their honey and wax, (7) Bee pollen and bee vitamins have become popular, ^{, and} (8) Even bee venom is being used to treat ailments. (9) The honeybee may be man's best friend.

WE: 3.20

Vary Placement of Important Information

Readers become sensitive to patterns in writing. If the important information is always located at the end of the sentence, then they may stop reading the entire sentence and just skim the writing for information. Therefore, it is important to vary the placement of important information.

Dan: When I wrote my paper for my health class, I knew that I'd fallen into the pattern of placing the important information at the end of each sentence.

Heart Disease

Medicine has pinpointed the risk factors for heart attacks. First of all, there is age. Heart failure occurs overwhelmingly in those sixty-five and older. People are at risk when they have a history of heart disease in their family. Another cause of heart attacks is cholesterol. People are at risk with high cholesterol and low HDL cholesterol. Other risk factors include high blood pressure and diabetes. Finally, heart disease can be caused by smoking and obesity. Most of the causes of heart disease we can't change, but some we can.

Group Activity 21.11   **Read the paragraph above out loud. Underline the important information in each sentence. This information names the risk factors. How might the writer move some of the information to the beginning or middle of sentences?**

One way to change the placement of important information is to rearrange sentences.

Move important words and ideas to the beginning of some sentences, and combine some sentences to include information in the middle of sentences.

First of all, **age** is predictor of who will have heart disease. **Those sixty-five and older** are in danger of heart failure.

Practice 21.12   **Rewrite the sentence so that the words in italics are at the beginning of the sentence.**

1. People are at risk *when they have a history of heart disease in their family.*

   When they have a history of heart disease in their family, <u>people are at risk</u>   .

2. Another cause of heart attacks is *cholesterol.*

   Cholesterol <u>is another cause of heart attacks</u>   .

3. People are at risk with *high cholesterol and low HDL cholesterol.*

   High cholesterol and low HDL cholesterol <u>put people at risk</u>   .

4. Other risk factors include *high blood pressure and diabetes.*

   High blood pressure and diabetes <u>are other risk factors</u>   .

5. Finally, heart disease can be caused by *smoking and obesity.*

   Finally, smoking and obesity <u>can cause heart disease</u>   .

Practice 21.13   **Rewrite Dan's paragraph using the techniques for varying the placement of important information.** Answers will vary.

Dan: Some of the new guidelines from the end of sentences should be placed at the beginning or in the middle of sentences. For example, in sentence 3 *the saturated fats and cholesterol* should be placed at the beginning of the sentence to add variety. In sentence 5, *grains, dried beans, fruits, and vegetables* could come at the beginning or in the middle of the sentence instead of at the end. Sentence 6 also could have the important information come nearer the beginning of the sentence.

Controlling Cholesterol

New guidelines from the government are aimed at helping people control

cholesterol, which is a major cause of heart disease. (2) First, everyone twenty and

Saturated fats and cholesterol should be
older should be tested for cholesterol. (3) People should reduce the saturated fats
reduced in people's diet.
and cholesterol in their diet. (4) They may need to cut down on the fast foods and

F
meats they eat. (5) Also, ~~they should eat~~ fiber foods like grains, dried beans, fruits,

help control cholesterol. Losing weight is important for over-
and vegetables. (6) Overweight people should lose weight. (7) Proper management
weight people.
of cholesterol will reduce the risk of heart disease.

Review Exercise 21.14   **Revising for sentence variety**

Rewrite the following paragraph using the sentence variety techniques. Answers will vary.

The Highwaymen

A group of African-American artists called the Highwaymen have become

popular with art collectors. The group created art back in the 1960s and 70s. , ', and ~~The~~

~~group~~ got its name because the artists sold their paintings from the trunks of their cars. ~~They~~ parked along the major highways of south Florida and sold to tourists.

; for example,

They painted nature scenes of Florida/They drew palm trees, billowy clouds, and

sunsets on the beach. They also painted pictures filled with marshes and cypress

, but now

trees. ~~They~~ sold their paintings for as little as ten or twenty dollars./ ~~Now~~ the work of

these artists commands thousands of dollars.

Review Exercise **21.15**   **Editing your own writing**

Revise a journal entry using the sentence variety techniques. Use a different colored pen to rewrite the entry so that no two consecutive sentences start with the same words, sentences are of different lengths, and the placement of important information is varied. Write "sentence variety" in the upper right-hand corner of the page to let your instructor know that you have edited the entry by combining sentences.

Review Exercise **21.16**   **Writing practice**

Write a one-page journal entry in which you respond to the following writing prompt. Try to use the sentence variety techniques to vary the sentences.

Choose a senior citizen you know and explain what you have learned from this person. Or explain why the elderly should be respected in our culture.

Part IV
Readings

Successful Reading Strategies

You will learn a variety of active reading techniques including:

- SQ3R
- Cooperative learning strategies
- Using a Reader's Journal

All of your college classes will require that you read and comprehend material from textbooks and a variety of other sources. Reading means more than passing your eyes over the words on a page. It means understanding the content well enough to be able to explain it. This chapter will introduce you to a variety of active reading techniques that will help you become a more successful reader. We suggest you use one or more of the techniques with each reading you are assigned this semester. Even though not every class will allow you to use the cooperative learning techniques we introduce you to, you can apply these techniques out of class with a study partner or study group. You can also learn to apply many of these techniques individually to become a more effective reader.

Active Reading

Active reading means just that—being active as you read. Most students find that to understand and remember what they have read, they must "do it, say it, and write it." Let's take a simple example.

Read this list of ten words once or twice.

smell	refrigerator	fountain	teddy bear	sand
fireman	rose	milk	beach	fly

Now cover the words and see how many of the words you can write from memory.

Now read this second list of ten words once to yourself. Next, read the words aloud. Last but not least, write each word once.

starfish	milkshake	car	tree	fountain
monkey	footstool	pear	lamp	taste

Now, cover the words and see how many you can write from memory.

If you are like most people, you could remember more words after you said them aloud and wrote them. "Do it, say it, write it" is a tried and true method of learning material, and you should apply this principle to your reading.

Do it: Apply the principles you learn in this chapter to your reading. Read every word of a selection and look up any words you are not familiar with. Identify the main idea of each paragraph and of the entire selection. Review what you have learned when you finish reading the selection.

Say it: Read the title, headings, subheadings, and any end-of-reading-questions aloud. Try to turn the headings into questions that you ask aloud. Look for answers as you read.

Write it: Take a pencil or pen in hand before you start reading, and use it to write down questions and comments in the margin of your text. Underline words, write question marks in the margins, and write out one-sentence summaries of each paragraph.

Working with a group on reading assignments will help you see how effective the "Do it, say it, write it" rule is in helping you to understand and remember what you read. The rule can be just as effective when you practice it alone.

SQ3R

You may or may not already be familiar with SQ3R from taking a reading class. SQ3R is an acronym (a word made up of the first letters of a phrase) that will help you remember the steps to active reading. SQ3R stands for

Survey

Question

Read

Recall

Review

These five steps will help you become a better reader:

Step 1: Survey
Look through the entire reading selection and preview what the piece will be about. Try to get a general idea of what the piece covers.

Read the title. What does the title tell you about the piece? Make a guess about what the piece will be about based on the title.

Read the summary, if there is one, or the introduction. Can you pick out the author's main idea statement? After reading the summary or introduction, what do you think the piece will be about?

Read all headings and subheadings, if there are any. Jot down one or two words for each heading and subheading. What do the headings and subheadings tell you about the organization of the piece? Can you see a rough outline of the piece through the headings?

Look at all graphs, charts, diagrams, and/or graphics. What are the graphics about? What do they tell you about the piece? Notice words that are in italics or bold. Are certain vocabulary words defined? Are there end-of-chapter questions? Read the questions to see what you will need to answer as you read the selection.

Step 2: Question

Turn any headings into questions and look for answers as you read the selection. For example, a heading such as "Run-ons" could be turned into the question, "What is a run-on?" The more you are actively involved in looking for answers to questions, the more you are likely to remember.

If there are no headings, ask yourself questions about each section of the reading. For example, if you are reading a narrative about a series of events, pause every paragraph or two and ask yourself, "What has happened so far?" Summarize the reading to yourself one paragraph at a time. Ask yourself how what you are reading relates to what you already know or have experienced.

Step 3: Read

Read the selection one paragraph at a time, answering the questions you have created for yourself and summarizing the main idea of each paragraph. Ask yourself, "What is this paragraph about?" Try to write a one-sentence summary of each paragraph. As you read, keep asking yourself how each paragraph fits into the overall structure of the essay. How does each paragraph support the main idea of the essay? As you read, keep revising or refining your idea of the main point of the essay.

Step 4: Recall

At the end of each section or at the end of the reading, try to summarize the main points of the reading. Look back at the questions you created based on the headings and see if you can answer the questions without looking back at the passage itself. It helps to answer the questions aloud.

Step 5: Review

Identify what you think the main idea of the essay is. Does the author state the main idea or thesis in a sentence or two? If so, underline it. If not, write the main idea in your own words. See how well you were able to answer the questions you created before you began reading. Answer any questions at the end of the chapter or selection. Look back at the reading to answer any questions you are uncertain of.

Group Activity **1**   **In pairs or groups of three, go through the five SQ3R steps together for an assigned reading.**

Step 1: Each group member skims the assigned reading. Group members take turns sharing the information they gathered in doing so. Each shares his or her prediction of what the reading selection will cover.

Step 2: Each group member writes out questions from the boldfaced headings and attempts to answer the question. Group members take turns sharing their questions and answers.

Step 3: Each group member reads the selection silently, looking for answers to the questions generated by the group.

Step 4: Each group member writes out the major points of the selection. Group members take turns sharing their summary of important points.

Step 5: The group discusses the differences in the summary of major points given by each group member and looks back at the reading selection to find answers and check for accuracy and balance. The group then agrees on a summary of major points.

> ### Problem Solving
>
> Cedric has difficulty concentrating when he reads. His mind wanders the moment he starts reading, and as a result, he doesn't remember much of what he has read. His strategy for dealing with this problem is to go to class without having done the reading, listen to the class discuss the reading, and complete the assignment based on the class discussion. What advice can you offer Cedric?

Cooperative Learning Strategies

The following group activity is intended to introduce you to active reading techniques that will help you learn to be a more effective reader. Even though you will not be able to use these cooperative learning strategies for every reading and in every class, once you learn the techniques, you should be able to apply them on your own.

Group Activity **2**   **Read and summarize in pairs**

Procedure: In pairs, go through the following steps for an assigned reading.

1. Read the first paragraph silently. Student A is the first summarizer and Student B is the accuracy checker.

2. The summarizer explains the content of the paragraph in his or her own words. The accuracy checker listens carefully, corrects any misstatements, questions the meaning of unfamiliar vocabulary, and adds anything that has been left out.

3. Move to the next paragraph, switch roles, and repeat the procedure. Continue until you have completed the assigned passage.

4. Answer the comprehension and discussion questions individually, and share your responses and clarify differences. Together you should summarize and agree on the overall meaning of the material.

5. An alternative to this procedure is for each student to read and summarize each paragraph at home and share their summaries with a partner in class.

Using a Reader's Journal

What Is a Reader's Journal?

We all have a little voice in our heads that comments on what we are reading. The voice might make comments such as "I like this," "I don't get it," "No way, I don't buy that," or "That reminds me of. . . ." Keeping a reader's journal is a way of harnessing and exploring that little voice in your head.

The purpose of a reader's journal is to allow the reader to respond to the ideas encountered in reading. The reader's journal engages the reader in a dialogue with what the writer says (content) and how the writer says it (form).

Dan: Writing a reader's journal helps me figure out the readings. I try to do a journal entry on each of the assigned readings—I just let myself think out loud on paper, and the interesting thing is that when I go to class the next day, I find I have a lot more to say than I would have otherwise. I'm usually pretty quiet in class, but keeping a reader's journal helps me have something to contribute.

One use for a reader's journal is to explore what you like and don't like about the essays you read, what seems effective and what doesn't. Think about the strategies the writer uses and how you might use similar strategies in your own writing. Another advantage of a journal is that you can come up with ideas that you might develop in a paper. As you read, ask yourself what connections you can make to your own experiences. Often such ideas can be expanded and developed into an essay of your own.

Questions to Ask about Readings

1. How does the writer begin the essay? Does the writer begin with a story or something personal or give background on the subject?

2. How does the writer get your attention and interest?

3. How does the writer help you see the scene he or she is describing?

4. Does he or she appeal to the senses?

5. What sort of language and images does he or she use?

6. How does the writer help you understand his or her ideas?

7. Does the writer use examples?

8. How does the writer end the essay?

9. If you had written about the same subject, what would you have done differently?

Peer Reader's Journal Selections

Here are example reader's journal entries from the four student peers. Tony and Alicia share reader's journal entries in which they respond to professional essays contained in *Writer's Resources: From Sentence to Paragraph*. You may be asked to respond to the professional or student essays in a similar fashion. These examples are intended to help you understand how to use a reader's journal.

Alicia on "Papa, the Philosopher"

I guess I identified with this reading because my family, like Buscaglia's, is foreign. As a kid I was embarrassed because my parents didn't speak English at home, so I never wanted any of my friends to come home with me. I spoke English at school and didn't have an accent, so I didn't want my friends to know my parents barely spoke English. My father was killed in a car accident when I was seven, and after that my mom had to go to work. Because she wasn't there when my sisters and I got home from school, we weren't allowed to have friends over. When I was in high school, I remember being ashamed of what my mother did for a living (she is a beautician). Most of my friends' moms were professionals or didn't have to work. It's weird being proud of your mom and ashamed of her at the same time. I admire her for how hard she's worked, but I was afraid my friends wouldn't see through her rough exterior to the heart of gold beneath. It was stupid of me, but I guess that's part of growing up. It made me feel better that Buscaglia could admit that he was embarrassed by his father even though he clearly admires his father's wisdom. He hits the nail on the head when he talks about kids wanting to be like everyone else rather than be different. As you get older, you start valuing the differences more.

Tony, on "Boys to Men"

This reading dealt with issues that hit pretty close to home for me.

I wish I had had friends like the three guys in "Boys to Men." None of my friends wanted to go to college, so it was hard to work up much of a head of steam to do anything but hang out when I was around them. My sister is the only one who encouraged me to make something of myself. She kept telling me I had lots of potential and I could be anything I wanted to be (even when everyone else had pretty much given up on me). She got me a job in the restaurant she managed, and she kept encouraging me to go to college. She even offered to help me with tuition. Her encouragement helped me believe I could be more than just a good waiter or bartender. I can see from my own life how important it is to have someone to believe in and encourage you.

Writing Topic **3**   Write a reader's journal entry on one of the readings in Part IV.

Measles, Mumps, and Chicken Pox

Faith Andrews Bedford

Imagination takes wing even when the body is confined to bed.

1   A winter rain slides slowly down Sarah's bedroom window. She watches as the school bus stops at the end of our farm road, and she waves as her sister boards. It is the third day of a sick-enough-to-be-in-bed illness, and Sarah is tired of her confinement. She turns her face away from the steam-fogged window, asking, "Mommy, were you ever this sick when you were little?"

2   I smooth wisps of hair off her hot forehead and begin telling her stories of the years when childhood illnesses kept boys and girls home from school for weeks at a time. For me, mumps came first. The sight of my chipmunk face in the mirror made me laugh, but the pain of swallowing even tiny sips of liquid brought tears. Meals were served to me on a tray whose four legs folded down to make a little table over my knees. Hand-painted leaves and flowers decorated the edges of the pale-yellow tray, which my grandmother had once used for her children. Sometimes, next to my dinner of consommé and weak tea, a fresh flower would stand in a vase.

3   Mother made the long trip to our village library twice a week and brought books home for me by the armload. When I was particularly feverish, she would read to me, her soothing voice rising and then fading as I drifted in and out of sleep. I loved to read everything from fairy tales to Nancy Drew mysteries and worked my way through every book about horses that the library owned.

4   I had saved my allowance for months to buy three little model horses: a palomino mare, her colt, and a rearing black stallion. Then I turned my rumpled blankets into a miniature landscape. The plastic horses galloped over the high mountain made by my knees, wound their way through wrinkled foothills, and peacefully grazed in the smooth, flat expanse at the foot of the bed. On a card table that Dad had set up beside my bed, I made a stable for my horse family amid paper dolls, coloring books, and the radio on which I listened to "The Lone Ranger" and "Roy Rogers."

replenished: *to furnish a new supply*

heady: *strong, intoxicating*

masking: *hiding*

pervading: *spread throughout*

5   Measles followed the mumps, and Mother's arsenal of amusements was replenished.* The little four-legged tray became an art studio where I turned clay into turtles, bowls, people, and, of course, horses. Paint by Numbers kits filled my room with the heady* smell of turpentine and linseed oil (only partially masking* the pervading* aromas of mustard plasters, Vicks VapoRub, and eucalyptus oil). Mother taught me to knit and to crochet. The card table soon became a jumble of knitting needles and balls of yarn, paintbrushes and cups of water, scissors and crayons.

buoyed: *floating on or held up by*

frantically: *wild with worry*

6   With measles came fevers so high that my room was darkened and my eyes were bandaged shut. Grandmother sent over dishes designed to tempt my almost-nonexistent appetite—Floating Island, a delicate mound of meringue buoyed* by a sea of lemon custard, and baked custard drizzled with maple syrup from the sugarhouse down the road. She and my parents frantically* coaxed me to drink endless glasses of water after the doctor mentioned the word hospital.

7   Lying in darkness, I made up stories that I intended to write and to illustrate with the watercolors I knew were somewhere on the card table. In the meantime, I learned to wiggle my ears and perfected my whistling.

quell: *stop*

8   When chicken pox appeared, Mother turned into an artist. To quell* the terrible itching, she painted my spots with calamine lotion and turned me into a clown. It was my responsibility to write down the total number of spots on a notepad. When the count began to drop, she told me, I would soon be well.

9   Sarah hardly remembers her own bout with chicken pox and, fortunately for her, measles and mumps are no longer a serious threat. As I help her sit up to drink orange juice mixed with ginger ale, she asks, "Is this one of Grandy's recipes?" Yes, I reply, recalling the many combinations of fruit juice and ginger-ale Mother created to get me to drink the liquids so important to my recovery—concoctions made even more special by the addition of a straw.

10   My children have a special straw that twirls and curls around and around, finally delivering juice to the thirsty patient. We use it only when someone is sick. As I set the glass back down on the table, I realize that among my three children I've only had to use this straw five times in the past 16 years; modern medicine has certainly worked miracles. By the time Sarah has children of her own, perhaps even chicken pox will be a thing of the past.

11   Sarah has only been sick for two days; in two more, she will probably be well. Not for her the weeks in bed, darkened rooms, hot plasters on the chest. She reaches over for the little horse family and begins to trot the palomino mare and her colt down one knee and up the other. I reach for the black stallion and begin to gallop him across the quilt to meet them. When I was 14, I packed these little horses carefully away, figuring that I would be a mother someday and would need a way to amuse my children when they were sick.

12   "Mommy?" Sarah calls after me as I head downstairs to prepare her a lunch of consommé, rice pudding, and chamomile tea. "This afternoon can you bring up your scrap basket so we can make some blankets for the little horses?"

13   "Sure," I call back. Mother and I once created a stable for my horses from an old shoe box. Perhaps Sarah and I will make one, too. Then I will teach her how to wiggle her ears.

Comprehension Questions

1. Sarah is the author's only child.

   T/(F)

2. What illnesses did the author have as a child?

   A. mumps
   B. measles
   C. chicken pox
   (D). all of the above

3. Fever accompanied which of the author's childhood illnesses?

   A. mumps
   (B). measles
   C. chicken pox
   D. polio

4. What toys did the author save for her children to play with?

   A. dolls
   B. boats
   Ⓒ horses
   D. paints

5. The author describes childhood illnesses as

   A. more severe today than when she was a child.
   Ⓑ less severe today than when she was a child.
   C. about the same as when she was a child.

Discussion Questions

1. What actions did the author take that reveal the author's love for her child, and the author's mother's love for her?

2. What positive, comforting images does the author recall from her childhood illnesses?

3. How does the author make her experiences of childhood illness vivid for the reader?

4. How did the author amuse herself when she was ill?

5. How do your experiences of childhood illness or your children's differ from the author's?

Journal Topic

Describe an illness you experienced. Who cared for you? What did you do to amuse yourself? What special foods did you eat? How was your experience different from the experiences the author describes?

Writing Topics

1. Describe an illness that kept you home from school as a child.

2. What similarities and differences does the author describe in her childhood illnesses and her children's illnesses?

3. Do you agree or disagree with the author's assertion that childhood illnesses are less severe today than they once were? Are children healthier today or have the types of illnesses merely changed?

Papa, the Philosopher

Leo Buscaglia

deviate: *differ*
intensify: *become stronger*

animated: *lively*

apt: *likely*

stigma: *mark of shame*

distress: *discomfort, pain*

acutely: *sharply*

epithets: *negative terms used to characterize a person or thing*

prospect: *possibility*
distraught: *upset*

1   It's not easy being different, especially as a child. The normal process of growing up presents enough problems, but when we discover that we deviate* from the norm in some way, the problems can only intensify*.

2   There can be no doubt that my family was different. My parents spoke little English, and when they did, it was thick with Italian flavor. Our lifestyle was obviously unlike most others—a little bit of Mediterrania transferred to the shores of America. We ate different, exotic foods; our conversations were more animated*; our voices a bit louder; our gestures more generous. The world we lived in was decidedly more foreign.

3   As a young child I was neither aware nor concerned about our many differences. Children are naturally more accepting of things as they are, less apt* to notice, let alone judge, differences in people unless influenced by adults. But this changed as I grew to adolescence and entered junior high school.

4   At that time Papa and Mama, whom I have loved without question, suddenly became an embarrassment. Why couldn't they be like other parents? Why didn't they speak without the telltale accents? Why couldn't I have cornflakes for breakfast instead of hard rolls and caffe *latte?* Why couldn't I take peanut butter and jelly sandwiches in my school lunches rather than calamari? ("Yuck," the other kids would say, "Buscaglia eats octopus legs!") There simply seemed no way for me to escape the painful stigma* I felt in being Italian and the son of Tulio and Rosa. Buscaglia—even my name became a source of distress*.

5   It was common in those days to label Italians wops and dagos. (Look at him and watch a day go by!) I was never really certain what either of those terms meant, but I nevertheless felt their sting. This pain was acutely* felt one day as I prepared to leave school. I found myself unexpectedly surrounded by a group of boys shouting the familiar epithets*.

6   One of them threw a cake at me, the sugary icing splashing across my face, into my hair, and over my clothing. "Dirty dago!" they shouted. "Your dad's a Chicago gangster and your mom's a garlic licker and you're a son of a dirty wop. Why don't you all pack up and go back where you came from?"

7   It seemed an eternity before I was released from their circle of pushes and punches. Humiliated and in tears, I broke free and dashed home. As I ran, full of confusion, anger, and resentment, I realized I had not made a single attempt to fight back.

8   When I arrived home, I immediately headed for and locked myself in the bathroom, assuming that I would not be seen. I couldn't stand the prospect* of Mama or Papa finding me in my distraught* condition. I washed off the frosting that stuck to me like glue. I couldn't stop crying as tears mixed with my blood-smeared face. The frustration enraged and strangled me. I couldn't believe what had happened. It all seemed so very wrong, yet I felt helpless to do anything about it.

9   It was Papa who finally knocked on the bathroom door. "What are you doing in there? What's the matter?" he questioned. Only after much gentle persuasion did I finally unlatch the door and let him in.

10   "What happened?" he asked, taking me into his arms. "What's the matter? What is it?"

11   In his protective arms I allowed myself the release I sorely needed. I sobbed uncontrollably. He sat on the edge of the bathtub with me and waited for me to gain some control. A shattered ego takes much longer to heal than a bloody nose. "Now tell me what happened," he said.

12   I explained. When I finished the story, I waited. I expected Papa to make some healing comment or take some immediate defensive action that would soothe me and solve the problem. I envisioned* his taking off in search of the bullies who had hurt me, or at least finding their parents and demanding retribution*. But Papa didn't move.

envisioned: pictured

retribution: punishment, revenge

13   "I see," he said quietly. "It's finally happened. They finally found you. Those people who hurt us and make us cry. They don't know us, but they hate us all the same. Those cowards who are strong only in groups and pick on us because they know we're few and not likely to fight back. I know they hurt you, but what happened wasn't meant just for you. You just happened to come along. It could have been any one of us."

14   "I hate being Italian!" I confessed angrily. "I wish I could be *anything* else!"

15   Papa held me firmly, his voice now strong and threatening. "Never let me hear you say that again!" he said. "You should be proud to be what you are. Just think about it. America was discovered by and got its name from Italians. Italians make sweet music, sing gloriously, paint wonderful pictures, write great books, and build beautiful buildings. How can you not be proud to be an Italian? And you're extra lucky because you're American, too."

16   "But they don't know that," I objected. "I'd rather be like everyone else."

"Well, you're not like everyone else. God never intended us all to be the same. He made us all different so that we'd each be ourselves. Never be afraid of differences. Difference is good. Would you want to be like the boys who beat you up and called you names? Would you want to make others suffer and cry? Aren't you glad you're different from them?" I remember that I thought it was a weak argument, but I remained silent.

17   "Well, would you?" he insisted. "Would you want to be like them? Like the people who hurt you?"

18   "No."

19   "Then wipe your tears and be proud of who you are. You can be sure it won't be the last time you'll meet these people. They're everywhere. Feel sorry for them, but don't be afraid of them. We've got to be strong and always be proud of who we are and what we are. Then nobody can hurt us."

20   He dried my tears and washed my face. "Now," he said, "let's get some bread and butter and go eat in the garden."

21   Though I didn't find Papa's explanation very satisfying, it somehow made me feel better. Perhaps it was just that being heard, loved, and held made it seem enough. I was still frustrated about people who had the capacity* to be so cruel, who persisted* in using others as scapegoats* for their own inadequacies*, and letting them get away with it.

capacity: willingness, ability
persisted: continued
scapegoats: the ones bearing blame for others
inadequacies: weaknesses

22   Further experience has taught me that I was not alone, that these painful encounters—even worse—had happened to my Jewish friends, my Mexican friends, my black friends, my Catholic friends, my Protestant friends, my disabled friends.

23   Papa was right in teaching me that as long as there was ignorance there would be injustice, as long as there were those with unrecognizable

self-hate there would be persecution. It is an unfortunate fact of life that the scapegoats are almost always members of a minority group.

24   Still, Papa made loving the unlovable his greatest challenge. "Bring them home with you, *Felice*," he'd say. "When they know us, they won't be able to hate us anymore."

bigotry: *intolerance of differences*

intolerance: *inability to tolerate differences*

refuge: *hiding place*

25   Of course, Papa didn't solve the problems of bigotry* on that sunny California day when we ate bread and butter in the garden. But there was something in his explanation, a certain strength and determination, that has continued to help me to see intolerance* and discrimination for what they are: a refuge* for weakness and ignorance. Acceptance and understanding can be expected only from the strong.

Comprehension Questions

1. At the time of the incident that the author recounts, he is in

   A. elementary school.
   B. junior high.
   C. high school.
   D. college.

2. What nationality is the author's family?

   A. Russian
   B. Italian
   C. Spanish
   D. Romanian

3. What do the boys who surround the author after school throw on him?

   A. dirt
   B. tomatoes
   C. cake
   D. trash

4. What does Buscaglia's father recommend he do to the boys who assaulted him?

   A. beat them up
   B. report them to the police
   C. invite them home
   D. tell their parents

5. What does his father suggest they do after the assault?

   A. go to the movies
   B. eat bread and butter in the garden
   C. go to church
   D. cook a big meal

Discussion Questions

1. How does the author feel about his parents?

2. How does the author respond to his attackers?

3. How does his father respond?

4. What lesson about prejudice does the author learn from his father?

Journal Topics

1. Do you remember becoming aware of the differences between your family and others?

2. Do you remember being embarrassed by your parents?

Writing Topics

1. Have you ever been ridiculed or persecuted because you were stereotyped in some way? Describe the experience and your feelings.

2. Agree or disagree with the author's father's advice: "Be proud of who we are and what we are. Then nobody can hurt us."

3. The author learned to recognize "intolerance and discrimination for what they are: a refuge for weakness and ignorance. Acceptance and understanding can be expected only from the strong." Can you think of examples from your life or others that prove or disprove his conclusion?

Consider This

Jack Canfield

Effort only fully releases its reward after a person refuses to quit.   •   *Napoleon Hill*

History has demonstrated that the most notable winners usually encountered heart-breaking obstacles before they triumphed. They won because they refused to become discouraged by their defeats.   •   *B.C. Forbes*

1   Consider this:

2   Woody Allen—Academy Award-winning writer, producer and director— flunked motion picture production at New York University and the City College of New York. He also failed English at New York University.

3   Leon Uris, author of the bestseller *Exodus*, failed high school English three times.

4   When Lucille Ball began studying to be an actress in 1927, she was told by the head instructor of the John Murray Anderson Drama School, "Try any other profession. Any other."

5   In 1959, a Universal Pictures executive dismissed Clint Eastwood and Burt Reynolds at the same meeting with the following statement. To Burt Reynolds: "You have no talent." To Clint Eastwood: "You have a chip on your tooth, your Adam's apple sticks out too far and you talk too slow." As you no doubt know, Burt Reynolds and Clint Eastwood went on to become big stars in the movie industry.

6   In 1944, Emmeline Snively, director of the Blue Book Modeling Agency, told modeling hopeful Norma Jean Baker (Marilyn Monroe), "You'd better learn secretarial work or else get married."

7   Liv Ullman, who was nominated two times for the Academy Award for Best Actress, failed an audition for the state theater school in Norway. The judges told her she had no talent.

8   Malcolm Forbes, the late editor-in-chief of *Forbes* magazine, one of the most successful business publications in the world, failed to make the staff of the school newspaper when he was an undergraduate at Princeton University.

9   In 1962, four nervous young musicians played their first record audition for the executives of the Decca Recording Company. The executives were not impressed. While turning down this British rock group called the Beatles, one executive said, "We don't like their sound. Groups of guitars are on the way out."

10   Paul Cohen, Nashville "Artists and Repertoire Man" for Decca Records, while firing Buddy Holly from the Decca label in 1956, called Holly "the biggest no-talent I ever worked with." Twenty years later *Rolling Stone* called Holly, along with Chuck Berry, "the major influence on the rock music of the sixties."

11   In 1954, Jimmy Denny, manager of the Grand Ole Opry, fired Elvis Presley after one performance. He told Presley, "You ain't goin' nowhere . . . son. You ought to go back to drivin' a truck." Elvis Presley went on to become the most popular singer in America.

12   When Alexander Graham Bell invented the telephone in 1876, it did not ring off the hook with calls from potential backers. After making a demonstration call, President Rutherford Hayes said, "That's an amazing invention, but who would ever want to use one of them?"

13   Thomas Edison was probably the greatest inventor in American history. When he first attended school in Port Huron, Michigan, his teachers complained that he was "too slow" and hard to handle. As a result, Edison's mother decided to take her son out of school and teach him at home. The young Edison was fascinated by science. At the age of 10 he had already set up his first chemistry laboratory. Edison's inexhaustible energy and genius (which he reportedly defined as "1 percent inspiration and 99 percent perspiration") eventually produced in his lifetime more than 1,300 inventions.

14   When Thomas Edison invented the light bulb, he tried over 2,000 experiments before he got it to work. A young reporter asked him how it felt to fail so many times. He said, "I never failed once. I invented the light bulb. It just happened to be a 2,000-step process."

15   In the 1940's, another young inventor named Chester Carlson took his idea to 20 corporations, including some of the biggest in the country. They all turned him down. In 1947—after seven long years of rejections!—he finally got a tiny company in Rochester, New York, the Haloid Company, to purchase the rights to his electrostatic paper-copying process. Haloid became Xerox Corporation, and both it and Carlson became very rich.

16   John Milton became blind at age 44. Sixteen years later he wrote the classic *Paradise Lost*.

cellist: *one who plays a cello*

17   When Pablo Casals reached 95, a young reporter threw him the following question. "Mr. Casals, you are 95 and the greatest cellist* that ever lived. Why do you still practice six hours a day?" Mr. Casals answered, "Because I think I'm making progress."

18   After years of progressive hearing loss, by age 46 German composer Ludwig van Beethoven had become completely deaf. Nevertheless, he wrote his greatest music, including five symphonies, during his later years.

19   After having lost both legs in an air crash, British fighter pilot Douglas Bader rejoined the British Royal Air Force with two artificial limbs. During World War II he was captured by the Germans three times—and three times he escaped.

amputated: *cut off*

20   After having his cancer-ridden leg amputated,* young Canadian Terry Fox vowed to run on one leg from coast to coast the entire length of Canada to raise $1 million for cancer research. Forced to quit halfway when the cancer invaded his lungs, he and the foundation he started have raised over $20 million for cancer research.

21   Wilma Rudolph was the 20th of 22 children. She was born prematurely and her survival was doubtful. When she was 4 years old, she contracted double pneumonia and scarlet fever, which left her with a paralyzed left leg. At age 9, she removed the metal leg brace she had been dependent on and began to walk without it. By 13 she had developed a rhythmic walk, which doctors said was a miracle. That same year she decided to become a runner. She entered a race and came in last. For the next few years every

race she entered, she came in last. Everyone told her to quit, but she kept on running. One day she actually won a race. And then another. From then on she won every race she entered. Eventually this little girl, who was told she would never walk again, went on to win three Olympic gold medals.

> My mother taught me very early to believe I could achieve any accomplishment I wanted to. The first was to walk without braces.   •   *Wilma Rudolph*

22   Franklin D. Roosevelt was paralyzed by polio at the age of 39, and yet he went on to become one of America's most beloved and influential leaders. He was elected president of the United States four times.

23   Sarah Bernhardt, who is regarded by many as one of the greatest actresses that ever lived, had her leg amputated as a result of an injury when she was 70 years old, but she continued to act for the next eight years.

24   Louis L'Amour, successful author of over 100 western novels with over 200 million copies in print, received 350 rejections before he made his first sale. He later became the first American novelist to receive a special congressional gold medal in recognition of his distinguished career as an author and contributor to the nation through his historically based works.

collaborators: *those who work together*

25   In 1953, Julia Child and her two collaborators* signed a publishing contract to produce a book tentatively titled *French Cooking for the American Kitchen*. Julia and her colleagues worked on the book for five years. The publisher rejected the 850-page manuscript. Child and her partners worked for another year totally revising the manuscript. Again the publisher rejected it. But Julia Child did not give up. She and her collaborators went back to work again, found a new publisher and in 1961—eight years after beginning— they published *Mastering the Art of French Cooking*, which has sold more than 1 million copies. In 1966, *Time* magazine featured Julia Child on its cover. Julia Child is still at the top of her field almost 30 years later.

26   General Douglas MacArthur might never have gained power and fame without persistence. When he applied for admission to West Point, he was turned down, not once but twice. But he tried a third time, was accepted and marched into the history books.

demoted: *lowered in rank*

27   Abraham Lincoln entered the Blackhawk War as a captain. By the end of the war, he had been demoted* to the rank of private.

28   In 1952, Edmund Hillary attempted to climb Mount Everest, the highest mountain then known to humans—29,000 feet straight up. A few weeks after his failed attempt, he was asked to address a group in England. Hillary walked to the edge of the stage, made a fist and pointed at a picture of the mountain. He said in a loud voice, "Mount Everest, you beat me the first time, but I'll beat you the next time because you've grown all you are going to grow . . . but I'm still growing!" On May 29, only one year later, Edmund Hillary succeeded in becoming the first man to climb Mount Everest.

Journal Topic

1. How did you respond as you read this essay?

Discussion Questions

1. What was most surprising about the examples you read?

2. What point is Canfield supporting with all of these examples?

3. How effective and/or persuasive is his method of giving examples to support his thesis?

Writing Topics

1. Select one of the individuals Canfield highlights and explain why his or her story inspires you.

2. Do you know someone who has overcome obstacles to be successful? Tell his or her story.

3. What does it mean to be persistent?

4. How do you plan to overcome the obstacles you may face in your life?

5. Support Canfield's claim that many successful people have overcome obstacles by selecting three to five examples from his essay to illustrate his thesis.

The First Job

Sandra Cisneros

1   It wasn't as if I didn't want to work. I did. I had even gone to the social security office the month before to get my social security number. I needed money. The Catholic high school cost a lot, and Papa said nobody went to a public school unless you wanted to turn out bad.

2   I thought I'd find an easy job, the kind other kids had, working in the dime store or maybe a hotdog stand. And though I hadn't started looking yet, I thought I might the week after next. But when I came home that afternoon, all wet because Tito had pushed me into the open hydrant—only I had sort of let him—Mama called me into the kitchen before I could even go and change, and Aunt Lala was sitting there drinking her coffee with the spoon. Aunt Lala said she found a job for me at the Peter Pan Photo Finishers on North Broadway where she worked, and how old was I, and to show up tomorrow saying I was one year older, and that was that.

3   So the next morning I put on my navy blue dress that made me look older and borrowed money for lunch and the bus fee because Aunt Lala said I wouldn't get paid until next Friday, and I went in and saw the boss of Peter Pan Photo Finishers on North Broadway where Aunt Lala worked and lied about my age like she had told me to and sure enough, I started the same day.

4   In my job I had to wear white gloves. I was supposed to match the negatives with their prints, just look at the picture and look for the same on the negative strip, put it in the envelope, and do the next one. That's all. I didn't know where these envelopes were going. I just did what I was told.

5   It was real easy, and I guess I wouldn't have minded it except that you got tired after a while and I didn't know if I could sit down or not, and then I started sitting down only when the two ladies next to me did. After a while they started to laugh and came up to me and said that I could sit when I wanted to, and I said I knew.

6   When lunchtime came, I was scared to eat alone in the company lunchroom with all those men and ladies looking, so I ate real fast standing in one of the washroom stalls and had lots of time left over, so I went back to work early. But then break came, and not knowing where else to go, I went into the coatroom because there was a bench there.

7   I guess it was time for the night shift or the middle shift to arrive because a few people came and punched the time clock, and an older Oriental man said hello and we talked for a while about me just starting, and he said we could be friends and next time to go to the lunchroom and sit with him, and I felt better. He had nice eyes and I didn't feel so nervous anymore. Then he asked if I knew what day it was, and when I said I didn't, he said it was his birthday and would I please give him a birthday kiss. I thought I would because he was so old and just as I was about to put my lips on his cheek, he grabs my face with both hands and kisses me hard on the mouth and he doesn't let go.

Comprehension Questions

1. How does the author get her first job?
   A. through a friend
   B. through a newspaper advertisement

C. through her church

D. through an aunt

2. What is the author told to lie about when she applies for the job?

A. where she is from

B. her age

C. where she lives

D. her experience

3. Where does the author go to work?

A. a fast food restaurant

B. a drug store

C. a photo shop

D. a dry cleaners

4. Where does the author eat her lunch?

A. in a park

B. in the lunchroom

C. in a bathroom stall

D. in the cloakroom

5. Who does she meet in the coatroom during her break?

A. an elderly Oriental man

B. someone her own age

C. a helpful fellow employee

D. the manager

Discussion Questions

1. What do we know about where the author lives, who her parents are, what her society is like, how old she is, etc.? How do we know it?

2. What does the author's misuse of language (*real* instead of *really* in paragraphs 5 and 6) tell us about her as a girl?

3. What is the author's attitude about work before she starts? On her first day?

4. Describe the work the author does.

5. What does the author learn through her experiences?

Writing Topics

1. Describe your first job. What ideas did you have about a job before you started? How was the job different from what you expected?

2. Describe a boss you have had. What made that person a good or bad supervisor?

3. Describe the work you did. What made the work you did enjoyable or not enjoyable?

4. Describe a particularly memorable co-worker.

From *An American Childhood*

Annie Dillard

egoism: self-interest, focus on self

fancies: believes

paltry: unimportant

reason: the capacity for logical thought

1   The interior life is often stupid. Its egoism* blinds it and deafens it; its imagination spins out ignorant tales, fascinated. It fancies* that the western wind blows on the Self, and leaves fall at the feet of the Self for a reason, and people are watching. A mind risks real ignorance for the sometimes paltry* prize of an imagination enriched. The trick of reason* is to get the information to seize the actual world—if only from time to time.

2   When I was five, growing up in Pittsburgh in 1950, I would not go to bed willingly because something came into my room. This was a private matter between me and it. If I spoke of it, it would kill me.

3   Who could breathe as this thing searched for me over the very corners of the room? Who could ever breathe freely again? I lay in the dark.

4   My sister Amy, two years old, was asleep in the other bed. What did she know? She was innocent of evil. Even at two she composed herself attractively for sleep. She folded the top sheet tidily under her prettily outstretched arm; she laid her perfect head lightly on an unwrinkled pillow, where her thick curls spread evenly in rays like petals. All night long she slept smoothly in a series of pleasant and serene*, if artificial-looking, positions, a faint smile on her closed lips, as if she were posing for an ad for sheets. There was no messiness in her, no roughness for things to cling to, only a charming and charmed innocence that seemed then to protect her, an innocence I needed but couldn't muster*. Since Amy was asleep, furthermore, and since when I needed someone most I was afraid to stir enough to wake her, she was useless.

serene: peaceful

muster: raise

5   I lay alone and was almost asleep when the damned thing entered the room by flattening itself against the open door and sliding in. It was a transparent, luminous* oblong. I could see the door whiten at its touch; I could see the blue wall turn pale where it raced over it, and see the maple headboard of Amy's bed glow. It was a swift spirit; it was an awareness. It made noise. It had two joined parts, a head and a tail, like a Chinese dragon. It found the door, wall, and headboard; and it swiped them, charging them with its luminous glance. After its fleet*, searching passage, things looked the same, but weren't.

luminous: glowing

fleet: quick

6   I dared not blink or breathe; I tried to hush my whooping blood. If it found another awareness, it would destroy it.

7   Every night before it got to me it gave up. It hit my wall's corner and couldn't get past. It shrank completely into itself and vanished like a cobra down a hole. I heard the rising roar it made when it died or left. I still couldn't breathe. I knew—it was the worst fact I knew, a very hard fact—that it could return again alive that same night.

8   Sometimes it came back, sometimes it didn't. Most often, restless, it came back. The light stripe slipped in the door, ran searching over Amy's wall, stopped, stretched lunatic* at the first corner, raced wailing toward my wall, and vanished into the second corner with a cry. So I wouldn't go to bed.

lunatic: insane

9   It was a passing car whose windshield reflected the corner streetlight outside. I figured it out one night.

memorable: important, worthy of being remembered

10   Figuring it out was as memorable* as the oblong itself. Figuring it out was a long and forced ascent to the very rim of being, to the membrane of skin that both separates and connects the inner life and the outer world. I

climbed deliberately from the depths like a diver who releases the monster in his arms and hauls himself hand over hand up an anchor chain till he meets the ocean's sparkling membrane and bursts through it; he sights the sunlit, becalmed* hull of his boat, which had bulked* so ominously from below.

becalmed: *unmoved by wind*
bulked: *possessed bulk*   11
ominously: *threateningly*

I recognized the noise it made when it left. That is, the noise it made called to mind, at last, my daytime sensations when a car passed—the sight and noise together. A car came roaring down hushed Edgerton Avenue in front of our house, stopped at the corner stop sign, and passed on shrieking as its engine shifted up the gears. What, precisely, came into the bedroom? A reflection from the car's oblong windshield. Why did it travel in two parts? The window sash split the light and cast a shadow.

12

Night after night I labored up the same long chain of reasoning, as night after night the thing burst into the room where I lay awake and Amy slept prettily and my loud heart thrashed and I froze.

contiguous: *touching or next to* 13
patently: *obviously*

There was a world outside my window and contiguous* to it. If I was so all-fired bright, as my parents, who had patently* no basis for comparison, seemed to think, why did I have to keep learning this same thing over and over? For I had learned it a summer ago, when men with jackhammers broke up Edgerton Avenue. I had watched them from the yard; the street came up in jagged slabs like floes*. When I lay to nap, I listened. One restless afternoon I connected the new noise in my bedroom with the jackhammer men I had been seeing outside. I understood abruptly that these worlds met, the outside and the inside. I traveled the route in my mind: You walked downstairs from here, and outside from downstairs. "Outside," then, was conceivably just beyond my windows. It was the same world I reached by going out the front or the back door. I forced my imagination yet again over this route.

floes: *large masses of ice that float on the surface of the water*

coincidental: *accidental*   14

The world did not have me in mind; it had no mind. It was a coincidental* collection of things and people, of items, and I myself was one such item—a child walking up the sidewalk, whom anyone could see or ignore. The things in the world did not necessarily cause my overwhelming feelings; the feelings were inside me, beneath my skin, behind my ribs, within my skull. They were even, to some extent, under my control.

15

yield: *give in*

I could be connected to the outer world by reason, if I chose, or I could yield* to what amounted to a narrative fiction, to a tale of terror whispered to me by the blood in my ears, a show in light projected on the room's blue walls. As time passed, I learned to amuse myself in bed in the darkened room by entering the fiction deliberately and replacing it by reason deliberately.

nigh: *near*   16

When the low roar drew nigh* and the oblong slid in the door, I threw my own switches for pleasure. It's coming after me; it's a car outside. It's after me. It's a car. It raced over the wall, lighting it blue wherever it ran; it bumped over Amy's maple headboard in a rush, paused, slithered elongate* over the corner, shrank, flew my way, and vanished into itself with a wail. It was a car.

elongate: *stretched*

Comprehension Questions

1. Where is the author when the monster frightens her?

   A. in the woods
   B. in the car
   Ⓒ in her bed
   D. at school

2. Who is with the author when she is frightened?

   A. a friend
   Ⓑ her sister
   C. her dog
   D. no one

3. Why is her companion unable to help her?

   A. She is tied up.
   Ⓑ She is asleep.
   C. She isn't concerned.
   D. She hates her sister.

4. How does Dillard respond to the monster?

   A. She screams.
   B. She hits it.
   Ⓒ She is petrified.
   D. She calls the police.

5. What does the monster turn out to be?

   A. a neighbor
   B. a dog
   Ⓒ car headlights
   D. the shadow of a tree

Journal Topic

Describe the experience of falling asleep when you were a child.

Discussion Questions

1. How does Dillard describe or characterize the thing that enters her room?

2. How effective is the first person point of view Dillard uses?

3. How does she feel about figuring out that the oblong of light is the reflection of a car windshield?

4. What does the realization that the light is the reflection of a car windshield lead her to understand about the world and her place in it?

5. Why does she have to keep reminding herself what the light that enters her room is?

6. What game does Dillard play with the monster in her room?

7. How does Dillard gain control over her fear?

Writing Topics

1. Describe an experience in which you were frightened as a child.

2. Describe the experience of falling asleep when you were a child.

3. What does Dillard learn about the world by watching the light move across her wall?

4. What figurative language does Dillard use to describe her discoveries about the world?

5. Make a statement about Dillard's discoveries about the world and support it with evidence from the essay.

From *The Bats*

Chitra Banerjee Divakaruni

1   That year Mother cried a lot, nights. Or maybe she had always cried, and that was the first year I was old enough to notice. I would wake up in the hot Calcutta dark and the sound of her weeping would be all around me, pressing in, wave upon wave, until I could no longer tell where it was coming from. The first few times it happened, I would sit up in the narrow child's bed that she had recently taken to sharing with me and whisper her name. But that would make her pull me close and hold me tight against her shaking body, where the damp smell of talcum powder and sari starch would choke me until I couldn't bear it any longer and would start to struggle away. Which only made her cry more. So after some time I learned to lie rigid* and unmoving under the bedsheet, plugging my fingers into my ears to block out her sobs. And if I closed my eyes very tight and held them that way long enough, little dots of light would appear against my eyelids and I could almost pretend I was among the stars.

rigid: stiff

2   One morning when she was getting me ready for school, braiding my hair into the slick, tight pigtail that I disliked because it always hung stiffly down my back, I noticed something funny about her face. Not the dark circles under her eyes. Those were always there. It was high up on her cheek, a yellow blotch with its edges turning purple. It looked like my knee did after I bumped into the chipped mahogany dresser next to our bed last month.

3   "What's that, Ma? Does it hurt?" I reached up, wanting to touch it, but she jerked away. "Nothing. It's nothing. Now hurry up or you'll miss the bus. And don't make so much noise, or you'll wake your father."

4   Father always slept late in the mornings. Because he worked so hard at the Rashbihari Printing Press where he was a foreman, earning food and rent money for us, Mother had explained. Since she usually put me to bed before he came home, I didn't see him much. I heard him, though, shouts that shook the walls of my bedroom like they were paper, the sounds of falling dishes. Things fell a lot when Father was around, maybe because he was so large. His hands were especially big, with blackened, split nails and veins that stood up under the skin like blue snakes. I remembered their chemical smell and the hard feel of his fingers from when I was little and he used to pick me up suddenly and throw me all the way up to the ceiling, up and down, up and down, while Mother pulled at his arms, begging him to stop, and I screamed and screamed with terror until I had no breath left.

5   A couple of days later Mother had another mark on her face, even bigger and reddish-blue. It was on the side of her forehead and made her face look lopsided. This time when I asked her about it she didn't say anything, just turned the other way and stared at a spot on the wall where the plaster had cracked and started peeling in the shape of a drooping mouth. Then she asked me how I would like to visit my grandpa for a few days.

6   "Grandpa!" I knew about grandpas. Most of my friends in the third grade had them. They gave them presents on birthdays and took them to the big zoo in Alipore during vacations. "I didn't know I had a grandpa!"

7   I was so excited I forgot to keep my voice down and Mother quickly put a hand over my mouth.

8   "Shhh. It's a secret, just for you and me. Why don't we pack quickly, and I'll tell you more about him once we're on the train."

9   "A train!" This was surely a magic day, I thought, as I tried to picture what traveling on a train would be like.

10   We packed fast, stuffing a few saris and dresses into two bags Mother brought out from under the bed. They were made from the same rough, nubby jute as the shopping bag that Father used to bring home fresh fish from the bazaar, but from their stiffness I could tell they were new. I wondered when Mother bought them and how she'd paid for them, and then I wondered how she would buy our tickets. She never had much money, and whenever she asked for any, Father flew into one of his rages. But maybe she'd been saving up for this trip for a long time. As we packed, Mother kept stopping as though she was listening for something, but all I heard was Father's snores. We tiptoed around and spoke in whispers. It was so exciting that I didn't mind not having breakfast, or even having to leave all my toys behind.

11   I was entranced by the steamy smell of the train, the shriek of its whistle—loud without being scary—that announced when a tunnel was coming up, its comforting, joggly rhythm that soothed me into a half sleep. I was lucky enough to get a window seat, and from it I watched as the narrow, smoke-streaked apartment buildings of Calcutta, with crumpled washing hanging from identical boxlike balconies, gave way to little brick houses with yellow squash vines growing in the yard. Later there were fields and fields of green so bright and ponds with clusters of tiny purple flowers floating on them. Mother, who had grown up in the country, told me they were water hyacinths, and as she watched them catch the sunlight, it seemed to me that the line of her mouth wavered and turned soft.

12   After a while she pulled me close and cupped my chin in her hand. From her face I could see she had something important to say, so I didn't squirm away as I usually would have. "My uncle—your grandpa—that we're going to see," she said, "lives way away in a village full of bamboo forests and big rivers with silver fish. His house is in the middle of a meadow where buffaloes and goats roam all day, and there's a well to drink water from."

13   "A real well!" I clapped my hands in delight. I'd only seen wells in picture books.

14   "Yes, with a little bucket on a rope, and if you like you can fill the bucket and carry it in." Then she added, a bit hesitantly, "We might be staying with him for a while."

15   Staying with a grandpa-uncle who had a well and buffaloes and goats and bamboo forests sounded lovely, and I told Mother so, with my best smile.

16   "Will you miss your father?" There was a strange look in her eyes.

17   "No," I said in a definite tone. Already, as I turned my head to look at a pair of long-tailed birds with red breasts, his loud-voiced presence was fading from my mind.

Comprehension Questions

1. Where does the story take place?

   A. New York
   B. Calcutta
   C. San Juan
   D. Los Angeles

2. Who shares the girl's bed?

   A. her sister
   B. her mother
   C. her dog
   D. her grandmother

3. Why is the mother's face bruised?

   A. She had been in a car accident
   B. She has fallen.
   C. Her husband has hit her.

4. Where are the girl and her mother going?

   A. to the zoo
   B. to the movies
   C. to stay with her grandfather

5. How will they get there?

   A. by bicycle
   B. by train
   C. by bus
   D. by foot

Journal Topics

1. Did you identify with the narrator of the story? Why or why not?

2. Do you remember as a child trying to figure out the world of adults? Write one particularly vivid memory.

Discussion Questions

1. What senses does Divakaruni appeal to in the opening paragraph? How does her appeal to the senses help make the girl's experience come alive for the reader?

2. Describe the relationship between the girl's father and mother. How do you know?

3. In what ways are the girl's experiences universal—that is, they could take place anywhere? What details let you know that the story takes place in another country?

4. How does the girl feel about her father?

5. How does she feel about the trip?

Writing Topics

1. Summarize the events of the story.

2. Discuss the causes or effects of the mother's flight from her husband.

3. How universal are the girl's emotions and experiences? Give examples from the story to support your opinion.

4. Describe a relative or an event that you had trouble understanding as a child.

5. Make a statement about the narrator of the story and support it with details from the story.

The Girl Who Helped the Samburu

Cathy Dyson

safari: *a land expedition, especially to hunt or observe wild animals*

1 Christina Morin went on vacation this summer to Africa and hasn't been the same since. While on safari* with her family last summer, 17-year-old Christina Morin spent four days in Kenya with people of the Samburu tribe. She met men, women and children who were struggling to survive. Two years of drought had killed their cattle and left the tribe, which doesn't believe in hunting, with nothing to eat.

2 Christina helped the owners of a tourist lodge pass out flour and sugar rations, but she wanted to do more. She taught the children how to paint. "They came up with amazing drawings of animals that I couldn't do. And, I've been taking art for four years," she said, "and they'd never seen a paintbrush before." The Fredericksburg Academy senior decided to buy the paintings, turn them into notecards, and sell them back home. She paid the children $200 of her own money for the images. "That fed them for two and a half weeks," she said.

3 One idea led to another, and before Christina flew back to America, she had the makings of a nonprofit business she calls The Samburu Project. Now, she's paying the tribe to make crafts, which she'll sell in Fredericksburg. Tribal women are stringing beaded bracelets and making zebra ornaments and Santa Clauses from banana leaves. The green bead in each Santa's hand represents the Fredericksburg pear, Christina said. The spearmaker is turning pieces of metal into ornaments and the children are painting giraffes and zebras. "I still don't know how it all happened," said Christina. "It's actually turned into a huge project. Now, I have fabrics, I have gourds, I have tables, I have picture frames."

4 And, she has specific ideas on how to help the Samburu tribe whose kindness and simple lifestyle made such an impact. She hopes to raise enough money to provide food throughout the drought and to buy a cow for each family. She also wants to dam nearby springs—which are still trickling—so a drought can never devastate* the tribe again.

devastate: *seriously harm*

5 "If I sell everything I have, I will have enough," she said. "If not, I'm going to be stuck with a lot of stuff."

contagious: *easily spread*

6 Christina's enthusiasm for the project clearly is contagious*. She recently talked to some second-grade Brownies at the school, and they want to buy a cow. "We're all so excited about the whole thing," said Liz Barnes, the Lower School director. "Christina just glows when she talks about it. It's become all encompassing for her. In fact, her mother worries that it's taking over her whole life."

7 The teen-ager does sound like she spent four months, not four days, in Kenya. She and her family shot 66 rolls of film while there, and she filled an album with portraits of tribe members. Their names and ages are listed beside the photographs. Christina pointed to the dozen strands of necklaces the women wear—beads which, combined, can weigh up to 12 pounds and tell the story of a life's journey. For instance, a woman with twins puts a circular bead on the left and right sides of her necklace. A woman getting married wears strands made from the hairs of a giraffe's tail.

8 Christina's nonprofit business is also academic. She's making it her senior project, which is a requirement for graduation at the private school. Seniors have to choose a topic, do an activity related to it and complete research. Christina's project clearly qualifies, said Susanne Nobles, the

utmost: *highest or greatest*

9

hoarded: *saved and hidden away for the future*

school's senior exhibit coordinator. "I think it's tremendous," she said. "Christina has taken it to the utmost* level."

Christina has learned a thing or two about herself in the process. She wants to study archeology in college, and she's spent most of her recent years thinking about her own future—not someone else's, as she's doing now. She also has more respect for money, even though her mother says she's also hoarded* it. "If I save an extra dollar," Christina said, "that's another meal for somebody else."

Comprehension Questions

1. Christina Morin got to know the people of the Samburu tribe when she was

   A. in school.
   B. on vacation.
   C. in the Peace Corps.
   D. on the Internet.

2. What had left the Samburu without food?

   A. flood
   B. drought
   C. war
   D. disease

3. What did she teach the Samburu children?

   A. to paint
   B. to read
   C. to speak English
   D. to swim

4. How did she help the Samburu?

   A. brought tourists to their village
   B. brought trade to their village
   C. brought supplies to their village
   D. sold their arts and crafts in the United States

5. Christina's goal was to

   A. build a school.
   B. build a hospital.
   C. buy a cow for each family and dam the springs.
   D. send the children to school.

Journal Topics

1. Have you ever seen extreme poverty in this country or abroad? How did it make you feel? Did it ever occur to you that you might be able to do something about it?

2. How has reading about Christina's actions influenced your willingness to try to make a difference? Do you believe you can or cannot make a difference in the lives of others? Why or why not?

Discussion Questions

1. What was unusual about what Christina did?

2. Describe what she did for the Samburu. How did her project work?

3. Who was involved in her project?

4. What did she do with the profits?

5. How successful was her project?

Writing Topics

1. Describe what Christina did for the Samburu people.

2. How did Christina's actions make a difference for the Samburu?

3. Make a statement about Christina's actions and use examples from the article to support your statement.

4. How has reading about Christina's actions influenced your own attitudes and/or behavior?

5. Why is Christina's story inspirational?

The Coming Job Boom

Daniel Eisenberg

bleak: *not promising*

paralegal: *legal assistant*

wend: *work*

acupuncturist: *someone trained in the Eastern art of acupuncture*

prospects: *possibilities*

adept: *skilled*

pink slips: *notice of being fired*

demographics: *the statistical study of human population*

dotcom bubble: *brief financial success of Internet companies*

burnout: *exhaustion from overwork*

pounding the pavement: *walking the street in search of a job*

driver's seat: *in control*

savviest: *most aware of conditions, smartest*

demographers: *people who study the effect of the age distribution on a population*

waiting in the wings: *waiting its turn, literally waiting to come on stage*

mammoth: *huge*

1 At a time when the job market still seems bleak*, the outlook for Alex and Cindi Ignatovsky, both 33, could not be much brighter. After trying out a number of different careers, the Aptos, Calif., couple have recently discovered their true callings. Alex, who had been a paralegal* and had also done a brief stint as an insurance salesman, has just started working as a juvenile-probation officer, helping kids wend* their way through the crowded criminal-justice system.

2 Cindi, who previously was an editor and a graphic designer, is now busy finishing up an intensive, multiyear program to become an acupuncturist*. In her view, as she puts it, "there's as much opportunity as I make of it."

3 She's right, about both her and her husband's prospects*—but not just because they're passionate and adept* at what they do. They have also, as it turns out, each chosen fields—in his case, law enforcement and social services, in hers, health care—that are feeling the first effects of the coming job boom. That's right. Even as thousands of Americans are still getting pink slips*, powerful help is on the way. And it has more to do with demographics* than economics. The oldest members of the huge baby-boom generation are now 56, and as they start retiring, job candidates with the right skills will be in hot demand. As Mitch Potter of human-resources consultant William M. Mercer says, "The dotcom bubble* created a false talent crunch. The real one is coming."

4 In certain industries, especially those in which burnout* and early retirement are common and demand for services is rising, the crunch has already arrived. As the population ages, hospitals can't find enough nurses or medical technicians. Drugstores are competing to hire pharmacists, bidding some beginners' salaries above $75,000. School districts and universities will need 2.2 million more teachers over the next decade, not to mention administrators and librarians, and are already avidly recruiting.

5 Homeowners can't get their calls returned by skilled contractors, electricians or plumbers. Corporations are scooping up accountants and engineers. For job seekers who have the right skills or are willing to learn them, there are real opportunities in government, construction and technology.

6 To millions of laid-off workers still pounding the pavement*, of course, this might seem like wishful thinking. While the economy grew a whopping 5.8% in the first quarter of 2002, the job market usually lags by at least a few months. To land a job, record numbers of workers are taking pay cuts or switching industries, according to outplacement firm Challenger, Gray & Christmas; many others are starting their own small businesses. But as hard as it may be to believe, it should not be too long before employees are in the driver's seat*. A wave of retirements whose full effect is only starting to be felt will soon ripple through the entire economy. And the savviest* workers and employers are already preparing for it.

7 Though the average retirement age is creeping up—and a growing share of Americans, by choice or necessity, are planning to work at least part time well past 65—demographers* say there still will not be enough qualified members of the next generation to pick up the slack. So with 76 million baby boomers heading toward retirement over the next three decades and only 46 million Gen Xers waiting in the wings*, corporate America is facing a potentially mammoth* talent crunch. Certainly,

immigration: *people moving to this country from another*

breach: *gap or empty space*   8

initiative: *first step*

got the ax: *were fired*

biotech: *biotechnology or the study of the genetic structure of organisms*   13

labor-saving technology and immigration* may help fill the breach*. Still, by 2010 there may be a shortage of 4 million to 6 million workers.

Not enough Americans are trained for these jobs. They lack everything from computer literacy and leadership to critical thinking and communication skills. The recent slump, though, may be helping narrow the skills gap in a surprising way. Although generous social-welfare systems in industrialized countries such as Germany and Britain make it easy for the laid off to wait around for a factory to reopen, Americans tend to take the initiative* during a downturn, getting educated or trained for a better job and in the process adding to the country's stock of human capital. Applications to graduate programs in everything from law and business to education and engineering are up from last year by 30%–100%. That approach should pay off. Although 1.9 million Americans with a high school diploma or less got the ax* from September 2000 to October 2001—a time when the economy was slumping—1.2 million people with college or vocational degrees were hired, according to the Employment Policy Foundation.

9   It isn't just the younger generation that's going back to school, either. Bruce LeBel, 59, a veteran aircraft mechanic who lost his job after September 11, is learning how to service the computer networks that help run more and more factories and power plants. Many of his former colleagues "are afraid to try anything different. They want to stay with a dead horse," he says. "But the only thing that can save me is having a skill that's in demand." To help other job hunters follow LeBel's example, here's a guide to the best job opportunities today—and tomorrow.

A Healthy Prognosis

10   If lately you have had to wait to fill a prescription or get your doctor on the phone, you know why no industry holds more promise than health care.

11   • **Caregivers** Nurses and pharmacists aren't the only ones being snapped up by hospitals. All across the country, sonogram operators, who make a median salary of $42,000, and radiology technicians are being hired. The people who help patients get back on their feet are also hot properties. Over the next decade, according to the Bureau of Labor Statistics, there will be 255,000 openings for all manner of therapists, including physical and respiratory therapists and speech pathologists.

12   • **Drugmakers** Firms that dream up wonder drugs are in one of the few industries that have continued to hire in droves. Swiss-based Novartis AG, which has embarked on a major expansion in the U.S., hired more than 1,800 workers last year and plans to keep hiring at a brisk pace. That includes everyone from marketing and manufacturing staff to people in finance, human resources and, of course, research science. This array of jobs pays anywhere from $30,000 to $300,000 a year. Likewise, Abbott Laboratories hopes to fill 5,000 new positions this year, including posts for sales reps who can drive product launches.

13   • **Gene Hunters** The much hyped biotech* industry is finally starting to deliver on its promise, with more small companies shifting from basic research to drug development. That means more jobs, from lab work

to medical writing, are in the pipelines as well. Genentech, based in South San Francisco, Calif., is increasing its head count each year by 297, or about 6% annually, hiring everyone from Ph.D.s to community-college grads who can work in manufacturing. Just in the budding field of bioinformatics, in which specialists can make more than $100,000 a year using computers to plow through reams of genetic data, there will be an estimated 20,000 unfilled jobs by 2005. Chemists are also being wooed across industries.

Uncle Sam Wants You

14   Long before September 11 ushered in a new era of respect for government, Washington was poised to enjoy an unlikely job boom. Almost half the Federal Government's 1.8 million workers will be eligible to retire within five years. From the Food and Drug Administration (FDA) and Park Service to the Commerce, Energy and State departments, agencies are bracing for a brain drain*, especially at the managerial level. And these aren't your classic paper-pushing jobs—although many of those, as at the busy Social Security Administration, are also going begging.

brain drain: *loss of intellectual talent*

15   • **Law Enforcement** Organizations—from the FBI and the CIA to the Coast Guard and the Defense, Justice and State departments—are revving up their recruiting efforts, looking for everyone from computer programmers, budding young diplomats and spooks* to lawyers and linguists*. The Immigration and Naturalization Service wants to hire thousands of new border-patrol guards and immigration inspectors to process and keep better track of new arrivals to the country; these positions require just a high school diploma and, with overtime, can pay around $40,000 in the first year.

spooks: *spies*
linguists: *specialists in languages*

16   • **Big Thinkers** To help assess the growing tide of innovations* that washes across its desks, the Patent and Trademark Office is desperate to find more qualified engineers and intellectual-property lawyers. Other high-end specialists are needed, such as drug reviewers at the FDA; accountants and statisticians at the Labor and Treasury departments, the Internal Revenue Service and the Securities and Exchange Commission; and trade experts at Commerce.

innovations: *new inventions or ideas*

Get Your Hands Dirty

17   In the dotcom mania of the '90s, it was easy to forget that skilled tradespeople can make good money.

18   • **Construction** A recent industry study showed that at least one-third of St. Louis' 80,000 construction workers are expected to retire in the next five years—a microcosm* of the situation nationwide; the industry needs to attract 240,000 new workers each year, from project managers to iron workers, just to compensate* for the exodus. The top tradespeople in their fields, such as plumbers, electricians, carpenters, bricklayers, roofers, and painters, can make upward of $100,000 a year.

microcosm: *a tiny world that is similar to a larger one*
compensate: *make up*

19   • **Manufacturing** Even in this beleaguered* sector, in which many firms have made huge layoffs, companies are having a hard time finding the right people. More than 80% of firms say they face a shortage

beleaguered: *under attack*

of qualified machinists, craft workers and technicians, according to a recent survey by the National Association of Manufacturers. That deficit* is likely to widen. Although manufacturing will not grow much overall during the next decade, a rapidly aging work force will create more than 2 million job openings—with many positions paying more than $50,000—for welders, tool- and die-makers, line managers and others.

deficit: *shortage*

20 • **Technicians** As machines keep getting more complex, with tiny microprocessors governing their every move, finding enough people to repair and maintain them is becoming harder. Heating and air-conditioning technicians are in high demand. Nationwide there are about 60,000 vacancies for car mechanics, who can earn anywhere from $30,000 to $100,000.

Engineering the Future

abundant: *plentiful*

20 Despite the layoffs from busted dotcoms, jobs will be abundant* in other areas of technology. Computer storage, enterprise software and semiconductors are still growth areas. Analysts expect corporate information-technology spending to stabilize* this year and rebound in 2003.

stabilize: *even out*

21 • **Engineers** Over the past 15 years, the number of students graduating with a bachelor's degree in engineering dropped 50%, to 12,400. Companies like Texas Instruments are hiring electrical engineers for product-design, sales and marketing departments. Other engineers— software, mechanical, aerospace, civil and structural—are also hot properties.

22 • **Computer Monitors** Computer-related jobs will be among the fastest growing in the next decade. Leading the way will be those key employees who help large companies maintain their daunting* tangles of technology, from system analysis and support specialists to database administrators.

daunting: *difficult, discouraging*

The Desk Set

23 Thousands of investment bankers, consultants and lawyers have become casualties of the latest round of corporate downsizing. But the long-range picture looks better. As baby-boomers scale back their time at the office to concentrate on other activities, from golf to philanthropy, corporate America will be desperate to find qualified managers and executives as well as support staff, from administrative assistants to paralegals.

24 • **Finance and Accounting** H&R Block has been busy hiring 1,200 financial advisers and marketing staff members as it broadens its tax-preparing business. Financial services firms continue to look for financial planners and asset managers. Despite their role in Enron and in other corporate scandals this year, accounting and auditing are especially attractive fields, expected to grow nearly 20% in the next decade.

25 • **Energy** The oil, gas and utility sector is bringing on finance and marketing graduates to help navigate deregulation*. Companies such as TXU, Exxon Mobil and Koch Industries are still hiring. A graying

navigate deregulation: *steer a course through reduced government regulation*

work force means the industry also needs to find a new generation of petroleum engineers, geologists and geophysicists.

26   To keep pace in today's fast-moving economy, job hunters must be, above all, flexible. Steve Reyna, 28, who four years ago went to work at TDIndustries, a Dallas-based mechanical contractor that specializes in air-conditioning and plumbing projects for high-tech companies, knows this better than most. After training as a sheet-metal technician, Reyna moved on to work in the so-called clean rooms of semiconductor companies, learning a little welding and plumbing along the way. Just one of more than 1,300 employees at TDIndustries who are rigorously cross-trained, Reyna is now ready to work, "wherever they need me." If the number crunchers turn out to be right, that could soon mean just about everywhere.

Comprehension Questions

1. What is responsible for the coming job boom?

   A. economic trends
   B. demographics
   C. increasing natural resources
   D. technology

2. By 2010 there may be a

   A. labor surplus.
   B. labor shortage.
   C. labor migration.
   D. labor influx.

3. What do many workers lack?

   A. computer literacy
   B. critical thinking
   C. communications skills
   D. all of the above

4. Applications to graduate schools are

   A. remaining steady.
   B. down.
   C. up by 10%.
   D. up by 30%–100%.

5. What must workers do to keep pace in today's economy?

   A. become computer literate
   B. be flexible
   C. hold two jobs
   D. be willing to move

Discussion Questions

1. What is the best way to combat the current job slump?

2. In the current economic slump, how have workers with a high school diploma fared compared to workers with college or vocational degrees?

3. Why is the job prospect bright in certain job areas?

4. What are the "hot" industries in today's economy?

Journal Topic

1. How did reading the article influence your thinking about job possibilities for you?

Writing Topics

1. Analyze the causes and/or effects of the coming job boom.

2. Give examples of jobs in hot industries.

3. Of all the jobs mentioned in the article, what job is most attractive to you and why?

Too Good to Be True

John Garrity

A hundred-yard-plus rushing average is the least impressive credential on the resume of Colorado freshman Marcus Houston

1   Some kids are good at puzzles. Some learn to read early. Mozart wrote a symphony when he was eight, and now and then you hear about some Doogie Howser-type who, at 15, is chairman of the math department at Cal Tech.

prodigy: *person with exceptional talents*
preternatural: *exceptional*
leverage: *ability to achieve big results with a small action (mechanical advantage of a lever)*

2   Marcus Houston is a different kind of prodigy*—a kid with a preternatural* understanding of leverage*. When he was in kindergarten in Aurora, Colo., his teacher gave all the kids a mock $1 bill and asked them to finish the sentence, "If I had $100 I would buy. . . ." Marcus crossed out the word buy and wrote in "go to a colich." Another time, the little boy went shopping with his father, Herman, at a Cub Foods store near their home. Staring at the long aisles packed with food, Marcus asked, "How much does one of these cost?"—meaning, the store. Herman said, "I have no idea. A million dollars?" Marcus thought about it and said, "I'm going to get me one. I could feed a lot of people."

3   Leverage is an empowering concept; a little push here produces a big result there, and before you know it, you think you can move mountains. When Marcus was a junior at Denver's Thomas Jefferson High and on his way to the first of two all-state selections as a running back, twelve freshmen footballers were flunking two or more classes after the first six weeks of school and lost their eligibility*. Disturbed by their failure and looking for an avenue of action, Houston created a program called Just Say KNOW, in which he delivered a talk and showed a football video at six middle schools, using his credibility* as a star athlete to motivate the younger kids academically.

eligibility: *qualification*

credibility: *believability*

4   He then funded an eighth-grade essay contest at each of those schools with money he had earned mowing lawns and shoveling snow. "Win $50!" read the flier. "Write an essay letting us know what success means to you and what you are doing to make sure you are successful." To encourage involvement by the kids who didn't write well, he added, "If seventy-five percent of the class enters, your class will be given a free pizza party!" The essays poured in, and the middle school teachers raved about Marcus's skill as a motivational speaker. Just Say KNOW is now a nonprofit corporation, and Houston, at 19, is a budding Arthur Ashe, soliciting* corporate donations and making plans to go national.

soliciting: *asking for*

idealism: *ability to believe in and pursue ideals*

5   Marcus gets his idealism* from his parents, Herman and Patricia Houston. For the past five years they've run the Youth Education Institute, a nonprofit organization that conducts betterment programs for young people in Denver. "We taught our children that if you have blessings, you have a responsibility to share those gifts," says Pat.

6   When Marcus went to Washington, D.C., in May to receive one of Prudential's Spirit of Community awards, a nonprofit organization called K.I.D.S. gave him $25,000 worth of sports-logoed coats to distribute to needy kids in Denver. "Marcus was ecstatic* about that," says his mom. "That's what makes him tick, making a difference for others."

ecstatic: *extremely happy*

7   Marcus has also shown how celebrity, a warm smile and a way with words can work magic with middle schoolers. His Just Say KNOW literature

is strewn with Houstonisms like, "Sometimes success comes down to whether you reach for the opportunities or reach for the excuses" and "Is your character rich enough so that people will want to invest in your dreams?" Standing in front of an eighth-grade class at Gove Middle School in January 1998, he worked the audience like a seasoned motivational speaker. "I can tell just by looking which of you are not going to be successful in life," he said, and then walked around the classroom studying faces. Kids who were slouched at their desks discreetly* straightened up, sliding up their chair backs in slow motion. "Aw, I'm just kidding," Marcus said with a grin. "But didn't you feel your heart stop? That's because you want to be successful."

discreetly: not calling attention to itself

8   The essay contests, with their fifty-buck payoffs, reflect Houston's belief that it takes more than a lecture to get kids to establish goals and priorities. "Our schools pay attention to the problem kids and provide incentives for them to achieve," he says. "But you also need incentives* for the good students to keep on achieving." Some of the winners of the second Just Say KNOW essay contest got not only cash prizes but also a stretch-limousine ride to the 1999 Jefferson High homecoming game, paid for by Houston. Revealing a flair for showmanship, Marcus ripped off a 60-yard touchdown run on the first play of the game—something your average foundation head can't do. "I think eighth grade is critical," Marcus says. "It's when kids develop their own vision and decide what crowd they'll hang out with."

incentives: motivation

9   The real miracle is that the 6 feet 2 inch, 205-pound Houston is so approachable and unassuming. He answers all the mail he gets; he talks on the phone with kids who want to discuss a problem or get a pat on the back for a good report card; he even smiles at strangers. When he scored his first college touchdown, on a five-yard run against Colorado State in the season opener, he didn't grandstand in the end zone; he just grinned and handed the ball to the ref.

10   Ask Houston to finish the sentence, "If I had a multi-million dollar NFL contract, I'd buy . . . , " and he'll still cross out "buy" and insert some noble alternative like "rebuild Matsekopi" (a village in Ghana that invited him to be their development chief). "Football complements me," he explains, "but it doesn't define me."

11   His proud parents have only one worry: that their leveraging son may try to save the world all by himself and wind up disillusioned*. "When you start dealing with humanity, you will always be in over your head," his father warns. "You will be loved, but you will also be hurt, and there will be times when you cannot make a difference."

disillusioned: disappointed, having lost belief in ideals

12   True enough. But Herman and Pat have clearly convinced their son of this corollary truth: Sometimes you can.

Comprehension Questions

1. What does Marcus Houston do to help kids?

   A. lecture in schools
   B. establish Just Say KNOW program
   C. fund essay contests
   D. all of the above

2. What sport does Marcus Houston play?

   A. soccer

B. wrestling

C. football

D. baseball

3. What motivated Marcus's efforts?

A. His brother was having trouble in school.

B. Twelve freshman football players lost their eligibility because of poor grades.

C. His school had low scores.

D. He flunked out of school.

4. What message does Marcus bring to kids?

A. the importance of staying off drugs

B. the importance of being responsible and doing well in school

C. the importance of helping others

D. the importance of family

5. What grade does Marcus think is critical in a youth's development?

A. first

B. eighth

C. tenth

D. twelfth

Discussion Questions

1. Describe Marcus Houston.

2. What did he do to help kids?

3. What message does he bring to kids?

4. How successful have his efforts been?

Journal Topic

1. Have you or someone you know done something to help others? Describe what you did and why you did it.

Writing Topics

1. Describe what Marcus Houston has done to help kids.

2. Make a statement about Marcus's actions and use examples from the article to support your statement.

3. If you could do one thing to help others locally, nationally, or internationally, what would it be?

The Man Who Planted Trees

Jean Giono

Provence: *region in the south of France*

embarked: *set out on a journey*

barren: *without vegetation*

lavender: *sweet smelling purple flower*

coarse: *rough*

1   About forty years ago, I was taking a long trip on foot over mountain heights quite unknown to tourists, in that ancient region where the Alps thrust down into Provence*. All this, at the time I embarked* upon my long walk through these deserted regions, was barren* and colorless land. Nothing grew there but wild lavender*.

2   After five hours' walking I had still not found water, and there was nothing to give me any hope of finding any. All about me was the same dryness, the same coarse* grasses. I thought I glimpsed in the distance a small black silhouette, upright, and took it for the trunk of a solitary tree. In any case I started toward it. It was a shepherd. Thirty sheep were lying about him on the baking earth.

3   He gave me a drink from his water-gourd and, a little later, took me to his cottage in a fold of the plain. The place was in order, the dishes washed, the floor swept, his rifle oiled; his soup was boiling over the fire. He shared his soup with me, and afterwards, when I offered my tobacco pouch, he told me that he did not smoke.

4   The shepherd went to fetch a small sack and poured out a heap of acorns on the table. He began to inspect them, one by one, with great concentration, separating the good from the bad. I smoked my pipe. I did offer to help him. He told me that it was his job. And in fact, seeing the care he devoted to the task, I did not insist. That was the whole of our conversation. When he had set aside a large enough pile of good acorns he counted them out by tens, meanwhile eliminating the small ones or those which were slightly cracked, for now he examined them more closely. When he had thus selected one hundred perfect acorns he stopped, and we went to bed.

5   There was peace in being with this man. The next day I asked if I might rest here for a day. He found it quite natural—or, to be more exact, he gave me the impression that nothing could startle him. The rest was not absolutely necessary, but I was interested and wished to know more about him. He opened the pen and led his flock to pasture. Before leaving, he plunged his sack of carefully selected and counted acorns into a pail of water.

6   I noticed that he carried for a stick an iron rod as thick as my thumb and about a yard and a half long. Resting myself by walking, I followed a path parallel to his. He climbed to the top of the ridge, about a hundred yards away. There he began thrusting his iron rod into the earth, making a hole in which he planted an acorn; then he refilled the hole. He was planting oak trees. I asked him if the land belonged to him. He answered no. Did he know whose it was? He did not. He supposed it was community property, or perhaps belonged to people who cared nothing about it. He was not interested in finding out whose it was. He planted his hundred acorns with the greatest care.

Providence: *God*

7   After the midday meal he resumed his planting. I suppose I must have been fairly insistent in my questioning, for he answered me. For three years he had been planting trees in this wilderness. He had planted one hundred thousand. Of the hundred thousand, twenty thousand had sprouted. Of the twenty thousand he still expected to lose about half, to rodents or to the unpredictable designs of Providence*. There remained ten thousand oak trees to grow where nothing had grown before.

Elzeard Bouffier: *pronounced* 8
'El-zay-ard Boof-ee-ay

remedy: *cure*

His name was Elzeard Bouffier*. He had once had a farm in the low-lands. There he had had his life. He had lost his only son, then his wife. He had withdrawn into this solitude where his pleasure was to live leisurely with his lambs and his dog. It was his opinion that this land was dying for want of trees. He added that, having no very pressing business of his own, he had resolved to remedy* this state of affairs. I told him that in thirty years his ten thousand oaks would be magnificent. He answered quite simply that if God granted him life, in thirty years he would have planted so many more that these ten thousand would be like a drop of water in the ocean.

9   The next day, we parted.

10   The following year came the War of 1914, in which I was involved for the next five years. An infantryman hardly had time for reflecting upon trees. To tell the truth, the thing itself had made no impression upon me; I had considered it as a hobby, a stamp collection, and forgotten it.

demobilization: *to be dis-charged from military service* 11

The war over, I found myself possessed of a tiny demobilization* bonus and a huge desire to breathe fresh air for a while. It was with no other objective that I again took the road to the barren lands. I had begun to think again of the shepherd tree-planter. "Ten thousand oaks," I reflected, "really take up quite a bit of space."

12   The oaks of 1910 were then ten years old and taller than either of us. It was an impressive spectacle. I was literally speechless and, as he did not talk, we spent the whole day walking in silence through his forest. In three sections, it measured eleven kilometers in length and three kilometers at its greatest width. When you remembered that all this had sprung from the hands and the soul of this one man, without technical resources, you understood that men could be as effectual* as God in other realms than that of destruction.

effectual: *producing an effect*

13   Creation seemed to come about in a sort of chain reaction. He did not worry about it; he was determinedly pursuing his task in all its simplicity, but as we went back toward the village I saw water flowing in brooks that had been dry since the memory of man. This was the most impressive result of the chain reaction that I had seen.

14   The wind, too, scattered seeds. As the water reappeared, so there reap-peared willows, rushes, meadows, gardens, flowers, and a certain purpose in being alive. But the transformation took place so gradually that it became part of the pattern without causing any astonishment. Hunters, climbing into the wilderness in pursuit of hares or wild boar, had of course noticed the sudden growth of little trees, but had attributed it to some nat-ural caprice* of the earth. That is why no one meddled* with Elzeard Bouffier's work.

caprice: *sudden change of mind*
meddled: *interfered*

delegation: *official group* 15

In 1935 a whole delegation* came from the Government to examine the "natural forest." A friend of mine was among the forestry officers of the del-egation. To him I explained the mystery. One day the following week we went together to see Elzeard Bouffier. We found him hard at work, some ten kilometers from the spot where the inspection had taken place. Before leaving, my friend simply made a brief suggestion about certain species of trees that the soil here seemed particularly suited for. He did not force the point. "For the very good reason," he told me later, "that Bouffier knows more about it than I do." At the end of an hour's walking—having turned it over in his mind—he added, "He knows a lot more about it than anybody. He's discovered a wonderful way to be happy!"

16   I saw Elzeard Bouffier for the last time in June of 1945. He was then eighty-seven. Everything was changed. Even the air. Instead of the harsh dry winds that used to attack me, a gentle breeze was blowing, laden with scents. A sound like water came from the mountains: it was the wind in the forest. Most amazing of all, I heard the actual sound of water falling into a pool. I saw that a fountain had been built, that it flowed freely and—what touched me most—that someone had planted a linden beside it, a linden that must have been four years old, already in full leaf, the incontestable symbol of resurrection.

17   Besides, Vergons bore evidence of labor of the sort of undertaking for which hope is required. Hope, then, had returned. Ruins had been cleared away, dilapidated walls torn down and five houses restored. Now there were twenty-eight inhabitants, four of them young married couples. The new houses, freshly plastered, were surrounded by gardens where vegetables and flowers grew in orderly confusion, cabbages and roses, leeks and snapdragons, celery and anemones. It was now a village where one would want to live. Counting the former population, unrecognizable now that they live in comfort, more than ten thousand people owe their happiness to Elzeard Bouffier.

tenacity: *persistence*
benevolence: *goodness, charity*
immense: *huge*

18   When I reflect that one man, armed only with his own physical and moral resources, was able to cause this land of Canaan to spring from the wasteland, I am convinced that in spite of everything, humanity is admirable. But when I compute the unfailing greatness of spirit and the tenacity* of benevolence* that it must have taken to achieve this result, I am taken with an immense* respect for that old and unlearned peasant who was able to complete a work worthy of God.

19   Elzeard Bouffier died peacefully in 1947 at the hospice in Banon.

Comprehension Questions

1. The man who planted trees was

   A. a farmer.
   Ⓑ a shepherd.
   C. a nurseryman.
   D. a camper.

2. The kinds of trees the man planted were

   A. elms.
   B. poplars and hickory.
   Ⓒ oaks.
   D. sycamore and ash.

3. The trees were planted on land that belonged to

   A. the man himself.
   B. the author.
   Ⓒ unknown owners.
   D. a baron.

4. According to the author, what was the most impressive result of the old man's actions?

   A. the trees
   Ⓑ the water

C. the roads

D. the towns

5. What was the year when the writer last saw the old man?

A. 1973

B. 1955

C. 1945

D. 1910

Discussion Questions

1. Explain the process that the man used to plant trees.

2. Why does the writer believe that this humble shepherd is exceptional?

3. Was Elzeard Bouffier's accomplishment more remarkable because he worked alone and without appreciation from anyone besides the author?

4. Discuss how the shepherd's work enlivened the region and gave it hope.

5. Discuss the reasons that the author's friend, after visiting the shepherd, stated, "He's discovered a wonderful way to be happy!"

Writing Topics

1. Summarize the story of the man who planted trees in one to three paragraphs. Include the actions of the author and how he discovered the man who planted trees.

2. Explain why this humble shepherd could be considered a hero. You may want to consider his actions and the results of his actions.

3. Choose someone you know about who has made the community a better place to live and argue that this person could be called a hero because of his or her actions and their effects on the community.

4. Propose an action or actions that you could take that might have some of the same results as the man who planted trees.

5. Explain the changes to the land and the people of the region that were brought about by the trees the man planted.

From *Long Quiet Highway*

Natalie Goldberg

1   My family were pioneers, among the first to move out from Brooklyn to savage nature, to Long Island. From Levittown, we moved even farther out when I was six, about to enter first grade, to that green split-level in Famingdale, practically the jungle. They were still paving the roads of the development as we rolled up in our blue Buick, my grandparents close behind in their green Plymouth station wagon. The land behind our house was undeveloped. That first year I discovered "my" oak tree and climbed it, found a cave, roamed through a trail of wild berries. The next year they built a GM plant in "my" woods, right in back of our house, and I don't remember even one whimper of a complaint from my parents. After all, wasn't this progress? The plant was lit brightly for the evening shift. I remember going down into the kitchen in the middle of the night to get a glass of cold water from the refrigerator, the GM lights falling in a large square pattern through our bay window onto the green linoleum.

2   My family read *Newsday*, but there were no books in my home. In my middle teens my father bought a hi-fi and we put it in the cocoa-carpeted sunken living room. We sat on the couch opposite the wooden console and were honestly stumped at what to play on it. Then my father had an inspiration: He ran out and bought a Mantovani record. My mother, my sister, and my grandparents approved when they heard it, and we played that one record over and over, nothing else for the first year. Then my father's brother died, Uncle Sam, who lived in a rent-controlled flat on the lower East Side, kept his money stuffed in a mattress, and carried it around with him in a brown paper bag when he went out. He was also a classical music aficionado, and we inherited his record collection. Suddenly we had a pile of Tchaikovsky, Berlioz, and Mozart next to the stereo. My family was curious about these records, and one day we tried Bizet's *Carmen* on the turntable. We frowned: It was too loud, too excitable. We put on Mantovani, something familiar, and relaxed again on the couch.

desolation: *loneliness, unhappiness*

3   My desolation* was that no one knew me and I did not know myself. My family's life was my life. I knew nothing else. I was clothed, fed, given a bed to sleep in, encouraged to marry early and rich, and loved in a generic way—I was "the big one," which meant the older and my sister was "the little one"—but no one spoke to me, no one explained anything.

4   In all fairness I think my family was stunned to be alive in the twentieth century, eating white bread, buying new products, removed from a community or religious context. Even now when I see my parents, who are in their seventies, they seem a little dazed that they "may" die someday, that they are in Florida far from their children, and that their children are so different from them.

5   Once when I was visiting my parents, my father and I sat up late one night to watch a movie. The end came earlier than we expected. My father turned to me. "That's just what it's like. You're in your life and suddenly it goes blank. They flash 'The End' across your face."

6   Everyone in my family was busy, but busy doing what? My mother was busy being on a diet. She ate thin, dried white toast, which she cut diagonally, leaving a line of brown crumbs on the white paper napkin. Then she spread lo-cal cottage cheese over it and drank black coffee. She bought things with credit cards in department stores and then returned them. My

father was busy running a bar, the Aero Tavern, in downtown Famingdale, going to the race track, eating T-bone steaks with lots of ketchup, and a wedge of iceberg lettuce with ranch-style dressing from the bottle. My grandfather mowed the lawn with the new power mower that automatically collected the cut grass in an attached pouch. He read the Yiddish paper, smoked stogies, and sat in a brown suit on a lawn chair in our driveway. Grandma told me stories and baked cookies. My sister, I suppose, was lost in her own activities of being the youngest. I never really got to know her, though we had slept side-by-side in the same bedroom all our lives.

alienation: indifferent separation

7　This alienation* is the American disease. It is our inheritance, our roots. It can be our teacher. Mother Teresa, who works with India's poorest of the poor, has said that America has a worse poverty than India's, and it's called loneliness. Mr. Cates once asked us in class after we read *King Lear*— after Gloucester plucked out his eyes and Lear anguished* over the betrayal by his daughters—"Which would you prefer? Physical torment, or mental and emotional suffering?" When we thought about it enough, no one in class could honestly choose.

anguished: suffered

Buddhists: Buddhism is founded on the belief that suffering is an inescapable part of existence but that the extinction of the self leads to illumination

neurosis: psychological disorder

8　Tibetan Buddhists* say that a person should never get rid of their negative energy, that negative energy transformed is the energy of enlightenment, and that the only difference between neurosis* and wisdom is struggle. If we stop struggling and open up and accept what is, that neurotic energy naturally arises as wisdom, naturally informs us and becomes our teacher. If this is true, why do we struggle so much? We struggle because we're afraid to die, we're afraid to see that we are impermanent, that nothing exists forever. My childhood suburbs gave the impression that they would exist forever, placid*, plastic, timeless, and monotonous*, but natural wisdom, the other side of neurosis, embodies* the truth of transiency*.

placid: calm, tranquil
monotonous: repetitious, dull
embodies: gives physical form to
transiency: remaining for only a brief moment
imminent: about to occur

9　I graduated from high school and planned to go away to college. My family never discussed my imminent* departure. I simply filled out applications to universities and was accepted at one. I did this all on my own. No one in my immediate family had gone to college and I knew they could not help me.

10　The end of August arrived. We loaded up my parents' brown Buick convertible and off we went to Washington, D.C. I'd never been there before. I was amazed when we arrived. There were big parks and white buildings, but no skyscrapers. Unlike Manhattan, I didn't have to bend my head all the way back to see the sky between tall rows of apartment houses. My parents helped me carry my suitcases into Thurston Hall and then up to the elevator to the eighth floor. One of my roommates—there were four per room— was already there. She was from Shaker Heights, near Cleveland. We all said hello to her, then my parents and I went back down in the elevator and stood looking at each other in the dormitory lobby. What else was there to do? They had delivered me to college. We hugged good-bye and they walked out the door. I stood there. My mother told me years later that she cried, back in the car. "We just left her. We should have taken her out for juice." I was all alone. My childhood in Farmingdale was over.

11　But I couldn't get away from home so easily. I studied Plato, Descartes, John Milton, William Black, Shakespeare. All of it was far away from my roots. It all seemed exciting for a while. I had done it: I had broken out. But I wandered around at George Washington University in a daze. Half of me was still in Farmingdale: I wore clothes my mother had picked out back on

Long Island; I dated boys my mother would like. There was no one like Mr. Clemente or Mr. Cates at the school to make what I read alive in my present life. I didn't have a way to digest the new influences of college.

12   I went to the symphony because my new friends from Boston and Philadelphia went, but I didn't know how to listen to the music. In the audience I mostly daydreamed and curled the program sheets in my lap; then suddenly the music would be over and we would be clapping. One roommate's family had a cook; the girl down the hall had a mother who worked as a scientist. She also swam laps every day. I had never heard of a mother doing that. I tried Mexican food; I tried coq au vin*. I made a friend from Georgia and she cooked honey-fried chicken, the way they made it in the South. I called my family every week on the phone, each one taking a turn to speak with me. My sister bought two tickets for a Richie Havens concert, she told me, for when I came home to visit. And my parents told me long distance that they were afraid for us to go to the concert, because of blacks rioting around the country.

coq au vin: chicken in wine

13   Ultimately, all this new college atmosphere wasn't enough to yank me from my roots. I carried my life in Farmingdale within me wherever I went. Personal power could not come from college or an English book. It had to come from deep within me. I had to go back and reclaim, transform, what I had inherited at home. Eventually I had to stop running from what I had been given. If I opened to it, loneliness could become singleness; lethargy* and boredom would transform into open space. Those fearful, negative feelings could become my teacher. I did not understand this consciously at the time I was in college. I did not know about Tibetan Buddhism then nor what I experienced on that train ride with Kate and her kids so many years later. But if I wanted to survive—no, not just to survive, I wanted glory, I wanted to learn how to grow a rose out of a cement parking lot—I had to digest the blandness and desolation* of my childhood and make them mine. I couldn't run away, even though I tried, because in fact, my roots were all I had. If I didn't transform that energy, no matter where I went—Washington, D.C., Ann Arbor, Chicago, California, New Mexico—I would still carry it with me. I would walk around like a numb* ghost—and for many years I did walk around numb. Writing became my vehicle for transformation, a way to travel out of that nowhere land. And because writing is no fool, it brought me right back in. There was no place else to go, but moving my hand across the page gave me a way to eat my landscape, rather than be eaten by it.

lethargy: lack of energy

desolation: emptiness

numb: unfeeling

Comprehension Questions

1. Where did Natalie Goldberg grow up?

   A. Miami, Florida
   B. Famingdale, Long Island
   C. New Jersey
   D. The Bronx

2. What was built behind her house?

   A. a playground
   B. a mall
   C. a library
   D. a GM plant

3. How many records did her family play?

   A. twenty
   B. five
   C. hundreds
   D. one ⓓ

4. How many sisters does Goldberg have?

   A. one ⓐ
   B. two
   C. three
   D. none

5. Where does Goldberg go to college?

   A. New York City
   B. Washington, D.C. ⓑ
   C. Seattle
   D. Miami

Journal Topic

1. Write about your memories of growing up.

Discussion Questions

1. How does Goldberg describe her house, her family, and her childhood?

2. Is she able to escape her family's influence when she goes to college?

3. How does her description of going to the symphony help us understand her college experience?

4. According to Goldberg, how does one move beyond one's childhood experience?

5. What happens if one doesn't "digest" one's childhood experience?

Writing Topics

1. Describe the place you grew up.

2. Compare and contrast your parents' tastes and your tastes in music, movies, entertainment, food, or reading.

3. How did you want to be different from your parents when you were growing up?

4. Describe an incident from your childhood that explains how you felt about yourself, your family, or your neighborhood.

5. Using examples from the essay, support the statement that Goldberg felt her childhood was bland and desolate.

Blind to Failure

Karl Taro Greenfeld

1   When he saw Erik Weihenmayer arrive that afternoon, Pasquale Scaturro began to have misgivings about the expedition he was leading. Here they were on the first floor of Mount Everest, and Erik—the reason for the whole trip—was stumbling into Camp 1, bloody, sick and dehydrated*. "He was literally green," says fellow climber and teammate Michael O'Donnell. "He looked like George Foreman* had beat the crap out of him for about two hours." The beating had actually been administered by Erik's climbing partner, Luis Benitez. Erik had slipped into a crevasse*, and as Benitez reached down to catch him, his climbing pole raked* Erik across the nose and chin. Wounds heal slowly at that altitude* because of the thin air.

2   As Erik passed out in his tent, the rest of the team gathered in a worried huddle. "I was thinking maybe this is not a good idea," says Scaturro, "Two years of planning, a documentary movie, and this blind guy barely makes it to Camp 1?"

3   This blind guy? Erik Weihenmayer, 33, wasn't just another yuppie trekker* who'd lost a few rounds to the mountain. Blind since he was 13, the victim of a rare hereditary* disease of the retina*, he began attacking mountains in his early 20s. But he was having the same doubts as the rest of them. On that arduous* climb to camp through the Khumbu Icefall, Erik wondered for the first time if his attempt to become the first sightless person to summit* Mount Everest was a colossal* mistake, an act of Daedalian hubris* for which he would be punished. There are so many ways to die on that mountain, spanning the spectacular (fall through an ice shelf into a crevasse, get waylaid by an avalanche*, develop cerebral edema* from lack of oxygen and have your brain literally swell out of your skull) and the banal* (become disoriented* because of oxygen deprivation* and decide you'll take a little nap, right here in the snow, which becomes a forever nap).

4   Erik, as he stumbled through the icefall, was so far out of his comfort zone that he began to speculate* on which of those fates might await him. For a moment he flashed on all those cliches about what blind people are supposed to do—become piano tuners or pencil salesmen—and thought maybe they were stereotypes* for good reason. Blind people certainly shouldn't be out here, wandering through an ever changing ice field, measuring the distance over a 1,000-ft.-deep crevasse with climbing poles and then leaping, literally, over and into the unknown.

5   The blind thrive* on patterns: Stairs are all the same height, city blocks roughly the same length, curbs approximately the same depth. They learn to identify the patterns in their environment much more than the sighted population do, and to rely on them to plot their way through the world.

6   But in the Khumbu Icefall, the trail through the Himalayan glacier, is patternless landscape, a diabolically* cruel obstacle course for a blind person. It changes every year as the river of ice shifts, but it's always made up of treacherously* crumbly stretches of ice, ladders roped together over wide crevasses, slightly narrower crevasses that must be jumped, huge seracs,* avalanches, and—most frustrating for a blind person, who naturally seeks to identify patterns in his terrain—a totally random* landscape.

7   In the icefall there is no system, no repetition, no rhyme or reason to the lay of the frozen land. On the other hand, "it is so specific in terms of

dehydrated: *medical condition that results from lack of water*
George Foreman: *heavyweight boxing champion*
crevasse: *a deep crevice or space*
raked: *scratched*
altitude: *height*

trekker: *hiker*
hereditary: *inherited through genes*
retina: *delicate membrane inside the eye*
arduous: *difficult, strenuous*
summit: *climb to the top or summit of*
colossal: *huge*
Daedalian hubris: *pride, presumption*
avalanche: *the slide of a large amount of snow down a mountain*
cerebral edema: *swelling in the brain*
banal: *commonplace*
disoriented: *lose one's bearings*
deprivation: *to be deprived of, lack of*
speculate: *guess*
stereotypes: *oversimplified concepts*
thrive: *do well*

diabolically: *devilishly*

treacherously: *deceptive and dangerous*
seracs: *towers of ice on a glacier*
random: *unpredictable*

where you can step," Erik recalls. "Sometimes you're walking along and then boom, a crevasse is right there, and three more steps and another one, and then a snow bridge. And vertical up, then a ladder and then a jumbly section." It took Erik 13 hrs to make it from Base Camp through the icefall to Camp 1, at 20,000 feet. Scaturro had allotted* seven.

allotted: *assigned*

8   A typical assault on Everest requires each climber to do as many as ten traverses* between Base Camp and Camp 1 through the icefall, both for acclimatization* purposes and to help carry the immense amount of equipment required for an ascent*. After Erik's accident, the rest of the National Federation of the Blind (N.F.B.) team discussed letting him stay up in Camp 1, equipped with videotapes and food, while the rest of the team and the Sherpas* did his carries for him. No way, said Erik. No way he was going to do this climb without being a fully integrated* and useful member of the team. "I wasn't going to be carried to the top and spiked like a football." He would eventually make ten passes through the Khumbu, cutting his time to five hours.

traverses: *movements across*
acclimatization: *getting used to the climate*
ascent: *climb up*

Sherpas: *Tibetan people living in northern Nepal*
integrated: *included*

9   Sometimes, when Erik is giving a motivational speech for one of his corporate clients, such as Glaxo Wellcome or AT&T, a fat, balding middle-aged middle manager will approach him and say, "Even I wouldn't do that stuff." Erik calls it the "Even I" syndrome*, where people assume that sight will trump* all other attributes and senses combined. Neither impatient nor smug*, he resists the impulse to say, "You're fat, out of shape and you smoke. Why would you even think of doing this stuff? Just because you can see?"

syndrome: *pattern of symptoms that indicate a disease*
trump: *beat*
smug: *overly confident*

10   Many pros wouldn't go near Erik's team, fearing they might have to haul the blind guy down. "Everyone was saying Erik was gonna have an epic," says Charley Mace, a member of the film crew. (Epic is Everest slang for disaster.) Another climber planned to stay close, boasting that he would "get the first picture of the dead blind guy."

11   For Erik, who knew almost as soon as he could speak that he would lose his vision in his early teens, excelling as an athlete was the result of accepting his disability rather than denying it. Growing up with two brothers in Hong Kong and Weston, Conn., he was always an athletic kid, a tough gamer who developed a bump-and-grind one-on-one basketball game that allowed him to work his way close to the hoop. He was, his father Ed says, "a pretty normal kid. While bike riding, he might have run into a few more parked cars than other kids, but we didn't dwell on his going blind."

12   His blindness was a medical inevitability*, like a court date with a hanging judge. "I saw blindness like this disease," he explains. "Like AIDS or something that was going to consume me." Think about that—being a kid, ten, eleven years old, and knowing that at some point in the near future your world is going to go dark. Certainly it builds character—that mental toughness his fellow climbers marvel at—but in a child, the natural psychological defense would be denial.

inevitability: *unable to be avoided or prevented*

13   When he lost his vision, Erik at first refused to use a cane or learn Braille*, insisting he could somehow muddle on as normal. "I was so afraid I would seem like a freak," he recalls. But after a few embarrassing stumbles—he couldn't even find the school restrooms anymore—he admitted he needed help. For Erik, the key was acceptance—not to fight his disability but to learn to work within it; not to transcend it but to understand what he was capable of achieving within it; not to pretend he had sight but to build

Braille: *a system of printing for the blind in which raised dots represent letters*

systems that allowed him to excel without it. "It's tragic—I know blind people who like to pass themselves off as being able to see," Erik says. "What's the point of that?"

14   He would never play basketball or catch a football again. But then he discovered wrestling. "I realized I could take sighted people and slam them into the mat," he says. Grappling was a sport where feel and touch mattered more than sight. As a high school senior, he went all the way to the Junior National Freestyle Wrestling Championships in Iowa.

fray: *battle*

15   Wrestling gave him the confidence to re-enter the teenage social fray*. He began dating when he was seventeen; his first girlfriend was a sighted woman three years older than he. Erik jokes that he is not shy about using his blindness to pick up women. "They really go for the guide dog," he explains. "You go into a bar, put the guide dog out there, and the girls just come up to you." He and his friends devised* a secret handshake to let Erik know whether a girl was attractive. "Just because you're blind doesn't make you any more selfless or deep or anything. You're just like most guys, but you look for different things," Erik says. "Smooth skin, nice body, muscles—that stuff becomes more important." And the voice becomes paramount*. "My wife has the most beautiful voice in the world," Erik says. Married in 1997, he and his wife, Ellie, have a one-year-old daughter, Emma.

devised: *developed*

paramount: *most important*

16   Erik first went hiking with his father when he was 13, trying to tap his way into the wild with a white cane and quickly becoming frustrated stubbing his toes on rocks and roots and bumping into branches and trunks. But when he tried rock climbing at 16 while at a camp for the disabled in New Hampshire, he was hooked. Like wrestling, it was a sport in which being blind didn't have to work against him. He took to it quickly, and through climbing gradually found his way to formal mountaineering.

17   Watching Erik scramble up a rock face is a little like watching a spider make its way up a wall. His hands are like antennae, gathering information as they flick outward, surveying the rock for cracks, grooves, bowls, nubbins, knobs, edges and ledges, converting all of it into a road map etched* into his mind. "It's like instead of wrestling with a person, I am moving and working with a rock," he explains. "It's a beautiful process of solving a puzzle." He is an accomplished rock climber, rated 5.10 (5.14 is the highest), and has led teams up sections of Yosemite's notorious El Capitan. On ice, where one wrong strike with an ice ax can bring down an avalanche, Erik has learned to listen to the ice as he pings it gently with his ax. If it clinks, he avoids it. If it makes a thunk like a spoon hitting butter, he knows it's solid ice.

etched: *clearly imprinted*

18   Despite being an accomplished mountaineer—summiting Denali, Kilimanjaro in Africa and Aconcagua in Argentina, among other peaks, and, in the words of his friends, "running up 14ers" (14,000-ft. peaks)—Erik viewed Everest as insurmountable* until he ran into Scaturro at a sportswear trade show in Salt Lake City, Utah. Scaturro, who had already summited Everest, had heard of the blind climber, and when they met, the two struck an easy rapport*. A geophysicist* who often put together energy-company expeditions to remote areas in search of petroleum, Scaturro began wondering if he could put together a team that could help Erik get to the summit of Everest.

insurmountable: *unable to be gotten around or over*

rapport: *trusting relationship*
geophysicist: *one who studies the physics of the earth*

19   "Dude," Scaturro asked, "have you ever climbed Everest?"

20   "No."

scuttling: *moving quickly, scurrying*

21 "Dude, you wanna?"

22 Climbing with Erik isn't that different from climbing with a sighted mountaineer. You wear a bell on your pack, and he follows the sound, scuttling* along using his custom-made climbing poles to feel his way along the trail. His climbing partners shout out helpful descriptions: "Death fall two feet to your right!" "Emergency helicopter-evacuation pad to your left!" He is fast, though, often running up the back of less experienced climbers. His partners all have scars from being jabbed by Erik's climbing poles when they slowed down.

23 For the Everest climb, Scaturro and Erik assembled a team that combined veteran climbers and trusted friends of Erik's. Scaturro wrote up a Braille proposal for the Everest attempt and submitted it to Mark Maurer, president of the National Federation of the Blind. Maurer immediately pledged $250,000 to sponsor the climb. (Aventis Pharmaceuticals agreed to sponsor a documentary on the climb to promote Allegra, its allergy medication; Erik suffers from seasonal allergies.) For Erik, who already had numerous gear and clothing sponsors, this was the greatest challenge of his life. If he failed, he would be letting down not just himself but all the blind, confirming that certain activities remained the preserve of the sighted.

24 He argued to anyone who would listen that he was an experienced mountaineer and that if he failed, it would be because of his heart or lungs or brain rather than his eyes. He wasn't afraid of physical danger—he had made dozens of skydives and scaled some of the most dangerous cliff faces in the world—but he was frightened of how the world would perceive him. "But I knew that if I went and failed, that would feel better than if I didn't go at all," Erik says. "It could be like the wrestling Junior Nationals all over again. I went out to Iowa, and I got killed. But I needed to go to understand what my limits were."

25 Oxygen deprivation does strange things to the human body. Heart rates go haywire, brain function decreases, blood thickens, intestines shut down. Bad ideas inexplicably pop into your head, especially above 25,000 feet, where, as Krakaer famously wrote in *Into Thin Air*, climbers have the "mind of a reptile."

26 At that altitude, Erik could rely on no one but himself. His teammates would have to guide him, to keep ringing the bell and making sure Erik stayed on the trail, but they would be primarily concerned about their own survival in some of the worst conditions on earth. Ironically, Erik had some advantages as they closed in on the peak. For one thing, at that altitude all the climbers wore goggles and oxygen masks, restricting their vision so severely that they could not see their own feet—a condition that Erik was used to. Also, the final push for the summit began in the early evening, so most of the climb was in pitch darkness; the only illumination was from miner's lamps.

Dante's Inferno: *the Italian poet Dante (1265–1321) described hell in a book called* The Inferno

27 When Erik and the team began the final ascent from Camp 4—the camp he describes as Dante's Inferno* with ice and wind—they had been on the mountain two months, climbing up and down and then up from Base Camp to Camps 1, 2, and 3, getting used to the altitude and socking away enough equipment—especially oxygen canisters—to make a summit push. They had tried for the summit once, but turned back because of weather. At 29,000 feet, the Everest peak is in the jet stream, which means that winds can exceed 100 m.p.h., and that what looks from sea level like a cottony wisp of clouds is actually a killer storm at the summit. Bad weather

played a fatal role in the 1996 climbing season documented in *Into Thin Air*.

28 On May 24, with only seven days left in the climbing season, most of the N.F.B. expedition knew this was their last shot at the peak. That's why when Erik and Chris Morris reached the Balcony, the beginning of the Southeast Ridge, at 27,000 feet, after a hard slog up the South Face, they were terribly disappointed when the sky lit up with lightning, driving snow, and fierce winds. "We thought we were done," Erik says. "We would have been spanked if we made a push in those conditions." A few teammates gambled and went for it, and Jeff Evans and Brad Bull heroically pulled out fixed guidelines that had been frozen in the ice. By the time Base Camp radioed that the storm was passing, Erik and his team were coated in two inches of snow. Inspired by the possibility of a break in the weather, the team pushed on up the exposed Southeast Ridge, an additional 1,200 vertical feet to the South Summit. At that point the climbers looked like astronauts walking on some kind of arctic moon. They moved slowly because of fatigue from their huge, puffy down suits, backpacks with oxygen canisters, and regulators and goggles.

29 With a 10,000-foot vertical fall into Tibet on one side and a 7,000-foot drop into Nepal on the other, the South Summit, at about 28,700 feet, is where many climbers finally turn back. The roughly 656-foot-long knife-edge ridge leading to the Hillary Step consists of ice, snow and fragmented shale*, and the only way to cross it is to take baby steps, anchoring your way with an ice ax. "You can feel the rock chip off," says Erik. "And you can hear it falling down into the void."

shale: crumbly rock made of layers of sediment

30 The weather was finally clearing as they reached the Hillary Step, the 39-foot rock face that is the last major obstacle before the summit. Erik clambered up the cliff, belly flopping over the top. "I celebrated with the dry heaves," he jokes. And then he walked 45 minutes up a sharply angled snow slope to the summit.

31 "Look around, dude," Evans told the blind man when they were standing on top of the world. "Just take a second and look around."

32 It could be called the most successful Everest expedition ever, and not just because of Erik's participation. A record 19 climbers from the N.F.B. team summited, including the oldest man ever to climb Everest—64-year-old Sherman Bull—and the second father-and-son team ever to do so—Bull and his son Brad.

33 What Erik achieved is hard for a sighted person to comprehend. What do we compare it with? How do we relate to it? Do we put on a blindfold and go hiking? That's silly, Erik maintains, because when a sighted person loses his vision, he is terrified and disoriented. And Erik is clearly neither of those things. Perhaps the point is really that there is no way to put what Erik has done in perspective because no one has ever done anything like it. It is a unique achievement, one that in the truest sense pushes the limits of what man is capable of. Maurer of the N.F.B. compares Erik to Helen Keller. "Erik can be a contemporary symbol for blindness," he explains. "Helen Keller lived 100 years ago. She should not be our most potent symbol of blindness today."

34 Erik, sitting in the Kathmandu international airport, waiting for the flight out of Nepal that will eventually return him to Golden, Colorado, is surrounded by his teammates and the expedition's 75 pieces of luggage. Success has made the group jubilant*. This airport lounge has become the

jubilant: joyful

mountaineering equivalent of a winning Super Bowl locker room. As they sit amid their luggage, holding Carlsberg beers, they frequently raise a toast. "Shez! Shez!" shouts a climber. That's Nepali for drink! drink! "No epics," a climber chimes in, citing what really matters: no one died. In between posing for photos and signing other passenger's boarding passes, Erik talks about how eager he is to get back home. He says summiting Everest was great, probably the greatest experience of his life. But then he thinks about a moment a few months ago, before Everest, when he was walking down the street in Colorado with his daughter, Emma, in a front pack. They were on their way to buy some banana bread for his wife, and Emma was pulling on his hand, her little fingers curled around his index finger. That was a summit too, he says. There are summits everywhere. You just have to know where to look.

Comprehension Questions

1. The essay describes Erik Weihenmayer's attempt

   A. to climb Mount Everest.
   B. to climb Mt Kilimanjaro.
   C. to swim the English Channel.
   D. to bike cross country.

2. What was unusual about Erik's attempt?

   A. He had a new baby.
   B. He had never attempted anything of the sort before.
   C. He is blind.
   D. He had lost a leg in an accident.

3. Erik was handicapped since he was

   A. born
   B. five
   C. thirteen
   D. eighteen

4. Erik's condition was caused by

   A. an accident
   B. a hereditary disease
   C. a sports injury
   D. a fire

5. What sport(s) did Erik take up after he became handicapped?

   A. swimming
   B. wrestling
   C. rock climbing
   D. both b and c

Journal Topics

1. Describe something you have done or attempted to do that took courage.

2. How do you think Erik would have felt if he had not succeeded in this particular climb?

Discussion Questions

1. How is Erik's story inspirational?

2. In what ways was Erik's condition not a handicap in climbing the mountain?

3. How was Erik particularly well suited for this challenge?

Writing Topics

1. What characteristics did Erik possess that enabled him to achieve his goals?

2. Describe the difficulties Erik faced and how he overcame them.

3. Recount Erik's ascent of the mountain.

4. How was Erik particularly well suited for this challenge?

5. Make a statement about Erik's character and support it with examples.

Deferred: *put off,*
postponed

What Happens to a Dream Deferred*?

Langston Hughes

fester: *putrefy, rot*

1   Does it dry up
Like a raisin in the sun?
Or fester* like a sore—
And then run?
Does it stink like rotten meat?
Or crust and sugar over
like a syrupy sweet?

2   Maybe it just sags
like a heavy load.

3   Or does it explode?

The River

Bruce Springsteen

1   I come from down in the valley
Where mister, when you're young
They bring you up to do like your daddy done
Me and Mary we met in high school
When she was just seventeen
We'd drive out of this valley to where the fields were green
We'd go down to the river
And into the river we'd dive
Oh down to the river we'd ride

all she wrote: *it was all over*

2   Then I got Mary pregnant
And, man, that was all she wrote*
And for my 19th birthday I got a union card and a wedding coat
We went down to the courthouse
And the judge put it all to rest
No wedding day smiles, no walk down the aisle
No flowers, no wedding dress
That night we went down to the river
And into the river we'd dive
Oh down to the river we'd ride

3   I got a job working construction for the Johnstown Company
But lately there ain't been much work on account of the economy
Now all them things that seemed so important
Well, mister they vanished right into the air
Now I act like I don't remember
Mary acts like she don't care
But I remember us riding in my brother's car
Her body tan and wet down at the reservoir
At night on them banks I'd lie awake
And pull her close just to feel each breath she'd take
Now those memories come back to haunt me

They haunt me like a curse
Is a dream a lie if it don't come true
Or is it something worse
That sends me
Down to the river
Though I know the river is dry
That sends me down to the river tonight
Down to the river
My baby and I
Oh down to the river we ride

Comprehension Questions

1. Which author likens a dream to rotten meat?

   A. Bruce Springsteen
   B. Langston Hughes

2. The speaker in "The River" and Mary met

   A. in the neighborhood.
   B. on a bus.
   C. in high school.
   D. at the beach.

3. According to Langston Hughes, what might dry up like a raisin in the sun?

   A. a lake
   B. a piece of fruit
   C. the river
   D. a dream

4. What has dried up in "The River"?

   A. a lake
   B. the river
   C. a piece of fruit
   D. a dream

5. The speaker in "The River" works in

   A. construction
   B. a factory
   C. law enforcement
   D. medicine

Journal Topics

1. What goal do you have that you feel is important to your future?

2. Tell about someone you know who has fulfilled a dream or lost a dream.

Discussion Questions

1. Do Langston Hughes and Bruce Springsteen have the same opinion about dreams?

2. If a dream explodes, as Langston Hughes says, would that be good or bad?

3. Has the speaker in "The River" lost his dream? What evidence from the poem can you give for your answer?

4. What advice would Hughes and Springsteen give to someone with a dream?

Writing Topics

1. Does Langston Hughes have a positive or negative view of deferred dreams and goals? Give three examples of images he uses and explain whether they are positive or negative.

2. What happened to the speaker in "The River"? Narrate or tell the story of the events of his life.

3. What are your dreams and goals and how do you plan to make them come true?

4. How can you safeguard your dreams and goals or the dreams and goals of someone you love? Give two ways you believe you can protect your dreams or the dreams of another.

Saying Good-Bye

Cynthia Jabs

1 Humans have a longer life span than most other creatures on the planet. So, with the possible exception of parrots, we tend to outlive most of our animal companions. Although seeing an animal friend through its final days can be a sad and trying time, it is also an opportunity to participate in a natural stage of life that may be unfamiliar territory for many of us.

2 One of the most difficult things about the death of a pet is that, all too often, its importance is largely overlooked. Friends, family, co-workers—even other pet owners—may fail to recognize the significance of a pet's passing. And without proper recognition of the life change involved in losing a pet, recovery becomes a harder, slower, and lonelier process than it otherwise would be.

integral: *necessary, essential*
void: *empty space*

3 Whether or not we consider our pets to be "part of the family," they are certainly integral* members of our household. Their leaving, however it happens, creates a void* that affects every member of the household. The entire family—adults, children, other pets, even family members who never got along with the pet—is affected by the loss.

plagued: *periodically troubled*
erupted: *exploded*
skirmishes: *brief fights*
intravenous: *inserted in the veins*

4 Our 18-year-old cat, Gypsy, died quietly last year when her ailing kidneys gave out. I was surprised by how much her death affected our other cat, Hobbes. These two creatures had never been buddies—their love-hate relationship was plagued* by power struggles that often erupted* in noisy nighttime skirmishes*. In the weeks immediately after Gypsy died, however, Hobbes steadily lost his appetite, and by the time we took him to the vet, he had to be hospitalized for intravenous* feeding and medication. For a few intense days, our family was afraid that we might lose him as well.

adapted: *gotten used to*

5 After a while, he came around and has since adapted* well to being our household's only cat. But losing Gypsy hit him harder than I would have expected, and in ways I had never imagined. We can't know how—or how hard—someone will be hit by the loss of an animal friend. We can only try to allow for the unexpected.

copes with: *handles*

6 The circumstances that surround a pet's death greatly affect the way the owner copes with* loss, according to John and Suzanne Hampton, longtime dog breeders and the authors of *Senior Years: Understanding Your Dog* (Macmillan, $25). When a pet's death follows a long illness, the authors say, people often suffer feelings of guilt or failure. If a pet dies suddenly, the loss may be too much for the owner to absorb all at once and may cause him or her to experience a temporary state of denial. Other stages of grieving include anger and depression. All of these emotions surface in one form or another before the grieving process reaches its final stage of resolution, in which a pet is fondly missed, but without the pain felt earlier.

euthanasia: *mercy killing*
arises: *comes up*
terminally ill: *near death, certain to die*
contradictory: *opposing or the opposite of*
option: *choice*
sympathize: *ability to share feelings*

7 In our pets' final days, we must often make a difficult choice. The question of euthanasia*, for example, arises* when animals are terminally ill* and suffering. Although it offers a way to relieve an animal's pain, euthanasia may feel contradictory* to a person who has spent years providing for all of an animal's health needs. For those who choose this option,* another question evolves: whether or not to be present during the procedure. These are highly personal choices, and many veterinarians now refer pet owners to experienced counselors for help in dealing with these difficult decisions.

8 Sharing the experience of loss with someone who can understand and sympathize* is one sure step in dealing with the healing process. Talking

either to a counselor or to someone who has recently had a similar loss can provide relief from bottled-up emotions. Sharing memories of your pet with others who knew him or her can also be very helpful.

9 When Gypsy died, we buried her in the corner of our garden where she liked to hide when she ventured* outside. Our children offered fond recollections* of her and said their good-byes. Finally, we passed around the picture of her that now sits on our mantel.

ventured: dared to go
recollections: memories

10 A child's first experience with death often comes with the passing of a pet, and rituals like these can be especially helpful for them. I remember how hard it was to explain to my four-year-old son that Gypsy wasn't going to wake up. I don't think he really understood until we buried her.

11 For some families, a burial ceremony can provide comfort. If you plan to bury your pet in your backyard, check local ordinances first. In some towns, especially in urban areas, it may be best to let a veterinarian arrange for the burial or for cremation.

12 If you have trouble settling on a place or procedure that feels proper, there are professionals to whom you can turn for products and services. The International Associations of Pet Cemeteries (5055 Rte. 11, Ellenburg Depot, N.Y. 12935; 518-594-3000) can help you find services nearby or answer other questions.

acknowledge: recognize

13 One way or another, it is a good idea to take some time to acknowledge* your pet's passing. Give yourself some space before you take on another pet. There is no way to replace a lost pet, and it is hard to begin a satisfying relationship with a new animal friend while you still are grieving for an old one.

14 As much as we would like to think that our pets will live forever, at some point we have to face the fact that they don't. Being with out pets straight through to the end of their lives helps us realize just how precious they are to us.

Comprehension Questions

1. According to the author, most people recognize the significance of the death of a pet.

   T / (F)

2. The death of a pet can affect
   A. the owner.
   B. other family members.
   C. other pets.
   (D). all of the above.

3. The author recommends
   A. euthanasia.
   B. replacing the lost pet within a few weeks.
   (C) acknowledging feelings of grief.

4. A burial ceremony can be especially helpful
   A. if the pet is buried in the back yard.
   (B). if it involves a child's first experience with death.
   C. if performed by a professional mortician.

5. The author's thesis can best be stated as the following:
    A. Pets are important members of the family.
    B. We learn who our friends are when we lose a pet.
    ⓒ Proper recognition of the life change involved in losing a pet can aid in the healing process.

Discussion Questions

1. How can the death of a pet affect other pets?

2. How do the circumstances of a pet's death affect an owner's feelings?

3. What are the stages of grief discussed by the author?

4. What are some of the difficult choices a pet owner has to make in a pet's final days?

5. What steps can aid in the healing process?

Journal Topic

1. Did you experience the death of a pet as a child or as an adult? Describe your feelings.

2. What helped you recover from the loss?

Writing Topics

1. Use examples from the article and from your experience to illustrate the grieving and healing process.

2. Describe the grieving and healing process.

3. How can the death of a pet affect various members of a household? (Consider other pets, children, adults.)

4. Relate a personal experience with the loss of a pet to the author's discussion of the grieving and healing process.

5. Relate the author's discussion of the grieving and healing process to another type of mourning (for a possession, a house, a job, a friend, a relative).

When Life Imitates Video

John Leo

1   Was it real life or acted-out video game?

2   Marching through a large building using various bombs and guns to pick off victims is a conventional video-game scenario*. In the Colorado massacre, Dylan Klebold and Eric Harris used pistol-grip shotguns, as in some video-arcade games. The pools of blood, screams of agony, and pleas for mercy must have been familiar—they are featured in some of the newer and more realistic kill-for-kicks games. "With each kill," the *Los Angeles Times* reported, "the teens cackled and shouted as though playing one of the morbid* video games they loved." And they ended their spree by shooting themselves in the head, the final act in the game Postal, and, in fact, the only way to end it.

3   Did the sensibilities* created by the modern video kill games play a role in the Littleton massacre? Apparently so. Note the cool and casual cruelty, the outlandish arsenal* of weapons, the cheering and laughing while hunting down the victims one by one. All of this seems to reflect the style and feel of the video killing games they played so often.

4   No, there isn't any direct connection between most murderous games and most murders. And yes, the primary responsibility for protecting children from dangerous games lies with the parents, many of whom like to blame the entertainment industry for their own failings.

5   But there is a cultural problem here: We are now a society in which the chief form of play for millions of youngsters is making large numbers of people die. Hurting and maiming* others is the central fun activity in video games played so addictively by the young. A widely cited* survey of 900 fourth-through-eighth-grade students found that almost half of the children said their favorite electronic games involve violence. Can it be that all this constant training in make-believe killing has no social effects?

6   The conventional argument is that this is a harmless activity among children who know the difference between fantasy and reality. But unstable youngsters often play the games unsure about the difference. Many of these have been maltreated* or rejected and left alone most of the time (a precondition* for playing the games obsessively*). Adolescent feelings of resentment, powerlessness, and revenge pour into the killing games. In these children, the games can become a dress rehearsal for the real thing.

7   Psychologist David Grossman of Arkansas State University, a retired Army officer, thinks "point and shoot" video games have the same effect as military strategies* used to break down a soldier's aversion* to killing. During World War II, only 15 to 20 percent of all American soldiers fired their weapons in battle. Shooting games in which the target is a man-shaped outline, the Army found, made recruits more willing to "make killing a reflex action."

8   Video games are much more powerful versions of the military's primitive* discovery about overcoming the reluctance* to shoot. Grossman says Michael Carneal, the schoolboy shooter in Paducah, Ky., showed the effects of video-game lessons in killing. Carneal coolly shot nine times, hitting eight people, five of them in the head or neck. Head shots pay a bonus in many video games. Now the Marine Corps is adapting* a version of Doom, the hyper violent game played by one of the Littleton killers, for its own training purposes.

---

scenario: *story outline*

morbid: *gruesome, unhealthy*

sensibilities: *feelings, perception of the world*
arsenal: *storehouse or stockpile of weapons*

maiming: *crippling or mutilating*
cited: *quoted or referenced*

maltreated: *badly treated*
precondition: *prerequisite, something that is required before something else*
obsessively: *behavior that cannot be resisted or controlled*
strategies: *plans of action*
aversion: *unwillingness, distaste*

primitive: *simple or unsophisticated*
reluctance: *unwillingness, hesitation*

adapting: *adjusting, changing to fit other conditions*

sociopath: *someone who hates people*

vulnerable: *weak, unprotected*

exploiting: *taking advantage of weakness*

9   More realistic touches in video games help blur the boundary between fantasy and reality—guns carefully modeled on real ones, accurate looking wounds, screams, and other sound effects, even the recoil of a heavy rifle. Some newer games seem intent on erasing children's empathy and concern for others. Once the intended victims of video slaughter were mostly gangsters or aliens. Now some games invite players to blow away ordinary people who have done nothing wrong—pedestrians, marching bands, an elderly woman with a walker. In these games, the shooter is not a hero, just a violent sociopath*. One ad for a Sony game says: "Get in touch with your gun-toting, testosterone-pumping, cold-blooded murdering side."

10   These killings are supposed to be taken as harmless over-the-top jokes. But the bottom line is that the young are being invited to enjoy the killing of vulnerable* victims picked at random. This looks like the final lesson in a course to eliminate any lingering resistance to killing.

11   SWAT teams and cops now turn up as the intended victims of some video-game killings. This has the effect of exploiting* resentments toward law enforcement and making real-life shooting of cops more likely. This sensibility turns up in the hit movie *Matrix:* world-saving Keanu Reeves, in a mandatory Goth-style, long black coat packed with countless heavy-duty guns, is forced to blow away huge numbers of uniformed law-enforcement people.

12   "We have to start worrying about what we are putting into the minds of our young," says Grossman. "Pilots train on flight simulators, drivers on driving simulators, and now we have our children on murder simulators." If we want to avoid more Littleton-style massacres, we will begin taking the social effects of killing games more seriously.

Comprehension Questions

1. The author argues that _____ contributed to school shootings.

    A. violent movies
    B. violent TV shows
    C. violent video games
    D. violent song lyrics

2. Shooting at a man-shaped target has what effect on soldiers?

    A. It improves accuracy.
    B. It helps make shooting a reflex action.
    C. It increases aggression.
    D. It decreases emotion.

3. During World War II, what percent of American soldiers fired their weapons during battle?

    A. 90–100%
    B. 70–80%
    C. 50–60%
    D. 15–20%

4. New video games are

    A. decreasing in violence.
    B. becoming more realistic and violent.
    C. making ordinary people and policemen targets.
    D. both B and C.

5. The author cites an expert who compares violent video games to

    A. violent TV shows.
    (B) murder simulators.
    C. harmless entertainment.
    D. military training.

Discussion Questions

1. How popular are the types of games described by the author? What do you think accounts for their popularity?

2. Do violent video games turn all players into killers? Why or why not?

3. What effects do you think violent video games have on regular players?

Writing Topics

1. What effect(s) does playing violent video games have on young people? Use examples to support your ideas.

2. Should violent video games be banned or restricted? Why or why not?

3. As a parent, would you want your middle or high school children playing violent "kill-for-kicks" games? Why or why not?

4. Should parents control their children's entertainment choices? Under what circumstances?

5. Write a letter to the editor of your local newspaper arguing that parents should monitor the video games their children play or that violent video games should be removed from movie theater lobbies and/or video arcades.

From *I Just Wanna Be Average*

Mike Rose

1   Students will float to the mark you set. I and the others in the vocational classes were bobbing in pretty shallow water. Vocational education has aimed at increasing the economic opportunities of students who do not do well in our schools. Some serious programs succeed in doing that, and through exceptional teachers—like Mr. Gross in *Horace's Compromise*—students learn to develop hypotheses* and troubleshoot, reason through a problem, and communicate effectively—the true job skills. The vocational track, however, is most often a place for those who are just not making it, a dumping ground for the disaffected.* There were a few teachers who worked hard at education; young Brother Slattery, for example, combined a stern voice with weekly quizzes to try to pass along to us a skeletal outline of world history. But mostly the teachers had no idea of how to engage the imaginations of us kids who were scuttling* along at the bottom of the pond.

2   And the teachers would have needed some inventiveness, for none of us was groomed* for the classroom. It wasn't just that I didn't know things—didn't know how to simplify algebraic fractions, couldn't identify different kinds of clauses, bungled Spanish translations—but that I had developed various faulty and inadequate ways of doing algebra and making sense of Spanish. Worse yet, the years of defensive tuning out in elementary school had given me a way to escape quickly while seeming at least half alert. During my time in Voc. Ed., I developed further into a mediocre* student and a somnambulant* problem solver, and that affected the subjects I did have the wherewithal* to handle: I detested* Shakespeare; I got bored with history. My attention flitted here and there. I fooled around in class and read my books indifferently*—the intellectual equivalent of playing with your food. I did what I had to do to get by, and I did it with half a mind.

3   But I did learn things about people and eventually came into my own socially. I liked the guys in Voc. Ed. Growing up where I did, I understood and admired physical prowess*, and there was an abundance of muscle here. There was Dave Snyder, a sprinter and halfback of true quality. Dave's ability and his quick wit gave him a natural appeal, and he was welcome in any clique, though he always kept a little independent. He enjoyed acting the fool and could care less about studies, but he possessed a certain maturity and never caused the faculty much trouble. It was a testament to his independence that he included me among his friends—I eventually went out for track, but I was no jock. Owing to the Latin alphabet and a dearth* of R's and S's, Snyder sat behind Rose, and we started exchanging one-liners and became friends.

4   There was Ted Richards, a much-touted Little League pitcher. He was chunky and had a baby face and came to Our Lady of Mercy as a seasoned street fighter. Ted was quick to laugh and he had a loud, jolly laugh, but when he got angry he'd smile a little smile, the kind that simply raises the corner of the mouth a quarter of an inch. For those who knew, it was an eerie signal. Those who didn't found themselves in big trouble, for Ted was very quick. He loved to carry on what we would come to call philosophical discussions: What is courage? Does God exist? He also loved words, enjoyed picking up big ones like *salubrious** and *equivocal** and using them in our conversations—laughing at himself as the word hit a chuckhole

---

Glossary (margin notes):

hypotheses: *tentative explanations of facts*

disaffected: *unhappy*

scuttling: *scurrying*

groomed: *prepared*

mediocre: *ordinary, unexceptional*
somnambulant: *sleepwalking*
wherewithal: *ability*
detested: *hated*
indifferently: *without interest*

prowess: *superior skill or ability*

dearth: *lack of*

salubrious: *healthy*
equivocal: *uncertain, inconclusive*

The Daily Worker: *a Socialist newspaper*

The Old Man and the Sea: *a novel by Ernest Hemingway*

hindsight: *understanding that comes after events have happened*   5

learned: *learning that comes from books and formal education*

apocryphal: *of questionable origin*

assured: *confident*

hodad: *greaser*

parable: *story that illustrates a moral lesson*

restive: *restless*

laryngectomize: *remove the larynx, area of throat containing vocal cords*

platitudinous: *filled with platitudes or trite expressions*   6

melee: *brawl*

disorienting: *to cause to lose orientation*

assumptions: *beliefs accepted without proof*

dissonant: *harsh, discordant*

ethnic: *people who share racial, religious, or cultural similarities*

linguistic: *language*

elite: *group with superior status*

constrained: *limited*

liberate: *free*

esteem: *value*

vengeance: *desire to punish*

stimuli: *excitement*

diffuse: *spread out, scatter*   7

sarcasm: *cutting remarks*

cultivate: *nurture, refine*

rolling off his tongue. Ted didn't do all that well in school—baseball and parties and testing the courage he'd speculated about took up his time. His textbooks were *Argosy* and *Field and Stream*, whatever newspapers he'd find on the bus stop—from *The Daily Worker** to pornography—conversations with uncles or hobos or businessmen he'd meet in a coffee shop, *The Old Man and the Sea**. With hindsight*, I can see that Ted was developing into one of those rough-hewn intellectuals whose sources are a mix of the learned* and the apocryphal*, whose discussions are both assured* and sad.

And then there was Ken Harvey. Ken was good-looking in a puffy way and had a full and oily ducktail and was a car enthusiast . . . a hodad*. One day in religion class, he said the sentence that turned out to be one of the most memorable of the hundreds of thousands I heard in the Voc. Ed. years. We were talking about the parable* of the talents, about achievement, working hard, doing the best you can do, blah-blah-blah, when the teacher called on the restive* Ken Harvey for an opinion. Ken thought about it, but just for a second, and said (with studied, minimal affect), "I just wanna be average." That woke me up. Average?! Who wants to be average? Then the athletes chimed in with the clichés that make you want to laryngectomize* them, and the exchange became a platitudinous* melee*. At the time, I thought Ken's assertion was stupid, and I wrote him off. But his sentence has stayed with me all these years, and I think I am finally coming to understand it.

Ken Harvey was gasping for air. School can be a tremendously disorienting* place. No matter how bad the school, you're going to encounter notions that don't fit with the assumptions* and beliefs that you grew up with—maybe you'll hear these dissonant* notions from teachers, maybe from other students, and maybe you'll read them. You'll also be thrown in with all kinds of kids from all kinds of backgrounds, and that can be unsettling—this is especially true in places of rich ethnic* and linguistic* mix, like the L.A. basin. You'll see a handful of students far excel you in courses that sound exotic and that are only in the curriculum of the elite*: French, physics, trigonometry. And all this is happening while you're trying to shape an identity, your body is changing, and your emotions are running wild. If you're a working-class kid in the vocational track, the options you'll have to deal with this will be constrained* in certain ways: You're defined by your school as "slow"; you're placed in a curriculum that isn't designed to liberate* you but to occupy you, or, if you're lucky, train you, though the training is for work the society does not esteem*; other students are picking up the cues from your school and your curriculum and interacting with you in particular ways. If you're a kid like Ted Richards, you turn your back on all this and let your mind roam where it may. But youngsters like Ted are rare. What Ken and so many others do is protect themselves from such suffocating madness by taking on with a vengeance* the identity implied in the vocational track. Reject the confusion and frustration by openly defining yourself as the Common Joe. Champion the average. Rely on your own good sense. Fuck this bullshit. Bullshit, of course, is everything you—and the others—fear is beyond you: books, essays, tests, academic scrambling, complexity, scientific reasoning, philosophical inquiry.

The tragedy is that you have to twist the knife in your own gray matter to make this defense work. You'll have to shut down, have to reject intellectual stimuli* or diffuse* them with sarcasm*, have to cultivate* stupidity,

malady: *illness, disorder*

flaunt: *show off*
materialize: *to make material*
neutralizes: *to make neutral*

have to convert boredom from a malady* into a way of confronting the world. Keep your vocabulary simple, act stoned when you're not or act more stoned than you are, flaunt* ignorance, materialize* your dreams. It is a powerful and effective defense—it neutralizes* the insult and the frustration of being a vocational kid and, when perfected, it drives teachers up the wall, a delightful secondary effect. But like all strong magic, it exacts a price.

Comprehension Questions

1. What track in school is Mike Rose on?

   A. College prep
   B. Advanced placement
   C. Vocational
   D. Technological

2. According to Mike Rose, vocational education is for students who

   A. don't do well in school.
   B. have an aptitude for mechanics.
   C. want to learn to make things.
   D. none of the above.

3. Mike Rose's problems in class included all of the following *except*

   A. not knowing basic information like the different kinds of clauses.
   B. having flawed ways of solving math problems.
   C. being distracted by the girls in the class.
   D. daydreaming.

4. What interests Rose most in his classes?

   A. the teacher
   B. the material
   C. other students
   D. writing

5. Who said "I just wanna be average"?

   A. Mike Rose
   B. Dave Snyder
   C. Ken Harvey
   D. Ted Richards

Journal Topic

1. Describe an incident that was typical of your high school experience.

Discussion Questions

1. Describe the school Rose attends.

2. Describe Rose's fellow students.

3. In what ways, according to Rose, can high school be disorienting?

4. According to Rose, how and why do students "tune out" in high school?

5. What price do they pay for evading reality?

Writing Topics

1. Describe a good or bad teacher from your high school.

2. Make a statement about your attitude toward school when you were in high school and support it with examples.

3. According to Rose, what are the causes or effects of students "tuning out" in school?

4. Why do you think students have trouble learning in high school?

5. Who or what did you admire when you were in high school? How did they or it influence you?

6. What, according to Rose and/or your own experience, are some methods students develop to defend themselves against the "suffocating madness" of high school?

Boys to Men

Ellen Sherman

1   Rameck Hunt can recall being ten years old, hanging out with friends on street corners in Plainfield, N.J., a city with more than its share of crime and poverty. It was 1983, and down the block, teenagers—boys who a few years earlier dreamed of becoming firefighters or police officers—were selling marijuana and crack. By age 14, they'd lost hope. They were just trying to survive. No way was he going to end up like that. He was going to get out.

2   But getting out would take more than just a boy's dreams—it would take time and work and planning. And it would require the support of a remarkable pair of friends Rameck Hunt had yet to meet.

3   In the beginning, the odds were stacked against him. Hunt's mother, Arlene, had wrestled with a drug problem. His father had done time for nonviolent charges and was seldom around. "For years I thought everybody's pops lived in jail," Hunt says. Rameck and seven relatives lived in a small, crowded house in Plainfield owned by his grandmother, a postal worker who largely supported the extended family on her own. Hunt shared a bed with his mother, uncle, and little sister.

4   Fortunately, he was a natural student. "I liked studying," Hunt says with a smile. "It's not like they had to trick me into it." But the streets, and some tough friends, were a constant distraction. He developed an attitude, and a swagger to go with it. "By about age ten, I started getting into trouble," he says. "Little things—roughing up other kids, stealing. I wasn't a bully inside. It was me trying to emulate* my friends."

emulate: *imitate*

5   Whatever her shortcomings, Arlene could see that her son was gifted and should be in a different environment. "You need a good education," she'd tell Rameck. Through a friend, she learned about Newark's University High, a magnet school for gifted students. Hunt, with his good grades, was admitted, and a new chapter of his life began.

6   In the fall of 1987, a wary 14-year-old showed up for the first day of school. "I thought there'd be all these geeks and nerds," Hunt says. Instead, he met George Jenkins and Sampson Davis—two guys just like him. Both of them dressed "cool," in jeans and Nikes. Both were smart. And both were growing up in single-parent homes with mothers who wanted more for them. "My mother was a rock," says Jenkins. Echoes Davis, "Mine was determined to make sure her family did well. She was always saying, 'Go to school.'"

7   All three took the advice to heart, but it didn't always keep them out of trouble. On Thanksgiving eve 1989, Hunt and a handful of friends were drinking beer behind Plainfield's Clinton Elementary School. As Hunt tells it, a crackhead lit up nearby, and Hunt and his pals told the man to get lost. When he didn't, the boys kicked and punched him. "We kept on beating him, then left to get something to eat," Hunt says. They returned to find the police waiting. Their victim identified them before being transported to the hospital.

8   The following morning Hunt awoke not to the smell of roasting turkey, but on the cold floor of the Herlich Juvenile Quarters. "I thought, Wow. I had this bad dream that I got thrown in jail," he recalls. "Then it hit me. I wanted to cry." He spent the holiday and part of the next week in detention. While waiting for a court appearance, he was able to look out a window. "I

could see kids on their way to school—like I should have been," he remembers. With no previous record, Hunt was released. "You think, this could never happen to me," he says. "But it did. I couldn't let that kind of peer pressure get to me again."

9   Hunt poured himself even more into his studies. And he spent more time with Jenkins and Davis. The three hung out, shared books, gave one another rides. During their senior year, they made an oath. "It wasn't like a blood oath, but whatever needed to be done, we'd do it for the other guy," says Hunt, "so we could make it out—together."

10   Jenkins, who for years had dreamed of becoming a dentist, encouraged his two friends to apply to Seton Hall University, which offered financial aid to low-income premedical and dental students. "I was selfish," Jenkins says with a smile. "I didn't want to go by myself."

11   When Hunt visited Seton Hall, he liked what he saw. "A whole lotta grass, a whole lotta trees," he says. "No graffiti. It was so pretty."

12   Carla Dickson, then a student-development specialist, interviewed Hunt. "He wanted to be a success, but he also wanted the program to work, not just for him but for his two friends," she says. "I was so impressed by that." In 1991 the three were among ten recipients of scholarships for the prestigious* program.

prestigious: recognized due to success

13   In many ways, Seton Hall was like a home for Hunt. When he moved into his dorm room, he had his own bed, desk and phone for the first time in his life. But because fewer than ten percent of Seton Hall's students were African American, Hunt and his two friends sometimes seemed like strangers in a strange land. In the halls, Hunt sometimes felt invisible. "People acted as though we weren't even there. We were just black kids from the ghetto."

isolation: separation

14   The three friends fought the isolation* by sticking close to one another. They studied together and looked out for each other. "If I needed money," says Davis, "Rameck was there to see me through."

15   They took jobs as tollbooth clerks to earn extra cash while maintaining grade point averages of 3.0 or higher. Still, balancing work and study wasn't always easy. "I must have quit college 300 times," Davis recalls. "Then I'd remember I was doing this for more than myself."

16   Hunt and Davis went on to Robert Wood Johnson Medical School in Piscataway. Jenkins stayed in Newark for dental school. At Robert Wood, Hunt sometimes felt that old isolation. During rounds, he'd jump in with his opinion, but his classmates seemed not to hear. "Sometimes I'd [have to] stand in front of them and repeat myself just to make them acknowledge* me," he recalls. When school vacations approached, his fellow students would buzz with plans for trips to Europe or the Caribbean. "Where are you going?" they'd ask Hunt, who'd shrug and say, "Oh, I'll just hang at my apartment."

acknowledge: recognize

17   Each weekend, the three friends got together. "It was important to have that link, to walk this path together," says Davis, "to have someone you could identify with."

18   On a sunny day in May 1999, Hunt and nearly 1200 other students gathered at a New Jersey amphitheater for graduation. Hunt spotted his mother and grandmother, now wheelchair-bound, applauding in the audience. "No one in our family has ever done something like this," he says. Rameck Hunt, one-time resident of the Herlich Juvenile Quarters, had become Rameck Hunt, M.D. And Hunt's two best friends were embarking* on careers as doctors alongside him.

embarking: starting

residency: *period in which doctors work in a hospital and receive specialized training*

postgraduate: *after graduate school*

sustain: *support*

mentoring: *guidance*

19 Later, at a celebration party at the Jenkins home, the three doctors accepted congratulations from friends, neighbors, even unknown well-wishers. "To them, if we could do it, they could do it," says Hunt.

20 The trio took a short vacation—their first—to Cancun. Then Hunt began his residency* in internal medicine at Robert Wood, and Davis in emergency medicine at Newark Beth Israel Medical Center. Jenkins continued postgraduate* studies in dentistry at the University of Medicine and Dentistry of New Jersey.

21 The pact that bound the friends for so long remains strong today because Hunt, Davis, and Jenkins want to sustain* the next generation. "We want them to see education as the way," says Hunt. The story of the three guys who made it out—with professional diplomas—will be told in *The Pact*, a book due out in May. The three doctors have also established the Three Doctors Foundation (www.threedoctorsfoundation.org), an outreach program that will offer mentoring*, scholarships and a summer camp for inner-city kids. They speak at universities, to business groups, even at the local library in an effort to spread their message. "The Cosby characters aren't real—they're on TV," Hunt tells kids. "We're living proof you can do it."

22 All three doctors intend to remain in the Newark area. "People are hanging pictures of us on their kids' walls hoping something rubs off on them," Jenkins says. "We want to be here for those kids," adds Hunt.

Today, Dr. Davis gives his full attention to an older black patient in the Newark Beth Israel ER. She smiles as if her grandson were in charge. "I want to take care of the people I grew up with," Davis says. On a cool November night, Dr. Jenkins, in an oversize sweatshirt and plaid hat, walks through his old neighborhood. Two kids approach him shyly just to say hi.

23 At Robert Wood, Dr. Hunt makes rounds. Several medical students listen as he charts a patient's treatment. "It feels good to have them listen," he says. "It feels well deserved."

24 The three doctors hope to heal their community—not just physically, but by taking on the disease of hopelessness and despair. They seem well on the way to finding a cure.

Comprehension Questions

1. Where did the three friends grow up?

   A. New York
   B. California
   C. New Jersey
   D. Washington, D.C.

2. Where did the three become friends?

   A. juvenile detention center
   B. school
   C. the neighborhood
   D. church

3. What did the boys pledge in high school?

   A. never to break the law
   B. to make it out of the ghetto together
   C. to become doctors
   D. to give back to their community

4. What college did the three friends attend?

  A. New York University
  B. Seton Hall University
  C. University of California
  D. Harvard

5. What do the men see as the surest way out of the ghetto?

  A. sports
  B. education
  C. family support
  D. money

Discussion Questions

1. How did their friendship help them succeed?

2. How were the boys like their peers? How were they different?

3. How have the three friends chosen to contribute to their community?

Journal Topics

1. What obstacles have you overcome in order to attend college?

2. Who or what do you have to support you in your life the way the three boys supported one another?

Writing Topics

1. What obstacles did the three boys have to overcome in order to succeed?

2. What factors contributed to their success?

3. Choose one factor in their success and explain how it contributed to their success.

4. How did their attitude contribute to their success?

5. In what ways are the three friends role models for others in their community?

From *The Knock Out*

Brent Staples

1   The sky over Miss Pell's algebra class saw heavy traffic in paper planes. The needle-nosed gliders flew beautifully—when they flew—but often spiraled straight onto the floor. Box-nosed planes showed better loft* and distance. The folds that squared off the nose displaced weight toward the front of the plane and made all the difference. I made the planes, but left it to braver boys to fly them, which they did, with great regularity, when Miss Pell turned her back to write on the board. Good planes reached her desk or landed on the floor near the wastebasket. The best and most glorious plane banked off the blackboard and floated to a perfect landing on the ledge, with the chalk and erasers. The room exploded in cheers.

loft: *ability to arch and stay in the air*

2   The class tortured Miss Pell in ways that were unheard of at Pulaski Junior High. Hatred of her burned especially bright in two Polish boys who were said to have been booted from Catholic school for monstrous behavior. They were a pair. Both short, they sported glistening pompadours, one dirty blond, one black. Miss Pell reminded them of the nuns, which was unfortunate because she lacked the habit* and crucifix that would have kept them at bay.

habit: *uniform worn by nuns*

3   Planes were the least of it. The boys rose as twin assassins* when she turned her back, hurling* erasers and lengths of chalk that thumped and thwacked off the board near her quaking* hand. The room neared riot and stayed that way until the principal, Mr. Rhoades, thrust his balding dome through the door and scowled us into submission. Miss Pell put on a show of sternness for him, but the sternness never reached us. We tore at her with smirks, even while Mr. Rhoades was present. The wildness started to build again as soon as he withdrew.

assassins: *killers*
hurling: *throwing*
quaking: *shaking*

4   Miss Pell's fear of us incited* cruelty and belligerence*. I felt the lure* but resisted as much as I could. I was always on the brink of failure and needed the mercy that good behavior would bring.

incited: *provoked*
belligerence: *aggressive, hostile behavior*
lure: *temptation, attraction*

5   My mind fled the room when Miss Pell filled the board with equations. I punched through the windows, through the blue roof of the sky, and into the deepest, darkest space, where I roamed the void with The Silver Surfer. Space travel left me ignorant of algebra, hence* the need for mercy. Civics and English I could pass even with poor citizenship, so I howled with the best of them. But in algebra I was a saint. My soul leaped to its feet when others got up to bombard Miss Pell, but my body stayed firmly in its seat. Good behavior could transform an "F" into a life-saving "D."

hence: *therefore*

6   The burning plane placed me beyond redemption. I made a plane with my usual care and passed it to David, who sat in the next row, a few desks behind me. This time David put a match to the plane before he launched it. The plane limped across the room, trailing smoke and ash, and crashed in the aisle a few desks ahead of me. Miss Pell whipped around and burned her eyes into mine. Perhaps she'd seen me make it. Perhaps she'd traced the line of flight to me. Whatever the evidence, she clearly thought me the culprit*.

culprit: *person guilty of a crime*

7   Only candy asses squealed. The code of the class dictated that I keep my face barren* of emotion, except for a smirk that said, "Torture me, I'll tell you nothing." My resolve* evaporated as Miss Pell's gaze burned into me. Her eyes were slits, her face red and heated, her hair plastered in damp hackles* to her forehead. This burning plane had tapped a rage that we had never seen. She accused; I pleaded: neither of us said a word. The year was

barren: *empty*
resolve: *firm decision*

hackles: *feathers on a rooster's head or hairs on a dog's neck* redeem: *rescue*

telepathy: *communicating through the mind*

insight: *understanding*

immunity: *freedom from prosecution or disease*

mocked: *made fun of*

odysseys: *extended wandering*

riding shotgun: *in the passenger seat*

nearly finished. There was not time to redeem* myself by studying and paying attention. Silently I screamed: "It wasn't me. It was David!" I motioned with my eyes to the next row. "I made the plane! But I didn't set it on fire! It was him!"

8   My telepathy* went unheard. I failed algebra and would spend the summer in summer school. I'd be sweating over equations while everyone else slept late and ranged free in the streets.

9   The first day of summer school I stepped out into the barren morning feeling sorry for myself. Then I saw Wesley standing at the bus stop, his sneakered feet spread wide apart, his arms swinging, the fist of one hand punching the open palm of the other. There was only one reason for him to be there: He was going to summer school, too. That made failing seem like good luck.

10   Wesley was beginning his junior year at Chester High. Hanging out with him would give me a boost and insight* into the mysteries. Girls would be sympathetic to another boy named Staples, even if he wasn't as handsome as Wesley and had never played on a championship basketball team. Tough guys who ruled the territory near the high school would certainly have failed as well. I'd be introduced to them as Wesley's cousin and thereby receive immunity*. All this I calculated in the short distance between my doorstep and the bus stop.

11   The summer school was held at a junior high school on the far east side of town. Wesley moved easily among the students. Girls threw themselves in his path. Time after time, he introduced me as his cousin, and each time was a baptism, like being born again.

12   Wesley and I met after school, lingered too long in the crowd, and ended up running for the bus. His strides were smooth and powerful, and I could barely keep up with him. He mocked* my awkwardness, but there was gentleness and even something like love in the way he did it. Normally I was deeply embarrassed at any reference to my body, but from Wesley I welcomed any attention at all. We caught the bus and collapsed breathless into our seats. Sometimes we talked, but mainly we didn't. I sat across the aisle and slightly behind him, so that I could watch him without his knowing. He looked out of his window, lost in his own thoughts. When we were together, my thoughts were always with him.

13   Wesley was killed after summer school ended. The weekend that killed him nearly killed my father and Brian and me as well. My father was taking Brian and me on a trip to Virginia. This was unexpected, since the honor of traveling with my father had always been set aside for Yvonne. Mr. Tommy was our driver. He owned an enormous Mercury Scenicruiser, as big as a Pennsylvania Railroad boxcar, with power everything. The trip seemed wrong. My odysseys* to Virginia had always included my mother and my uncle Bunny. We always left in the late afternoon and drove at night, with me riding shotgun*. This time we left early in the day with Mr. Tommy behind the wheel and my father riding shotgun in my place. Brian and I rode in the back seat. My mother stayed behind, thus adding to the strangeness.

14   We were driving toward the highway when the black Crown Victoria came roaring toward us, its front end high in the air. Mr. Tommy veered to the right, but the Crown Victoria veered with us. There was an explosive crunching of metal, and I felt myself being slammed around against the seats and ceiling. I came to sitting on the curb, blood running into my eyes from a gash in my forehead. Brian was clutching a broken shoulder. My

15   father and Mr. Tommy were barely scratched. The Crown Victoria's windshield was smashed, the driver's head a mass of cuts.

I was lying on the table awaiting my stitches when I saw that the doctor was not a doctor at all, but an intern*. A spasm of terror ran through me. My face would be ruined. I could see the sausagelike scar ballooning out of my forehead, girls at Chester High averting their eyes in horror. "Go away and send me back a real doctor," I said. The intern frowned and leaned in for a closer look. His hand touched down beside my face, smelling of soap. I grabbed at his wrist, and just missed, the hair of his arm like sandpaper on my fingertips. He stalked out of the room and came back with a bigger, hairier man, also in surgical greens. "This man is an orderly," he said. "You can lie here and be treated of your own free will. Or he can hold you down. Which would you prefer?" The intern scowled and awaited my answer. There was an animal force about him. Hair grew uninterrupted from his head, down his neck, and onto his upper arms. Fighting him would worsen the disfigurement*. I agreed to lie still. The intern threaded the stitch hook and sewed me up.

16   That night Wesley was shot to death. My thoughts were still blurred from the blow to my head; people and buildings floated at odd angles. The phone rang with the news. Whoever answered it repeated to those of us who were in the room: "Wesley has been killed. Someone shot him. It happened down at the corner of 3rd and Reaney." That was three blocks from our front door. Earlier in the evening I'd heard an ambulance and wondered what hapless soul it carried. Now I knew.

17   I stepped outside onto the porch. I squinted, trying to make tears, but none would come.

18   Wesley was sixteen years old. Hubert Dixon, the man who had killed him, was twenty-one. The death was ruled an accident. The police said that Wesley and Hubert were passing a gun back and forth when the gun went off. Later I heard that Hubert had jokingly held the gun to Wesley's chest and that Wesley said, "I dare you." The gun went off and he was dead.

intern: *graduate of medical school undergoing specialized training*

disfigurement: *spoiled appearance*

Comprehension Questions

1. What class does Staples describe?

   A. English
   B. algebra
   C. history
   D. economics

2. Why is Staples failing the class?

   A. He can't read.
   B. He doesn't do his homework.
   C. He daydreams in class.
   D. He misses class because of illness.

3. Why doesn't Staples misbehave in class?

   A. He feels sorry for the teacher.
   B. He dislikes the other kids in class.
   C. He hopes to get a D in class for good behavior.
   D. He fears his parents will be told if he misbehaves.

4. What incident gets him in trouble with the teacher?

   A. talking in class
   Ⓑ a burning paper airplane
   C. a fight

5. What happens to Brent Staples the day his cousin is killed?

   A. He goes shopping.
   B. He reads a book.
   C. He gets in a fight.
   Ⓓ He is in a car accident.

Journal Topics

1. Does Staples' description of his classroom bring back memories of classes of your own? Describe a particularly vivid memory of being in class.

2. Have you ever experienced the sudden death of someone you knew or loved? Describe what happened and how you felt.

Discussion Questions

1. Describe Staples' attitude toward school.

2. Describe Wesley Staples. How does Brent Staples feel about him?

3. How is Wesley Staples killed?

4. How does Brent Staples' car accident influence his response to Wesley's death?

5. How do you think the car accident and Wesley's death affect Brent Staples?

Writing Topics

1. Describe a relative you particularly admired or disliked.

2. Describe a particularly good or bad teacher.

3. Have you ever had to deal with sudden violence or loss? Describe the events and how they affected you.

4. Make a statement about Brent Staples' attitudes or experiences and support it with evidence from the essay. For example, "Brent Staples admires his cousin Wesley' or 'Brent Staples is not a particularly good student" or "Brent Staples must cope with sudden violence and death."

5. Compare and contrast Brent Staples' and Mike Rose's (pg. 339) views of the classroom.

Part V

Appendixes

Appendix A

English as a Second Language (ESL)

In this appendix, you will review the following topics:

- Nouns: singular and plural, count and noncount
- Adjectives: articles (a/an/the), this/that, many/much, few/a few, little/a little, some/any, another/other, no -s on adjectives, participles as adjectives
- Verbs: modals, verb tenses, passives, gerunds and infinitives, two-word verbs
- Position of adverbs
- Prepositions of time, location, travel and distance, and transportation
- Word order
- Common ESL errors

This section of the textbook reviews common English problems experienced by many American students who have one or more parents who speak another language and by students who learned another language before or at the same time they learned English. Your instructor will refer you to this appendix if he or she notices certain types of errors in your writing. You may also choose to review these skills and complete the practice exercises on your own. Some of the terms used in this appendix will not be familiar to native English speakers, but these terms are useful in explaining the subtleties of the language that many native speakers pick up by hearing the language from the time they are born.

English is full of idiosyncrasies. You can best become familiar with parts of the language that don't fit the general rules through long-term exposure to the language. If you are learning English as your second language, we recommend that you listen to and read English as much as possible. Listen to the radio and watch TV; read the newspaper; listen to the conversations of people around you; take every opportunity you can to practice your English.

Nouns

1. **Plural nouns** have an -*s* or -*es* ending.

   boys, cars, institutions, chairs

1.1   Irregular plural nouns do not end in *-s* or *-es*.

Examples: men, women, children, policemen, firemen, deer, sheep

For spelling rules, see Appendix B: Spelling (page 375).

Count/Noncount Nouns

1.2   **Count nouns** can be counted and have plural forms.

a horse   horses

a chair   chairs

1.3   **Noncount nouns** cannot be counted and do not have plural forms. Do not use *a* or *an* in front of noncount nouns. Noncount nouns may be preceded by indefinite adjectives (some, a lot, more, any, much) and may be preceded by units of measure.

advice	some advice	a piece of advice
homework	a lot of homework	3 pages of homework
information	much information	2 pieces of information
coffee	some coffee	2 cups of coffee
bread	some bread	3 slices of bread

1.4   Noncount nouns are singular and take singular verbs (with an s).

More information **is** needed before we make a decision

Some milk ha**s** been spilled on the floor.

1.5   **Categories of Noncount Nouns:**

Abstract nouns:

Emotions: love, hate, jealousy, misery

Qualities: beauty, honor, justice, wisdom

Abstractions: health, success, friendship, freedom

Activities: swimming, football, dancing, camping, baseball

General categories: homework, information, jewelry, furniture, machinery, music

Mass nouns:

Liquids: water, tea, cream, soup, gasoline, milk

Solids: sugar, butter, lettuce, tin, bacon, toothpaste

Gases: air, nitrogen, oxygen, smoke, steam, smog

Natural phenomena or weather terms: darkness, rain, sleet, wind, thunder, lightning

Subject areas: history, music, biology, politics

Practice **1**   **Identify each noun as count (C) or noncount (U) and provide a plural form for each.**

	Noun	Plural form
Example:	U lightning	three bolts of lightning Answers will vary.
1.	U silver	several pieces of silver
2.	C letter	three letters
3.	U loyalty	a great deal of loyalty
4.	U trash	a large amount of trash
5.	C husband	two husbands
6.	U honesty	some honesty
7.	U milk	a lot of milk
8.	C job	many jobs
9.	U sunshine	some sunshine
10.	C truck	three trucks

Adjectives

Indefinite Articles

2.1   *A* is used before singular, nonspecific nouns or adjectives that begin with a consonant sound.

I would like to read a book.

I never learned to ride a horse. (h sound)

I'm attending a university. (you sound)

I saw a tired woman.

2.2   *An* is used before singular, nonspecific nouns that begin with a vowel sound (a, e, i, o, u).

I want to eat an orange.

We are leaving in an hour. (ow sound)

That is an old house.

He is an honorable man. (o sound)

Practice **2**   **Write *a* or *an* before each noun or noun phrase.**

1.   a   hallway
2.   an uncle
3.   a   history class
4.   a   honey jar
5.   an eager boy

6.   an underwater camera
7.   a   hot stove
8.   a   hen
9.   an egg
10.   an awful dinner

2.3   *The* is used with singular or plural nouns that have been specified.

I want *a* parakeet. (singular, nonspecific noun)

I want *the* parakeet I saw in *the* pet store. (singular, specific nouns)

2.4   *The* is used before a superlative.

My mother is *the* best cook in town.

2.5   *The* is used before ordinal numbers.

the first, *the* second, *the* tenth

2.6   Use *the* before political unions, groups of islands, mountain ranges, rivers, oceans.

the United States, *the* Republic of China, *the* Himalayas, *the* Hawaiian Islands, *the* Nile, *the* Pacific Ocean, *the* Red Sea

Pitfalls

2.7   Do not use *the* before a possessive noun.

Incorrect: *the* Alice's dog

2.8   Do not use *the* in front of names of streets, cities, states, countries, continents, lakes, islands, mountains.

Incorrect:

the San Francisco

the Argentina

the Lake Superior

Practice 3   **Write *the* in the blank, if needed.**

1. _____ Jay's sister works in the Adirondack Mountains.

2. Put the broken glass in the trash can.

3. _____ Alexa's brother moved to the Unites States last year.

4. The busiest time of the year is _____ Christmas.

5. _____ New York is the most popular destination for _____ tourists.

6. Juanita wants the doll she saw in the department store on _____ Main Street.

7. The New York Yankees play at _____ Yankee Stadium.

8. The Golden Gate Bridge is in _____ San Francisco.

9. The puppy in the window is barking at the girl.

10. The Andes are in _____ South America.

Practice 4   **Write *a, an, the* in the blanks, if needed.**

1. The first chapter of a book is the most important.

2. The Mississippi River is the longest in the United States.

3. _____ Octavio's aunt is the only one who likes the movie.

4. _____ trust is a_____ necessary ingredient in a_____ good marriage.

5. _____ air is necessary for _____ humans to live.

6. _____ broccoli gives us _____ important nutrients.

7. _____ children learn by imitating _____ adults.

8. The_ air in the_ room is full of _____ smoke.

9. _____ Bill's car is the_ loudest one on the_ block.

10. _____ wedding rings are usually made of _____ gold.

2.9   Use *this* and *that* with singular nouns. Use *these* and *those* with plural nouns.

>   this dog   that dog
>   these dogs   those dogs

2.10   Use *many* with plural countable nouns. Use *much* with noncount nouns.

>   many girls
>   much gold

2.11   Use *few* (meaning not many) or *a few* (meaning several) with plural countable nouns.

>   We have *few* workers.
>   He has *a few* dollars.

2.12   Use *little* (meaning not very much) or *a little* (meaning a small amount) with noncount nouns.

>   She has *little* patience.
>   Paul wants *a little* cream in his coffee.

Note: Little (meaning small) can be used with countable nouns.

>   A little chair, a little dog

2.13   Use *some* with positive statements about count or noncount nouns. Use *any* in negative statements about count or noncount nouns.

>   He would like *some* cookies.
>   He owns *some* gold.
>   He doesn't want *any* cookies.
>   He doesn't own *any* gold.

2.14   Use *another* with singular nouns. Use *other* with plural nouns.

>   I want to read *another* book.
>   I want *another* piece of pie.
>   I'd like to read *other* books.
>   I have eaten *other* pies.

Practice 5   **Label each noun as count (C) or noncount (U) and then write a phrase expressing quantity for each word.** Answers will vary.

phrase expressing quantity

Example: __U__ toast   many pieces of toast

1. __C__ egg   two eggs
2. __U__ coffee   two cups of coffee
3. __U__ love   a great deal of love
4. __U__ butter   two teaspoons of butter
5. __U__ lightning   several bolts of lightning
6. __C__ pizza   three pizzas
7. __U__ glass   several pieces of glass
8. __U__ violence   too much violence
9. __U__ luck   a little luck
10. __U__ machinery   many pieces of machinery

Practice 6   **Write a phrase with the each of the following words.** Answers will vary within category.

Example: many   many students

1. other   plural nouns
2. few   plural countable nouns
3. a little   noncount nouns
4. any   negative statements about count or noncount nouns
5. some   count or noncount nouns
6. another   singular nouns
7. these   plural nouns
8. that   singular nouns
9. those   plural nouns
10. much   noncount nouns

2.15   Adjectives are not made plural in English.

I own one red car.

I own two red cars.

a two-car garage

three baby carriages

Participles Used as Adjectives

2.16   Present participles (*-ing* form) and past participles can be used as adjectives.

crying baby	broken plate
dining room	boiled cabbage
exciting movie	excited children

Practice **7**   **Circle the correct word in parentheses.**

1. Many Americans like (frying/fried) chicken.
2. I love to see your (smiling/smiled) face.
3. I like (freezing/frozen) desserts.
4. The movie was (exciting/excited).
5. The book was (boring/bored).
6. The puppy was (exciting/excited) to see us.
7. The (painting/painted) desert is very colorful.
8. I find that book (amusing/amused).
9. The students in my class are (confusing/confused) about the assignment.
10. Lisa was (surprising/surprised) by the flowers.

For comparative and superlative forms, see Chapter 9, "Parts of Speech," page 123.

For correct order of adjectives, see Chapter 10, "Word Choice," page 135.

Verbs

Modals

3.1   Modal auxiliaries (can, could, will, would, shall, should, may, might, must, had better, would rather, have to, ought to, have got to) take **no** endings to show agreement or tense.

Juan can walk. (No ending on *can walk*)

Eliza would rather run than walk. (No ending on *would* or *run* or *walk*)

Verb Tense Review

Tense	Form	Use	Example
Present	-verb -verb +s	Current fact, opinion, or habit	Chile is in South America. Ramon studies hard.
Present progressive	(am, is, are) + verb + ing	Event or condition happening right now	It is raining. He is studying.
Past	-verb + ed Irregulars	Past fact, opinion, habit	The meal was excellent. The car hit a wall. I cried last night.
Past progressive	(was, were) + verb+ ing	Action in progress in past, especially one interrupted by another past action	The boy was sleeping when the phone rang.
Present perfect	(has, have) + past participle	Action that occurred at unspecified time in past, several times in past, or that began in the past and continues in the present	They have already left. She has seen that movie. I have lived here since 1995.
Past perfect	had + past participle	The first of two past actions (the second is in past tense)	I had eaten by the time he arrived. We had finished when the bell rang.
Future	-will +verb (am, are, is) + going to + verb	Action that is expected to happen in future	I will fly to Italy this summer. I am going to study tonight.

Practice   8   In each blank, write the correct tense of the verb in parentheses.

1. Every morning, Paula _____ jogs _____ three miles. (jog)

2. We _____ will buy _____ a new car next month. (buy)

3. The United States _____ has sent _____ many men into space. (send)

4. Last night, Elena _____ ate _____ too much fried food. (eat)

5. Isabel _____ loves _____ chocolate. (love)

6. Yesterday, Susana _____ bought _____ two pairs of shoes at the mall. (buy)

7. The baby _____ is crying _____ right now because she is hungry. (cry)

8. She _____ was dreaming _____ when suddenly she woke up. (dream)

9. I _____ went _____ to the doctor twice this week. (go)

10. Last week, I _____ caught _____ a terrible cold. (catch)

Practice   9   In each blank, write the correct tense of the verb in parentheses.

1. Rosario _____ has seen _____ that movie already. (see)

2. Alaska _____ is _____ the largest state in the union. (be)

3. We _____ have owned _____ the same house for ten years. (own)

4. The dog _____ was sleeping _____ when I arrived home. (sleep)

5. It _____is raining_____ outside, so I cannot go out. (rain)

6. Peter _____fell_____ out of a tree when he was a child. (fall)

7. The children _____were playing_____ when their mother arrived. (play)

8. Next week, Luz _____will move_____ into a new apartment. (move)

9. While it was raining, our roof _____began_____ to leak. (begin)

10. Last year, a ticket only _____cost_____ two hundred dollars. (cost)

Passives

3.2   English speakers prefer the use of active voice to the passive voice.

In active voice, the subject performs the action.

S   V   Obj.
Erica cooked dinner.

S   V   Obj.
The puppy chewed the bone.

In passive voice, the subject receives the action.

S   + be +   past participle + by + doer of action
The dinner was cooked by Erica.

The bone was chewed by the puppy.

The book was sold in France.

You will be rewarded for good work.

He has been chosen to speak at the meeting.

Passives are acceptable if the doer of the action is unknown or unimportant.

The apartment was robbed.

The bridge was built in 1995.

Practice 10   **Rewrite the following passive sentences as active sentences.**

1. Seven books were read by Jack.

Jack read seven books.

2. The dinner was cooked by my mother.

My mother cooked the dinner.

3. Attendance is taken every day by the instructor.

The instructor takes attendance every day.

4. The movie was enjoyed by everyone.

Everyone enjoyed the movie.

5. The mail is delivered by the postman.

The postman delivers the mail.

6. The newspaper was brought in by the dog.

The dog brought in the newspaper.

7. The exam was graded by the instructor.

The instructor graded the exam.

8. This house was built by my father.

My father built this house.

9. The prize was awarded by the mayor.

The mayor awarded the prize.

10. The suspect was arrested by the police.

The police arrested the suspect.

Gerunds and Infinitives

3.3   A **gerund** is a verb + ing used as a noun (reading, swimming, running). Use a gerund after a preposition (a word like *by, of, in, about*).

He is tired of studying.

3.3a   Use a gerund after these phrases:

to be accustomed to _____ing.

to be used to _____ing.

to look forward to _____ing.

to object to _____ing.

3.3b   Use a gerund after these verbs:

finish	mind
keep (on)	postpone (put off)
stop (cease)	consider (think about)
enjoy	delay
quit (give up)	discuss (talk about)
appreciate	go
avoid	

He finished studying at midnight.

We discussed going fishing tomorrow.

3.4   An **infinitive** is *to* + the simple form of the verb (to run, to sit, to play). Infinitives can be used as a subject or an object:

To succeed in college was her only goal.

He hopes **to succeed** in college. (object)

3.4a Use an infinitive after these verbs:

hope	agree	want
offer	forget	appear
promise	ask	need
refuse	expect	demand
decide	seem	claim
remember		

Maria hopes to pass her exam.

They claim to have seen nothing.

3.5 When using a negative form, put **_not_** before the infinitive.

My mother decided **not** to cook dinner.

3.5a Use a noun or pronoun and an infinitive after these verbs:

tell	force	permit
allow	encourage	except
remind	order	want
require	warn	need
advise	ask	

My father always tells me to think before I act.

My sister allowed Gino to borrow her car.

3.5b Certain verbs may be followed by either a gerund or an infinitive:

start	intend	remember
hate	like	stop
begin	try	regret
can't stand	prefer	forget
continue		

I like to swim.

I like swimming.

3.5c Most verbs that can take either a gerund or an infinitive have no change in meaning. However, "stop," "remember," and "forget" are different. Although either a gerund or an infinitive can be used with these verbs, the meaning changes.

My mother stopped to smell the roses. (She stopped in order to smell the roses.)

My mother stopped smelling the roses. (She no longer smelled the roses.)

Juan remembered to mail the letter. (He remembered to do it.)

Juan remembered mailing the letter. (He remembered the act of mailing it.)

Cynthia forgot to do her homework. (She didn't do the homework.)

Cynthia forgot doing her homework. (She didn't remember doing the homework.)

3.5d   Both gerunds and infinitives may be used as singular subjects.

Swimming is good exercise.

To swim against the current is difficult.

Practice 11   **Circle the correct gerund or infinitive.**

1. They want me (going/to go) ice-skating.

2. Enrique delayed (visiting/to visit) his family.

3. William appears (to be/being) drunk.

4. I want (to go/going) shopping.

5. We asked our friends (to come/coming) over at nine.

6. I refuse (to give/giving) you my keys.

7. I hope (to see/seeing) you soon.

8. I enjoy (to read/reading).

9. The policeman asked (to see/seeing) my driver's license.

10. Jose told his sister (to stop/stopping) talking.

Two-Word Verbs

3.6   Two-word verbs are a verb and a preposition that have special meaning.

3.6a   Nonseparable two-word verbs (cannot be separated by a noun or pronoun):

call on	grow up
catch up	keep up with
check into	look after
check out of	look into
come across	look out for
drop by	pass away
drop in	put up with
drop off	run into
get along with	run out of
get in (into), get off, get on, get over, get through	show up
	take after
go over	

3.6b　Separable two-word verbs (can be separated by a noun or pronoun):

call ___ back	find ___ out	put ___ away
call ___ off	give ___ back	put ___ off
call ___ up	give ___ up	take ___ off
cheer ___ up	hand ___ in	take ___ out
clean ___ up	hang ___ up	take ___ over
cross ___ out	look ___ over	tear ___ down
cut ___ out	look ___ up	think ___ over
do ___ over	make ___ up	try ___ on
drop ___ off	pick ___ out	turn ___ in
figure ___ out	pick ___ up	turn ___ off
fill ___ out	point ___ out	turn ___ up

Practice　12　　**Circle the correct verb phrase.**

1. Ignacio came at seven o'clock to (pick up me/**pick me up**).

2. Tamil wanted to (**call Jennifer back**/call back Jennifer).

3. At the party, the crowd yelled, "**Turn it up**/turn up it."

4. I promised my friend I would (**look into the problem**/look the problem into).

5. My father tells me I (**take after my mother**/take my mother after).

6. I hope we don't (**run out of food**/run food out of).

7. My boyfriend promised to (**drop me off**/drop off me) before ten.

8. (**Look out for your brother.**/Look your brother out for.)

9. I told Trevor to (**give it back**/give back it).

10. I hope you can (**put up with me**/put me up with).

Practice　13　　**Editing for verb errors**

Correct all the verb errors in the passage below. Do not make any unnecessary changes.

This coming June, Alejandro, a friend of mine from Spain, will visits me. I ~~had~~ ^{have}

not seen him for a year. Last summer, I flew to Spain and stay^{ed} with him and his

family in Madrid. We traveled around the country, and I was able to see the Prado,

the Alhambra, and the Spanish Riviera. Because I ~~study~~ ^{studied} a little Spanish before I went

to visits my friend, I could asks directions and exchanges a few words about the

weather, the scenery, and the food. Of course, I ~~taste~~ ^{had tasted} Spanish food before, but I

~~never eat~~ ^{had never eaten} it like his mother ~~make~~ ^{made} it. Because her cooking ~~are~~ ^{was} so good, I gained ten

comes · have
pounds! When my friend Alejandro ~~come~~ to the United States, I'll ~~has~~ to take him to
written · practicing
the beach. He has ~~write~~ me to say that he has been ~~practice~~ his English to use while
will
he is here. I'm sure we have a lot of fun.

Adverbs

Adverbs modify verbs, adjectives, and other adverbs.

Position

4.1 Adverbs generally come before the verb, adjective, or adverb they modify.

V
Antonio *slowly* **completed** his homework.

Adj
Rosa is a *very* **pretty** girl.

Adv
The job is *quite* **easily** done.

4.2 Many adverbs may be placed after the object or verb.

Antonio completed his homework *slowly*.

The job is done *quite easily*.

4.3 Frequency adverbs (*often, always, never, usually, sometimes, seldom, frequently, never, occasionally*) are placed before most verbs, but after the *be* verb, and between a helping verb and a main verb.

We *always* eat in the dining room. (before main verb)

Shaquira *is* rarely upset. (after *be* verb)

The boys have *never* seen their aunt. (between helping verb and main verb)

Pitfalls

Do not place an adverb between a verb and its object.

Incorrect: He closed quietly the door.

Correct: He quietly closed the door or He closed the door quietly.

Practice 14 **Place the adverb correctly in the sentence.**

1. Jose locked the car. (quickly)

Jose quickly locked the car. or Jose locked the car quickly.

2. Antonio and Julie are playing. (always)

Antonio and Julie are always playing.

3. He washes his clothes. (never)

He never washes his clothes.

4. Sandra read the book. (quickly)

Sandra quickly read the book. or Sandra read the book quickly.

5. Su-ling is laughing. (always)

Su-ling is always laughing.

6. The twins make good grades. (frequently)

The twins frequently make good grades.

7. My dog likes to run on the beach. (at night)

My dog likes to run on the beach at night.

8. They called their father. (excitedly)

They excitedly called their father.

9. My mother flew to California. (yesterday)

My mother flew to California yesterday.

10. I wish I were rich. (sometimes)

I sometimes wish I were rich.

Prepositions

Prepositions show relationships between things. They indicate where something is in relation to something else (*over, under, through, by, with*). They can also indicate direction, time, or origin (*to, toward, by, at, from, of*). For a more complete list of prepositions, see Chapter 9, "Parts of Speech," page 128.

Prepositions of Time

5.1   Use **on** for a day of the week, a holiday, and a calendar date.

on Wednesday, on Christmas, on March 6th

5.2   Use **in** for a year or a part of a day.

in 1995, in the evening

5.3   Use **at** for a specific time.

at two o'clock, at noon

Practice 15   Write *in*, *on*, or *at*, if needed, in the blanks.

1. There are no classes <u>on</u> the 4th of July.

2. I was born <u>in</u> 1983 <u>at</u> three o'clock <u>in</u> the afternoon.

3. <u>In</u> 1995 a hurricane hit South Florida <u>at</u> midnight.

4. The train will arrive <u>at</u> noon <u>on</u> Friday.

5. The test will be <u>at</u> four o'clock <u>on</u> Tuesday.

6. <u>On</u> January 6th, we will have a party <u>in</u> the late afternoon.

7. I hope I arrive <u>at</u> school <u>on</u> time.

8. Dinner will be served <u>at</u> two o'clock <u>on</u> Christmas.

9. I love to walk <u>on</u> the beach <u>in</u> the evening.

10. The accident occurred <u>at</u> three o'clock <u>in</u> the morning.

Prepositions of Location

5.4   Use *in* for inside of.

in a room, in a house, in a building

5.5   Use *in* with a city, state, or country.

in Dallas, in Texas, in the United States

5.6   Use *on* for a surface.

on a table, on a wall, on a field

5.7   Use *by* for beside.

by the school, by the tree

5.8   Use *near* for close to.

near the school, near me

Practice 16   Write *in*, *on*, *at*, *by*, or *near*, if needed.

1. Jose threw his backpack <u>on</u> the table <u>by</u> the door.

2. Your present is <u>in</u> the box <u>on</u> the floor.

3. The candy is <u>on</u> the top shelf <u>in</u> the cabinet.

4. We met <u>near/in</u> the biggest store <u>in</u> the mall.

5. Your shirt is <u>in</u> the bottom drawer of the dresser <u>in</u> your room.

6. The picture hung <u>on</u> the wall <u>in</u> the living room.

7. We played tennis <u>on</u> a clay court.

8. The boy balanced the book <u>on</u> his head as he walked <u>by</u> the tree.

9. Because the mall is <u>near</u> my house, I can walk there.

10. His house is <u>near</u> here.

Prepositions of Transportation

5.9   Use *on* if the means of transportation carries one person or many people.

> on a bike, on a horse, on roller skates, on a motorcycle, on a plane, on a boat, on a train, on a bus

Use *in* if the means of transportation carries two to six people.

> in a car, in a taxi, in a small plane

Practice   17   **Fill in the blank with *on* or *in*.**

1. on   an ocean liner
2. in   a helicopter.
3. on   a barge
4. in   a jet
5. in   a van
6. on   a submarine
7. in   a Rolls-Royce
8. in   a canoe
9. in   a rowboat
10. on   a cruise ship

Practice   18   **Fill in the blank with the appropriate preposition (in, on, by, at, of, near), if needed.**

1. At   4:00 we got on   a train.
2. On   New Year's Eve, you kiss your sweetheart at   midnight.
3. I was born on   December 3rd in   1983.
4. They got married in   1985 and celebrated their anniversary on   June 4th.
5. The best part of   the party was when we sat on   the floor and told ghost stories.
6. I rode in   a taxi and arrived at   the play on   time.
7. I live near   the school, so I don't have to get up early in   the morning.
8. They left at   6:00 to get to the movie in   time for the opening credits.
9. In   the United States, many people eat ham on   Easter.
10. The party begins at   8:00 on   Saturday.

Word Order in Basic Sentence Patterns

6.1   Subject + Verb

> **S**   **V**
> The girl dances.

Other words and phrases may be added to modify or describe the subject or verb.

The girl in the blue dress dances like an expert.

6.2   Subject + Verb + Direct Object

S   V   D. O.
Raul hit the ball.

Other words and phrases may be added to modify or describe the subject, verb, or direct object.

S   V   D. O.
Exhausted by the long game, Raul barely hit the ball over the pitcher's head.

6.3   Subject + Verb + Indirect Object + Direct Object

S   V   I.O.   D. O.
I wrote my sister a letter.

Other words and phrases may be added to modify or describe the subject, verb, or direct object.

S   V   I.O.   D. O.
Mary and Jose bought their father an expensive present.

6.3a   If *to* or *for* appear before the object, then the sentence ends in a prepositional phrase rather than a direct object.

S   V   I.O.   prep. phrase
Mary and I wrote a letter to our father.

6.3b   Do not use the words *to* or *for* before an indirect object.

S   V   I.O.   D.O.
Rosario sent↑Juan a letter.
       ↑ **No *to***

Ex: My mother bought↑me a dress.
              ↑ **No *for***

6.4   Subject + Linking Verb + Adjective or Noun

S   V   Adj
Maria seems sad.

S   V   Noun
My brother is an electrical engineer.

6.5   Questions

In questions, the subject comes after the verb.

V   S
How are you?

V   S
Where is the test?

      V   S   V
When are you going?

6.5a *Not only... but also* phrases require the inverted word order of questions in the first clause.

    V   S   V   S   V
Not only does Enrique dance well, but he also sings well.

6.6   Sentences That Begin with *There* or *Here*

In sentences that begin with *there* or *here*, the subject comes after the verb.

    V   S
There are fifteen chairs in this room.

    V   S
Here are the papers that you requested.

6.7   Placement of Adjectives and Participles

Adjectives are generally placed before the noun or pronoun that they modify, but they follow a linking verb.

    Adj   N   Adj   N
I bought three dresses at the new mall.

    N   V   Adj
Sarah is talented.

6.8   Placement of Adverbs

See sections 4.1–4.3, page 366.

6.9   Pronouns

Use either a noun or a pronoun, but do not follow a noun with a pronoun.

Incorrect: Sung-Li she writes well.

Correct: Sung-Li writes well.

She writes well.

Practice 19   **Correct the faulty word order in the following sentences.**

1. The instructor explained slowly the exam.

The instructor slowly explained the exam. or explained the exam slowly.

2. I have read many times the book.

I have read the book many times.

3. Rosario has seen never that movie.

Rosario has never seen that movie.

4. My sister gave to me a watch.

My sister gave me a watch.

5. Not only Maria does play tennis well, but she also plays basketball well.

Not only does Maria play tennis well, but she also plays basketball well.

6. You are when leaving?

When are you leaving?

7. I gave a record my sister.

I gave my sister a record. or I gave a record to my sister.

8. My father a doctor is.

My father is a doctor.

9. Claudia she is a good sport.

Claudia is a good sport.

10. She is tired never.

She is never tired.

Common ESL Errors

7.1   Independent clauses need a subject (except for command sentences that have an understood *you* subject).

Incorrect: Is raining now.

Correct: It is raining now.

7.2   One of _____s (plural noun) _____s (verb with -s ending)

One of the boys is coming over after school.

One of the chairs has a hole in it.

7.3   Do not use double negatives in English.

Incorrect: He doesn't want no broccoli.

Correct: He doesn't want any broccoli.

He wants no broccoli.

Practice **20**   **Correct the errors in the following sentences.**

1. One of the flower̂s̄ is wilted.
2. Because the car is dirty, ît needs to be washed.
3. My sister doesn't want to do nô a̅n̅y̅ dishes.
4. Ît Smells good in here.
5. The teacher said she wouldn't accept nô a̅n̅y̅ excuses.
6. One of my friend̂s̄ got a speeding ticket.
7. Because I passed the test, Î am going out.
8. My baby sister won't eat nô a̅n̅y̅ vegetables.

9. After I play tennis, ~~I~~ shower.

10. ~~It~~ Won't rain.

Practice   21   **Editing for "s"**

In the passage below, correct words with missing -s endings. Also, correct the words that have unnecessary -s endings

     My three sister**s** have many bad habit**s**. One of their bad habit**s** is not picking up their clothes. My mother remind**s** them every day to pick~~s~~ up their clothes, but they never seem~~s~~ to remember. My oldest sister, Anna, has curly hair~~s~~ and a friendly disposition~~s~~. She is always singing in the shower~~s~~, but unfortunately she never remember**s** to hang up her towel. My second oldest sister, Flora, loves book**s**, but she always leave**s** her book**s** lying on the floor~~s~~. My youngest sister, Irene, dream**s** of traveling to foreign land**s**, but she ~~have~~ has her head in the cloud**s** and doesn't remember~~s~~ to make her bed. I love~~s~~ my three sister**s**, but sometime they drive~~s~~ me crazy.

Practice   22   **Editing for basic errors**

Correct all the errors in the passage below. Do not make any unnecessary changes. Watch for different kinds of errors such as mistakes with run-ons, fragments, verbs, spelling, homonyms, and capitals. You should also find common ESL errors.

     Being a policemen **a** ~~are a~~ **is** hard work. First of all, policemen **don't** ~~doesn't~~ earn more **than** ~~then~~ one thousand dollars a month, and they risk their **lives** ~~life~~ for these small amount**s**. There **are** ~~is~~ never enough policemen to fight ~~effectively~~ the crime effectively. Also, there **is much contra-** ~~are many contra-~~ **band** ~~band~~ because **it** is easy to throw~~n~~ the merchandise **off** ~~in~~ the coast and then a boat pick**s** **it** up. Because of the low pay~~s~~, there are many corrupt policemen~~s~~. Also, the policemen **are afraid of being** ~~have fear to be~~ killed by drug dealer**s**.

Practice   23   **Editing for basic errors**

Correct all the errors in the passage below. Do not make any unnecessary changes. Watch for different kinds of errors such as mistakes with run-ons, fragments, verbs, spelling, homonyms, and capitals. You should also find common ESL errors.

     People in **the U.S.** ~~united states~~ **have** ~~has~~ an interesting eating habit~~s~~ **in** ~~on~~ the morning. Some peo-ple~~s~~ wake up regularly late in the morning and just **have** ~~has~~ coffee~~s~~. **A**nother people get up early. They **cook** ~~cooking~~ ~~the~~ **a** big breakfast~~s~~ with ~~the~~ eggs, bacon, and toast~~s~~. Many American~~s~~ children **choose** ~~chose~~ cereal because it **has a lot of** ~~have many~~ sugar~~s~~ and toys in **the** box.

s are
Other sweet breakfast food ~~is~~ coffeecake and ~~the~~ pastry. ~~The~~ doctors recommends fre-

eating   in order to live
quently to eat a healthy breakfast ~~for~~ ~~living~~ longer.

Appendix B
Spelling

Most of us would like to be better spellers. Fortunately, we are increasingly using computerized word processors that include spell-check programs. However, sometimes we still must write by hand, and we need to know how to spell common words. The spelling rules and the list of commonly misspelled words will help you become a better speller. Also, the information on using a dictionary and spell checker will help you avoid misspellings.

Common Rules for Spelling

Spelling rules are needed to keep the pronunciation correct when word endings such as *-ing* and *-ed* are added to words. The rules have to do with combinations of **vowels** (a, e, i, o, u and sometimes y) and **consonants** (all letters except vowels) and the rules for adding endings onto words.

GPM: 2.4

1. i before e

Use **i** before **e** except after **c**.

Examples:

i before e	**e before i**
believe	receive
reprieve	deceive
friend	conceive

1.1 When the word makes a long **a (*ay*) sound**, use **e** before **i**.

Examples:

neighbor	weight
eight	freight

Exceptions to the rule:

either	h**ei**ght
n**ei**ther	w**ei**rd
for**ei**gn	l**ei**sure
s**ei**ze	

2. Single Syllable Word Endings

GPM: 2.7–2.8

Double the final consonant of a word when adding an ending that begins with a vowel such as *-ing, -ed, -er, -est* if the word is one syllable and a vowel comes before the consonant. (The last consonant is doubled to preserve the sound of the vowel.)

Examples:

bat + ed = batted

pen + ed = penned

rob + ing = robbing

sit + ing = sitting

run + er = runner

slim + est = slimmest

2.1　Multisyllable Word Endings

GPM: 2.9

When adding an ending that begins with a vowel such as *-ing, -ed, -er, -est,* double the final consonant of multisyllable words when the final syllable is stressed and a vowel comes before the final consonant.

Examples:

control + ed = controlled

permit + ed = permitted

prefer + ed = preferred

refer + ed = referred

begin + er = beginner

admit + ing = admitting

commit + ing = committing

patrol + ing = patrolling

GPM: 2.12

3. Dropping the Final e

Drop the final **e** on a word when adding an ending that begins with a vowel.

Examples:

believe + er = believer

like + able = likable

rake + ing = raking

move + ed = movable

3.1   Keep the final **e** when adding an ending that begins with a consonant.

Examples:

achieve + ment = achievement

rare + ly = rarely

like + ness = likeness

Exceptions:

argue + ment = argument

judge + ment = judgment

true + ly = truly

GPM: 2.16

4. Dropping the Final y

Drop the final **y** and add **i** when adding an ending if there is a consonant before the **y.**

Examples:

pretty + er = prettier

funny + est = funniest

try + ed = tried

rely + able = reliable

reply + ed = replied

happy + ness = happiness

beauty + ful = beautiful

4.1   Keep the final **y** when adding an ending if there is a vowel before **y.**

Examples:

delay + ed = delayed

donkey + s = donkeys

play + er = player

4.2   Always keep the final **y** when adding *-ing* to words ending in **y**.

Examples:

rely + ing = relying

reply + ing = replying

try + ing = trying

Exceptions:

lay + ed = laid

pay + ed = paid

say + ed = said

Frequently Misspelled Words

GPM: 2.22

You can improve your spelling significantly by studying the following list of frequently misspelled words. Try to remember how they are spelled by looking at the bold letters that show what's unusual or tricky about the spelling of these words.

ac**ross**	cloth**e**s	h**ei**ght
actua**ll**y	com**i**ng	hun**gr**y
ag**ai**nst	d**ea**lt	int**e**rest
a lot (two words)	de**s**troy	**lai**d
all right (two words)	din**i**ng	lib**ra**ry
a**lm**ost	dur**i**ng	lik**e**ly
a**lth**ough	eas**i**ly	marr**ia**ge
alway**s**	e**ff**ect	m**ea**nt
am**ong**	exer**c**ise	m**ere**
an**swer**	experi**e**nce	natura**ll**y
around	exp**erie**nce	n**ei**ther
arti**cle**	fav**o**rite	ni**e**ce
at**t**ack	fi**el**d	nin**e**ty
befor**e**	fina**ll**y	nin**th**
begi**nn**ing	for**t**y	**pai**d
beli**e**ve	**fou**rth	perso**nal**
br**ea**th	for**w**ard	perso**nnel**
breath**e**	fri**e**nd	pla**nn**ed
business	genera**ll**y	p**oi**son
careful	**g**rateful	po**ss**ible
carri**e**d	g**ua**rd	prob**ably**
	happiness	

pro**ving**	**since**	studying
quiet	shining	suppose**d**
rea**lly**	sh**ou**lder	themsel**ves**
rec**ei**ve	simp**ly**	therefor**e**
re**ga**rd	sophomore	tog**e**ther
re**mem**ber	sour**ce**	truly
roo**mm**ate	spee**ch**	unti**l**
saf**e**ty	sto**pp**ed	u**si**ng
sci**e**nce	stor**ie**s	vie**w**
sense	str**aigh**t	writing
sentence	stren**gth**	**yie**ld
se**ve**ral	stri**ct**	

Keep a Record of Your Misspellings

It's important to keep a record of the words you misspell. Usually your instructor will circle misspellings. You should look up the spelling of every word marked as a spelling error. By becoming aware of common misspellings in your writing, you will improve your spelling dramatically.

Use the Error List on pages 390–391 to record your misspellings and their correct spellings. Study your personal list of misspellings every time you prepare to write a paper. Go down the list of misspellings and mentally correct the spelling, and then check your answers using the list of corrections.

Example:

Error	Correction	Rule
beleive	believe	i before e except after c
convience	convenience	missing letters

Use a Dictionary to Check Your Spelling

Unless you are writing on a computer, the most valuable resource you have to check spelling is the dictionary. You should carry a college-level paperback dictionary with you to any class in which you will write. Use the headwords at the top of the page; these are the first and last word on the page. For example, "bazaar/beard" tells you that any word starting with the letters *bazaar* up to and including *beard* is on this page. If the word you have spelled starts with "baz" and is not on the page, your spelling is incorrect. You must guess again with another spelling of the word and look this spelling up in order to confirm the spelling.

The dictionary can give you more information about the words it lists than just the spelling. It will also tell you the part of speech and the definition of the word.

Example:

bazaar/beard

bead (bēd) *n*. 1. A small piece of material pierced for stringing. 2. A narrow projecting strip of molding. -*v*. 1. To decorate with beads.

Use a Spell Checker to Check Your Spelling

The problem with using a dictionary to check your spelling is that you must know which words to look up. Often writers don't know which words they are misspelling. Also, you must be fairly close to the correct spelling in order to find the word listed in the dictionary. If the misspelling is very far off, such as "sickology" for psychology, you won't find the word.

Writing on a word processor with a spell check takes care of both of these problems. Any word you misspell will be underlined in red. When you click on the word, you will get a list of words with similar spellings. It will be important that you choose the correct word to replace your misspelling. If you are in doubt, check the definition of your choice to confirm that you are using the correct word. You should also pay careful attention to the words identified as misspelled and add them to your personal list of spelling errors in order to improve your spelling.

You can also buy small spell checkers to bring to class with you. You simply type in a word to get a read-out of the correct spelling.

Appendix C
Creating a Portfolio

A writing portfolio is a selection of your writings. Often, writers build a portfolio at the end of a term from the writings they have done during the term. The portfolio is a record of what you have accomplished and the progress you have made in your writing class. In assembling the portfolio, you may also write an introduction that explains why you have chosen the writings in the portfolio and a conclusion that reflects on your learning experience this term.

Understanding the Assignment

You should make sure that you understand what your instructor wants to be included in your portfolio.

Writing Practice **Determining what to include in your portfolio**

Fill in the information for your assignment.

Parts of the portfolio: _____

Number of journal entries to include: _____

Number of paragraphs to include: _____

Other requirements:

_____

_____

Due date: _____

Determining the Writing Context

It is important that you understand the purpose of the portfolio and its intended audience before you begin selecting writing to include.

Purpose

Most writers agree that no one piece of writing can fully represent their ability, hard work, and creativity. Each assignment calls for different skills. Writing is a form of expression like speaking or singing. To appreciate our written expression, we have to look at a number of pieces of writing, just as we appreciate a singer for different songs and even styles of songs. You are helping your instructor assess your performance this term by assembling a portfolio, and you are in charge of determining which writings to include.

Also, your writing has improved during the term. You are not the same writer today that you were at the beginning of the term. To appreciate your progress, you need to review all the writing you have done during the term.

Finally, building a portfolio will give you an opportunity to reflect on your experience this term. Your learning cannot be summed up simply by a final grade. You have learned a great deal about how to express yourself in writing, and the portfolio will be a product that you can present with pride.

Audience

Your instructor will read your portfolio as part of assessing your progress. You may also want to present your portfolio to family, friends, employers, and your next writing teacher. Most important, you yourself are part of the audience for this portfolio. The work you include is concrete proof to the world of the hard work you have done and the gains you have made.

Writing Practice ② **Determining the writing context**

Indicate the purpose and audience of your current assignment.

Purpose: _____

How will the portfolio be graded? _____

How much will the portfolio grade count in your final grade?

_____

Audience (Who will see this portfolio?):

_____

As with any longer paper or essay, you should begin with the body of the portfolio and leave the introduction and conclusion until after you have selected the writings you wish to include.

Selecting Writings to Include in the Portfolio

1. Select two or three journal entries (or the number that your teacher requests).

   Reread your journal entries. Choose entries in which the subject matter and content are interesting or meaningful.

2. Choose three to five paragraphs to include in the portfolio.

   Think about your audience (including yourself) when choosing the papers to include. You probably want to include paragraphs that earned the highest grades, and you may want to include the paragraphs that taught you valuable lessons about writing. It is also effective to include paragraphs using the different patterns of development you learned this term such as persuasion, exemplification, narration, description, and compare and contrast.

3. Consider revising and editing the writings you select for your portfolio.

   A. Review Chapter 21 for methods of improving the sentence variety in your paragraphs.

   B. Add more specific detail to weak supports.

   C. Review Chapter 10 for ideas on how to improve the word choice in your writing. In particular, try to replace vague wording such as weak verbs and abstract nouns with specific and concrete language. Identify and replace slang and clichés. Use appropriate vocabulary when possible. (Remember that you are showing off what you have learned through the term; make your writing as strong as you can.)

   D. Edit your writing for English errors using the Editing Checklist in the appendix.

Writing Practice 3 **Determining the writing selections**

Titles of journal entries to include:

_____

_____

Titles of paragraphs to include:

_____

_____

Titles of other papers to include:

_____

_____

Writing an Introduction to Your Portfolio

Think of the introduction as a letter to those who will see the portfolio. What do you want them to know before they start reading the selection? The introduction should be a paragraph (a minimum of five sentences). It should answer the following questions that a reviewer might have upon opening your portfolio.

Writing Practice   4   **Writing an introduction to your portfolio**

What does writing mean to you?

_____

_____

_____

_____

How has your view of writing changed through taking this course?

_____

_____

_____

_____

Why have you chosen these writings for your portfolio?

_____

_____

_____

_____

Example

Tony's Introduction

My writing has changed a lot this term. Writing was always a chore to me. I like expressing myself, but I don't like worrying about whether what I've written is correct or not. After taking this course, I'm not so afraid any longer of making mistakes because I understand the mistakes and how to correct them. I also feel much more comfortable writing papers because I have practiced the writing process. Using the steps of the writing process helped me generate more ideas, organize my ideas before I started writing, examine what I had written (with a little help from my peers), and improve my first draft before I turned the paper in. By taking it step by step, I came up with a much better paper than I would have otherwise.

I chose the writings in my portfolio because they represent the ways that I have grown this term. I see myself making peace with my past and figuring out my future in my journal. My papers and paragraphs were a proving ground for me. I showed my instructor and myself that I could follow instructions and come up with a decent paper. I also found that I could make my papers much better by revising them with the help of my teacher and classmates.

Writing a Conclusion to Your Portfolio

The conclusion is a reflection on your experience in this course this term. It should be a paragraph of five or more sentences. Use the following questions as prompts to help you generate ideas.

Writing Practice ⑤   **Reflecting on what you have learned**

How does this portfolio represent your learning this term?

_____

_____

What were the two or three most meaningful assignments or experiences in this class?

_____

_____

_____

_____

How do you feel about your writing now compared to when you started the class?

_____

_____

_____

_____

Example

Tony's Conclusion

Effort brings improvement. I have learned the truth of this statement this term. I came into this course nervous about my writing ability, and I leave confident of my ability to write at a college level. What I don't know, I will learn. The most important experiences in this class came when I overcame my nervousness and made a total commitment to learn and achieve. There was the night in the library when I admitted to myself that I was procrastinating about writing the paper due the next week.

I took out my notes and textbook and then just started through the writing process steps. I told myself that I wouldn't get up until I had a first draft. By following the steps and filling out the writing process prompts, I got a draft in an hour! I couldn't believe it. From then on, I just did what I was asked because I knew I just had to have faith in the process.

Appendix D

Paragraph Writing Checklists

In this chapter, you will find the following forms to guide your writing:

- Map Template
- Outline Template
- Paragraph Review Questionnaire
- Paragraph Revision Checklist
- Editing Checklist
- Error List
- Paragraph Writing Process Prompts

Map Template

Topic sentence:

_____

_____

Area of Support _____

Specific Details _____

Relation to Topic Sentence

1. _____

2. _____

3. _____

4. _____

5. _____

Outline Template

Topic sentence: _____

I. Support 1 _____

    A. Specifics_____

    B. Relation _____

II. Support 2 _____

    A. Specifics_____

    B. Relation _____

III. Support 3 _____

    A. Specifics_____

    B. Relation _____

IV. Support 4 _____

    A. Specifics_____

    B. Relation _____

V. Support 5_____

    A. Specifics_____

    B. Relation _____

Paragraph Review Questionnaire

Directions: Read the paragraph carefully and answer the following questions as specifically as possible. Remember, your goal is to help your peer improve his or her paper.

1. Is the topic sentence clear? Restate it in your own words.

2. Does the paragraph adequately explain or develop the topic sentence? List the areas of support used.

3. Does the order of supports seem logical?

4. Is there enough information or support to develop the topic sentence? What additional information or supporting ideas could the writer have included?

5. What did you like most about the paragraph?

6. What seemed most unclear about the paragraph?

7. Did you notice mechanical errors in the paragraph?

Paragraph Revision Checklist

1. **Form**
Title: Are the major words (including the first and last words) capitalized?
☐ yes ☐ no
Does the title reveal the topic and slant of the paragraph?   ☐ yes ☐ no
Does it catch the reader's attention?   ☐ yes ☐ no
Is the first sentence indented?   ☐ yes ☐ no
Does the paragraph have the required number of sentences?   ☐ yes ☐ no
Does the paragraph have the required organizational pattern?   ☐ yes ☐ no

2. **Topic Sentence**
Does the topic sentence fit the assignment?   ☐ yes ☐ no
Is it appropriate for the intended audience and purpose?   ☐ yes ☐ no
Is the main idea clear?   ☐ yes ☐ no

3. **Support**
Is there enough support (three to five supports, depending on the assignment) to explain or prove your topic sentence?   ☐ yes ☐ no
Does each support clearly relate to or develop the topic sentence?
☐ yes ☐ no
Are there enough specific details, facts, and examples to convince the reader?   ☐ yes ☐ no
Are any supports repeated?   ☐ yes ☐ no
Does anything in the paragraph not relate to the main idea?   ☐ yes ☐ no
Is the relationship between support sentences clear?   ☐ yes ☐ no
Are there clear transitions within and between sentences?   ☐ yes ☐ no
Is the order of supports clear and logical?   ☐ yes ☐ no
Are the sentences varied in length and structure?   ☐ yes ☐ no
Is appropriate vocabulary used?   ☐ yes ☐ no
Is the language clear and precise? (Are there strong verbs, specific nouns, colorful adjectives and adverbs?)   ☐ yes ☐ no

4. **Conclusion**
Does the conclusion tie the paragraph together?   ☐ yes ☐ no
Does it introduce any new ideas or arguments that might confuse the reader?   ☐ yes ☐ no

Editing Checklist

As you learn about the following skills, add them to your editing checklist.

1. Check for run-ons and fragments. Is there one complete sentence—and no more than one complete sentence—between every two periods? (Identify the subject and the verb, and make sure the word group makes sense.) ☐ yes ☐ no

2. Check every verb. Do subjects and verbs agree? Is proper verb tense used? Be sure to check the problem phrases such as *there is/there are* and pay attention to singular subjects such as *everyone*. ☐ yes ☐ no

3. Check pronouns. Do they agree with their antecedents? ☐ yes ☐ no

4. Use the dictionary or computer spell check to catch capitalization errors and misspellings. Remember, however, that the spell check will not catch errors with problem words such as *there/their*. ☐ yes ☐ no

5. Remember your personal list of errors. Check your writing for any of these errors. ☐ yes ☐ no

6. Look for any missing words or letters by reading the writing slowly from the last sentence to the first. ☐ yes ☐ no

7. Check for apostrophes in contractions and possessives. ☐ yes ☐ no

8. Check commas. ☐ yes ☐ no

Error List

Error	Correction	Explanation/Rule
Ex: This fine bike shop are	This fine bike shop is	verb error

1. _____

2. _____

3. _____

4. _____

5. _____

6. _____

7. _____

8. _____

9. _____

10. _____

11. _____

12. _____

13. _____

14. _____

15. _____

16. _____

17. _____

18. _____

19. _____

20. _____

Paragraph Writing Process Prompts

The following prompts will guide you in writing paragraphs. You may wish to consult these prompts each time you write a paragraph until the process becomes second nature.

1. Understanding the Assignment

Assignment: _____

Length: _____

Due date: _____

2. Narrowing the Topic

Use one or more brainstorming methods to narrow your topic.

3. Determining the Writing Context

Decide on your purpose, audience, and tone. Then choose a tentative main idea.

Purpose: _____

Audience: _____

Tone: _____

Tentative main idea: _____

4. Generating Ideas

Generate ideas by brainstorming, free writing, listing, clustering or dividing. You may find it helpful to use scratch paper. Come up with as many ideas as possible. Keep your purpose and audience in mind as you generate ideas to support your topic sentence.

5. Organizing Ideas

1. Examine the ideas you have generated and revise your tentative topic sentence.

2. Select your strongest support ideas and place them in the map or outline template in the order you would like to use them. Do more brainstorming if you do not have enough supports to develop your topic sentence.

3. Generate specific details for each of your supports.

4. You may wish to state how each support relates to or proves the topic sentence.

Map Template

Topic sentence: _____

_____

Area of Support	Specific Details	Relation to Topic Sentence
1. _____		
2. _____		
3. _____		
4. _____		
5. _____		

Outline Template

Topic sentence: _____

_____

I. Support 1 _____

    A. Specifics_____

    B. Relation _____

II. Support 2 _____

    A. Specifics_____

    B. Relation _____

III. Support 3 _____

    A. Specifics_____

    B. Relation _____

IV. Support 4 _____

    A. Specifics_____

    B. Relation _____

6. Drafting

Write a draft of the paragraph by creating a sentence or sentences for each area of support on your map or outline. Incorporate your specific details and, where appropriate, the relation to the topic sentence.

7. Revising

If possible, get feedback on your paragraph from peers or your instructor. If feedback is not available, analyze the strengths and weaknesses of your paragraph using the Paragraph Revision Checklist on page 389.

8. Editing

Use the Editing Checklist on page 390 and the suggestions of your peer editors to find and correct errors in your paragraph.

Index

Credits

This page constitutes an extension of the copyright page. We have made every effort to trace the ownership of all copyrighted material and to secure permission from copyright holders. In the event of any question arising as to the use of any material, we will be pleased to make the necessary corrections in future printings. Thanks are due to the authors, publishers, and agents for permission to use the material indicated.

Andrews Bedford, Faith, "Measles, Mumps, and Chicken Pox," from *Country Living,* February 1995. Reprinted by permission of the author.

Buscaglia, Leo, "Papa, the Philosopher" from *Papa, My Father,* pp. 60–65. Published by Slack, Inc. Reprinted by permission of the publisher.

Canfield, Jack, "Consider This" compiled by Jack Canfield from *A Second Helping of Chicken Soup for the Soul.* Copyright © 1995 by Jack Canfield, Mark Victor Hansen. Published by arrangement with Health Communications.

Cisneros, Sandra, "The First Job" from *The House on Mango Street.* Copyright © 1984 by Sandra Cisneros. Published by Vintage Books, a division of Random House, Inc., and in hardcover by Alfred A. Knopf in 1994. Reprinted by permission of Susan Berholz Literary Services, New York. All rights reserved.

Dillard, Annie, excerpt from *An American Childhood,* pp. 20–23, by Annie Dillard. Copyright © 1998 by Annie Dillard. Reprinted by permission of HarperCollins.

Divakaruni, Chitra, excerpt from "The Bats" from *Arranged Marriage,* pp. 1–4, by Chitra Divakaruni. Copyright © 1995 by Chitra Divakaruni. Used by permission of Doubleday, a division of Random House, Inc.

Dyson, Cathy, "The Girl Who Helped the Samburu" (original title, "Local Student Sells Artwork, Crafts to Help Kenyan Tribe"), from *The Free Lance-Star in Fredericksburg.* Reprinted by permission of the author.

Eisenberg, Daniel, "The Coming Job Boom," from *TIME,* May 6, 2002, pp. 41–44. Copyright ©2002 TIME Inc. Reprinted by permission.

Garrity, John, "Too Good to Be True," from *Sports Illustrated,* October 9, 2000, pp. 78–84. Copyright © 2000 Time, Inc. All rights reserved.

Giono, Jean, "The Man Who Planted Trees." Copyright © 1985 Michael McCurdy, Chelsea Green Publishing Co., White River Junction, VT. Reprinted by permission.

Goff, Ted, "Successes/Learning Experiences" cartoon by Ted Goff. Reprinted by permission of the artist.

Goldberg, Natalie, excerpt from *Long Quiet Highway,* pp. 23–31, by Natalie Goldberg. Copyright © 1993 by Natalie Goldberg. Used by permission of Bantam Books, a division of Random House, Inc.

Greenfeld, Karl Taro, "Blind to Failure," from *TIME,* June 18, 2001, pp. 52–63. Copyright ©2001 TIME Inc. Reprinted by permission.

Photo Credits